American Food
The Gastronomic Story

Books by Evan Jones

Hidden America
(with Roland Wells Robbins)

The Father: Letters to Sons and Daughters

Trappers and Mountain Men

The Minnesota: Forgotten River

Citadel in the Wilderness

American Food: The Gastronomic Story

Evan Jones

American Food

The Gastronomic Story

Including a Personal Treasury
of More than 500 Distinctive Regional,
Traditional and Contemporary Recipes

E. P. Dutton & Co., Inc. | New York | 1975

Grateful acknowledgment is made to the following publishers for permission to cite passages:

Atheneum Publishers, Inc.: *The Margaret Rudkin Pepperidge Farm Cookbook* by Margaret Rudkin. Copyright © 1963 by Margaret Rudkin. Reprinted by permission.

The Bobbs-Merrill Company, Inc.: *Soul Food Cook Book.* Copyright © 1969 by Bob Jeffries. Reprinted by permission.

Chilton Book Company, Radnor, Pa.: *The Gold Cook Book* by Louis P. De Gouy. Copyright 1947 by Louis P. De Gouy. Reprinted by permission.

Fawcett Publications, Inc.: *The Farmer's Daughter Cookbook* by Kandy Norton Henely. Copyright © 1971 by Fawcett Publications, Inc.

Houghton Mifflin Company: *Sam Ward "King of the Lobby"* by Lately Thomas. Copyright © 1965 Houghton Mifflin Company. Reprinted by permission.

Little, Brown and Company: *West Coast Cook Book* by Helen Evans Brown. Copyright 1952 by Helen Evans Brown.

Random House, Inc.: *Invisible Man* by Ralph Ellison. Copyright 1947, 1948, 1952 by Ralph Ellison. Reprinted by permission.

Alfred A. Knopf, Inc.: *All Manner of Food* by Michael Field. Copyright © 1965, 1966, 1967, 1968, 1970 by Michael Field. Reprinted by permission.

Simon & Schuster, Inc.: *The Wonderful World of Cooking* by Edward H. Heth. Copyright © 1956 by Edward H. Heth. Reprinted by permission.

Published simultaneously in Canada by
Clarke, Irwin & Company Limited, Toronto and Vancouver
ISBN: 0-525-05353-0

Library of Congress Cataloging in Publication Data

Jones, Evan, 1915–
    American Food: The Gastronomic Story

    Includes index.
    1. Cookery, American.   2. Food. I. Title.
TX715.J76 1975   641.5'973   74–22467

For Robert Lescher

Contents

Recipes

Indexes

American Food

The Gastronomic Story

Chapter I

Puritans and Plantations

ALMOST ANYONE who ever has been host to a friend from another country has had to deal with the question, "What is American food?" A visitor from abroad—in whatever region his discovery of the United States may begin—encounters so many public eating places that specialize in dishes from Europe or the Orient that it would be surprising if he failed to ask when he might sample indigenous food. It's a question that seldom gets a satisfactory answer. Public food in America is apt to be pretentious and derivative, or vulgarized like hot dogs and hamburgers oozing with spicy-sweet sauces. But there is a difference between restaurant talk of cuisines and the reality of good home cooking. The true style of American food is the sum of many parts, and most of it came over with immigrants. In addition, there developed after World War II a new generation of lovers of food who, having traveled or lived abroad, returned with recipes and whetted palates as well as with enthusiasm for the art of creating good things to eat. They were repeating the pattern of bringing from abroad new ways of cooking to be incorporated into an American style that has been evolving since the arrival of the first settlers.

Like the vegetables discovered in the New World, much of the best indigenous food is simple but good. Foreign travelers are apt to consider wild rice a delicacy to be as coveted as truffles from France or Italy. Pompano from American waters, filleted and sautéed in butter with lemon juice and parsley, and served with tiny boiled potatoes, or Long Island duckling, roasted with sage and onions, can be worth a special journey. Abundance and the quality and variety of raw ingredients are basic to the American way with food, and they have been from the earliest years. Basic, too, is the assimilation of ideas from many other cuisines.

1

Even a primitive American cooking style cannot be said to have simmered into being over the first campfire beside Virginia's James River. No more so on that cold winter day at Plymouth when Miles Standish and friends shot and roasted over coals an eagle "which was excellent meat—" so they said, thinking of Merrie England, "hardly to be discerned from mutton." Not even the penchant among Indian tribal cooks for stewing corn and dried beans into palatable meals can be assessed as a distinguishable branch of epicurism.

Nevertheless, the first important influences evolved in the colonial period. Britishers had come to the New World in many cases to gain religious freedom, yet they were intent also on emulating the daily life of their homeland. Their feelings were well expressed when they used the term, New England. For their part, those who were Puritans exercised "the plain style," as they called it, as a fundamental of life. The preparation of food, quite naturally, was affected by this philosophy.

To both Plymouth and Jamestown, colonial women brought the incontestably British cooking style they had learned at home. There was a forthrightness about their preparation of various raw ingredients, and nothing at all about the way they cooked (in contrast to the French, for instance) could be described as tricky. The kitchens they left behind were rudimentary—open-hearthed and usually equipped with a spit or two. The limited character of their utensils can be recognized in John Winthrop's admonition to his wife to be sure to bring to Massachusetts Bay "2 or 3 skillets of several sizes, a large frying pan, a small stewing

pan, and a can to boil a pudding in. . . ." They were women who always had done a good deal of their own work, but many of them had come from urban rather than rural homes and some had to accustom themselves to the care of poultry and dairy animals and to such chores as butchering.

In Virginia, where life generally was easier—as well as in chilly New England—colonial housewives continued to prepare meals as their forebears had. Except for fair-weather days when they might cook outdoors, all their roasting, broiling, boiling, and baking were done in the blistering temperatures of the wide kitchen fireplace with its spits and its heat reflectors, its trivets, its drip pans, griddles, Dutch ovens, hanging pots and trammels and cranes, and its long-handled peels with which to recover food or containers buried in the coals. The challenge was to apply English methods to whatever food supplies there might be, whether sent from England or grown or caught in the colonies. The earliest inventory at Jamestown showed sixty-odd domestic pigs, offspring of three English sows, in addition to some five hundred similarly bred chickens; but great damage had been done to other food supplies by rats, which had arrived on the first ships and had persistently multiplied.

No problems attended the boiling or broiling of chickens or pork, but in order not to tax these resources, more than sixty colonists in 1610 were packed off down the James to live on oysters and other seafood at the river's mouth. There they found sturgeon in such great abundance that they dried the surplus, then pounded the hard flesh and mixed it with roe and sorrel to provide, as some said, both bread and meat.

"Baked sturgeon" was apt to be cooked by those early Virginians in a cast-iron oven-pot which sat with its heavy, deeply edged iron cover on three squat legs among the glowing fireplace coals. Sometimes more coals were packed in, red-hot, on the rimmed top when the objective was to brown the surface of a meat roast, for instance. This was pure, untainted English cooking of the period, as are these instructions: "To roast a piece of fresh sturgeon, fasten it on the spit, and baste it well with butter for a quarter of an hour, then with a little flour, then a grate of nutmeg all over it, and a few sweet herbs. . . ." Average English tastes called for the use of some spices, and all but the very poor bought pepper, cloves, mace, cinnamon, and ginger when an occasional ship brought new supplies. Even the Pilgrims, who had to eat groundnuts during the first hard winter, preferred such conventional seasonings when they were available. And some early Virginians insured the succulence of their spitted sturgeon with an artful sauce: an anchovy, an onion, a little lemon peel, a bundle of sweet herbs and spices simmered in white wine and walnut catsup, with "the inside of a crab bruised fine"—or with lobster, shrimps, prawns, and about a dozen oysters, all of it thickened with butter rolled in flour.

Untainted Yankee cooking has never been quite so profligate with the sea's bounty. Yet fish was a staple of life for all the men and women who had come to colonize. The Pilgrims, after they had managed to stay alive

To Roast a Large Fish

Take a large [fish of any kind], gut it and clean it, and lard it with Eel and Bacon, as you lard a Fowl; then take Thyme and Savory, Salt, Mace, and Nutmeg, and some Crumbs of Bread, Beef-suet and Parsley; shred all very fine, and mix it up with raw Eggs; make it a long Pudding, and put it in the belly of your Pike, skewer up the Belly, and dissolve Anchovies in Butter, and baste it with it; put two Splints on each Side of the Pike, and tie it to the Spit; melt Butter thick for the Sauce, or, if you please, Oyster-sauce, and bruise the Pudding in it. Garnish with Lemon.

—Eliza Smith,
  The Compleat Housewife, 1742

Eel Stifle

Cut the eels into pieces about four inches long; take two onions, two shallots, a bunch of parsley, thyme, two bay leaves, a little mace, black and Jamaica pepper, a pint of good gravy, the same of Port wine, and the same of vinegar, six anchovies bruised; let all boil together for ten minutes; take out the eels; boil the sauce till reduced to a quart; strain and thicken it with a table-spoonful of flour, mixed smooth in a little cold water. Put in the eels, and boil them till they are tender. Eels may also be roasted with a common stuffing.

—"A Boston Housekeeper," 1832

on the *Mayflower* on a diet of "salt horse" (as they called dried beef), hardtack, beer, dried fish, and cheese, sent enthusiastic messages about their food sources back to England. As Edward Winslow wrote a friend, "Fresh cod, in the summer, is but coarse meate with us." He reported the bay full of lobsters all summer, and said that in September a hogshead of eels could be taken in a night. All winter Winslow and his neighbors had mussels and clams "at our doors. Oysters we have none near," he wrote cheerfully, "but can have them brought by the Indians when we will." Also for the taking, they found wild fruits and herbs and a "great store of leeks and onions."

All those eels that Winslow valued were cooked as simply as possible—not with dozens of shrimps and mushrooms and parsley roots sautéed in herbs (as in a popular Pennsylvania Dutch soup)—but with nothing more than a morsel of fat and a little onion, wild or otherwise, whichever should be handy. The Pilgrims called so unadorned a dish an Eel Stifle which, accented with salt pork and potatoes, evolved into a classic Yankee repast.

English cookery was described by contemporary observers as fare that required no imagination. At home the British then were dining on pork that had been fed on apples, or juicy roast beef, stubble geese, and other earthily good British things like cheddar. Colonists, not surprisingly, were inclined to eat just that way when they settled in America. In 1622 en route to London, after a short residence in Jamestown, John Pory described Plymouth Bay's bluefish as "of a taste requiring no addition of sauce," and he spoke for the average English palate as well as for New World plenitude.

"What but plenty makes hospitality and good neighbourhood?" asked another seventeenth-century Englishman traveling through Virginia and Maryland. Everywhere he looked he had found "as sweet and savoury meat as the world affords," along with good butter and cheese, fish, fowl, and venison, orchards and gardens. Many later travelers were as lyric as their predecessors about the abundant wild fruit, the strawberries and wild grapes that had been successfully transplanted into domestic plots, the variety of melons, the pumpkins and squash, the corn that was sometimes white, sometimes blue, sometimes yellow or red. Pilgrim women had brought seeds to grow cabbages, turnips, carrots, onions, parsnips, peas, herbs, and other English vegetables; they even had planted some string beans which they called French beans. Virginians planted artichokes, asparagus, beets, broccoli, cauliflower, cress, cucumbers, and the mustard and other greens that were to help make the South famous for its "pot likker." Robert Beverly, who wrote Virginia's first history, emphasized the cultivation of "all the Culinary Plants that grow in England."

To incorporate such garden produce into the kind of meals they liked, housewives of the southern colonies turned for culinary guidance to their English cookbooks, and their European guests often noted that the colonial Virginia hostess who wished to be fashionable invariably proffered dishes suited to the taste of affluent families back in England

and served in the English mode. She herself ladled the soup as a first course, to be followed by large roasts of meat, whole fowls, boiled or baked fish, with supplementary meat dishes, game birds, sometimes seafood dishes, and the home-grown and variously prepared vegetables— all at a single meal. Desserts included distinctly Anglo-Saxon puddings, pastries, jellies, and the inescapable sweetmeats of seventeenth- and eighteenth-century menus.

In Virginia—to lessen their dependence on English food by adapting what they could from Indian ways—a number of families among the earliest settlers had been billeted with friendly tribes to learn how to recognize strange varieties of edible roots and how to prepare them, as well as to master the imaginative ways that the local Indians had devised for making use of corn. All the colonists quickly accepted the need for using corn meal as well as flour in making bread, and gradually one good recipe followed another—from the most primitive ash cakes to hoecakes ("so called because baked on a Hoe before the fire," a colonial Williamsburg tutor wrote) to corn pones to corn sticks to Johnny cake (spelled "Jonny" and made with white corn meal in Rhode Island) to hush puppies fried in deep fat, which were as necessary to fried fish, a southern cook once said, as woman is to man.

Among the young women who set out to adapt to the produce of New World harvests were Joane Pierce, Elizabeth Joones, and Temperance Flowerdieu. Those who were first to live side by side with Indian women in order to learn their cooking secrets are not named, but it isn't hard to imagine them as they experimented with the aboriginal way of pounding parched corn into meal. Or to share the wonder as the squaws built fires beside the cornfields, heated water to a boil into which to toss the freshly picked and husked ears of corn, then to watch the eating, the moving of cobs across hungry mouths like harmonicas. Never had they seen a vegetable eaten in such fashion, but they and their menfolk took to the idea immediately. They also quickly accepted the various Indian ways of mixing corn with beans and meat, both summer and winter (when the vegetables that were dried in the fall were soaked before cooking).

Virginia cooks did more than accept the hulled dried corn called hominy; they made a sort of southern fetish of it. Those young Jamestown women camping among the squaws observed the Indian use of ashes and water to remove the skin from dried corn kernels and tasted the difference in flavor when the now white puffed morsels were cooked as a soup, mixed with meat and wild greens, or ground somewhat coarsely to become famous, under the influence of future southern cooks, as grits. "Hawg 'n' hominy," that special combination of corn and salt pork, is often

Old Salem Hominy

Soak corn overnight. Add 3 heaping teaspoons lye to 6 quarts shelled corn. Cover with water and cook until hulls come off. Wash in cold water and rub between palms of hands until rest of hulls come off. Put in cold water and bring to a boil. Drain and cook in boiling water all day. When water has cooked up and hominy is dry, add ½ cup table cream and ¼ pound butter. Then continue cooking for about 2 more hours.

given credit for keeping the pioneers alive in every phase of the westward trend of settlement. Colonial women were most apt to cook grits as a stick-to-the-ribs gruel to which they added maple syrup, as the Indians sometimes did. They boiled the plump, unground kernels of whole hominy and served the result as a vegetable with meat. Or they soaked equal amounts of dried beans and whole hominy overnight, then simmered them in water with a little salt pork and seasonings for five hours or more.

This latter combination was a variation of the Narragansett *msickquatash* introduced to colonial cooks by the Indians and subsequently known as succotash. A similar corn-bean dish may have been served by Pilgrim housewives at the first Thanksgiving dinner in 1621 (along with venison, roast duck, roast goose—no turkey has been reported—clams, eels, wheat and corn breads, leeks, watercress, wild plums, homemade wine), and it became without question a staple in the colonial diet, especially in New England. The oldest succotash recipe on record requires the boiling of two fowls in a large kettle of water. Meanwhile, two quarts of dried white beans are simmered with a half-pound of lean salt pork "until like soup." Fat is skimmed off the broth from the fowls and in goes a four-pound freshened piece of corned brisket, a diced turnip, five or six sliced potatoes; the cooked chicken and pork are set aside to keep warm. The beans "like soup" are added to the broth along with salt, pepper, and four quarts of cooked dried corn.

"Before serving, add the meat of one fowl," the original recipe says firmly. "The second fowl should be served separately, as also the corned beef and pork." Such a succotash, made according to these instructions, was the *pièce de résistance* in 1769 when a dozen or so Plymouth young men of *Mayflower* stock formed the Old Colony Club at a dinner to celebrate the landing of the Pilgrims.

There may be a dozen "authentic" ways to make succotash. Indian women, who tutored those first English cooks, would freeze their winter succotash (made of dried vegetables) and use an idle tomahawk to chop off chunks to melt over a fire as needed. In summer they made a similar stew with corn cut from the cob at the milky stage and stewed with fresh beans along with whatever meat was available. Southern cooks developed the use of fresh limas or butter beans as the ideal accent to young corn. A professed authentic version from Maine stipulates cranberry beans, never limas, as does a Connecticut recipe that prescribes kernels stripped from boiled corn-on-the-cob with a few small pieces of cob to "cook the sweetness out." In his unpublished diary, a pioneer Vermont farmer was moved to mention food only once in an entire year. "This day," he noted in mid-August 1808, "I din'd upon Succotash." That succotash must have been a noble dish to warrant mention by so taciturn a frontiersman.

The English colonists not only had learned Indian ways of cooking corn and beans together but, as every school child *should* know, they had learned from Squanto how to make use of the growing corn stalks to support the bean vines by planting the two together. They had also found that corn, unlike other grains which require smooth and well-tilled fields, could be grown in patches where trees had been cut down, leaving stumps behind; they accepted the boon that corn could be raised easily on land that not long before had been heavily forested. This fact alone may have made America a corny country. The adjective when applied to sentimental things is said to derive from the supposedly unsophisticated humor of the early farmer; it might as well apply to a provincial American style of cooking.

A contemporary American cookbook with encyclopedic intentions may include, perhaps, twenty to thirty recipes for preparing corn. Most of these, basically, are the dishes that English cooks devised in modifying Indian food to conform to the familiar things of the British Isles. In both early New England and the South of plantations those cooks made corn puddings, sometimes as one-dish meals, sometimes to accompany meat, sometimes to finish the meal as a dessert. The legendary Yankee Hasty Pudding is nothing more than cornmeal boiled with a modicum of seasoning. Indian puddings, as they are made in many parts of the country, are sweet and baked, as often as not, with accents of maple syrup, New Orleans molasses, even grated orange.

Pudding made with corn kernels, baked with eggs and milk, and sometimes enlivened (like Yorkshire pudding) with meat drippings, is a standard in the American repertoire. The sweet and custardy dessert version, however, seems to thrive only among frugal Yankees who have been known to serve it with a hard sauce, or with butter and sugar. Honey or maple syrup added with discretion also deflects the pure vegetable quality of corn pudding, and a little nutmeg or mace can underscore the

natural flavor. It is, in any case, a uniquely American way to end a meal.

In the smoothest, most luscious corn pudding I know, much depends on the amount of liquid in the corn pulp. Some Kentucky cooks say this delicacy must be made with young field corn, and served as a vegetable. A razor-sharp knife cuts down the center of each row of kernels. No husk or skin is supposed to come close to the finished product. The blunt, noncutting edge of a knive is used to depress the kernels when the ear is held upright over a bowl. Out spill the tender insides only, to be mixed with eggs, milk, or cream, butter, salt, pepper, and a hint of sugar. This mixture is baked in a buttered casserole at about 350° for about forty or forty-five minutes. "When it doesn't shake," say southern cooks, "it is ready."

Corn oysters, which are sometimes called mock oysters and are considered by some to taste like marine oysters fried in deep fat, are usually made with whole kernels, but are incomparably better when prepared as is the pudding above. In this fashion they sometimes fool the unalert into thinking they are real oysters, and they are given a very precise title by M.F.K. Fisher in this recipe she got from a southern lady.

Such recipes provided ways to use corn when colonists found it impossible to cook it immediately upon picking, as the Indians did every chance they got. "They delight much," Robert Beverly wrote of the natives, "to feed on Roasting-ears; that is, the Indian corn, gathered green and milky, before it is grown to its full bigness, and roasted before the Fire, in the Ear." Even when he had a garden in Paris, Thomas Jefferson cultivated Indian corn "to eat green in our manner," that is, as quickly after it left the stalk as possible. Fresh-picked vegetables, it has been said, should be "run from garden row to the kettle boiling for them, before the shock of being picked has had a chance to make them nervous or revengefully tough. Green-corn, of course, is the most immediate of all vegetables. It should be cooked before the flow of honey has stopped on the stem it has been pulled from."

When not so swiftly managed, about 90 percent of the sugar in sweet corn turns to starch within an hour of picking, and no store-bought corn remotely compares to that cooked in the field. The early American cooks learned this lesson well, but twentieth-century urbanization makes the practice almost impossible. To help a little, some modern cooks add sugar to the boiling water and refrain from any salt whatever, for salt-water-cooking toughens the kernels even more than prolonged exposure to air. An even better recipe for those who cannot toss their corn directly from the stalk into the pot is this one still used in Coahoma County, Mississippi (a good enough method, incidentally, to have been adapted by a Paris restaurant known for its *Mais Frais Americaine*):

For a dozen ears, as fresh as availability permits, southern cooks bring to a boil two quarts of milk mixed with an equal amount of water and a half-pound of butter. They say the corn may be cooked as much as eight to ten minutes, depending upon how fresh it is. And some say it will keep

One-and-Only Unique Real Corn Oysters

Shuck 1 dozen ears of corn and score each row of kernels. Cut from cobs and put through fine food grinder, saving all the milk. Let set about 3 hours, or until milk is set into custard. Beat 1 or 2 eggs, using 2 if mixture is stiff, and add salt and pepper to taste. Drop from spoon into hot fat, and turn once when brown. Serve immediately.

in the milk-water mixture for at least an hour after the pot is taken from the fire, tasting as fresh as when cooking stopped.

Just as Jefferson brought corn to France so he could pick the ears from his Paris garden, Benjamin Franklin hungered for it in cooked form when in 1768 he was representing the colonies in London. He wrote to his wife asking her to send his favorite Pennsylvania fruits, along with buckwheat flour and cornmeal, then he put his English cook through her paces until she mastered various corn breads and cakes. Earlier he had taken British prejudice to task by responding to a letter in the London *Gazetteer:* "Pray let me, an American, [affirm] that Indian corn, take it all in all, is one of the most agreeable and wholesome grains in the world . . . and that johnny or hoecake, hot from the fire, is better than a Yorkshire muffin. . . ."

Beans—and the Yankee Character

Other Americans have become convinced that Boston brown bread, also made from Indian corn, is equally superior to the Yorkshire product, and along with Boston beans the steamed bread from Benjamin Franklin's birthplace has remained a gastronomical standard wherever Yankees have settled in the United States. I remember this from my own childhood in Minnesota, more than a thousand miles removed from Boston but nevertheless a place, like so many other not-so-long-ago frontiers, influenced by a kind of New England hauteur. Our home-steamed Boston brown bread was served by my mother with her own all-night-long baked New England beans, sometimes even as a repository for what in our house was invariably a cheese (of domestic manufacture) called "Olde English," very orange-yellow and, as my parents would say between appreciative munches, "good and sharp."

The beans were the genuine article. They related my part of America to one of its beginnings, to the dour climate of New England that helped to produce a style of cooking no more given to subtle embellishments than the food of that isle, that realm, that blessed plot so many had left behind. Early New Englanders very soon discovered—as should be proved by whatever case there may be for brown bread—that sweeteners added *something* to the quality if they did not necessarily improve the taste of food; the sugar content fortified their bodies against bitter and seemingly endless winters. They had learned this, perhaps, watching Narragansett and Penobscot squaws mixing maple sugar in with beans to bubble gently for a day or so in pots buried in pits lined with coals.

Few real Yankees admit to disliking baked beans, no matter what the recipe, and some colonists may have tasted one or another version in England. George III is said to have been fascinated when he—having had few of the advantages of his more humble subjects—first found beans cooked with bacon and being eaten by workmen constructing a military establishment at Woolwich, not far from London; the king ate baked beans al fresco with his subjects and so liked the taste (or the idea

Boston Brown Bread

One cup of sweet milk,
  One cup of sour,
One cup of corn meal,
  One cup of flour,
Teaspoon of soda,
  Molasses one cup;
Steam for three hours,
  Then eat it all up.

—Old Yankee Cookbook

of so democratic a repast) that he instituted an annual bean feast. No such example by any king ever was required to establish "baked bean days" as community celebrations in many parts of the United States. Recipes vary with the region, naturally. Throughout New England the various ways of cooking beans comprise a controversial subject, as energetically debated as the differences among Frenchmen who argue the fine points of the *cassoulets* of Castelnaudary and Toulouse. Yankee cooks have been equally opinionated since they traveled in oxcarts with frozen slabs of beans—to be heated at midwinter campfires—hanging from the wagon sides.

Salt pork is considered the heart and soul of Maine beans because, some say, it should constitute about a quarter of the pot's contents. My feeling is that the pork should have an instantly recognizable stripe of red down the middle and that its rind should be severed at about one-and-a-half-inch intervals so the meat rests flatly instead of curling. But some real down East Yankees would say that every bean in a real Maine bean pot "should be treated like a voter in an election. You must understand each bean to bake a collection of them," according to a Lewiston newspaper that emphasized that meat is much less important than the beans. "Leaving aside our different families of beans, such as peabeans, 'yallereyes,' 'marrer-fats,' kidney, lima and 'crambry,' we note a difference among themselves in each tribe. They never wholly assimilate or mash. That is, they never do in Maine. You do get in Boston a sort of brown paste with small nubbly particles in it, dejected in appearance. It should be called 'bean butter.' "

Some Vermont purists still demand that yellow-eye beans be accented in the old Indian way with maple syrup—four cups of beans to a pound of salt pork and a quarter-cup of syrup—while others in the same Green Mountains, where people are equally apt to be snowed in, speak for a quart of soldier beans to half a pound of salt pork and a half-cup of

shaved maple sugar rather than syrup. Still others are happy, and produce marvelous results, using navy or pea beans instead of yellow-eyes, with no other deviations. Pea beans were also the stuff of which "Algonquin Maple Baked Beans" were made in Depression days when literary New Yorkers used to dine regularly at the Algonquin Hotel on American fare; this recipe called for *two* pounds of salt pork and some molasses heightened by maple syrup.

True to British heritage, more Americans put gluttonous emphasis on meat, and at least one version of the recipe, in traveling from New England to Missouri, added an equal amount of country ham to the salt pork, tossing out maple, molasses, and sugar in favor of New England rum. In pioneer Michigan, in the rough country of that state's peninsula, apparently almost nobody used molasses—the style being to bake beans in a dripping pan with a layer of sliced salt pork covering the top; these beans were cut out of the dripping pan in slices and served with a colorful sauce of homemade tomato catsup.

New England baked beans have been modified in other regions, but ritual prevails in the skiing country north of Boston where some Yankees still emulate Puritan forebears with beans for Saturday night supper—and they have it again for breakfast on Sunday when churchgoers once refrained from cooking as well as other forms of work. There and elsewhere, outdoor types still follow the "bean-hole" method of digging a pit into which to sink an iron pot full of beans, with coals close to top and bottom surfaces and a covering of earth to prevent the heat from escaping. Some other carry-overs from the past prevail. People who own old New England houses still make use, on rare occasions, of the brick ovens built into colonial fireplaces. About two hours before putting the bean pot in to bake they build a fire and let it burn until the black soot comes off the oven walls and the top surface has turned white. The coals are then swept out (for this job a turkey wing was long ago settled upon as just the right natural tool); the pot is put in to bake and the iron door of the oven latched tight for the nocturnal slow cooking.

In colonial days such preheated brick ovens would turn out at the same time not only baked beans, but bread, Indian puddings, meat pies, and pandowdies among other things. Although lexicographers say that the origin of this last term is obscure, pandowdy has a fine Yankee ring to it and, according to some cooks, it also has synonyms that stretch from Apple Jonathan and Apple Potpie [*sic*] to Yankee Apple John and Apple Betty.

Pandowdy recipes themselves are equally various, calling sometimes for stale bread as a retainer, sometimes for biscuit dough. A maple-flavored apple pandowdy, even now, can be baked overnight in a brick oven after comparatively simple preparation. You simply get some good tart New England apples—Rhode Island greenings, pink candy-striped Duchess from Vermont, for instance, or York, or Minnesota's Wealthy, or Newtown Pippins. Slice them and put them into an earthen baking dish and pour over them maple sugar mixed with water; sprinkle with finely

Traditional New England
Baked Bean Soup

Let 3 cups beans, 4 cups water, 1 small onion and 1 stalk celery simmer for half an hour. Strain. Try out about ¼ cup diced salt pork, blend a tablespoon of flour with fat, and add a cup and a half of tomatoes. Let cook one hour, season with salt and pepper, and serve.

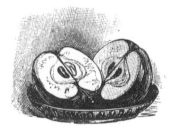

Mrs. Israel Putnam's Apple Jonathan

According to a great-great-great-great-grandson of the Connecticut Revolutionary War patriot, the descendants of Israel Putnam have been eating this version of apple pandowdy for more than 200 years: Arrange about 4 cups apples in buttered baking dish. Add ½ cup cider. Mix ½ teaspoon of cinnamon, ⅛ teaspoon of cloves, ⅛ teaspoon of nutmeg with 1 cup of brown sugar and sprinkle over apples; dot with butter. Cover ¼ inch thick with biscuit dough, making slits on top with knife to let steam escape. Bake in medium heat until apples are tender, time depending upon texture and quality of apples. Serve warm.

diced salt pork (butter will do, of course). Add a little nutmeg if you like. Mix corn meal, flour, and lard with enough water to make a dough and roll it out to about an inch in thickness, then put this pastry atop the apple slices, pricking it at regular intervals with a fork. The pandowdy will cook along with the beans and can join them on this typically Yankee breakfast menu, the encrusted apples brought to old-time glory with a topping of thick unpasteurized cream and shaved maple sugar.

Pork—and the Anatomy of Boiled Beef

Pork in its various forms served early New England because pigs required almost no supervision and could be raised on edible discards of all kinds. Porkers did their bit for southern cooks as well, but not so inclusively as they abetted the northern pattern of frugal life. Long, bitter, blustery winters kept menus anchored to the pork barrel in the cellar of the house where red-streaked creamy slabs of sidemeat had been laid down in brine thick enough to let the pork pieces float when the heavy hewn-oak cover was lifted. This is an image of treasury—in this bursary of food one gets telling glimpses of the American past; the old political reference to dipping into the pork barrel still turns up in accounts of lawmakers' machinations.

And America moved west with pigs in droves, foraging on mast in virgin woods, rooting and snorting and running untended in the streets of burgeoning towns and cities. When venison and wild birds were in short supply, pork was the staple meat in every diet, and instead of wearing out its welcome it incited sentimentality in hundreds of memoirs. One such remembrance of a Midwest childhood reports, "For breakfast we had bacon, ham, or sausage; for dinner smoked or pickled pork; for supper ham, sausage, headcheese or some other kind of pork delicacy." Salt pork, this choice of language makes it easy to believe, could be cooked with skill and undoubtedly love, could be served three times a day in such variety that it did not pall. No wonder it has been said, perhaps too often, that America's forests and prairies were turned into farms, and "her railways laid, her canals dug, her ships kept at sea on a porcine diet."

It is doubtful that anyone recently has had three consecutive meals based on no other meat than pork. But of course such redundant menus were the result of necessity, despite the cheerful memoirs. More often, the meat preserved in brine was an accent, to enrich flavor in a more substantive dish. Daniel Webster's mother, so her Yankee son told friends, was an artist at simmering together chicken and salt pork "in her own rare manner" to serve with pork gravy whenever Webster visited her in New Hampshire.

There are twentieth-century cooks who maintain the art of preparing the traditional Yankee "salt pork dinner," which combines winter vegetables like turnips, carrots, beets, and potatoes, sautéed sliced apples, with salt pork that has been boiled, then slowly fried until its dusting of cinnamon-scented flour is browned into the meat and all the excess fat is rendered. The meat slices are served on a platter surrounded by sliced apples, mounds of boiled vegetables, a separate dish of potatoes baked in their skins, and a gravy boat steaming with a delicate sauce made by stirring flour into a little of the pork fat and blending in thick sweet cream; sometimes an equal amount of sour cream gives extra piquancy. "Sounds awful," a good cook once said, "but it's heavenly." In Vermont this salt pork dinner is ritual eating: diners open and mash the potatoes, strewing them with bits of pork they have cut up; then they cut in the vegetables they like; the fried apples go alongside, and there is usually a New England relish like piccalilli or small green tomatoes pickled in dill.

Most times when a New Englander says boiled dinner, however, he means corned beef—good red meat that was preserved in the old days for hot-weather use by a coating of grains of dry salt rather than brine. Like the salt pork repast above, New England's boiled dinner dates back to days when cooking was done at the open fire and meat and vegetables could be combined in a single pot that hung from a crane, bubbling gently for hours while the housewife pursued her dozens of other chores. It is a meal for the heartiest of appetites, and it is delicious when carefully prepared.

The average recipe calls for corned brisket. Down East, however, no tradition-conscious State-of-Mainer would consider using this mixed lean and fat meat from the animal's chest. Voluble Maine cooks say that brisket is the toughest part of beef; for corning those cooks want the rump, the thick rib, or the flank next to the loin. Brisket, they say, affords no way of being made genuinely tender, for they believe that four hours of cooking leaves it stringy and, as one of them said, "tooth resistant." To avoid such catastrophe, they rub a three- or four-pound piece of rump, thick rib, or flank with coarse salt, then cover the piece with water so heavily salted it will float a potato or an egg. They take an old-fashioned Yankee doorstop and put it on a plate to weight down the meat which then bathes in the brine overnight.

Some, surprisingly, cook the beef the next day, but others leave their meat in a quiet pickle for anything from a week to a month. The independence of Maine cooks cannot be overemphasized. Indeed, some practice the art of "corning in the kettle," which simply requires putting fresh meat in heavily salted water and cooking it about two hours until it is tender; it is left to cool in its own liquor, then is lifted out and laid in a deep bread pan, the fibers of the beef running the long way. "Pull up layers of meat with a fork," say these directions, "and into the interstices press pieces of fat from the outer edge. When the meat has been well larded, put a shingle on top of the meat, and weight it down with a window weight or a flat-iron." Thoroughly chilled, this Maine corned beef—becomingly congealed into a shimmering loaf—is sometimes served with the hot vegetables of a New England boiled dinner.

As must night the day, red flannel hash follows a boiled dinner because

Lucy Emerson's Fine Sausages

You must take six pounds of good pork, free from skin, gristles, and fat, cut it small, and beat it in a mortar till it is very fine; then shred six pounds of beef suet very fine and free from skin . . . take a good deal of sage, wash it very clean, pick off the leaves, and shred it very fine; spread your meat on a clean dresser or table, then shake the sage all over, about three large spoonfuls, shred the thin rind of a middling lemon very fine and throw over, with as many sweet herbs, when shred fine, as will fill a large spoon; grate two nutmegs over, throw over two teaspoonfuls of pepper, a large spoonful of salt, then throw over the suet, and mix it all well together . . . roll them up with as much egg as will make them roll smooth; make them the size of a sausage, and fry them in butter or good dripping; be sure it be hot before you put them in, and keep rolling them about. . . . You may clean some guts and fill them.

—*The New-England Cookery*, 1808

New England beets, carrots, potatoes, and other vegetables provide the right colors as well as flavors to complement the last of the corned beef. Hashes are common to almost every cuisine, and this one undoubtedly owes something to the culinary techniques brought over by the English colonists. Also, it achieved perfection in the era of the wood-burning black iron stove; cooked over very low heat at the back of the stove until the bottom is brown and has taken on crispness, a good hash is characteristic of the New England art of eating. And red flannel hash, with a poached egg or two topping each portion, is also ornamental.

If the beets that tint this dish generally cause Yankees to think of winter underwear, they also are said to have reminded members of the Yale Club of Harvard's crimson battle colors; as a result, beets prepared in a sweet and sour sauce have been nationally known for several generations as Harvard beets. And beets distinguish red fish hash—made by combining them with potatoes and codfish or halibut instead of meat. In Maine's saltwater country the tender red-spined green leaves of young beets that thrive in that sandy soil are simmered with salt pork as greens; the small roots are cooked separately, then both are combined and dished up with lots of butter, and with vinegar and chopped eggs as accessories.

July 4th Salmon and Aristocratic Codfish

Even as early as 1630 a passing traveler said that the Maine coast "had the smell of a garden." That image still prevails, though much of the terrain is rugged and the soil stony. Produce of the sea and earth are brought together in special ways in this state, particularly in the traditional New England Fourth of July menu that calls for freshly-picked green peas, gently simmered Maine salmon, and a creamy sauce containing hard-cooked eggs.

Like Independence Day salmon, salt cod seems synonymous with New England. In addition, shellfish were so abundant in the beginning that Pilgrim cooks at Plymouth, according to early cookbook writers, had nearly fifty ways of serving clams and lobsters. There may be fewer ways to prepare cod for the table, but the Massachusetts affection for it is such that a wooden replica of the codfish is enshrined in the state legislature, and in the nineteenth century it was the source of status and fortunes for families who belonged to what was known as the "codfish aristocracy." In those days in every home there was a box containing hard, whitish slabs in the back pantry, and in many cracker-barrel stores a long, dried fillet of salt cod hung next to the rum barrel as a kind of free lunch to whet the thirst. Cod was considered a must for Saturday dinner for generations of seagoing New Englanders and was known as Cape Cod Turkey when it was cooked with pork scraps and served (like fresh salmon) with an egg sauce, and with boiled potatoes and beets decorating each side of the platter. Cooks in Gloucester, Massachusetts, are famous for their codfish balls, and in Rhode Island fresh cod is stuffed with onions, celery, bread-

Broiled Boston Scrod

Split a young codfish and remove all bones. Sprinkle with salt and pepper and dip in olive oil. Again sprinkle with salt and pepper and dip in bread crumbs and broil on a medium fire (charcoal is best) about 20 minutes, or until tender. Put on hot platter and cover lightly with butter to which chopped parsley and a little lemon juice have been added. ½ to ¾ pound scrod serves 1 person.
—Parker House, Boston

crumbs, and oysters before baking, or it is made into a custard and served with that state's famous white-meal Jonny cake.

However, haddock may be New England's favorite fish, and the fact that it has considerably more flavor than its cousin the cod is reason enough for such popularity. Like cod, it is sometimes served under a mantle of egg sauce, and there are numerous New England ways of stuffing haddock—one with minced clams, onion, and buttered and crumbled crackers being very good indeed. In Maine whole haddock is notched and wedged with salt pork, then baked slowly, sometimes for several hours.

This is fine food that doesn't threaten the budget—but then neither did lobster when New England was young; so plentiful was it then that it was used as bait for codfish. One early traveler after another reported his surprise over these long-clawed crustaceans, grown to five or six feet in length and weighing twenty-five or thirty pounds. Somewhat wryly, perhaps, one writer said that these giants began to disappear from New York harbor as the result of "incessant cannonading" during the Revolutionary War. Sixty years or so later, however, the visiting English Captain Frederick Marryat, of the Royal Navy, noticed the prodigious size of lobsters off the Boston coast and said that each one "could stow a dozen common English lobsters under their coats of mail." By the end of the nineteenth century lobsters no longer were permitted to grow so large, and the going price in Maine—per *dozen* whole lobsters—was reported to be twenty-five cents.

Homarus americanus is not only different from European lobsters but does not inhabit Atlantic waters south of Long Island; the clawless crayfish of Florida and the West Coast are widely known either as spiny lobsters, rock lobsters, or Key West crawfish, but are slightly tougher and lack the true lobster's exotic flavor. Thus in this single instance, Puritan food had a great advantage over that of the plantations, opulent though the southern cuisine was soon to become.

The two regional cooking styles had many shellfish in common in their beginnings, but the Indian way of cooking seafood packed in seaweed, with ears of corn added, failed to catch on in the South. These so-called clambakes have remained a New England ritual for three hundred and fifty years.

The Pilgrims learned the ingenious technique from the Indians; seaweed was laid over stones hot enough to cause it to steam, thus cooking corn and shellfish in perfect concordance. In southern New England clams have given their name to this outdoor banquet, but no such occasion would be complete without lobsters; and in Maine, substantially the same kind of picnic is advertised by hundreds of resorts as a "lobster bake."

In either case some seaside chefs add various fish, along with chicken or sausages, and potatoes usually join the ears of field-fresh corn. One white-haired clambake patriarch I know substitutes a domestic washboiler for the Indian's method of digging a pit. This man's fire is laid in a

Fannie Farmer's Baked Stuffed Haddock

Clean and wipe a four-pound haddock, removing eyes, but leaving on head and tail. Rub over with salt inside and out, stuff, and sew. Cut five diagonal gashes on each side of back bone, and insert narrow strips of fat salt pork, having gashes on one side come between gashes on other side. Shape with skewer in form of letter S and hold in shape with small twine. Arrange strips of fat salt pork on fish sheet, put fish on sheet in dripping pan, and bake in hot oven one hour, basting with fat in pan every eight minutes. Serve with Hollandaise Sauce.

Lobster Stew

Bring 2 cups Maine sea water to boil in a steamer and lay in 12 medium lobsters shell-side down to steam in their own juice: cover tightly, keep heat high 10 to 15 minutes. Remove and pick meat from shell while hot, discarding intestinal vein and lungs. Let picked meat cool overnight. Melt ½ pound butter in large pot and in it heat lobster meat until it seethes. Turn heat low and slowly add 1 quart milk, stirring clockwise to keep mixture from coagulating. Add second quart of milk a little at a time. Bring to a froth and immediately stir in third quart of milk, stirring constantly. Let come to a boil and stir in 1 pint light cream; when this starts to bubble add remaining pint of cream. Simmer a few minutes without permitting it to boil, then remove from heat. Cool 12 to 24 hours while flavor develops. Reheat before serving. Season to taste. This will serve 10 to 12.

—Robert P. Tristram Coffin

    Take the meat out of the Tail and claws of a boiled Lobster & cut them in Slices, & season them with grated Nutmeg, Pepper and Salt; then take the Meat out of the Body, and season it with the Yolk of an Egg, a little Flour, Nutmeg, Pepper and Salt. Make these Ingredients into [small meatballs] and fry them brown with Butter; then [make a pie crust to line] your Dish and lay the pieces of Lobster in with some Oysters, an Anchovy shred, & the Force-meat balls over them, to which add half a pound of good fresh Butter, laying it uppermost. Close your Pie and bake it half an Hour, and then put in a Layer of good rich Gravy [made with fish stock].

              —Mrs. Sylvester Gardiner

trench, and he covers the bottom of his boiler with about three inches of common rockweed on which he spreads about a dozen hard sea clams, which he describes as too tough to eat but good for flavor. He layers these with more seaweed and spreads out a piece of cheesecloth to receive six small broiling chickens, split in half, and a pound of frankfurters. More rockweed is needed to bury a dozen each of white and sweet potatoes, then come ears of corn with the silk removed, followed by split lobsters wrapped in butcher's paper, more seaweed and cheesecloth, and three pecks of soft steamer clams. Rockweed has tiny sacs containing sea water which jetties, when heated, into the steaming meat and seafood. Thus when cooked, chicken tastes like something between fish and fowl; lobster gathers subtlety from the other meats; and the vegetables acquire an aromatic marine flavor from the steam.

    Lobsters that escaped immolation in clambakes were always easy for cooks to obtain, and cookbooks (*The Cook's Own Book*, Boston, 1833, for one) made note that lobsters were sold already boiled in Boston markets "and are always fresh and good." A pie made of boiled lobster was a great Yankee favorite in colonial days and remained so for generations after the Revolution. Here, recorded sometime before 1763, are the instructions of Mrs. Sylvester Gardiner:

    A lobster pie recipe recorded in the 18th century by Mrs. Sylvester Gardiner (and other versions popular in colonial New England) was in the tradition of British meat pies. So is the common clam pie, variations of which will be found from the saltwater farms of Maine—where a simple combination of minced clams, clam liquor, cracker crumbs, butter, eggs, and milk is encased in a shell—to a vegetable and salt pork melange of Cape Cod or Long Island. A Towd Point recipe has only a single onion competing with the flavor of the clams but, in the Hamptons, Long Island potatoes are included as well, along with the sophistication of lemon juice and minced parsley. Around Chatham on the Cape some good cooks think a delectable clam pie can be made only after a night of a full moon. They disdain quahogs, or common long-necked hard shell clams, insisting on giant sea clams, so large that four are sometimes sufficient. When the round white moon fills the sky over Monomoy Point, and the tide is way out, diggers walk out as far as possible toeing the oozing sand with investigatory feet. When it is time to make the pie, they wash away the grit from the clams and strain the liquor, chopping off the heads and cutting away the stomachs. The body meat is chopped fine and combined with minced onion fried with salt pork, some flour, milk, and cayenne. Sometimes diced potatoes take the place of the flour-and-milk white sauce.

Mashed potatoes, carrots, and celery may be incorporated in the pies made from Chesapeake Bay clams in Virginia and Maryland, but in no other region is the clam so esteemed as in New England. True enough, sentimental Yankees who established their old place names like Salem and Portland in the Pacific Northwest also brought their appetite for clams—to the extent that a verse entitled *The Old Settler* includes this quatrain:

> No longer the slave of ambition,
> I laugh at the world and its shams
> As I think of my pleasant condition,
> Surrounded by acres of clams.

There were, as pioneers came to expect, some hard times for those New England settlers of Oregon and Washington, and a Judge Cushman of Tacoma has read into the record the fact that Puget Sound people had to rely so heavily on products of the sea, particularly the many Pacific varieties of clams, that "their stomachs rose and fell like the tides." These transplanted Yankees, according to a story sometimes told in Seattle, were so disheartened when they found themselves without corned beef that they replaced it with easily available local clams when they made hash. As they worked it out, clam hash has crumbled bacon and sautéed onion bits mixed with the clams, diced potatoes and two beaten eggs, and the conglomerate is baked in a moderate oven for about half an hour.

Yankees who haven't left home continue to do ingenious things with their native clams—there is a very heady soup of clams puréed with fresh green peas, a little celery, onion, carrot, and the inevitable salt pork. Clams served on Maryland tables are most often "deviled" with a mustardy sauce, or fried in cornmeal or pancake batter. Some are chopped into a fritter mixture and become famous further down the coast, as well as in New England.

When Oysters Were in Season

American oysters are still frequently served as they were in colonial times, and a real afficionado may insist there is no better way to eat them

Chowder for Ten or Twelve

Take of salt pork cut in thin slices, as much as will make half a pint of fat, when tried, which will do for a sufficient quantity of clams instead of two good sized cod, the heads or hard leathery part being first cut off. Be careful not to burn the fat. First, put your fat in the pot. Secondly, put a layer of clams on the fat; pepper, salt and a few cloves, then a layer of the slices of pork, strewed over with onions cut fine; then a layer of ship-bread or hard crackers dipped in water; then your thickening. Go on again with clams, &c. &c. as above, till your pot is nearly full, then put in water until you can just see it, and let it stew slowly. After coming to a boil, it will be done in twenty-five or thirty minutes. N.B.—Some like potatoes cut in slices, which may be introduced between each layer. Likewise wine or cider, as you fancy. This Recipt is according to the most approved method, practised by fishing parties in Boston harbor.

—*The Cook's Own Book*, 1833

than as they were first tasted at Jamestown, fresh from the water and unadorned. Virginia colonists in 1609 were kept from starving to death when sent to the oyster beds on the Elizabeth River with no other food than ground corn rationed at a pint a week per person. But by the middle of the nineteenth century, far from being used to stave off starvation, oysters were being eaten as a between-meals snack, and they were at least as popular as hot dogs a hundred years later.

Even Americans who had never visited coastal regions knew and loved the taste of oysters. Entrepreneurs set up "oyster expresses" which in one instance started oysters off in Baltimore, in a packing of seawater-soaked hay. Driven in fast wagons to Pittsburgh, barrels of the Baltimore oysters were loaded on Ohio steamboats for the next leg that took them to Cincinnati; there they were kept alive in saltwater tanks until they were sold. Chicago is reported to have celebrated its first oysters in 1842, when mollusks that had arrived alive in Ohio were boiled, packed in ice, and shipped by rail to the head of Lake Michigan. And Vermonters a hundred years ago could sit down to a supper in Montpelier, St. Johnsbury or Burlington and eat oysters that had spent the day in barrels of ice on the train from Boston. Even earlier, oysters had traveled similar distances in saddle bags or packed in kegs of flour or meal. At hinterland taverns they were kept alive, along with clams, buried in beds of sea sand and Indian meal that was faithfully watered twice a week or so. Oyster caravans, the spring wagons rattling along unpaved roads, served upper New York housewives who swapped butter, cheese, homespun, or their own carded yarn for some of the sea's bounty.

Such things helped to change the American cuisine more quickly from regional to national in character. Here's a diary entry of a late nineteenth-century St. Louis girl that tells us ". . . oysters and other shellfish come by boat from New Orleans in barrels, and when a family is fortunate enough to get a barrel, all their friends are invited for the evening . . . what a treat this is considered!" The word treat only begins to suggest the enthusiasm virtually all America had for oysters while the great plenty lasted. People bought and ate them on the street from wheelbarrows and wagons. Men, sometimes a little sneakily perhaps, went downstairs into cellars to purchase their fill of bivalves in smoky places called "oyster saloons." Some were fancy enough to cause a British visitor to note "the pleasant addition of curtains to inclose you in your box." With amenities like that, some of these oyster rendezvous were even called parlors.

Almost every town of any size had somewhere to sit and eat oysters, and a note of elegance in the decor usually indicated, in that Victorian age, that ladies would be welcome. A place called Gobey's in San Francisco advertised its "Ladies and Gents Parlor," perhaps to dispose of rumors that such hostelries may have been illicitly inclined. During the Gold Rush, in other places in that town, the company was overwhelmingly male as oysters were greedily eaten at twenty dollars a plate—and the greed was still there during the nineties when a dozen on the half shell, along with a small steak and a cup of coffee, could be had for a

quarter. A Philadelphian recalled a time when few blocks in his home city were without oyster cellars, and he added, somewhat longingly, that he was born too late "to have been taught that oyster eating, especially the eating of raw oysters, was the indulgence of low taste." He remembered that in that era of active temperance societies there were people who thought the eating of raw oysters was a form of cruelty to animals.

It is apparent that few Americans paid attention to such hard criticism—even when William Makepeace Thackeray, dining in Boston's Parker House and eating his first Wellfleet oyster, was widely quoted as having said that he felt as if he had just swallowed a baby. Another Englishman said that "a first rate American oyster is as big as a cheese-plate" and he added that a half-dozen—"their flavor undeniable"—were enough for a complete dinner. And there are reports that complete meals of nothing but oysters were not infrequent in New England; presenting them in several ways could and did result in a menu of variety. Community suppers, prepared by women with Yankee inventiveness, might go something like this:

Oysters on the Half Shell with Lemon and Horseradish
Pickled Oysters   Pigs in Blankets
Oyster Stew, Montpelier Crackers or Oyster Crackers
Escalloped Oysters, Brown bread sandwiches
Oyster Pie   Fried Oysters
Creamed Oysters with Pastry Diamonds
or Oyster Patties
Potato Salad
Apple Pie, hot or cold   Mince Pie, hot or cold
Cheese   Coffee

It is doubtful that any country ever went as crazy over oysters as the United States seemed to do in those years between the end of the Revolutionary War and the end of westward expansion. Dozens of ways of cooking them were devised, many of them bearing an undeniably American stamp. Their plenitude made them a natural addition to the stuffing that filled birds and turned various combinations of oysters and turkey—whether in pies or appetizingly stuffed buckwheat pancakes—into Yankee dishes. They have inspired top secret recipes like that for Oysters Rockefeller and Cream of Squash Soup. They have even, as they did to John and Adam Exeter in 1847, driven two Trenton, New Jersey, brothers to invent for special oyster uses a new kind of cracker one and one-quarter inches in diameter and three-quarters of an inch thick—just the right size to be accepted universally as "oyster crackers."

Oyster stew was often a Sunday supper in itself for families throughout the land during what might be called the "oyster century." The enthusiasm coincided with a wide acceptance of the chafing dish, not only as a boon to bachelors, but also to households left to their own resources when the cook had a day of leisure. In chafing dish cooking, more often

Oyster Soup

Three pints of large fresh oysters. Two table-spoonfuls of butter, rolled in flour. A bunch of sweet herbs. A quart of rich milk. Pepper to your taste. Take the liquor of three pints of oysters. Strain it, and set it on the fire. Put into it, pepper to your taste, two table-spoonfuls of butter rolled in flour, and a bunch of sweet marjoram and other pot-herbs. When it boils add a quart of rich milk—and as soon as it boils again take out the herbs, and put in the oysters just before you send it to the table.
—*The Cook's Own Book*, 1833

Olympia Oyster Omelet

Heat up 1 cup of rich cream sauce made with best cream. Add 1 cup of Olympia oysters and cook until they plump. Season with salt, pepper and a little dry sherry; keep warm. For 2 persons, make a 4-egg omelet of French type, spoon ½ of oysters and sauce into omelet before folding. Turn out on hot plate and garnish with remaining oysters and sauce.

than not, the man of the family presided over the alcohol lamp and its heating pans, and equally often he was apt to consider oyster stew the finest, if not the only, dish in his repertoire. To judge by the memories of children who have written about such Sunday suppings, *pater familias* may well have been talented.

"It is more than a quarter century," says one of these tributes, "since I have had an oyster stew comparable to those Father used to do on the chafing dish on the table. He had a properly heavy hand with the sherry and a properly light hand with the red pepper." Less adventurous Yankees were likely to have a proper hand with paprika and nutmeg, or even celery salt. In my own boyhood it was the butter that got very proper attention, being cut into a thin pat that was dropped into each dish at the last, edge-of-boiling minute, so that it was a disappearing golden island as the first sip was taken.

If oyster stew is a dish for family suppers, roast oysters are for larger celebrations and, like clambakes in New England, oyster roasts draw big crowds below the Mason-Dixon line. Biloxi, Mississippi, where there are streets paved with oyster shells and shaded by moss-draped oaks, won fame throughout the South for its "oyster bakes"; and over on North Carolina's coastline where the Outerbanks throw up a narrow, sandy breakwater, the sea-hemmed-in village of Roadanthe year after year boasted of having the world's biggest oyster roast. Plantation owners on rivers like South Carolina's Combahee still entertain with oysters by the bushel freshly dug from local streams. (One bushel for fifteen guests is the rule.) They are washed and scrubbed and shoveled onto iron mesh or grills or sheet iron over a hot, crackling fire made of brush. A blanket of wet gunnysacking provides steam, and when the oysters pop and are spread out on a great table the hungry fall to and devour them in typically informal American style.

There was even a feeling of informality in antebellum days when Southerners went outdoors to feast on oysters and other good things as guests of the country gentleman who ran for political office—at least plantation aristocrats thought it was informality. Handymen carted big stoves onto the meadow and set them up in long lines facing each other. In between these lines serving girls set tables, also in long lines, impeccably decorating them with ancestral napery, fine china, and gleaming silver. When, at the appointed hour of one P.M., a hunting horn sounded from the portico of the great house, oysters by the barrelful were spread out to roast. A butler discharged his troops with whiskey punch for men and eggnogs for women. After the leisurely drinks, a guest once recorded, there came "battalions of pickaninnies bearing platters of sputtering oysters." And after an hour or so of feasting on oysters, there was an hour's rest while the linen was changed and order restored to the dining tables. Then crayfish in aspic, shrimp and watercress salad, red snapper baked whole with a wine sauce, terrapin stew and venison patty, pudding made of palmetto hearts and yams "baked so tenderly they fell into the mold of any hand they touched." Not until sundown was there a hint of the real reason for the picnic; then the host announced to his sated guests that he was standing for office and would appreciate their votes.

There was a landed-gentry Englishness to scenes like this. Much of the colonial South, said Sir William Berkeley, a Virginia governor in the The average plantation owner was a man of the middle class who acquired land and devoted his energies to building a life of greater security and more evidence of affluence than he or his forebears had known. Social status was of grave concern and was marked by an emphasis on horse racing and fox hunting, six-in-hand coaches and ten-gallon punch bowls. Hospitality, above all, was *de rigeur,* not only because there were in early days few taverns, but because guests added interest to the isolation of plantation life. Entertaining was easy enough, with so many servants, easier because so many had an affinity for cooking well. The colonial South, said Sir William Berkeley, a Virginia governor in the seventeenth century, was "the land of good eating, good drinking, stout men and pretty women." With these planters' wives a good table was a point of honor. Meals on most plantations were prepared in detached kitchens and sped to the table under cover by waiters recruited from the slave population—"long trains of slaves," as an early traveler wrote, "passing to and fro, with different viands. . . ."

Henry Clay's Own Mint Julep Recipe

From his diary: "The mint leaves, fresh and tender, should be pressed against the goblet with the back of a silver spoon. Only bruise the leaves gently and then remove them from the goblet. Half fill with cracked ice. Mellow bourbon, aged in oaken barrels, is poured from the jigger and allowed to slide slowly through the cracked ice. In another receptacle, granulated sugar is slowly mixed into chilled limestone water to make a silvery mixture as smooth as some rare Egyptian oil, then poured on top of the ice. While beads of moisture gather on the burnished exterior of the silver goblet, garnish the brim of the goblet with choicest sprigs of mint."

Plantation Breakfast Salt Herring

Take fresh herring, remove the head and insides and split the fish so that it can lie flat. Use as little water as possible in rinsing the fish. Pack herring in a wooden or earthen crock, a layer of fish and layer of coarse salt. Have the last layer one of salt and put a large plate, with a rock on top, so that all the fish will be in the cure. So prepared they will keep indefinitely. When you are ready to use the fish, soak them at least 24 hours in cold water, changing the water several times. Salt herring may be fried, but are best broiled with lots of butter. That is the way my father enjoyed them for his breakfast.
—"Uncle Morris," in an
old Virginia
newspaper

Toward a Uniquely Southern Cuisine

Aside from the service, the southern menu itself, of course, had little of the New England puritanism. Plantation breakfasts were generally so luxurious that one traveler after another described them in detail, and one reported that the ample breakfasts of England were, in comparison, "meager repasts." More often than not a man's day started with a julep "made of rum, water and sugar," or sometimes the eye-opener was brandy. Grilled fowl, prawns, ham and eggs, "potted salmon from England," cornmeal mush, varieties of hominy, and vegetable dishes might follow. A visitor in 1774 observed that the average planter rose early, had his drink (because "a julep before breakfast was believed to give protection against malaria"), then inspected his stock and his crops before breakfasting at about ten o'clock on "cold turkey, cold meat, fried hominy, toast and cider, ham, bread and butter, tea, coffee and chocolate." There was no pie to help break the night's fast, as there was in New England, but there was almost invariably hominy in one form or another and several kinds of hot bread—wheaten rolls, apple bread, for example, and cornmeal cooked in myriad forms.[1]

Northerners seem always to have been impressed. A Massachusetts man who visited Virginia during Madison's administration applauded the southern use of hominy, no matter how it might be prepared, because, as he said, it was a good substitute for potatoes which in the South "don't keep sound during the winter." While he noted that puddings and pastries were seldom served, there was always a great array of meats, "six or seven kinds . . . flesh, fowl and fish." And while neither cider nor home brew was as prevalent as in New England, Virginia tables offered weak toddies for the ladies, and for the men whiskey, apple or peach brandy, "with decanters on the sideboard." People said in those days that one could get good beef and bad bacon north of the Potomac, and south of the river there was good bacon and bad beef. It is true that pork was and remains a Dixie favorite. During the colonial period on one plantation alone twenty-seven thousand pounds of pork were annually consumed but only about one third that amount of beef. When Frederick Law Olmsted made his rather well-known tour of the South before the Civil War he described a meal at which there were "four preparations of swine's flesh"; and beside a variety of fowl there was opossum that the traveler found "somewhat resembled baked suckling pig."

Whether in the form of ham, bacon, or jowl, pork was always on the table, and most travelers agreed that Virginia ham was the best—good enough in very early colonial years to cause Sir William Gooch, royal governor, to send his home-cured hams regularly to his brother the bishop of Norwich, as well as to the bishops of Salisbury, London, and Bangor. William Byrd, who built up the great tidewater plantation called

[1] A nineteenth-century writer decided that in northern New England "all the hill and country towns were full of women who would be mortified if visitors caught them without pie in the house." As he saw things, the absence of pie at breakfast "was more noticeable than the scarcity of the Bible."

Westover, considered ham so important that his recipe was written in the flyleaf of his Bible:

> To eat ye Ham in Perfection steep it in half Milk and half Water for thirty-six Hours, and then having brought the Water to a boil put ye Ham therein and let it simmer, not boil, for 4 or 5 Hours according to Size of ye Ham—for simmering brings ye Salt out and boiling drives it in.

In the South hams have been a serious subject ever since the days of Gooch and Byrd. British methods of curing were employed from the first years along the James estuary but it was the planting of peanuts, used for cheap food on slave ships, that helped to give Viriginia hams their special flavor. Many of them were cured and smoked at a tidewater settlement called Smithfield after the London market area, and soon hams bearing that name were being favorably compared with the long-famous hams of York, Westmoreland, Suffolk, and Bradenham. By the nineteenth century in England, Gloucester and Buckingham hams were considered the best in the kingdom because the pigs in those countries were fed on beech mast. Yet the American peanut-fed hams appealed to Queen Victoria and a standing order went out from the palace for six of these Virginia hams each week.

Fame of this sort caused other American ham producers to appropriate the Smithfield name, while paying little attention to the quality exacted in the Virginia community. As a result, in 1926 the General Assembly of Virginia finally got around to trying to protect the trademark that had become the most famous in this country. The legislators legally defined "genuine" Smithfield hams as those "cut from carcasses of peanut-fed hogs, raised in the peanut-belt of the State of Virginia or the State of North Carolina, and which are cured, treated, smoked, and processed in the town of Smithfield, in the State of Virginia."

"A good Virginia Ham ought to be 'spicey as a woman's tongue, sweet as huh kiss, an' tender as huh love.'" So, they say, spoke one of the most talented country cooks as he demonstrated ways to prepare a perfectly aged ham. Most Virginia cooks, like Mrs. D. W. Sykes, whose colonial inn in Smithfield was widely known in the first half of the twentieth century, cook hams as simply and as carefully as suggested by William Byrd, above. Thomas Jefferson, at Monticello, had a boiled ham stuck with cloves, covered with brown sugar, and baked for two hours while it was intermittently laced with a good white wine. A variation in nearby Charlottesville calls for cutting end-to-end gashes an inch apart and deep enough to touch the bone. These apertures are stuffed with brown sugar mixed with chopped sweet pickles and crumbs of corn bread, and the ham is basted while baking with a sauce made from the water in which the ham simmered, plus vinegar and brown sugar. In southern Maryland the most typical old-fashioned way of stuffing is with a combination of greens—seasoned spinach, or mixtures of kale, watercress, cabbage, and celery—plus red pepper, mustard seed, and Tabasco. Real country hams often were simmered in cider or beer, but more modern housewives

To Cure Virginia Hams

For each hundred pounds of hams, ten pounds of salt, two ounces of saltpetre, two pounds of brown sugar, and one ounce of red pepper, and from two to four and a half gallons of water, or just enough to cover the hams after being packed in a water-tight vessel (or enough salt to make a brine to float a fresh egg high enough, that is to say, out of the water). From five to six weeks in brine; then hang up, smoke, and put in papers before the fly appears in spring—and bagged with the hock turned down, and hung till wanted. Boil till well done, for bad cookery can spoil the best ham.

—*Virginia Cookery-Book*, 1885

have been known to boil their hams in ginger ale or Coca-Cola on the theory that no other seasoning is needed.

The rich, nutty, pungent flavor of authentic American smoke-cured ham made this country famous (in ways different from other countries) for ham and eggs as a feast for breakfast, lunch, or dinner; and it made the South famous for red-eye gravy, which goes better—they say in Blue Ridge and Blue Grass country—with the hot biscuits and boiled hominy grits traditionally served with fried ham.[2] In the days of a cavalier style of life below the fortieth parallel, assertive ham was accompanied by baked yams or home-grown sweet potatoes baked with Virginia apples and chestnuts flamed in rum brought down the coast from New England.

Southern colonists, following English tradition, added slices of ham to beefsteaks cooked in gravy, sealing in the meats with a crusty top to make a meat pie. They maintained the Tudor custom of spiced beef, marinated a fortnight at least, then roasted and served cold; slices as thin as parchment are still eaten with beaten biscuits made by pounding (for half an hour until the dough blisters and is therefore full of air) a mixture of flour, lard, and water. In Baltimore and on the Eastern Shore, where these little hot breads are still made, sometimes with a machine designed to do the work of the tedious pounding, they are known as Maryland biscuits. (Beat, they say in Caroline County, at least thirty minutes, and forty-five for company.) At a buffet supper in Annapolis, tiny Maryland biscuits might accompany deviled Maryland ham, crabmeat balls, hot chicken mousse, deviled crabs, a casserole of rice, oven creamed mushrooms, spiced beef, lobster salad, green salad, sweet rolls, strawberry ice, lemon sherbet, and a fluffy vanilla cake.

Southern ham is a natural foil for birds and fish, and it often is served side by side with wild turkey or shad roe, for instance, just as it has frequently been combined with shrimp or crab or duck in so-called made dishes (casseroles) typical of the cooking style that may be called southern. One of the best of such collaborations between ham and seafood calls for crabmeat rolled in thin slices of ham, served straight from the fire, piping hot.

Early Virginians were apt to serve crab, shrimp, and lobster in traditional English fashion: very simply. They minced the meat of the crab, cooked it in some white wine and vinegar touched up with gratings of nutmeg; they made an anchovy sauce with plenty of butter and a couple of egg yolks, then combined sauce and crabmeat and served it hot in the shell. Along the Eastern Shore and in the Carolina Low Country soups and stews made with crabs and a milk-and-butter stock, or chicken broth, have been popular since the seventeenth century.

[2] They also say in the South that the smell of frying ham is enough to make a body dissatisfied with anything else he might be served. To enhance ham with red-eye gravy, put the fried slices aside and add one-half cup of iced water to the drippings, letting it bubble until it turns red. Some cooks use strong black coffee; others stir in one teaspoon of brown sugar until it caramelizes, then add the ice water.

18th Century Way to Butter Shrimps

First take your shrimps after they are boiled & set them on coles till they are verry hot; then melt your butter & beat it very thick & poure it on them when they are served up, & strew on some pepper.

—Frances Parke Custis

The blue crab necessary to dishes like these is brought in from Chesapeake Bay and the coastal waters of the Carolinas, Georgia, and the Gulf of Mexico. Soft shell crabs are another matter. They are blue crabs, all right, but in that biological state when they have molted one shell and have not yet grown a new one. In this period of about forty-eight hours, crabs seek peace and protection in vegetation-sheltered water near the shoreline. For the so-called "she crab," this idyll is the moment when she may welcome love. She waits for a hard shell male and then, after whatever ecstasies, she develops a new carapace and moves on toward maturity. When such soft shell crabs are caught they should be kept alive until they are put into the vessel in which they are to cook. An expert at shellfish cooking told me, "The only good crab is a live one. Hard crabs should be fighting their grim end when they are dropped into the pot of boiling water, and soft shell crabs should be alive through their last-minute preparation for the skillet or the broiler."

Crab meat may *seem* edible when bought frozen or canned, but none can compare with that fresh from the water. The blue crabs of the Eastern Shore that turn so brilliant a red when boiled alive are the basis of a considerable variety of cooked dishes. Sometimes this variety increases when a hero passes through town, inspiring the creativity of local chefs. (This happened a good deal in the nineteenth century when the world seemed more heroic.) When Admiral George Dewey returned from his Spanish-American War victory, the chef of the Maryland Yacht Club dipped into his French culinary background and invented Crab Meat Dewey—white mushrooms, black truffles, shallots, crab, all in a white wine sauce finished with thick scalded cream glazed under the broiler.

The last crab I had was not done *à la George Dewey;* it had no French sauce at all. It was just a plain, steamed Dungeness crab, a good deal bigger than that of the Atlantic Coast and named for a promontory just off the Pacific Coast in Juan de Fuca Strait.

Dungeness are found all the way from Mexico to the Aleutians and I doubt that any were ever better in flavor than the great piles from a Palo Alto fish man that we had on a recent Thanksgiving in a California ranch house, vaguely Spanish, in the Sonoma Valley. Our hostess was a California native for whom this arched room with its beams and its stippled walls and its expansive open-doored, warming Franklin stove had been designed. She sat at the end of the massive refectory table delicately stripping away shell and piling fat shreds of crab meat neatly on her plate before she began to eat. Most of the guests were less dignified—there were small sounds of shells being cracked by impatient teeth, fingers licked, monosyllables of appreciation. This crab had no hot pepper as in Louisiana, nor hint of nutmeg common in Charleston and on the Carolina coast. The meat was so sweet and delicately pungent that it seemed to me it needed nothing, not even the lemony melted butter with which it was served.

The first colonists ate crabs by the shore, and so do seafood addicts

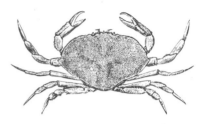

To Dress Crabs

Take out the meat and clean it from the Skin. Put it into a Stew-pan with half a pint of white wine, a little nutmeg, pepper and salt, over a slow fire,—throw in a few crumbs of bread, beat up one yolk of an egg with one spoonful of vinegar, then shake the Sauce pan round a minute, and serve it upon a plate.

—*Miss Ann Chase's Book,* 1811

today. A crab feast is one more American ritual, like clam and lobster bakes, and oyster roasts, that may take place on the grass, at an outdoor table, or in someone's screened-in porch. After white-sailed boats cross the finish line of a Tred Avon River regatta, sailors gather on the Chesapeake shore for a feast that may augment the steamed crabs with crab loaf sandwiches, corn roasted in the husks, tomatoes and cucumbers from a nearby garden, and watermelons.[3] The feast centers around an accommodating container, usually something like a large lard can with some sort of grating in the bottom. Steam is made by vaporizing two or three cups of cider vinegar or flat beer which has been seasoned strongly—mustard, red pepper, mace, and ginger for starters. Scrambling crabs are dropped into the container, the cover clamped on, the fire licking around the bottom. Cooking takes about twenty minutes, and eating is every man for himself; the eating surface is spread with newspapers while each guest operates with knife, nutcracker, or another device to break the claws. The job is to remove the top shell, feelers and apron, discarding the gray-white spongy "dead man's fingers" and the intestines. Break the claw shell and split the body to get at the meat. And don't overlook the greenish crab fat—that's a delicacy.

Cookbooks before Miss Fannie

The crab loaf that is sometimes on the menu at organized roasts represents an old English custom that may first have been described in a cookbook in 1741 when Edward Kidder published his *Recipts of Pastry*. Kidder described hollowed rolls fried in deep drippings, then filled with a stuffing of chopped oysters and eels covered by an anchovy-mushroom wine sauce; lobster meat was similarly bound into rolls in those days. Today a crab loaf is made with a crusty loaf of bread from which the top is cut and the interior hollowed out. A crab meat filling is prepared by mixing shredded crab with mustard, celery seed, salt, and pepper, and a good deal of butter with a little of the bread crumbs doused in sweet cream. The top is put back on the loaf which is then heated in a fast oven (or wrapped in foil and toasted over coals), then cut into sizzling slices.

The Kidder book was published in London, and it was there that a Virginia printer named William Parks in the same year found one of the ten editions of *The Compleat Housewife* by Eliza Smith and decided it was time Virginia colonial women had a cookbook of their own. In the style of the times, Parks simply appropriated from Mrs. Smith's various editions recipes (including one for oyster loaves) he considered useful and adaptable to the colonial life; he left out those containing ingredients not obtainable or those which would merely "swell out the Book and increase its Price." His pirated version went on sale in Williamsburg, and soon other English cookbooks were made available to colonists. The first

[3] When one has tasted watermelons, Mark Twain wrote, "one knows what angels eat. It was not a Southern watermelon that Eve took; we know it because she repented."

truly American cookbook did not appear, however, until George Washington was retiring as the new nation's first president. *American Cookery* was published in Connecticut in 1796, for the first time giving printed instructions for the cooking of corn and other colonial produce.

"An American Orphan," designated as the author of this book, turned out to be a New England cook named Amelia Simmons, who gave the earliest professional directions for making Indian pudding, Johnny cake, and watermelon pickles. Between 1796 and 1808 *American Cookery* was published in four editions, and its repertoire widened to include Independence Cake, Election Cake, and Federal Cake, titles that spoke of a new nationalist fervor. There was talk of an "American mode of cooking." Lucy Emerson of Vermont did to Miss Simmons what William Parks had done to Mrs. Smith—she reprinted most of the Simmons recipes in a volume she called *The New England Cookery*. But she didn't succeed in making her usurpation any less English or more endemic to the homeland of the Yankees.

The first genuinely regional cookbook available to Americans was *The Virginia Housewife* by Mary Randolph published in 1824. In Mrs. Randolph's pages there was a candid breaking away from the English past and an admission of other influences in the gastronomy of the United States. Hers was the first book to devote an entire section to vegetables and to feature some not commonly served in England such as sweet potatoes, pumpkins, squashes, and tomatoes. She was loyal enough to her region to be the first to recommend fresh, young turnip tops which, she declared, "are still better boiled with bacon in the Virginia style. . . ."

At last there was a Virginia style. And if it differed from that of those Yankees up north, it differed also from the culinary ways of Huguenot Carolina, of creole Louisiana, and Catholic Maryland. Yet throughout the South the gentle pace of everyday life linked one region to another. The common affluence before the Civil War helped to make ideas from abroad more easily acceptable. Some of these seemingly new ways of looking at things had to do with what goes on in the kitchen, and—inevitably, perhaps—there were some changes made in that abstraction we tend to call American food.

Amelia Simmons' Coriander Cookies

Cream ½ cup butter till soft; add 1½ cups sugar gradually and cream till fluffy. Sift flour with a little baking powder and salt, and stir in 1 tablespoon of coriander. Add dry mixture alternately with some sour cream and milk, beat after each addition. Dough will be quite firm and can be handled and baked at once. Pinch off pieces about size of hazlenut. Roll in balls, flatten out in circles on greased cookie sheet. Bake in hot oven 12 to 15 minutes, or until edges begin to brown. Cookies may be sprinkled with colored sugar, cinnamon and sugar, or chopped nuts before baking. Makes about 75.

Mrs. Randolph's "To Scallop Tomatos"

Peel the skin from very large, full, ripe tomatos—put a layer in the bottom of a deep dish, cover it well with bread grated fine; sprinkle on pepper and salt, and lay some bits of butter over them—put another layer of each, till the dish is full—let the top be covered with crumbs and butter—bake it a nice brown.

—1831

Chapter 2

The French Touch

SOME TRAVELERS from abroad viewed this country in its earliest epochs not only with alarm but with alimentary disdain. The initial criticism was based not on notions of French *haute cuisine*—which Puritan England found sinful—but on the recognition that raw materials too often were treated without sufficient respect. Travelers were always, in those days, impressed by the abundance of fish, meat, and vegetables, but they deplored what happened in the kitchen to such good things. In 1796 on a visit to New York's city market one observer counted sixty-three kinds of fish, fourteen kinds of mollusks and crustaceans, fifty-two of meat and fowl, along with twenty-seven garden vegetables for sale. (A whole pig, it was noted, could be bought for fifty cents.) Bounty has rarely, however, had very much to do with culinary excellence.

England's seagoing novelist Captain Frederick Marryat made it a matter of record that in the early nineteenth century there were "plenty of good things for the table in America; but. . . ."

It was a big "but" that Marryat managed to soften by a frequently used quotation: " 'God sends meat, and the devil sends cooks,' " he wrote in his *Diary in America,* adding, "such is and unfortunately must be the case for a long while, in most of the houses of America, owing to the difficulty of obtaining or keeping servants." The situation was no different in public hostelries. Traveling through shingle-roofed hamlets and tree-stump studded countryside, visitors generally agreed that taverns themselves were dreadful, and the food served in them was occasionally close to inedible.

One of these Britons, for half a dozen years a consul for Her Majesty in Transcendentalist Boston, had no doubt that the worst of the trouble was in the cooking. "The great evils," Thomas Colley Grattan said in a book he chose to call *Civilized America,* "are the odious attempts at *la cuisine française,* and the bad butter used in the sauces." It was the first of these evils that upset Mr. Grattan the most. "Every broken-down barber, or disappointed dancing master . . ." he declared, "sets up as a cook. . . . In a word, the science of the table is at the earliest stage of infancy in the United States. In all the doubts and fears expressed as to their future fate, nothing sounds so terribly ominous as that aphorism in [Brillat-Savarin's] 'Physiologie du Gout,' which solemnly says, *'La destinée de Nations dépend de la manière dont elles se nourrissent.'* "

Ominous, no doubt—but it isn't too easy to find a direct connection between this nation's destiny and the way it nourishes itself, Brillat-Savarin to the contrary. Almost thirty years before he published *The Physiology of Taste* in 1825, this most celebrated of France's gastronomes did spend a couple of years in New York, for a time as a fiddler in a theater orchestra, but he wasn't enough impressed with the city's food to mention it in his classic volume. He was in fact a little like the more pretentious American cooks of the period. He went out one day in Connecticut and shot a turkey, then served it, of course, with the most subtle French touches he could devise. Naturally, this Gallicized repast was a resounding success with the guests who gathered near Hartford.

Another Debt to Jefferson

Brillat-Savarin had no effect on American culinary ways, but by this time Thomas Jefferson's admiration for the food of France had begun to have limited influences, especially in his native South. In his five years in Paris, where he followed Benjamin Franklin as U.S. envoy, as much of Jefferson's attention as he could spare was devoted to recipes rather than treaties, to the intimate secrets of the kitchen rather than those of state. Jefferson, as Marshall Fishwick put it a little too neatly, "wed Virginian and French cooking in one of the happiest unions recorded in the history of cookery."

At any rate, he did his best to do so. It was Jefferson who ensconced the first French chef in the White House. And he carried his point further when, bringing eleven servants to staff the executive mansion, he assigned two black girls, Edy and Fanny, as apprentices to Chef Julien so that they might learn advanced culinary ways. He was convinced that the Paris influence in the kitchen was worth paying for. "I have understood that twenty dollars a month is what is given to the best French cook," he wrote a friend, going on to say that he was so determined to find a superlative chef that he authorized his agent "to go as high as twenty-eight dollars." Forty percent more than the prevailing wage was simply not too great a premium for the assurance of having the best food in Virginia.

Patrick Henry permitted himself to get so riled by Jefferson's Gallic admirations that he once told a political rally that the author of the Declaration of Independence "abjured his native victuals." This was missing

the point. For at the same time Edy and Fanny arrived to develop their skills under Julien's tutelage, Annette, the Monticello children's governess, joined the White House crew to make sure that the president also got the kind of southern food he had grown up with. Annette knew "just how he liked batter cakes, fried apples, and hot breads served with bacon and eggs at breakfast." Far from abjuring anything, Jefferson was determined to surround the best of Virginia food with the best from the European cuisine.[1]

In this spirit Annette left a record of her way of making chicken hash, under the title *Capitolade* and with the stipulation, "This dish is for breakfast." Rich in chopped cooked chicken, mushrooms that came from the edges of nearby woods, home-grown shallots, onions, and garlic, *Capitolade* is the kind of dish that Southerners often have found at plantation breakfasts, and its sauce of dry white wine combined with chicken stock suggests Jefferson's encouragement of the use of his French vintages in the kitchen.

Waffles made by cooks like Annette were made from the same mixture of ingredients as batter cakes, the southern term that Yankees or Westerners might translate either as pancakes or griddlecakes. In Jefferson's South, the French urge for the thinnest of batters was more often than

Rice Woffles

Boil two gills of rice quite soft, mix with it three gills of flour, a little salt, two ounces melted butter, two eggs beaten well, and as much milk as will make it a thick batter—beat it till very light, and bake it in woffle irons.
—*The Virginia Housewife,* 1831

---

[1] Perhaps others in the fledgling U.S. government might have learned from Jefferson. A French traveler during Washington's administration pointed out the importance of food in some diplomatic situations. He said of his country's minister to the new nation that his "maladroitness was such that when he dined at the home of M. [Alexander] Hamilton . . . he took with him two or three dishes cooked in the French fashion on the pretext of being on a diet." Needless to say, had the French minister dined with Jefferson such precautions would have been even more gratuitous.

not suppressed. One New World pancake, for instance, blended unbolted wheat flour and corn meal with eggs and clabber or curd—another combined flour with yeast and cooked hominy grits whose pearly contribution made the cakes that sizzled on a hot griddle seem slightly heavy though smoothly textured and unlike any European forerunner. George Washington's mother was one of the cooks who made sure that cakes like these were even more American by serving them with a mixture of maple syrup and honey heated together. There were, as well, efforts to emulate French chefs more closely by making very thin dessert *crêpes,* still known in Virginia vernacular as "Quire-of-Paper Pancakes." These are mixtures of egg yolks, flour, butter, sugar, and white wine, and when they come hot off the griddle the paper-thin cakes are stacked, with sprinklings of maple sugar on each surface, then cut in wedges like pie. Dating back to the same colonial period, "Pink-Colored Pancakes" also sometimes turned up as dessert on Virginia tables. There was nothing very French about these; they got their color from beets pulled fresh from the kitchen garden and their sweetness from coatings of preserved fruits.

Jefferson's garden, surely, was a boon to his cooks. He had planted such continental delicacies as broccoli and endive, together with vegetables about which even Patrick Henry could find no reason to complain. It was also true that he grew and ate tomatoes when the relatively few Americans who had heard of them considered them poison apples. Jefferson's garden got his closest attention, and for years he joined his neighbors in vying for the earliest harvest of peas, the winner playing host to the losers and serving the victorious crop as a highlight of a celebratory meal.

Just how keen on "native victuals" Jefferson really was can be seen in these entries from his 1774 *Garden Book,* ending on August 3 in a crescendo of pride for home-grown things:

May 16. First dish of peas from earliest patch.
May 26. A second patch of peas comes to the table.
June 4. Windsor beans come to table.
June 5. A third and fourth patch of peas come to table.
June 13. A fifth patch of peas come in.
July 13. Last dish of peas.
July 18. Last lettuce from Gehee's.
July 23. Cucumbers from our garden.
July 31. Watermellons from our patch.
Aug. 3. Indian corn comes to table.
        Black-eyed peas come to table.

Indian corn on August 3, of course, would be corn on the cob, picked and husked and cooked in the swiftest progress from field to hungry mouths. The black-eyed peas Jefferson noted that day really belong in the bean family (botanically *Vigna sinensis*); they would have been picked and shelled early in the morning, when still a bit dewy, kept in spring water until an hour before dinner time, then cooked in the French manner with bacon or white meat (salt pork) just long enough to pre-

Arlington Quire-of-Paper Pancakes

In a note to a recipe-collecting committee of St. James' Episcopal Church, Pewee Valley, Kentucky, Mildred Lee said in 1898, "I send a recipe for pancakes, an old-fashioned Virginia dessert, which we used to use at Arlington." Her directions follow:

"Beat 4 eggs light and frothy; beat in ½ cup sugar. Sift together ½ cup flour and nutmeg gratings and add to egg mixture alternately with 1 cup milk. Use a rotary beater if necessary to remove lumps, then stir in ½ cup melted butter and ¼ cup Madeira or sherry. Heat 5-inch griddle or frying pan, painting with butter. Put about 2 Tbs batter on hot griddle, tilting immediately to spread thin layer over entire surface. Cook about 2 minutes till brown on bottom and well done on top. As each cake is finished stack on pie plate in 200° oven and dredge with powdered sugar; keep stack covered with another pie plate turned upside down. To serve, cut stack in wedge-shaped pieces like a pie."

serve their garden tenderness. Monticello cooks may also have picked black-eyed peas before they were ripe, snapping them from the vines when only two or three inches long and following a Paris recipe for cooking the pods as one would prepare so-called French beans.

During the winter, dried black-eyed peas—they've also been known as field peas, cowpeas, whippoorwills, Jerusalem peas, Tonkin peas, and Marble peas—from earliest times have served the South in the same fashion as baked beans often staved off hunger for most of the rest of the country. Like all other beans, these marbled black-and-white legumes are enhanced by the flavor and fat of one or more kinds of meat. They would not have been found *per se* by Jefferson during his stay in France. But while minister he had toured much of France and had seen the bean fields of Languedoc; there is at least a chance that he tasted a leguminous *cassoulet* at either Castelnaudary, Carcassonne, or Toulouse, for he stopped at each of these hometowns of the classic French baked-bean dish. He investigated the provincial food with enthusiasm, and he wrote his friend Lafayette that the traveler who would learn about French food "must ferret people out of their hovels, as I have done, look into their kettles, eat their bread. . . ." Though he told Lafayette he had considered "the throwing of a morsel of meat" into some of the pots he saw, he didn't, so far as we know, include a recipe for *cassoulet* among all his notes on food; nevertheless there remains in some parts of Jefferson's South a casserole recipe that seems to demonstrate how a little of that kind of French influence is still recognizable in a forthright American dish of black-eyed peas.

This version of baked beans requires some cooked country ham and some leftover duck, wild or domestic. Delicious as they can be, such elaborations are not considered necessary among many Southerners.[2] Sometimes, when black-eyed peas are served with sliced meat, no more than a dash of cream and some black pepper are added. When fresh

[2] A legendary southern bean dish is known as Hoppin' John, most closely associated with the Carolinas. Variations of Hoppin' John are served also in Georgia and Florida, in fact in most states of the Old South. The dish is traditionally a high point of a New Year's Day meal when a shiny dime is often buried among the beans before serving. He who gets the coin in his portion is assured good luck throughout the year.

Carolina Hoppin' John

Cover ham bone, hog jowl, or hunk of salt pork with water and cook for 2 hours. Add 1 cup dried black eyed peas which have been washed and soaked overnight. Cook until almost tender. Remove meat and add 1 cup washed raw rice with salt and pepper. Boil until rice is tender and liquid has evaporated.

—Old Salem Cookery

black-eyed peas accompany roast meat they are sometimes embellished with sour cream, cucumber, dill, caraway seed, orégano; this last may be the only one of the herbs listed that did not grow in Mr. Jefferson's garden.

In his years as president, Jefferson took time when he could to oversee all phases of supply and preparation of White House food. "He would get out the wagon early in the morning," his overseer Edmund Bacon later wrote, "and [his steward] Lamar would go with him to Georgetown to market. . . ." Bacon emphasized that "it often took fifty dollars to pay the marketing they would use that day." At Monticello, according to Bacon, guests came "in gangs," with or without invitations, "and they almost ate him out of house and home. . . . I have killed a fine beef and it would be all eaten in a day or two. There was no tavern in all that country that had so much company." Jefferson himself, said Bacon, "was never a great eater, but what he did eat he wanted to be very choice. . . . He was especially fond of Guinea fowls, and for meat he preferred good beef, mutton, and lamb." With a sense of the history he played a part in, Bacon added that "Meriwether Lewis' mother made very nice hams. And every year I used to get a few from her for [the president's] special use."

Edmund Bacon is one of many who has left impressions of both Jefferson as host and the French influences he brought to his table which the overseer described as "Chock-full [of] Congressmen, foreigners, and all sorts of people." He said they would sit down to a four P.M. dinner and talk on into the night. One of them, Congressman Manasseh Cutler of Puritan Massachusetts, preserved a Jefferson menu for February 6, 1802, that had offered White House guests "rice soup, round of beef, turkey, mutton, ham, loin of veal, cutlets of mutton, fried eggs, fried beef, and a pie called macaroni."[3] Desserts included "Ice cream very good, crust wholly dried, crumbled into thin flakes; a dish somewhat like a pudding—inside white as milk or curd, very porous and light, covered with cream sauce—very fine. Many other jim cracks, a great variety of fruit, plenty of wine (and good)." A list Jefferson had made of desserts fashionable at the French court when he lived in Paris included pastries, custards, cakes, sweet fritters, and a variety of fruit compotes. He had brought home a delicate recipe for blancmange made with almond paste and gelatin, and some of the French sauces he asked his Virginia kitchen to duplicate were those known as *hachée, tournée, piquante,* and *Robert.*

Margaret Bayard Smith, who played an active part in the first forty

---

[3] It seems that macaroni and Parmesan cheese were two of Thomas Jefferson's favorite foods. The macaroni pie that Cutler mentions belongs in this category, but it failed to enchant the Massachusetts congressman; his description says it "appeared to be a rich crust filled with strillions of onions, or shallots, which I took them to be, tasted very strong, and not agreeable. Mr. Lewis [TJ's secretary, later to be sent with William Clark to explore the Louisiana Purchase] told me there were none in it; it was made of flour and butter, with a particularly strong liquor mixed with it."

Thomas Jefferson's Ice Cream

Jefferson called his freezer "a cream machine for ice," the purchase having been made in 1784. His recipe: "Beat 6 egg yolks until thick and lemon colored. Add 1 cup sugar and a pinch of salt gradually. Bring 1 qt. heavy cream to a boil and pour it over the egg mixture. Put it into the top of a double boiler and cook until it thickens. Remove and strain through a fine sieve. When it is cold, add a teaspoon of vanilla. Freeze as usual."

years of the capital's social life, recalled long after Jefferson's death that the president's dinners were beyond comparison with any others given in the White House. She said succinctly that "republican simplicity was united to Epicurean delicacy" in a style of hospitality not emulated often enough in the new nation. Seeing things differently, John Adams was nonetheless still impressed when he wrote: "I held levees once a week that all my time might not be wasted by idle visits. Jefferson's whole eight years was a levee. I dined a large company once or twice a week. Jefferson dined a dozen every day."[4]

The open-handed hospitality that distinguished Jeffersonian dinners invested all the meals at which he presided. "The French style" was duly noted by the New England educator, George Ticknor, who was a Monticello visitor as a young man; and Ticknor was impressed as well with the breakfasts that might on the same day include braised partridges, eggs, bacon, cold meats, fried apples, various hot breads, along with the ever-present batter cakes, and a tansy pudding that may have softened the bitter taste of that herb by following an old recipe which mixed tansy with sweeteners, brandy, eggs, milk, citron, and spices. (In her chronicle of capital life Margaret Bayard Smith noted a similar menu in describing a "most excellent Virginian breakfast" when she visited James and Dolley Madison.) And "Pannequaiques," a festive recipe Jefferson had picked up from his chef in Paris, also became a favorite French addition to Monticello breakfasts.

Triumphs for La Haute Cuisine

Jefferson's luxurious dining was not unique. Increasingly French influences were acknowledged. Even the Williamsburg edition of Mrs. Eliza Smith's 1742 cookbook had a good share of recipes with French titles, albeit of bastardized spelling, as when *poupeton* came out as "pulpa-toon." Much the same is true of America's oldest manuscript cookbooks, some belonging to early eighteenth-century households. One of these, kept by Frances Parke Custis, the mother of Martha Washington's first husband, includes French bread, and in it the terms *à la mode, à la braise, à la daube* are common. No matter that Eliza Smith had written in an introduction to one of the editions of her manual: "To our disgrace, we have admired the French tongue and French messes. . . . [French chefs are] upstarts who do such preposterous recipes as stuffing a roast leg of mutton with pickled herring." No matter that the famous Mrs. Hannah Glasse warned, "If gentlemen will have French cooks, they must pay for French tricks." In her *The Art of Cookery, Made Plain and Easy,* one of the most popular cookbooks in colonial Virginia, Mrs. Glasse fairly

Tansy Pudding

Blanch and pound a quarter pound of Jordan almonds; put them in stew-pan, add a gill of syrup of roses, the crumbs of a French roll, some grated nutmeg, half a glass of brandy, two table-spoonsful of tansy juice, 3 oz. of fresh butter, and some slices of citron. Pour over it a pint and a half of boiling cream or milk, sweeten, and when cold, mix it; add the juice of a lemon, and 8 eggs beaten. It may be either boiled or baked.

—*Mackenzie's 5,000 Receipts, 1829*

The Custis Way to Stew Calves Feet

Boyle & pill them, then put them between 2 dishes over a chafing dish of coles, with some water, & put therein a little vinegar some currans, sugar cinnamon & mace & when they are enough you may if you pleas put in a piece of fresh butter and soe serve them up.

[4] Some clue to dinner à la Adams may be found in these lines by John Quincy Adams, second member of that family to be a White House host: "At home I find the table spread, / And dinner's fragrant steams invite, / But first the two fold stairs I tread, / My atmospheric tale to write. / Then seated round the social board, / We feast, 'til absent friends are toasted, / Though sometimes *my* delays afford / The beef or mutton *over-roasted*."

exploded at "the blind folly of this age, that would rather be imposed upon by a French booby, than given encouragement to a good English cook!"

French cooking threatened that of the English because it was better, of course, and also because of the enforced exodus of many of the best exponents of the Parisian cuisine. The French Revolution caused chefs like Louis Eustache Ude (Ude had been Louis XVI's cook) to seek refuge in Great Britain where they began to tantalize the upper classes with the joys of *haute cuisine*. An English translation of LeSieur Menon's *La Cuisinière Bourgeoise* had been published in London as early as 1763, and Ude's *The French Cook* came out in English in 1813 when the author was assuaging the palates of the Earl of Sefton's guests with the subtleties of Paris dining. "French tricks" were bound to gain acceptance in spite of Mrs. Glasse.

Reprints of French cookery manuals including Ude's were widely used on this side of the Atlantic early in the nineteenth century. Affluent Americans, turned Francophile by their hero-worship of men like the Marquis de Lafayette, were—much more than their English cousins— quick to show interest in recipes from French kitchens. As a consequence these tricks of chefs were pirated without shame or apology. One such

Miss Leslie's Indian Pound Cake

Cream six tablespoonfuls butter, gradually working in one cup sugar until mixture is fluffy. Beat in four eggs, one at a time. Sift together one and a quarter cups flour, three-quarters teaspoon baking powder, and one-quarter cup sifted white corn-meal, then stir in a dash of ground nutmeg, a good pinch of cinnamon, half a teaspoon of vanilla and two teaspoons applejack, a little at a time. Pour this batter into greased shallow cake pan and bake in slow oven about one and a half hours. Let it cool after baking, then turn upside down on rack.

Common French Omelette

Break as many eggs as you please into a saucepan; add salt, and mix in some parsley minced very small, and some onions for those who like them; beat up the eggs well; then melt some very good butter in a frying-pan till it no longer hisses—this is the precise moment when it begins to turn brown, and the moment for the throwing in the eggs. Place the frying-pan on a good, clear, quick fire, that the omelette may be of a good brown, and yet not too much done, which is a great fault, and serve it up hot.

—*The Carolina Housewife*, 1847

collection of loot, called *Domestic French Cookery,* was compiled in 1832 by Eliza Leslie of Philadelphia, five years after she had published *Seventy-Five Receipts* which she described as "in every sense of the word, American. . . ."

Miss Leslie's American book did offer New World ideas like "Indian Pound Cake," made with cornmeal, sugar, butter, eggs, spices, and brandy, and a boiled "Boston Pudding" for which she suggested a filling of cranberries. She also gave instructions for "New York Cup Cakes" and she balanced her recipe for "Common Gingerbread" with one entitled "Lafayette Gingerbread," which was richer for the use of lemon juice and a sweetening of brown sugar in addition to molasses. But French recipes dominated as Miss Leslie compiled other cookbooks in a career that kept her work in print for more than forty years. Even for her, French recipes in themselves were not enough. For Americans living in good-sized towns Miss Leslie defied Mrs. Glasse altogether. Her advice in 1837 stipulated that the "safest way to avoid a failure in an omelette soufflé . . . is to hire a French cook to come to your kitchen with his own utensils and ingredients and make and bake it himself."

In that same period the first real restaurants appeared in major American cities, and along with hotels, country inns, and local taverns they too began to persuade American housewives that keeping up with one's neighbors meant staying abreast of the French.[5] The Astor House, the preeminent New York hotel when Miss Leslie's second book appeared, pursued this trend as early as 1838 in somewhat haphazard fashion by presenting a menu with "Boiled Cod Fish" and "Oysters and Roast Turkey" listed alongside Paris dishes like *Ballon de Mouton à la Tomate* and *Rouleau de Veau de la Jardinière.*[6]

"Delmonico" Enters the Language

The previous fall had seen the opening of a restaurant that was to do perhaps more than any other to set high standards for Americans interested in good food. The soon-to-be-famous Delmonico's established a

[5] Reactions were sometimes mixed. In 1838 the distinguished Philip Hone, prominent Whig and long-time mayor of New York, protested the new style of serving one course at a time, instead of placing all dishes on the table at once. "One does not know how to choose," he wrote in his diary, "because you are ignorant of what is coming next, or whether anything is coming. Your conversation is interrupted every minute by greasy dishes thrust between your head and that of your next neighbor, and it is more expensive than the old mode of showing a handsome dinner to your guests and leaving them free to choose. It will not do. The French influence must be resisted. Give us the nice French dishes, *fricandeau de veau, perdix au chous,* and *cotelettes à la province,* but let us see what we are to have."

[6] It may be that this custom is not unknown today. At any rate, as late as 1855 one of the great hostelries of the period, the United States Hotel at Saratoga, New York's renowned resort, ineptly scattered its menu with compromise language: "Filet of Veal à la Gardiniere," "Tenderloin of Mutton à la Maire d'Hote," "Currie of Veal en Bordured de Riz."

cuisine that was exclusively Continental; the French-speaking family from Switzerland wrote their menu in French, then paid one hundred dollars for a translation and henceforward had their bills of fare printed with matching columns of English and French. Their two-language menu was widely imitated, and for the rest of the nineteenth century the Delmonico restaurants set many styles that increased the French influence on American food. Twentieth-century cookbooks continue to give instructions for dishes that have become standards: Delmonico potatoes are creamed and baked with cheese; finnan haddie got its Delmonico touch in a similar treatment, with cream, hard-cooked eggs, and cheese; a delicate, custardy pudding also bears the name. And good old-fashioned butchers, wherever they may be, can still offer a Delmonico steak which dictionaries define as a piece cut from the short loin.

Although "Delmonico" still carries with it a connotation of excellence, and although chefs who received training at those restaurants moved on to establish *la grande cuisine* in far-flung hostelries like San Francisco's elegant old Palace Hotel and the Broadmoor Casino in the Rockies, the name is as apt as not to remain attached to unsophisticated dishes that have no clear lines of heritage. I know of one, to be found in a "Collection of Choice Recipes from a Golden Era of St. Louis Living," and it takes the cookbook browser back a hundred years or so to "cook's night off" and the chafing dish that became so necessary a part of American dining room paraphernalia.

MENU

Huîtres

Potages

Consommé, Souveraine   Tortue verte à l'anglaise

Hors d'œuvre
Timbales, Périgourdine

Poisson
Bass rayée, Massena
Pommes de terre, fondantes

Relevé
Filet de bœuf aux olives farcies
Tomates, Trévise

Entrées
Chapon à l'Amphitryon
Petits pois, parisienne
Térrapène à la Newberg

—

SORBET TULIPE

—

Rot

Canvas-back Duck   Cailles

Froid
Terrine de foie-gras
Salade de laitue

Entremets de douceur
Pommes à la Condé
Gelée aux oranges   Gaufres, Chantilly   Pièces montées
Glaces fantaisies
Fruits   Dessert   Petits fours
Café

Mardi, le 21 Novembre, 1893.   DELMONICO'S

Cherry Delmonico

Drain thoroughly a can of large red sweet cherries. Remove the pits and replace with small blanched roasted almonds. Arrange nests of crisp watercress on individual chilled plates. Line each nest with mayonnaise and fill with stuffed cherries, each rolled in cream cheese softened with cream or undiluted evaporated milk, having the finished balls the size of a large walnut. Use three balls in each nest and dust with a few grains of paprika blended with cinnamon.

Charleston Potatoes à la Madame Genlis

Boil your potatoes, with a little salt; cut them in slices, and lay them in a stew-pan, with a good sized bit of butter, some parsley and skellion chopped fine, with pepper and salt; place on the fire and turn frequently, so that all will be covered with the butter sauce. When served up, a little lemon-juice is added.

Veal Hash Delmonico may not have earned its credentials from any chef, but the preponderance of precooked ingredients makes it an easy and savory meal to conjure up in a chafing dish, with little or no kitchen experience—and with egg yolks added at the end, there is a distinctive French touch hinting at the delicacy of *blanquette de veau.* Chopped onion is cooked gently in oil, diced veal and potatoes are scattered in and accented with chopped pimiento, chopped olives, and chopped eggs. Equal amounts of stock and good thick cream are then poured into the chafing dish, and as these cook down a bit a little of the resulting sauce is stirred into lightly beaten egg yolks so there will be no curdling over the heat. When this mixture has blended well it is turned into the hash and served hot, still quite liquid in consistency, over toast or English muffins.

Sometimes there seems no end to dishes of this sort, so clearly American in their amalgamation of various ingredients but with touches that betray a debt to Parisian cooks. While the Delmonico reputation was just beginning to affect some American householders, others more affluent were already going more directly to French sources by taking their cooks along when they traveled abroad. In the South generally, cooks who had been born as well as trained in France were common enough to cause one lady of a great Charleston family to point out that cookbooks published especially for the use of those cooks—and in their own language—were "to be found in every book store." There was no ignoring the various degrees of interest in the cooking of Paris. In and around Charleston many plantation cooks in late antebellum days were guided by a volume entitled *The Carolina Housewife,* described modestly by its author as "a selection from the family receipt books of friends and acquaintances who have kindly placed their manuscripts at the disposal of the editor"; in fact, it also included general hints from the French along with several recipes culled from *Maison Rustique,* a manual written by the accomplished Mme. Genlis, an intimate of the French royal household. The appearance in Charleston of the Genlis recipe for Lyonnaise potatoes seems to have been the first notice of that dish in these United States, setting off a chain reaction that has come close to making American restaurant menus seem incomplete unless they include potatoes fried with onions in the manner of France's second largest city.

Sarah Rutledge, the compiler of *The Carolina Housewife* who belonged to one of the South's first families, hoped that her selected foreign recipes would, as she said, add value to her book. On the other hand, Horace Mann's wife, one of the cultivated Peabody sisters of Boston, had a warning for her readers when she appended a section of French recipes to her no-nonsense book called *Christianity in the Kitchen.* It was all very well, she said, that citizens of France believe that health and happiness are connected to good cooking and that the French "have applied themselves to the task of improving the art"; nevertheless she thought they used too much butter, oil, and lard, and she exhorted Americans to eschew the Gallic penchant for "injurious ingredients."

As one who believed herself to be descended from Boadicea (early

Britain's warrior queen who defied the Roman occupiers), Mary Peabody Mann may have had reason for her aversion to any sort of Latin touch in Anglo-Saxon kitchens. Boadicea has gone down in history as having excoriated the southern invaders who wanted to impose fancy ways on straightforward Britons. Eyes flashing and untamed red hair flowing down her back, she told her troops that from across the Channel had come men "who bathe in warm water, eat artificial dainties, drink unmixed wine. . . ." Centuries later, in the Victorian times in which Mrs. Mann wrote, Boadicea had become for some Anglophiles a symbol of romantic revolt. In her own time the warrior queen had brought her cheering followers to their feet by praising them for eating the poorest of vegetables instead of bread, rejecting wine in favor of water, and using the juices of plants instead of fats or oils.

Paeans for the Food of Early New Orleans

Both Boadicea and Mrs. Mann fought losing battles. In America the invasion, albeit more specifically gastronomical, was not limited to a single front. As the immigration of chefs continued through eastern seaboard ports, the French influence emanating from the Gulf of Mexico became more and more recognizable in the repertoires of good cooks in other parts of the country. New Orleans, founded as a French town and surviving an interim of Spanish occupation, had developed its own cuisine early in American history. Some travelers who had tried Louisiana eating, and who damned the food of America generally, resorted to paeans when trying to do justice to the Crescent City of the South (so called because it is built on a curve of the Mississippi). And well-traveled William Makepeace Thackeray, whose appreciation of French gastronomy moved him to write the "Ballad of Bouillabaisse," was similarly affected by epicurean New Orleans. He described the city after his visit in the 1850's as the place where "of all the cities in the world, you can eat the most and suffer the least, where claret is as good as at Bordeaux, and where a 'ragout' and a 'bouillabaisse' can be had, the like of which was never eaten in Marseilles or Paris."

Such lavish praise was often earned by the food served in private homes as well as in restaurants, for Louisianans dining in public demanded that restaurant cooks be at least as talented as those employed by private citizens.[7] Such rivalry could not go unnoticed. Guests in New Orleans compared the food to that of Delmonico's and the equally outstanding dining room of the Hotel Brunswick in New York. And dining out in the Crescent City also brought to some minds favorable comparisons with Paris' Cafe Anglais, La Maison Dorée, Durand's, and Bignon's, some of the best of nineteenth-century Continental hostelries.

[7] "The Creole cookery in private houses is," British journalist George Augustus Sala wrote, "exquisite. The question whether Life be worth Living for can be immediately answered in the affirmative after you have partaken of white mulligatawny pepperpot and turkey with plantain sauce; and the New Orleans 'drip' coffee is the most aromatic and most excellent preparation of that beverage that I know."

Creole Bouillabaisse

First cut off the head of the Red Snapper and boil it in about one and a half quarts of water, so as to make a fish stock. Put one sliced onion and an herb bouquet consisting of thyme, bay leaf and parsley, into the water. When reduced to one pint, take out the head of the fish and the herb bouquet and strain the water and set it aside for use later on.

Take six slices of Redfish and six slices of Red Snapper of equal sizes and rub well with salt and pepper. Mince three sprigs of parsley, three bay leaves and three cloves of garlic, very, very fine, and take six allspice and grind them very fine, and mix thoroughly with the minced herbs and garlic. Then take each slice of fish and rub well with this mixture till every portion is permeated by herbs, spice and garlic. They must be, as it were, soaked into the flesh, if you would achieve the success of this dish. Take two tablespoons of fine olive oil and put into a very large pan, so large that each slice of the fish may be put in without one piece overlapping the other. Chop two onions very fine and add them to the heating oil. Lay the fish slice by slice in the pan and cover, and let them 'etouffe,' or smother, for about ten minutes, turning once over so that each side may cook partly. Then take the fish out of the pan and set the slices in a dish. Pour a half bottle of white wine into the pan and stir well. Add a pint can of tomatoes, or six large, fresh tomatoes sliced fine, and let them boil well. Then add half a lemon, cut in very thin slices, and pour over a pint of the liquor in which the head of the snapper was boiled. Season well to taste with salt, pepper and a dash of Cayenne. Let it boil until very strong and till reduced almost one-half; then lay the fish slice by slice, apart one from the other, in the pan, and let them boil five minutes. In the meantime have prepared one good pinch of saffron, chopped very fine. Set it in a small deep dish and add a little of the sauce in which the fish is boiling to dissolve well. When melted, and when the fish has been just five minutes in the pan, spread the saffron over the top of the fish. Take out of the pan, lay each slice on toast, which has been fried in butter; pour the sauce over and serve hot immediately. You will have a dish that Lucullus would have envied.

—*Creole Cook Book*, 1901

Sea Marsh Stew

Sauté for five minutes two cups of boiled, peeled shrimp with one cup of cooked and peeled crawfish tails. Add four cups of cream, a pinch of cayenne, one teaspoonful of Worcestershire sauce, a pinch of dry mustard, and salt. Simmer ten minutes. Add one cup of cooked green peas, drained, and a dash of fennel and paprika. Cook a few minutes longer and serve on toasted bread or in cooked pastry shells.

—*Mary Land's Louisiana Cookery*

Just east of New Orleans, along the Gulf of Mexico, nineteenth-century travelers could also find French food in Biloxi, Mississippi, and Mobile, Alabama, both of which predated the Crescent City as French settlements. In the twentieth century both towns (even though Mardi Gras is a gay and Gallic event in Mobile) have become more typically southern, with an emphasis on the provender netted in the Gulf. In the bayou country, west and south of New Orleans, however, French is still the predominant language, even if it is closer to the speech of Quebec than to that of Paris. And for similar reasons the cooking in this low country area may be closer to the earliest years of colonial America than any other. These water-logged counties of Louisiana are, as the inhabitants say, Cajun country, to which French-Canadians who refused to swear allegiance to the British crown were exiled. Coming from Acadia on the peninsula that helps to guide the St. Lawrence River toward the North Atlantic, these were fishermen and wetlands farmers who managed to preserve their folkways along southern lagoons and sluggish streams.

Cajun cuisine is not Parisian; it may in fact be closer to that of Brittany, from where thousands of colonists set out for the New World. Along the lacy Louisiana Gulf Coast fruits of the sea are as much a part of the good life as they are in Finistère and Morbihan. At Grande Isle and other fishing towns south of New Orleans, the shrimp fleet receives its annual blessing in an August dawn from an archbishop in golden cape and tall miter. After the chanting of litany, the newly painted fishing boats parade on the water and the day turns into a festival, with long board tables covered by newspapers, with steam redolent of red pepper rising from the maple-sugar kettles (otherwise idle at this season) in which shrimp are boiled, with fiddles stirring young and old to dance as they have for generations. Shrimp and crawfish—and oysters, mussels, eels, mullet—all echo the bounty of coastal France which has so influenced Louisiana cooking.

If Cajun food remains close to its roots in Brittany, the cooks of New Orleans, and of Louisiana's River Road plantations, have been responsible for the distinctive cuisine most often described as Creole. That word has French, Spanish, Portuguese, even Latin roots, and is applied to persons of European descent born in the New World. In culinary precincts it is used most frequently to describe spicy concoctions of tomatoes, green pepper, onions, and garlic. Creole is also used to describe the cooking of some of the Caribbean islands and their cooks have an undeniable claim to the term. But Louisianans have no doubt that it is *sui generis*, a label warranted only by the best of the state's local food.

The Louisiana Dowry

Sometimes cooks in other regions find that Louisiana's best seems to extend beyond reasonable limitations; the Creole repertoire is a formidable list, yet one that magnetizes those who like to cook. There is a tradition, one of their historians wrote in the mid-twentieth century, that

may help to explain: "When a girl marries she receives, as part of her dowry, the ancestral skillet. She is considered a social failure unless she develops a *haut ton* and applies it to her cookery. And in Louisiana today gastronomes may travel to the North, to the South, or to the City [of New Orleans] and find *un vrai régal* on the native tables."

This could mean a simple fish course of sea trout cooked with a sauce of green peppers, shallots, wine, and toast crumbs; or a dinner menu including shrimp in highly spiced oil and vinegar, turtle soup, Gulf trout filleted and served with sautéed soft shell crabs and a sprinkling of buttered almond slivers, along with new potatoes, broccoli from farms just up the river, a cabbage palm salad, and Louisiana pecan-molasses ice cream. It also could mean a preparation of shrimp that is one of the simplest yet most interesting ever devised. Sautéed in oil to which has been added several sticks of cinnamon, three or four cloves and a generous grating of nutmeg, the shrimp are left to steep in the spices a half-hour or so; then warm light rum is flamed and poured over them. Or a true Creole regalement might include thin pancakes stuffed with oysters in a hot Hollandaise-like sauce that is touched with the fire of *Tabasco à la Creole*, the sauce that Louisiana cooks make from home-grown peppers whose flavor, they maintain, is unsurpassed.

Not only do gifted Louisiana cooks prepare oysters in dozens of French-accented ways, the streets of the Vieux Carré of New Orleans are punctuated with oyster bars maintaining that nineteenth-century tradition which made ostreomaniacs of a majority of United States citizens. Oysters can be eaten in these quick-service places freshly opened, they can be popped steaming into one's mouth, or they may be carried home under a wondrous title, *La Mediatrice*—the famous "peacemaker" of New Orleans days when husbands sometimes stayed out long enough to want means to placate wives. "Right justly is the Oyster Loaf called the 'Peacemaker,'" a turn-of-the-century book says with a hint of Edwardian

Louisiana Molasses Ice Cream

Beat the yolks of four eggs and stir one cup of molasses into the eggs. Place in a double boiler and cook until thick. After the custard has cooled, add two cups of cream and one cup of minced pecans and freeze. The cream may be whipped before adding.

Nothing in New Orleans is better known than the 'Peace-Maker' and it is a foolish husband who does not rely on it in case of need. . . . The top crust of a loaf of French bread is cut off and the inside taken out, leaving a long, boat-like affair; this is buttered and slipped into the oven to toast. It is then filled with about 2 dozen fried oysters and the top, which has been buttered and toasted, replaced. It keeps hot for a long time and is fine.

Oysters Rockefeller

Take selected oysters, open them and leave them on the deep half shell. Place the shells containing the oysters on a bed of rock salt in a pie pan. The sauce for the oysters is compounded as follows:

Take the tail and tips of small green onions. Take celery, take chervil, take tarragon leaves and the crumbs of stale bread. Take Tabasco sauce and the best butter obtainable. Pound all these into a mixture in a mortar, so that all the fragrant flavorings are blended. Add a dash of absinthe.

Force the mixture through a fine-meshed sieve. Place one spoonful on each oyster as it rests in its own shell and in its own juice on the crushed rock salt, the purpose of which is to keep the oyster piping hot. Then place them in an oven with overhead heat and cook until brown. Serve immediately. Thus spoke Monsieur Alciatore to your humble servant.

—Louis P. De Gouy

naughtiness, "for, well made, it is enough to bring smiles to the face of the most disheartened wife."

Women needn't wait for men to turn wayward to enjoy an Oyster Loaf. It is identical in concept to the crab sandwiches of the Eastern Shore. But it still carries with it the connotation of a man making amends for indiscretions. Buttery sautéed oysters confined in a hollowed-out and toasted loaf of French bread became famous in San Francisco's gayest days as "the squarer"; even in puritan Connecticut the idea—there called "Boxed Oysters"—may have helped to get a mild philanderer out of trouble. Doubtless no such problems lurked behind the fact that Mrs. James Monroe noted that her recipe for Oyster Loaves came to her from Martha Washington, or that she sometimes substituted clams or shrimp in the same formula.

Seafood in all its forms distinguishes New Orleans menus. Oysters from Bayou Cook, Lac Barre, and Barataria Bay, once in almost unlimited supply, were as famous in the nineteenth century as Long Island's Lynnhavens, the Chincoteagues from Chesapeake Bay, or the tiny Olympias from Puget Sound. Louisiana's shellfish now are most apt to come from Houma or Morgan City, whence they are trucked by the ton across bayou country to French restaurants of New Orleans that have built worldwide reputations on their saltwater cuisines. Antoine's, where Jules Alciatore created Oysters Rockefeller, may be the "Frenchest" of them all, and the secret "Rockefeller" recipe has become so much a part of American cooking lore that its original similarity to the Burgundy sauce that sometimes dresses snails may have been lost. Yet whether oysters are blanketed in combinations of spinach, shallots, herbs, and anchovy, or lettuce, spring onions, anise, lime juice, and Tabasco sauce—to suggest only two of the secret's variations—Oysters Rockefeller remains one of the most appreciated discoveries of diners-out who like exploring unfamiliar culinary paths.

One way or another the Frenchness of Louisiana cooking has branched out and made its mark. Oysters Bienville, named for one of the heroes of New France, was concocted by a New Orleans restaurateur; the oysters are tucked into a sauce with a really Parisian elegance. When made in the Vieux Carré this Bienville sauce is dominated by minced shrimp. In a Baltimore modification the shrimp are joined by clams and are puréed. There is a similar variation on a theme in another French Quarter recipe, one that calls for frogs' legs: *Grenouilles en Fricassée à la Vieux Carré* embellishes a classic method by adding oysters. Up the Mississippi at St. Louis, cooks went even further afield with a dish of frogs' legs hidden behind the title of *Pigeons de Marais* because somebody at Tony Faust's oyster house thought a fastidious Victorian lady would be repelled at the image instilled by a more accurate description.[8] In this

[8] To utter the word leg in front of ladies was considered crude, vulgar, even insulting. The gallant Captain Marryat tells of such a blunder on his part, after which the lady involved instructed him always to use limb to placate tender female sensibilities. She is quoted by Marryat as saying, "Nay, I am not so particular as some people are, for I know those who always say limb of a table, or limb of a

preparation of "marsh pigeons" the shellfish is crab—instead of oysters which are used in the traditional New Orleans fricassee—and the meat of the frogs' legs is stripped from the bone before simmering in wine. As it is made today the final result—and it is delicious—is a combination of boned crab and frog meat cooked with mushrooms; there is a cream sauce accented with sherry and applejack, plus a dash of cayenne pepper that marks so many colonial Louisiana specialties.

Eighteenth-century settlers already had carried up the Mississippi and onto its tributaries much of traditional Gallic cooking. St. Louis was a thoroughly French community before Thomas Jefferson moved into the White House. So were smaller places like Terre Haute and Vincennes on Indiana's Wabash River. On the Ohio there is Louisville (named by an American admirer of Louis XVI), where French glimpses can be seen in recipes from down river that are now acclaimed as Kentucky's own. One of these is called Louisville Rolled Oysters, little more than fist-sized clusters of tiny bivalves from Mississippi Sound dipped in egg and seasoned cornmeal and deep fried; simplicity itself, this is an encrusted, seethingly hot bunch of oysters that can taste of the Vieux Carré when eaten at family gatherings in Blue Grass backyards.

Nothing about things of this sort seems remarkable enough to claim as a regional achievement. But good, simple cooks, loyal to their home turf, don't need to dazzle to establish their competence. They leave spell-binders, often enough, to those who cook for the public. In Louisville and Natchez and the plantations along the River Road, many of the best of the public cooks by 1850 were black and male and so well trained that those of them who took over the galleys of the luxury steamboats plying the Mississippi and the Ohio were masters of the intricacies of *haute cuisine*. Aboard the shining white, gold-trimmed sternwheelers and side-wheelers, these chefs created plantation meals for passengers from all over the country and many parts of the world. Among voyagers dining under chandeliers swaying to the boat's motion they spread the enthusiasm for food of the Vieux Carré and Greek revival mansions.

Chickens, pigs, lambs were shepherded on board—because of lack of refrigeration—and fish were hooked or seined from the waters that turned to foam as the steamboats churned forward. In the galleys pompano were plucked from tanks and prepared *en papillote,* and the succulent Mississippi catfish were trimmed into *paupiettes,* rolled around a stuffing of pecans and capers, poached in white wine, and finished with a wine sauce encompassing mushrooms and oysters. Surely, the chef of a vessel like the *Robert E. Lee* had his men regularly turn out a caldron of New Orleans Court Bouillon which, in some ways close to a bouillabaisse, is a soup of several chopped vegetables with fish fillets added at the end. Far better known and considered so great an example of the burgeoning

pianoforte." Sometime after this colloquy Marryat entered a room in which, he later wrote, there was a "pianoforte with four *limbs.* . . . [In order] to preserve in their utmost purity the ideas of the young ladies in her charge, [the mistress of the establishment] had dressed all these four limbs in modest little trousers, with frills at the bottom of them!"

How to Cook the Toothsome Terrapin as It Ought to Be

Immerse the live terrapin in spring water, boiling hot, for five minutes, to loosen the skin. The skin is then removed with a knife, thoroughly polished to free it from any foreign substance, with a piece of chamois leather. Then replace the terrapin in boiling water. When the claws become so soft as to pinch into a pulp by a moderate pressure between the thumb and forefinger, take it out and remove the bottom shell first, as the convexity of the upper shell catches the rich and savory juices that distinguish the terrapin from the mud turtle and the slider. Cut off the head and claws, and carefully remove the gall and sandbag. A little gall does not impair the flavor of the terrapin, but the sandbag requires the skillful touch of a surgeon, the heart of a lion, the eye of an eagle, and the hand of a lady.

Cut up the remainder into pieces about half an inch in length. Be careful to preserve all the juice. Put in a chafing dish, and add a dressing of fine flour, the yolks of eggs boiled so hard they are mushy, *quantum sufficit* of butter fresh from the dairy, salt to taste, red pepper, a large wineglass of very old Madeira (to each terrapin) and a small quantity of rich cream. The dish like everything else fit to eat except Roman punch and Stilton cheese, should be served smoking hot. Some persons have been known to season with spices, but this, like the rank perfume which exhales from the handkerchiefs of underbred people, is apt to arouse suspicion.

—Sam Ward

American style of cooking that Lafayette gave it as one of his reasons for returning to the nation he helped to liberate, turtle soup was termed a national dish from the bayou to the diamondback breeding grounds on Chesapeake Bay.

Louisianans maintain that only a good Creole cook knows how to brew the aromatic mixture they still sometimes refer to as "Soupe à la Tortue." The basic method is French. Sometimes ham is added to meld with the flavor of the green turtle, white wine or sherry is stirred in, or quenelles exuding the fragrance of laurel and nutmeg are floated on the surface. Louisiana ways with green turtle soup spread across the South, augmenting rather than nullifying the Gallic base from which this kind of good soup or stew is apt to evolve. And in Baltimore, where French-trained cooks, driven by Haiti's war of independence, arrived in small legions, the diamondback terrapin became the center of the gourmet rivalry that pitted Marylanders against Philadelphians.

The French influence never was overt in Baltimore, but Philadelphia, for many early decades the country's largest city as well as briefly the capital, was long a cosmopolitan center. It was the kind of place at which Puritans and perhaps some others looked askance. "A most sinful feast again," John Adams wrote in his diary while attending the Continental Congress, "everything that would delight the eye or allure the taste—meats, turtle and every other thing . . . Parmesan cheese, punch, wine, porter, beer, etc." That phrase "turtle and every other thing" gives one pause. Turtle soup and turtle steak appeared on most formal Philadelphia menus when, in the early nineteenth century, at least one Fairmont Park hostess emulated Mme. Recamier, priding herself not only on her "salons" of intellectuals, but on her superior French dinners. (She had a dining room large enough to seat one hundred guests on gilded chairs imported from Paris.) The turtle served with dinners in Philadelphia got talked about a good deal—by intellectuals from abroad and by connoisseurs with upturned noses in Baltimore.

Finally, in 1893, some historians insist, members of Philadelphia's Rittenhouse Club and Baltimore's Maryland Club considered the matter serious enough to sit down at the same table. In Philadelphia, old-time purists believed that cream sauce should be blended with the turtle broth just before pieces of the meat are dropped in; in Baltimore, Maryland Club Terrapin is a clear soup laced with butter and sherry and dominated by picked turtle meat untainted by herbs or cream. In the famous meeting of the two clubs, according to an account that comes to me from a Chesapeake Bay acquaintance, the latter, simpler version got the nod from the impartial jury.

In New York Ward McAllister, the bon vivant whose roots were in Georgia, would have agreed essentially, substituting Madeira for sherry.[9]

[9] McAllister was a nephew of the great American gastronome Sam Ward, who helped to focus the interest of socialite Easterners on the French cuisine. McAllister has become remembered most, however, as the arbiter who established "the Four Hundred"—the number of guests Mrs. William B. Astor II deigned to receive.

But in Savannah where this self-styled "Autocrat of the Drawing Rooms" had spent a good many youthful days, terrapin from a nearby terrapin farm on the Isle of Hope is still turned into a succulent stew incorporating steamed turtle that has been allowed to cool in its own aspic and is melded with chopped egg whites, yolks rubbed with butter and flour, cream, and a good wine accented with onion, nutmeg, red pepper, Worcestershire sauce, and lemon.

Lessons from Mrs. Habersham

This manner with terrapin represents more than a classic recipe of the South. The formula was given coinage by a Savannah woman whose family background was the kind that didn't cause one to think of her in the kitchen, let alone teaching others of her social set how actually to prepare meals. The historical-minded Harriet Ross Colquit looked in on this episode of southern gastronomical development: "Long before it was fashionable for society women to have a career, or do anything in the least practical, Mrs. Fred Habersham, who was famous for her table, conducted a cooking school at her home in Savannah, and here all the young society matrons gathered once a week, pencil in hand, and wrote down the words of wisdom which fell from her lips, while she illustrated by cooking as she talked. . . . teacher and pupils fell to and ate all the delicacies which she had wrought, so that the undertaking could not have been a very profitable one for the teacher."

Mrs. Habersham may have been the first Savannah "society woman" to share her ability to create exceptional American food, but by the last quarter of the nineteenth century there were scores of teachers available to any female American who wanted to cook. By the time Thomas W. Lawson sent each of his four daughters to a teacher ensconced in a cottage on his Cape Cod estate—and offered each of them $100,000 when she could cook a formal dinner, including the making of bread and butter—the study of the art of cooking had become to some degree fashionable.

Of the teachers who became fashionable, most were French. Probably the best known was Pierre Blot, who arrived about the time of the Civil War. Blot was a Paris-trained chef and, as he advertised himself, a "Professor of Gastronomy" who believed American women were interested in the finesse of the French approach to food; after his "tour of Lectures" in the East, the New York Cooking Academy which he established was successful enough to persuade many that his instincts were right. His book *What to Eat . . . And How to Cook It,* published in 1863, seems to reflect his classroom straightforwardness, and his school continued, under the aegis of Juliet Corson, to give Americans opportunity to learn the fundamentals of classic cookery for years after the professor returned to France.[10]

[10] A sixty-page pamphlet was published in 1866 after Blot's "immensely popular" lectures in Boston's Mercantile Hall. In it a series of the Frenchman's recipes is followed by questions and answers: "Is a cook a chemist?" Well, said the professor,

While some women studied French ways in classrooms, affluent American males of the nineteenth century prided themselves on mastering the art of French cooking by habitual dining out in the best hostelries. Others, like Thomas Jefferson, developed their epicurean sensibilities by dealing directly with their own French cooks.

General Winfield Scott failed to make it to the White House in the election of 1852 but he was as devoted as his Virginia forerunner to the French cooking he learned first from an aged French colonist forced to

"A cook is a person whose duty it is to keep in order the animal mechanism. A chemist is called when the mechanism is out of order." M.D.s please note. His successor, Miss Corson, conducted cooking classes in both the United States and Canada and was awarded a prize at the Columbian Exposition in 1893 for scientific cooking and sanitary dietetics. Her lectures and demonstrations at the University of Minnesota in 1884 drew 1,200 persons who learned about such topics as "Cheap Dishes for Rewarmed Foods" and—foreshadowing the health-food enthusiasm of the twentieth century—the strength-sustaining values of lentils, fresh and dried peas, and beans.

take shelter near Petersburg after the Haitian revolution. While still a boy, Scott was taught to cook by this émigré who was too poor to afford a servant but so respectful of the meals he prepared himself that he never failed to dress for dinner. These lessons Scott amplified by trips to Paris where he got to know the chefs of Les Trois Provençaux, Very's, and other great restaurants. Traveling to every out-of-the-way corner of the United States as a career officer, Scott knew all about the food available to Americans and—as few others did—what should be done to make it more palatable.

More than that, he talked food and touted French culinary tricks wherever he went. "I know of no flesh or beasts, or edible fishes, or fowl, or herb, or root, or grain, the preparation of which for food," his aide Erasmus Darwin Keyes wrote in a book largely about Scott, "was not many times the subject of his conversation." The general, who was chief of staff of the army, was known as "Old Fuss and Feathers," but in the memories of maître d'hôtels in New York, New Orleans, Washington, and throughout the country he was respected as the nation's best known gourmet (when that word had a meaning worthy of real respect). Opponents of Scott's presidential aspirations accused him of gustatory xenophilism, yet his mind was usually on the bounty of his native land. During the Civil War, after he had had to reassign General Benjamin Franklin Butler to a command at Hampton Roads on Chesapeake Bay, Scott softened the blow by writing, "You are very fortunate. . . . it is just the season for soft-shelled crabs, and hog fish have just come in, and they are the most delicious pan fish you ever ate."

Old Fuss and Feathers might have instructed General Butler to have his cook prepare the molting crustaceans for frying in deep fat, or he might have urged that lump back crab meat be dressed in mayonnaise, sending along a recipe published in Charleston in 1847. Far from being confined to Delmonico's for dishes prepared in the French manner,[11] even epicures like Scott took for granted the increasing number of Gallic recipes that had come to be accepted as American. Mayonnaise, in fact, was being prepared in U.S. kitchens very early in the nineteenth century.

By the end of that century, when Fannie Farmer was well on her way to a lasting reputation as the arbiter of Yankee dining habits, her cookbook proved how easily thousands of Americans took to the influence of *haute cuisine*. *The Boston Cooking-School Cook Book*, by Fannie Merritt Farmer, published in 1896, did not bother to Americanize such recipe titles as Hollandaise sauce, chops en papillote, soufflé au rhum—or scores of others. Quoting John Ruskin in her foreword, the author of the cookbook that was to sell more than three million copies in the United States alone defined the meaning of cookery as, among other things, a capacity for ". . . English thoroughness and French art. . . ." Thus Miss Farmer cited the two most important influences on what was to become—however tenuously—American food.

[11] Winfield Scott ended his days living in the same building as one of Delmonico's dining rooms; his enormous weight so curtailed his travel that he made sure of being close to the best of kitchens.

Purely American Crab Soup

Open and cleanse 12 young fat crabs (raw) and cut them into two parts; parboil and extract the meat from the claws, and the fat from the top shell. Scald 18 ripe tomatoes; skin them and squeeze the pulp from the seed and chop it fine, pouring boiling water over the seed and juice and, having strained it from the seed, use it to make the soup. Stew a short time, in the souppot, 3 large onions, one clove of garlic, in one spoonful of butter, 2 spoonfuls of lard, and then put in the tomatoes, and after stewing a few minutes, add the meat from the crab claws, then the crabs, and last, the fat from the back shell of the crab; sift over it grated breadcrumbs or crackers. Season with salt, cayenne and black pepper, parsley, sweet marjoram, thyme, half-teaspoonful lemon juice, and the [grated] peel of a lemon; pour in the water with which the seed were scalded, and boil it moderately one hour.

—Old Abingdon Cook Book

Chapter 3

Padres and Conquistadores

IN *Death Comes to the Archbishop* Willa Cather tells of two French priests who helped to bring civilization to New Mexico. As Spaniards had done before them, these missionaries planted orchards and gardens, and nurtured vineyards. But Father Vaillant and Bishop Latour[1] never succumbed to the peppery tastes in cooking that had evolved after the Spanish conquest. Once, visiting a parishioner near Santa Fe, Father Vaillant is told that his host's dinner of young lamb is to be stewed "with chili and some onion. . . ." The prospect causes the priest to ask leave to personally roast his portion quickly, as it would be done in France.

"Cook a roast in an hour! Mother of God, Padre," the *rancho* cook cries, "the blood will not be dried in it!"

"Not if I can help it!" says Miss Cather's priest, and she pictures him carving while watched by serving girls appalled at "the delicate stream of pink juice that followed the knife."

Priests so gastronomically inclined are far from unique, and this scene rings with the accuracy of many occasions never recorded in either fact or fiction. In the Southwest, nevertheless, there were few Frenchmen, in or out of cassocks. There the European influence on food established by clerics and settlers alike was Spanish, with some Aztec and other Indian overtones. In the Southeast, and in Florida particularly, the Continental Spanish influence has been modified by the produce of tropical islands. It developed the distinction that is described as Creole along the rim of the Gulf of Mexico.

In New Orleans, where that city's best restaurant food is still as French

[1] Father Joseph Machebeuf, and Jean Baptiste Lamy, who became Archbishop of Santa Fe in 1875, were the Franciscans whose letters and papers Miss Cather used to document her novel.

48

as it ever was, the most authentic Creole cooking is apt to be found in private homes. The cuisine indigenous to Louisiana took on its own aromas and tastes when the first colonial women, like their English counterparts on the Atlantic Coast, began to adapt the ingredients and some of the methods of Indian cooking. Louisianans were quick, for instance, to exercise the possibilities of the Choctaws' powdered sassafras leaves, the modern version of which is called gumbo filé and gives soups and stews of that name their characteristic flavor and texture.

Louisiana's French colonists became Spanish subjects only forty years after the settlement of New Orleans, and for another four decades, until the beginning of the nineteenth century, Spanish tastes prevailed among the ruling Creole cooks. New Orleans, as the principal port of the Gulf of Mexico, teemed with traffic in imported goods from Latin America and the islands of the Caribbean. Tropical foods and seasonings suited the city's indulgent climate. Most influential of all were the assertive spices, foreign to Gallic cooking, but so basic to Spanish cuisine that Columbus' discovery of the New World had been (as history has so often insisted) a by-product of his search for the Spice Islands. Hot peppers, especially, like cayenne from the Guiana coast and Tabasco from the jungle plains on the southern rim of the Gulf, were brought north by Spaniards, and today some Louisianans claim that more peppers are raised in their state than in any other section of the United States. Along the southern tier from Florida to California, the use of peppers in combination with to-matoes became the common way to turn standard recipes into Creole variations.

Rice and Beans—and Color No Matter

The hurried traveler in Louisiana is apt to get the impression that all the best food is French in style, but—as careful preservation of ancient architecture in the Vieux Carré also makes clear—Spaniards left several kinds of permanent changes in gastronomy. Like other Europeans, they planted the seeds and encouraged the appetite for beans, especially the red ones that are often kidney shaped, or those known in Spanish as *frijoles colorado* or *habichuelas*. Red beans combined with rice comprise a basic dish, as typical of southern Louisiana as Hoppin' John of the Carolinas, the good luck dish for New Year's feasts. In one form or another, bean dishes are even more intrinsic to Spanish-influenced American food than to that of other parts of the country. The conquistadores introduced black beans into Florida from their Caribbean islands, along with more exotic ingredients, like the oranges that sometimes seem synonymous with the name of the state.

Again in Florida, rice is mixed with beans—black beans and rice are a sobering dish considered by party goers in Tampa to be a fine way to mark the witching hour of midnight. The beans are cooked very slowly with a ham hock. Red onions are slightly sautéed with garlic and chopped green pepper, then added along with bay leaf and a little vinegar to the simmering beans. After about three or four hours, rice is cooked separately to a fine fluffiness. The combination is served with the ham-and-pepper-flavored beans topping the white rice, and on top of all a garnish of finely minced onion and a lacing of oil and vinegar; sometimes chili powder and cayenne are stirred into the beans. And sometimes, among those who haven't forgotten their Spanish history, this combination is still called "Moors and Christians," the pristine rice representing the good guys, of course.[2] Black beans are a variant of *Phaseolus vulgaris,* the botanical family to which kidney, navy, pea, pinto, and other New World beans belong. Their flavor is heartier than most others, tastier in my opinion, but for some reason they are reserved for soup in most parts of the country. Black bean soup may well be, in fact, the best of all bean soups, no matter what region influences the cook. Onion, carrots, celery, and garden herbs are common accents, and in some recipes a ham bone or some chicken broth can add a meaty flavor. In that old Spanish town of San Antonio, Texas, however, sausages float in the brew of black beans ladled out at the century-old Menger Hotel, and wine, garlic, and the zest of Tabasco underline this soup's south-of-the-border influences. Wine has been a factor in some Texas cooking since the Franciscan priests began to cultivate grapes at El Paso early in the eighteenth century.

[2] In Louisiana that particular ethno-religious slur has been forgotten and the combination is called simply "Red and White." It's considered a hearty workingman's meal, and is often accompanied (as at Kolb's, on St. Charles Street, New Orleans) by sliced country ham, garlic bread, and beer. Sometimes the "reds" are mashed with butter, the ham slices, or salt pork, laid on top, the boiled rice on the side; with a green salad this version is considered a Louisiana favorite.

Early in the sixteenth century, a hundred years before the first British settlement, Ponce de León, who was governor of both Florida and Puerto Rico, brought rum to the mainland; there, perhaps inevitably, that distillation of sugar cane, rather than wine, was used to point up the orégano and garlic flavors of baked black beans. In Florida today this recipe is dressed up with sour cream floating on each serving, with ham—smoked or baked fresh—as the accompanying meat. South Florida cooks make an appetizing paste of black bean soup by mixing it in condensed form with chili powder, tomato sauce, and mild Spanish-type cheese such as Monterey Jack. In Tampa, which is about 25 percent Spanish in ethnic background, this bean spread is often served warm at cocktail time with marquitas, the green plaintain (or banana) chips which are sliced thin and fried in deep fat like potato chips.

"Spanish beans" is a term that sometimes refers to black beans and sometimes to garbanzos, or chickpeas, and I've wondered occasionally why the conquistadores, who found the Indians using so many kinds of beans unknown to the Old World, went to all the trouble of shipping garbanzos across the ocean. A story for which I can't vouch has it that the Southwest tribes—who, say anthropologists, have been cultivating beans since the fifth century—developed many varieties. They valued most the yellow, blue, red, white, pinto, and black because they symbolized the six cardinal points, north, east, south, west, zenith, and nadir. The Spanish found the Indian cooks stewing beans, frying them in animal fat, making them into bread and cakes, and even serving them cold in a primitive sort of salad. Still, men who came in search of the Seven Cities of Cibola introduced the chickpea to the Indians and—as other settlers entered the regions that Spaniards had colonized—to the developing American cuisine.

In Louisiana chickpeas are cooked with various meats seasoned with green peppers, chili powder, cayenne, and cumin, and are proffered with sliced pimiento and plain boiled rice, much like "Moors and Christians." In New Mexico and Arizona, where they give way to the pinto and the red bean in popularity among legumes, chickpeas are mashed and baked as a sort of chili-flavored soufflé, or are stewed with lamb shanks and the scent of saffron, or simmered with the hot Spanish type of sausages, called *chorizo piquante*, and a sauce made from red and green chili peppers. A Los Angeles version, obviously modified for Anglo tastes, combines blander sausages, ground beef, cooked chicken, onions and tomato paste, but leaves out the hot peppers. A more typical California way with chickpeas makes them a part of a barbecue; the cooked legumes are mixed with green chilies, green onions, and green pepper, all finely minced, and tossed with cumin and seasoned oil and vinegar. When designated as an hors d'oeuvre this delicious concoction is served alone, but gets a lettuce cup if offered as a salad. A similar recipe in Florida substitutes Tabasco sauce for the minced chilies, adds orégano, garlic, a goodly quantity of avocado cubes, and shredded spinach. Another combination—served hot this time—mixes cooked chard, cooked

To Cook Dried Lima Beans

At night wash one pint of beans, put them in a small tin pail, pour over them one quart of boiling water, cover closely and let them stand until two and a half hours before dinner; then add more water, and let them boil until tender, keeping them well covered with water. When nearly done, throw in two even teaspoonfuls of salt; be careful to keep them from breaking. When perfectly soft, drain in the colander, return them to the kettle, and add three ounces of butter, half a teaspoonful of white pepper, and one gill of cream. Shake them about gently, and when very hot, serve.

—Old Recipe

tiny new potatoes, and chopped tomatoes, with sautéed onion, garlic, crumbled dried chilies, and grated cheese.

Some Like Them Hot

The Spanish first encountered chili peppers, which their descendants and other Americans have learned to use so profusely, when Columbus came upon some of them after his landing at Hispaniola. Mistakenly, the admiral called them peppers, as if they were related to *Piper nigrum,* the Asian plant whose berries are dried and ground and used as seasoning in all kinds of cookery. The peppers of the New World are *Capsicums,* and there is a profusion of them—they vary in color from red to green to yellow, and in flavor from mildly biting as is the common green or bell pepper to the aggressive heat of sixty or more kinds of chili peppers.

Out of all these varieties only green peppers gained full acceptance in northern gardens; in the sixteenth century the Puritans banned pepper and all other spices on grounds that they encouraged their users toward passionate excitation. Capsicums have appeared on other lists of aphrodisiacs, but no case has ever been proved. The excitement usually occurs, if at all, over the first taste of a dish enlivened by chili peppers. A report of one of the earliest U.S. visitors to Taos, while that region was a part of Mexico, tells us that he and his companions could not eat the first meal offered them because the food was so fiery. Another early pioneer in Brownsville, Texas, wrote that he could "quaff the Rio Grande at a draught" because he found the chili-ignited diet so full of heat.

Theories vary on why anybody tolerates food so hot with spices that the eater thinks his mouth is on fire. One speculation holds that diet based on such things as beans and rice are so bland that enhancement with stronger and stronger seasoning may have been inevitable. History has it that Portuguese circumnavigators found in India a ready market for chili peppers because the average palate there already had a high appreciation of *Piper nigrum,* the black pepper that had become harder for the average Asian to get after that spice became such a prized trade item in Europe.

China's province of Szechwan once was more closely related to India, and because of a somewhat tropical climate it also had a natural affinity for the hot peppers of the New World. Its cooks have used them exceedingly well. The increase in the number of Szechwan restaurants in the United States during the last decades of the twentieth century could be seen as the trail of Capsicums come full circle, for many of the distinguishing flavors of this Chinese cuisine originated in the Western Hemisphere. Yet Szechwan food is attractive to American diners-out because of the subtleties and range of flavors; the spices are not allowed to be domineering. On the other hand, any dish made with the same spices and labeled "chili"—i.e., any such dish made in the authentic manner of the Southwest—is apt to be forthright, to say the least.

Used alone, the word "chili," to most Americans, means *chile con carne,* which translates from the Spanish into "chili peppers with meat," and is rather the wrong emphasis in describing a mixture that is more meat (in canned form usually more beans) than pepper. There are infinite variations in the preparation of chili con carne, but chili cooks can generally be categorized in one of two ways—those who follow the old Spanish-American recipes calling for chili pepper in pod form and those who insist that no authentic chili—or "bowl of red" as it is known by some Texans—can be made without a mixed seasoning called chili powder.

In its most widely distributed form chili powder consists of dried chilies ground fine, with cumin, orégano, and garlic, also ground, the combination mixed to make a powder that looks a good deal like instant coffee. There is no doubt that the packaging of this formula by Texans toward the end of the nineteenth century helped to maintain the popularity of chili con carne in regions where there was Spanish influence in the kitchen, and across the northern tier of states as well. Almost anywhere, a good argument can be worked up about the ingredients of chili con carne. "No living man . . ." an Illinois writer who went east wrote, ". . . can put together a pot of chili as ambrosial . . . as the chili I make. . . . That is the way of us chili men. Each of us knows that *his* chili is light years behond all other chili in quality and singularity." Some recipes call for ripe tomatoes and red peppers, some for green tomatoes and green chilies—Texas purists say that the original San Antonio style rejects tomatoes of any kind, rejects onions and all other vegetables except peppers and garlic. Southwesterners in show business, like Will Rogers, have been known to refuse to travel without a supply of canned chili, and a swing band leader of the 1940s went so far as to suggest that

Chile Sauce

No mild compound of hashed vegetables, sugar, and imported spices is the Southwestern chile sauce. You start with three or four whole, dried, red chile peppers. They go in a pan, preferably enamel or earthenware, with a clove of garlic and a quart of water. When the mixture has boiled until the chiles are pulpy, put it through a sieve to remove the seeds and membranes of the peppers. The sauce can be thickened a little with flour, and it can be salted, but purists object to this tampering with Nature's experiment in spontaneous combustion. They eat it as is, and they eat it on everything. Often chile seems to replace salt in the Southwestern diet.

—Alice Marriott
in *The Valley Below*

Congress, as he wrote to a friend, "should pass a law making it mandatory for all restaurants to follow a Texas recipe."

Most chili is based on beef, which faithful cooks never grind, but cut into small cubes instead. In New Mexico lamb or mutton is substituted. In a Dallas recipe fresh ham is diced and mixed with cut up round steak in a proportion of one to two. There is much argument about the merit of suet, and when Lyndon Johnson was president there was considerable to-do because the White House version of the Texas hill country recipe called for no beans. To put the matter straight, beans may or may not be included—mixed in or served alongside of the chili concoction. Chili is meat flavored with hot peppers and herbs—and with other embellishments, depending upon the cook. Fresh chili peppers are cultivated, among other places, in California's Ventura and Orange counties, in Texas, Arizona, and New Mexico. Unfortunately, the names vary from place to place. The milder varieties may sometimes be called simply California, or *poblano*, or *ancho*; some of the hot ones are known as *seranno* and *jalapeño* and *pequin*.

In early fall anyone who drives Route 64 along the Upper Rio Grande toward Taos can see ropes of pepper pods hung against adobe walls and over roofs to dry in the sun until they are the color of live coals. Some of these red ones are large and very hot and are sold in markets as "New Mexico chili pods." Others are ground and packaged without the addition of other seasonings. In the Santa Cruz valley in southern Arizona both red and green dried chilies are prepared for market, and Santa Cruz chili powder is carefully marked "no spices added."

Cooks whose palates are conditioned to peppery flavors sometimes suspect the nationally distributed powdered chili compounds of being stretched with cornmeal. Whether this happens or not, most chili cooks who opt for pure dried peppers, or the powder derived therefrom, do so because they like to control precisely the amount of cumin, orégano—the wild marjoram native to the Southwest—and garlic. Generally speaking, no other spice is acceptable in a traditional chili con carne, yet a Florida cook who proclaimed her own product "as fine a chili con carne as I have ever tasted" included in her formula an amount of paprika equal to the chili powder she used plus a third as much allspice. I have tried this, and while the recipe may seem heresy to the Chili Appreciation Society of Dallas (which eschews tomatoes and grudgingly admits a smidgin of paprika may be used for color) it results in a superior Spanish-American feast.

Of Seeds and Sauces

There may be fewer chili con carne purists in Florida than in the Southwest, but much of the other peninsula food shows that Florida for centuries has been receptive to newcomers with Spanish leanings. In Ybor City, the cigar-making suburb of Tampa, the black beans and rice may be accompanied by roast beef stuffed with raisins, olives, and bacon that releases a sweetly pungent aroma when carved. Spaniards brought the same idea to southern California where today roast pork infused with orégano and garlic is covered by thick brown sauce containing as accents sliced ripe native olives, raisins, cumin seeds, chopped green pepper, tomatoes. But there is also an East Coast version that calls for a pork roast to be stuffed with rice ornamented with olives and raisins in a piquant tomato sauce.

In Spain *arroz con pollo* is a classic—chicken cooked with saffron rice and peas and garnished with either artichokes or young asparagus. In Mexico Spaniards substituted chilies for the milder vegetables, a treatment of chicken-and-rice that moved north with the Dons into California. In Puerto Rico and Key West and South Florida and Spanish Harlem the accents are sometimes olives and capers, and more and more in places like Ybor City a mélange that is also called *arroz con pollo,* on menus and in homes alike, is dominated by tomatoes and sweet peppers. The classic architecture submits to the materials at hand. *Arroz con Pollo a los Estados Unidos,* like the average American citizen, retains its Old World name and an affinity for its origins, but it will never be the same.

Poultry and pumpkin seed sauce is something else again. Indians who met the Spaniards on the Rio Grande included pumpkin seeds among their gifts of peace, and the conquerors of the Pueblo Indian towns soon began adapting Indian ways of using the seeds in cooking. Chicken in a sauce of blanched almonds, pumpkin seeds, cumin seeds, popped corn, ground chili, and garlic is one of the legacies of the conquistadores. It is exotic, it is delicious, and it is not difficult for anyone who owns a blender to make. Almonds and the two kinds of seeds are stirred in a hot dry skillet until lightly toasted, then spun in the blender along with almost as much popped corn, the chili, and the garlic. This amalgam is incorporated into some chicken stock, sometimes with tomatoes, and simmered until it is the consistency of a thick gravy. Sometimes the chicken is poached, sometimes browned before baking in the sauce. The combination of flavors seems to take this dish beyond its Spanish-Indian beginnings, and the ineffable quality baffles guests—no one ever spots the popcorn flavor.[3]

Seeds and nuts and an equally surprising ingredient distinguish the chili-flavored sauce that makes Turkey Mole a Spanish-American recipe—a recipe so firmly established in California that one company in Rosemead, in the citrus country east of Los Angeles, sells a ready-made mole powder. The surprise component is chocolate. Turkey Mole is rare and

[3] New Englanders made such dishes as popcorn pudding, saturating the popped corn in milk. Euell Gibbons, who grew up in the Southwest, tells in his *Stalking the Healthful Herbs* of devising a suet pudding that combines a meal made by spinning dry-popped corn in a blender with flour ground from dried roots of the chufa, or earth almond, that grows wild in Florida and the Southwest as well as other regions; Indians ate the roots like nuts, while Spanish soldiers drank *horchata de chufas,* a sweet but refreshing beverage. Gibbons' chufa pudding uses two parts of popcorn meal to one part of chufa flour along with sugar, eggs, and buttermilk. His recipe is, perhaps, an unwitting twentieth-century crossing of Spanish and Indian food lines.

delicious enough to need no romanticization, but an apocryphal story about its origin may be worth repeating.

In the early nineteenth century the American Southwest was still under the jurisdiction of the see of Durango, and when any member of the church hierarchy moved north to visit the colonial parishes there was great excitement. Legend has it that the first Turkey Mole was concocted at the Convent of Santa Rosa to mark the arrival of the archbishop.

In the kitchen the cooks, quite naturally, were inspired to outdo themselves. They managed to get hold of some chocolate, which ancient Aztec custom reserved for royalty, and which therefore seemed suitable for the head of the church.[4] They ground the usual variety of dried chilies, added sesame and anise and coriander, cloves and cinnamon, garlic and tomatoes. To this long-brewed mixture, already dark brown from hours on the fire, the nuns decided to add that regal touch; bitter chocolate was certain to mystify His Excellency, as well as to flatter him when he should ask to have it identified.

The late Michael Field, whose several books on food are among the best in print, once said he'd been told that the ambition of every Spanish-American was to be served Turkey Mole on his birthday. Part of the trouble in achieving such a wish is that a great deal of grinding (the word *mole* suggests the Spanish word for mill and derives as well from the Aztec *molli* for sauce) was necessary in the old days. Now the efficiency of modern blenders makes this recipe for Turkey Mole à la Michael Field[5] worth bringing to fruition in any American kitchen:

The turkey and the stock

9–10-lb. turkey, cut up
7–8 qts. water
2 medium onions, peeled
2 medium carrots, scraped
1 lge. bay leaf
3 stalks celery with leaves
20 (about) black peppercorns
1 Tbs. salt

The mole sauce

6 Tbs. chili powder
5 Tbs. sesame seeds

[4] Since chocolate was considered by Aztecs to be aphrodisiacal, foods made of chocolate were forbidden to women. However, Cortez found the elite of Tenochtitlán drinking a foaming potion of ground cacao beans, vanilla, and red pepper chilled by snow from the Sierras. A hundred years later when Louis XIV married the Spanish Infanta, his bride introduced a similar New World combination of vanilla and chocolate to both sexes at Versailles. Hot chocolate seems to have been served even in Puritan New England as early as 1670, perhaps a score of years before tea became the patriotic drink that helped in the next century to launch the Revolutionary War.

[5] From *All Manner of Food*, by Michael Field (New York: Alfred A. Knopf, 1970).

¾ cup blanched almonds
1 tortilla, or ¼ cup crumbled corn chips
½ cup seedless raisins
2 medium cloves garlic, peeled
½ tsp. anise seed
½ tsp. cinnamon
½ tsp. powdered cloves
½ tsp. coriander seeds or ground coriander
3 medium, ripe tomatoes, coarsely chopped
3 medium onions, peeled & quartered
2 tsps. salt
½ tsp. whole black peppercorns
4–5 cups turkey stock (or chicken stock)
1½ oz. unsweetened chocolate, grated
4–8 Tbs. lard

In ten- to twelve-quart soup pot combine turkey pieces, gizzard, heart, onions, carrots, and celery. Pour in water to cover by two inches, bring to boil, and skim off foam and scum. Lower heat, adding salt and peppercorns, then cover and simmer as slowly as possible about forty-five minutes, until turkey is almost but not quite tender. (A leg or thigh should show slight resistance when pricked with fork.) Put pieces on board and cut meat away from bone in fairly large serving pieces; leave as much skin intact as possible. Return bones to pot and let stock cook fairly briskly over moderate heat, uncovered, while you make mole sauce.

In large mixing bowl, combine chili powder, three Tbs. sesame seeds, almonds, tortilla torn in pieces (or corn chips), raisins, garlic, anise, cinnamon, cloves, coriander, tomatoes, onions, salt, peppercorns, and two cups strained stock; mix. Blend two cups at a time of this mixture until all is thoroughly puréed and smooth. Pour into four-quart casserole and stir into it two more cups of turkey stock; bring to boil, then lower heat and stir in grated chocolate while mixture simmers.

Melt four Tbs. lard in ten to twelve-inch skillet and add turkey pieces, skin side down, without crowding. Cook three or four minutes, turning frequently, until all pieces are golden; add lard as necessary. As each piece is finished, put it in mole sauce. Simmer, covered, about twenty minutes, until turkey is tender, but do not let mixture boil. Taste for seasoning, and serve sprinkled with remaining sesame seeds.

Once cooks learn the ease with which this seemingly complicated sauce can be made, they frequently apply it to other fowl, and often to pork—sometimes also to game, which might include anything from a roast leg of venison to cottontail rabbits so common in the Southwest. Some Californians say that generally they prefer rabbit to chicken, and those with Mexican tastes stew rabbit or hare with chilies and tomatoes. There are other Spanish-oriented rabbit recipes still hailed in places where missions were once the only signs of civilization. A California dish called *Conejo Casserole* calls for an herb-wine marination, then slow cooking with sliced mushrooms and at least a cup of sliced ripe olives. Apricots grown and dried by the padres crept—like chocolate—into rabbit recipes, and some are a part of current repertoires. One calls for the rabbit to be marinated in white wine and white wine vinegar seasoned with orégano and rosemary. The rabbit pieces are then sautéed and baked in the marinade with dried apricots for about an hour. The resulting flavor is as distinctly suggestive of the Southwest style of cooking as any chili.

The Circuitous Ways of the Avocado

The United States does not owe all the culinary uses of chocolate—or even chili—to pre-Columbian cooks. But *guacamole* is another matter. The sauce, which predates New World history, is made of avocado and is now so prevalent at cocktail parties that the word itself is accepted by recent American dictionaries as part of the language. In circles less than lexical it is not unusual to find the phonetic spelling, *waca molay*, serving to identify a recipe. In the centuries that passed after Hernando Cortez became, perhaps, the first European to taste the avocado at one of Montezuma's banquets, the record indicates that George Washington also had a bite of one when he went to Barbados as a young man. In his journal of that trip in 1751 he wrote that "the Avagado pair is generally most admired. . . ." adding that he himself preferred the pineapple.

A traveler from Latin America was responsible for avocados growing in the Hawaiian Islands as early as 1825, and a horticulturist named Henry Perrine cultivated some south of Miami in 1833. Known more commonly as alligator pears, they were grown as ornamental plants and occasionally were served as fruit at exclusive dining clubs. In fact, the San Francisco financier Henry E. Huntington was so intrigued when his own club offered them that he pocketed a huge pit and had it planted in his garden of exotica. There, so Californians say, that same seed bears fruit today.

"If reliable witnesses do not err," Lately Thomas wrote in his entertaining book about the Delmonico family, 1895 was the year the avocado was introduced to fashionable New Yorkers at the Madison Square hostelry. "Richard Harding Davis was co-sponsor of the delicacy. That Galahadian idol of the popular press toured Central and South America in 1895, and at Caracas he was served avocados. So intrigued was he with their buttery, musky flavor that he brought a basketful back to New York. He carried them to Delmonico's where 'Charley' [Ranhofer, the chef] peeled one, tasted, and approved. Thereafter a supply was shipped regularly to the restaurant, and the avocado's popularity began."

In California, however, it was not until about 1924 that Anglo farmers took this plant of the Spanish missions seriously enough to organize the Avocado Growers Exchange. That group now raises nineteen of the ninety-nine varieties and ships them—as do equally productive Florida growers—to markets around the world. They do thrive in many other parts of this planet, of course. Somerset Maugham once claimed at a

On Avocados

The alligator-pear—or let us call it avocado, please—is one of the Creator's masterpieces—what we would call a stroke of genius had a mortal originated it. . . . The avocado was undoubtedly created to serve as a salad. If you cut it in two, lengthwise, and take out the big stone, you have two halves like those of a small melon. The flesh, firm, though soft and custardy, has a most exquisite flavor—a faint flavor which, with oil and vinegar makes a symphony of fragrance.

After writing the above remarks I came across a clipping in which an evident epicure objected to "desecrating" the avocado pear by oil or mayonnaise dressing when served. "Eat it with a spoon slowly," he advises, "to give time for the pleasure it imparts to permeate the very soul, and let who will rail at fate. There are those who give it a slight sprinkling of salt, others who dust it over with a little white pepper, but personally I would as soon think of flavoring my currant jelly with garlic or my chateau Yquem with Trinidad rum."

—Henry T. Finck

small dinner party in Paris that he personally had been responsible for introducing them to French soil; he had brought seeds from a friend's California avocado ranch and had had his gardener plant and tend them at his villa on Cap Ferrat.

Maugham also confided to a friend that he was the inventor of avocado ice cream, a claim one might even find justifiable after remembering how often culinary minds hit upon the same ideas. The butter-fat texture is as tempting to the palate as rich cream, and the thought of chilling avocados in parfaits or turning them into a frozen dessert with added flavors of nuts or fruit juices comes easily. That texture also seems a natural complement to a simple green salad dressed with good California olive oil and lemon juice; but in a meal in full progress there is surprise, delightful and sprightly on the tongue, when pieces of avocado are mixed at the last minute with hot rice that has steeped in chicken stock flavored with saffron and the essence of garlic.

There are many other Spanish- or Latin American-influenced recipes for this bland vegetable which was sometimes called (in days when Britannia ruled the waves) "midshipman's butter." Creamed fish and chicken are considered by many contemporary cooks to be glamorized when served in the hollow of an avocado half. This sort of thing can be as pastily unappetizing as chicken à la king at any businessmen's lunch club, depending upon the cook. A hungry man might try instead a baked avocado stuffed with some ground cooked pork stirred into a little chopped tomato and flavored with three capers and a pinch of fresh marjoram; a spoonful or so of beaten egg and some bread crumbs top things off as the avocado goes into the oven.

In a Spanish colony in Florida chilled avocados are stuffed with marinated and finely minced white onions. I season an omelet with a stirring of cumin, coriander, cardamom, ginger, and perhaps some other tropical spices; then as the egg mixture begins to set, I decorate the center with small cubes of avocado. Breaking away from Hispanic influence, the New York chef Albert Stockli invented an avocado bisque that depends on tiny smelts, cooked in wine with mushrooms, onions and rice; when puréed this fish mixture is blended with avocado, seasoned with orégano, basil, and thyme, and enough light cream to make a smooth soup.

To start off a meal in any part of the Spanish fringe of this country, the average cook's avocado soup is more likely to be based on chicken stock, and there are dozens of variations. But in California the start of a meal is as apt as not to be a salad—not the Spanish salad soup, known as gazpacho on both sides of the Atlantic, that usually combines cucumber, tomatoes, and sweet pepper, and is aromatically seasoned in an icy broth —but such things as guacamole used as a mayonnaise-like dressing for marinated cauliflower; or pitted ripe olives, chopped green pepper, and mayonnaise tossed with diced stale bread that has been sealed in a jar for several days with a dried chili pod.

Why salad as a first course, instead of the delicately dressed greens of

Guspacha Salad

Slice *cucumbers* very thin, also *onions* and peel *tomatoes*; fill a glass dish with alternate layers of this mixture with *bread crumbs* (*stale*) sprinkled over each layer. Cover all with *French dressing* and garnish with *lettuce*, and serve icy cold.

—Col. Talbott

France that serve to cleanse the palate between one course and another? Eastern Americans have been known to sneer at this custom without even wanting to know from whence it sprang. Some gastronomes have surmised that salad as a first course was introduced by immigrants who brought the Italian way of eating a few fresh raw things before sailing into the heaviness of *pasta*. But I suspect it may be related also to the outdoor life of the Dons who came north to a climate that produced abundant fruits and vegetables and who may have savored the raw food as they waited for the meat to sizzle to the right degree of flavor and juiciness on the barbecue rack.

In the Beginning There Was Barbecue

Barbecue is the English adaptation of the Spanish *barbacoa*, a word applied first in the New World to the outdoor grilling of meat by the Indians of Haiti. When Ponce de León and de Soto and Spaniards after them probed the southern Atlantic Coast of North America they found the Indians using crude wooden racks to smoke or dry fish, fowl, and other meat over open fires. The Cherokees and Creeks of the Carolinas and the Gulf Coast applied their techniques of grilling cattle and pigs and the colonizers refined the practice when their *ranchos* took root in arid Texas, New Mexico, and Arizona and in the fertile valleys of California. The Spaniards added the sauces that have, for most barbecues of today, the accent of hot peppers and garlic, whether they are the simple marinade bastings of the old South, or the thick tomatoey variations on the *mole* theme that have proliferated in the Southwest and California.[6]

"Way back when the Dons first came to California," Helen Evans Brown wrote in her lively *West Coast Cook Book*, "grilled meat was a part of every festive gathering. A huge fire was made, a freshly killed beef hung in the shade of a tree, and *vaqueros* and their ladies cut off pieces every time that hunger called, and cooked it over the waiting fire. . . ." She added, "It wasn't only charcoal grilling that was practiced by those Californians of the past, they also had their huge pit barbecues even as today."

Traditional community barbecues still bring together people from the ranches, the range, and neighboring towns; and the cord wood piled in the long narrow ditches, dug for the purpose, is apt to burn all the night before. On iron bars and chicken wire stretched across the sunken fire the meat is placed to broil slowly throughout the morning. A cook with a bucket of vinegar and his own special seasoning treks back and forth

[6] Sarah Hicks Williams, a bride who left New York in 1852 to live in Clifton Grove, North Carolina, on the plantation of her husband's family, stressed the culinary differences between North and South in letters to her parents. "They live more heartily," she wrote of her new Carolina relatives. "There must always be two or three kinds of meats on Mrs. Williams' table for breakfast & dinner. Red pepper is much used to flavor meat with the famous 'barbecue' of the South and [the dish] which I believe they esteem above all dishes is roasted pig dressed with red pepper & vinegar."

along the pit's rim, swabbing the meat, occasionally turning it. At serving time when the juicy slices are carved, there is time for nostalgia: the traditional accompaniments were always homemade bread and baked beans—and freshly churned butter, pickles, preserves, and dozens of kinds of pies and cakes made by wives and daughters.

For years the Spanish-American sheriff of Los Angeles County held an annual barbecue that attracted as many as 60,000 people. Such enormous affairs ceased to be common, but ranchers still gather in Texas and the Mountain states for old-style range feeds, just as other families gather for community picnics. By the middle of the twentieth century observers of American mores might have been tempted to assess the custom of picnic-area or backyard barbecuing as one of the equations of affluence. A good deal of chicken, beef, pork, and chunks of lamb has been charred, scorched, and burned as the result of the availability of a myriad supply of outdoor cooking equipment. And all of this comes naturally to Americans in every part of the country—from the luaus of Hawaii to the cookouts of New England.

Actually, a fair amount of contemporary barbecuing is done—as was equally true in colonial days and on every frontier—because it is more pleasant to cook outside on a hot summer day. In the old days, with open-hearth kitchen fires, it was a warm-weather necessity. Outdoor cooking is in the American blood. At the same time the Dons were establishing the custom in the Southwest, British colonials were adopting the word to refer to the sizable gatherings at which people were fed on meat, game, and other food cooked over well-laid fires. Electioneering and barbecuing became virtually synonymous in the eighteenth and nineteenth centuries. And in the modern Deep South the old lavish *al fresco* hospitality, made possible by slavery, is emulated in some degree where estates are maintained—cooking hearths are sheltered by roofs on many contemporary plantations and the barbecue is frequently served in a summer house.

Chicken, spareribs, tenderloin, and other cuts of pork are still the prevailing choices among southern barbecuers, even as beef is the preference of most Texans and Californians. But the Spanish also introduced the first sheep and goats to American ranges, and their descendants in the Southwest have enormous appetites for barbecued *borrego*, baby lamb, and *cabrito*, suckling goat. So do the Basque herdsmen who were brought into the Mountain states toward the end of the nineteenth century. With the exception of a mighty few chop houses in cosmopolitan cities, mutton is easily available only in parts of the Rockies. In Winnemucca, Nevada, at the foot of Sonoma Peak, oven-roasted mutton and even mutton hash are fixtures on local restaurant menus. Down in the Four Corners country, in sight of the Sangre de Cristo mountains, lamb is considered fiesta meat, and the older and wiser heads among the Chicanos insist that butchers follow the Spanish way of cutting with the grain to seal in the juices; then they barbecue the roast over a hot fire and slice it thin.

There is no surprise in the fact that Americans have turned barbecues into a business. Lyndon Johnson made it all too clear that a successful

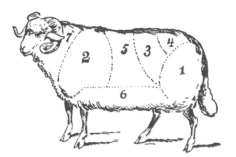

feast under the live oaks required the best professional barbecue man in Texas. Further west of Johnson City there used to be an outfit that showed up annually in places like Albuquerque with two truckloads of equipment, three cooks, and something like 650 pounds of meat—beef and lamb. Preparing a feast for a crowd took the professionals from five A.M. to 6:30 P.M., while logs burned down to the right kind of coals and great slabs of meat cooked in homemade barbecue sauce alongside skillets of Texas onions and pots of bubbling pinto beans. In northern New England, far from the incursions of the Spanish empire, halves of chickens are grilled over coals and the folks who gather for small-town Fourth of July celebrations salute the traveling barbecue expert as they stand around licking their fingers and biting into broilers that have a taste not to be duplicated outside of America. Here there is no palate-burning, vaguely Spanish barbecue sauce, but the principle is the same.

A Meal in the Hand

Literally taking things into one's own hands when it comes to eating has helped to encourage the American penchant for what too many women's magazines choose to call "finger foods"—whether they be vegetables or cracker variants, used to scoop up those "cocktail dips," or corn on the cob, or sausages or meat patties slapped between pieces of bread and labeled hot dogs, hamburgers, or Sloppy Joes. Indians showed Puritans and Cavaliers alike how easy the eating of freshly boiled corn on the cob could be. Cortez and his men reported that the Aztecs munched tamales on the street. Other conquistadores described how Pueblo tribesmen made their tortillas from ground corn and turned them into *tacos* by filling the flat cakes with beans or meat sauces and rolling them up to eat by hand.

Floridians, Puerto Ricans, and other Americans of Spanish heritage depend on an excellent European style of bread, but for many in California and the Southwest the pre-Columbian tortilla is still the staff of life. Except that it is made of cornmeal, it is identical to the *chapatis* of India—a mixture of meal and water that is patted into shape between the hands of the cook—or sometimes a final smoothing takes place on the suntanned surface of a bare thigh. Like a maid "setting her cap" in a Yankee springtime, the Chicano girl who finishes a round flat cake in this way is turning out a tortilla that is bound, of course, to cause the youth who eats it to fall in love. Nowadays *masa harina,* an "instant" corn flour mixture, is available in Spanish groceries, and tortilla presses can be bought by those cooks who aren't concentrating on the way to a young man's heart. In the old days tortillas were always baked on a round, flat *comal,* made of stone or pottery, but they can be cooked as well on a modern griddle.

Like bread, tortillas accompany meat dishes. When they are filled with one of the infinity of stuffings devised over centuries, i.e., when they are rolled around a mixture of fish, meat, and sometimes beans they are properly described as *tacos*. When a tortilla is fried crisp in fat it is transformed into a *tostada* and is folded once to enclose a filling; thus it becomes the Spanish-American Indian version of the sandwich. The process of turning tortillas into *enchiladas* begins with dipping the flat bread in a tomato sauce. Sometimes a delicious filling is made by combining Monterey Jack cheese with sautéed *chorizos*, the peppery, garlic-and-paprika pork sausages to be found where Mexican and Spanish foods are sold. Sausage and cheese are rolled up in the tortillas, laid side by side in a baking dish, and covered with more sauce, then a sprinkling of grated cheese, before going into the oven. Tamales (the Spanish simply added an *e* to the Indian word) are corn-husk envelopes filled with cornmeal mush or *masa harina* dough plus chili in one form or another, for flavor. They can be cooked in hot ashes like corn on the cob, but are more likely to be steamed.

As cooks from England, in their own good time, found many ways to adapt corn products to Old World recipes, so did those from Spain who settled in Texas, New Mexico, Arizona, and California. New World hominy, combined with Old World *menudo* (tripe) was for centuries a traditional Christmas breakfast among Spanish-Americans, and it is still celebratory fare. In most of the Southwest *menudo* is served on Sunday mornings as a marvelous stick-to-the-ribs soup when the night before has been a late one.

The trouble with tripe may be that Americans who have been caught in the maze of upward mobility think of it as poor man's food; instead,

Spanish Sausages

are made from the fat and lean of the back and loins of a well-fed two-year-old hog, finely minced or pounded together and strongly seasoned with cloves of garlic and green or red capsicums or chilies; but as these cannot always be conveniently procured in this country, cayenne pepper may be substituted. The whole should be covered with any sort of strong, dry wine, until absorbed by the ingredients, which will occupy perhaps a few days, according to the quantity. Fill the largest skins you can get with the meat, fat and lean alternately, occasionally adding some of the wine. Tie up in links, and hang them in a room where they will not get damp or become too dry, and they will keep twelve months.

especially when prepared with love and Spanish-Indian ingenuity, it is the kind of delicacy that converts cynics. The Chicano method with *menudo* does not produce as richly gelatinous a result as Tripes à la mode de Caen, nor is it dominated by tomatoes, in the style of Italian cooks. The *menudo* of the Great West should bubble lazily with a veal knuckle and the traditional Spanish-American herbs and spices. With the perfume of *Alta California* in the steam that rises from each bowl, and with plain *tostadas* at the ready, this is a beautifully simple midday meal when blessed with a glass of Joseph Heitz's Pinot Chardonnay from the Napa Valley. Even more—I've been informed by a man who has lived most of his life in New Mexico and Arizona—*menudo* is a sure cure for a hangover.

The Good Herbs

In her research into restorative soups and stews, Helen Brown discovered that *Sopa de Albondigas* so intrigued nineteenth-century California Anglos that those pioneers from the East recorded variations of a Spanish dish of meat balls under such spellings as avonigas, abondegas, abondas—"the early American ladies cooked it better than they pronounced it," Mrs. Brown said. Their successors still cook it, not because the idea of soup with meat balls is so unusual, but because a medley of herbal flavors distinguishes it. The taste of chili peppers is imperative, but broth and meat balls alike may be infused with a variety of herbs—most especially mint if the dish is made in New Mexico or Arizona. In the Southwest mint is found more useful than elsewhere.

Yerba buena, which translates as "good herb," and refers in Spanish to one of the native American herbs, was the name first given to the settlement on San Francisco Bay. It was an herb that ran wild over the hills and it came to add a very special savor to the cooking of meat and other foods in the early period. Some modern cooks substitute tarragon mixed with chervil or parsley on the theory that the combination is gentler as well as more civilized than wild *yerba buena*. But ordinary dried mint, available in virtually all food stores, is used in the New Mexico broth brewed from pork neckbones; mint flavors breaded pork chops that are served with fried chili peppers and—again as a balance to chili—is an accent for a braised round steak, popular around Santa Fe, that simmers with onions and tomatoes and Napa Valley Pinot Noir wine. When cooks of this region season lamb, they often use juniper berries, and they insist on the wild ones when they can find them in the field.

The Spanish, with their love of herbs and spices, have influenced the evolution of American cooking more than is generally recognized. The bright orange blossoms of the safflower plant, seen throughout New Mexico and Arizona, are there today because centuries ago seeds from Spain were planted by padres. Now safflower oil is common enough in American supermarkets, but this plant contributes in another way to Southwest cooking. According to a regional authority, local cooks learned early that safflower blossoms could be dried and crumbled to serve as a substitute for the extravagantly priced Old World saffron. Their flavor gives a somewhat more poignant taste to Rio Grande *arrozos* and various soups, and the plants that escaped the cloisters to grow wild continue to remind one of the padres who introduced them to the arid soil.

Three hundred years ago, when the Spanish priests arrived, they found the Southwest Indians making much use of nuts from the *piñon,* now the state tree of New Mexico. Much like the *pignoli* of southern Europe, the fruits of the *piñon* were eaten just as were the seeds of other plants, and the Pueblo tribes also added them to stews or ground them for use as thickeners. Spanish-American families (for some of the poorest of whom *piñons* are more of a necessity than a subtle addition to their cuisine) annually gather the nuts wild and store them for the winter or sell them in trade. Among affluent Southwesterners with an interest in distinguished food, sophisticated adaptations of primitive recipes are among the rewards of dining in their homes. A spicy filling for avocado halves mixes *piñons* with tomatoes and citrus juice. And a delicate soup, compared by some cooks to a deftly seasoned vichyssoise, is made by blending a quantity of pine nuts with chicken broth and light cream redolent of scallions, coriander, and mint.

H. L. Mencken noted that the American language has absorbed more Spanish influences than those of any other European tongue. I am not going to try to prove it, but a similar case can be made for the flavors of Spain in American food. The fancy for peppers, red, green, and yellow, hot and sweet, must seem to be the most prosaic of all items. Yet there are many others. Garlic was lifting the flavor of Southwestern gastronomy long before the arrival of Italian cooks in so many parts of the rest of the country. Olives were not left to the Greeks who infiltrated the restaurant business. Stuffed or not, the olives so prevalent in American living rooms at the cocktail hour have added piquancy to New World cooked dishes since the Spanish began to contrast their flavor with peppers and tomatoes in casseroles; sauces thus concocted have bathed many an otherwise

Spanish Friceo

This dish is made from good beef (the same kind as used for beef-steak), lean pork or young mutton. The best is beef and pork in equal quantities. Two pounds of meat is enough for six or eight persons. The meat is beaten till soft and then cut in thin slices; cut raw potatoes in thin slices, washing them before they are cut, but not after, and take two soup plates of them. Mix with potatoes two saucerfuls of onions cut in slices. Take a pudding dish and put the meat and potatoes in layers. Scatter over each layer some pepper, some Jamaica pepper, and salt; put on every layer of potatoes a piece of butter and at least three-quarters of a tablespoonful of thick sour cream. Close the pudding dish well and put it into boiling water, and let it boil for one and one-half hours.

—Hand-written recipe

staid conglomerate of fowl or fish in ointments new in fragrance and texture. Olives, too, were brought across the Atlantic by Spanish fathers who grew them first to make holy oils and soon enough to enhance the plain food of the missions. California has been olive country since the middle of the eighteenth century when trees were planted at Mission San Diego, foreshadowing the development of the U.S. variety called, appropriately, Mission olives. Driving through the Southwest, olive groves are to be seen in New Mexico and, along with dates and oranges, in Arizona's Valley of the Sun. Here the Spanish again were responsible for the first figs as well as dates (California's Coachella Valley has more than 5,000 acres in date palm orchards) and for numerous other fruits.

When visitors walk arcaded cloisters at the Franciscan mission in Sonoma and stand before the Spanish cathedral built by Willa Cather's archbishop in Santa Fe—especially, perhaps, in examination of the intricate stone work of San Antonio's mission of San Jose—wherever remnants of Spain remain in Florida or Louisiana, there are reminders of Spanish ways of living. Spaniards established the cultivation of many of the basic ingredients of the American diet and they left a legacy of style as well. Not something to be minimized as "Tex-Mex"—that's as unauthentic as a five-gallon hat. The real Spanish gastronomical influences have become so much a part of American cooking that they are virtually forgotten.

Chapter 4

Gemütlichkeit and Serious Eating

THE FARMERS' MARKET in Lancaster, Pennsylvania—established in perpetuity by royal charter of George II in 1742—is as indicative of German influence on American food in the twentieth century as it was in the years before the Revolution. Twice a week in the 1970s the turreted, mansard-roofed red brick building teemed with the dwindling romance and the unabated aromas of food products from hundreds of small farms in and around Lancaster County. Dairy products, vegetables, and baked goods, freshly killed poultry, hickory smoked meats, barrel-aged pickles, honey, apple butter, chow-chow, Pennsylvania Dutch corn relish, homemade fudge—most of the food taken home by people who browse through Lancaster's central market is raised or wrought by other people whose names are German and whose style of cooking has dominated many kitchens in other parts of America, wherever pioneer movements have led.

The Pennsylvania Dutch have no roots in Holland; their ancestors were German-speaking religious refugees who came to America by way of the Rhineland and other parts of Germanic Europe. Within a year of the arrival of Philadelphia's first Quakers from England and Wales, the Mennonites, who were to have so much influence in many rural sections of America, had established nearby Germantown. As these were followed by Amish from Switzerland, Bohemian Moravians, Schwenkenfelders, Dunkers, and others, word of the good food to be had in Pennsylvania began to spread to other colonies.[1] The self-denial that marked the reli-

[1] John Adams may have cast a cold eye on the extravagance of Philadelphia dining, but George Washington is said to have retained, after his wartime service, a lifelong appetite for Pennsylvania dishes. He was only one of the founding fathers who ate frequently at the Sun Inn, established by Moravians at Bethlehem in 1758. It was at this roadside tavern that many colonial Americans first tasted *schnitz und*

A MORAVIAN COMMUNAL MEAL

Sausage Scrapple

Bring 1 quart water to a rolling boil and add 1 cup white cornmeal a little at a time, letting pot boil up after each addition; crumble in 1 pound pork sausage, stirring to mix well with cornmeal. Add ½ teaspoon each dried thyme and sage and 1 teaspoon of salt. Cover pot and simmer 1½ hours, stirring frequently. Pour into loaf pan and set aside to cool; put in refrigerator for about 3 hours, until loaf is very firm. To serve, cut in slices about ⅓ inch thick and fry in bacon fat over medium heat, until crisp.

gious precepts of these groups did not apply to cooking and eating, fortunately for American gastronomy in general. Philadelphia, which was already a cosmopolitan and sophisticated community in the eighteenth century, had been swift to appreciate the culinary art of its rural neighbors, and Pennsylvania Dutch scrapple, an aromatic mixture of Indian cornmeal and pork scraps formed into a loaf compactly designed for slicing, became essential to a proper Philadelphia breakfast menu very early in colonial history. The acceptance by the Quaker city was such that most renditions of this mealy, sausage-like loaf are still known as Philadelphia scrapple, even though much of it is made on the farms or in such Pennsylvania Dutch towns as Reading.

"One wonders," the Pennsylvania historian Frederic Klees once wrote, "how the Philadelphians got along for a whole year—that of 1682—until the Pennsylvania Dutch arrived and gave them scrapple." Firm loaves of sage-and-marjoram-flavored scrapple are sliced thin and broiled, or fried very crisp, as the *pièce de résistance* of a hearty breakfast. Scrapple goes as well with eggs as with bacon or ham, and some Philadelphians insist upon daubing their sizzling slices with catsup. Others dress up scrapple with fried sliced apples, or applesauce, and on many Pennsylvania Dutch farms the accent is either maple or brown sugar syrup. At meals other than breakfast, green peppers and cabbages are stuffed with scrapple, potatoes are scalloped with scrapple, and fragrant croquettes are made by combining cooked rice, hard-boiled eggs, freshly minced parsley, and scrapple in an egg batter. Marylanders make their own scrapple by combining pork sausage and cornmeal, and Cincinnatians substitute oats for cornmeal, while Germans in St. Louis achieve a similar result by combining pork with oatmeal and rice or barley.

knepp, raisin pie, sauerkraut, *schmierkäse,* and many kinds of cake. An eighteenth-century traveler who stopped for a couple of days at the Sun reported being "constantly supplied with venison, moor game, the most delicious red and yellow bellied Trout, the highest flavoured wild strawberries, the most luxuriant asparagus, and the best vegetables . . . I ever saw. . . ." He was clearly impressed by not only the bounty but the appetizing preparation of meals at this Pennsylvania Dutch hostelry.

In the nineteenth century scrapple gained fame not only in the United States, but also among foreigners. Edward VII, then Prince of Wales and nineteen years of age, made a North American tour that took him from Canada to Washington where he was entertained by President James Buchanan, the only chief executive to come from Pennsylvania Dutch country. There is no record that scrapple was on the White House menu (Buchanan had established a French cuisine) for the prince, but he undoubtedly sampled scrapple when he visited Philadelphia. The joke is still told—as one of the hoariest in the Philadelphia repertoire—that the prince remarked, "I met a large and interesting family named Scrapple, and I discovered a rather delicious native food they call biddle." Distinguished bearers of the Biddle family name have handled the matter with aplomb.

In any form, scrapple is apt to be a homely dish, even though more nostalgia-inducing than most, and it is one of the gastronomical divertissements from Pennsylvania that turn up in other parts of the country to underscore the German influence. Emigration from Pennsylvania began a score of years before the Revolution when Moravians from Bethlehem, on the Lehigh River, pulled stakes and moved along the Blue Ridge to a new settlement in North Carolina. Here they made scrapple from pork liver and called it, as often as not, pon haws (from the German *pfann hass*), as it is still sometimes referred to in Pennsylvania.

Wherever Germans migrated, and they traveled singly and in groups to settle in almost every region of the country, they made lasting contributions, adding zest to the plain dishes English colonizers had borrowed from the Indians, and enlarging the general American repertoire in ways so subtle that few people today may be aware of how many "standard American" dishes are Germanic in origin.

Pennsylvania Dutch cooks apparently were as swift to make use of spices and subtropic vegetables brought into the crowded docks of eighteenth-century Philadelphia as were others who lived in such ports as Charleston and New Orleans. Like New England housewives, those in Pennsylvania adapted the basic Indian succotash; inhibited by few if any moral attitudes toward food, they enlivened the mixture of corn and beans with green peppers and other vegetables from the West Indies. Thomas Jefferson's interest in the tomato as a source of food failed to influence the average cook until some time after Jefferson's death, yet tomatoes were also added to succotash by Pennsylvania cooks early in the nineteenth century, and their variation is a vegetable stew that combines sautéed onions, green pepper, fresh tomatoes, and potatoes cubed with corn and lima beans. On farms in southeast Pennsylvania this version of succotash is topped with featherweight dumplings, sometimes made of potatoes, onions, and bread, or of poached liver and beaten eggs.

There is kinship between this mélange of New World vegetables and the North Carolina recipe for Brunswick stew which, whatever its true

Pennsylvania Dutch Succotash

Melt 2 tablespoons bacon fat or butter in heavy pot and sauté 2 onions and 1 diced green pepper about 3 minutes; add 1½ cups diced potatoes, cover with about a quart of boiling water and cook about 15 minutes. Add 2 cups lima beans (fresh or soaked overnight) and cover, simmering 15 minutes more. Add 2 cups chopped tomatoes, 1 teaspoon sugar, 1 cup fresh corn and 1½ teaspoons salt plus some freshly ground black pepper, cooking just long enough to make kernels tender.

origin, is now claimed as the invention of pioneer cooks in every state south of the Mason-Dixon line. Brunswick stew uses all the vegetables of the Pennsylvania succotash, involving also a good many other items, as well as endless arguments about whether or not chicken is a poor substitute for the traditional squirrel meat. (Most North Carolina recipes call for both, as well as beef and sometimes veal, but after visiting in Mississippi's uplands, the New York chef Louis P. De Gouy reported that he was ridiculed there for even mentioning domestic chicken as an acceptable ingredient.) There also are sotto voce debates as to whether or not to borrow the okra that is organic to gumbo recipes and makes Brunswick stew, after long hours of simmering, as thick as old-fashioned porridge.

Pepper Pot at Valley Forge

Old-fashioned may be as appreciative a way as any for labeling American food that has German antecedents. These recipes reach deep into the past. One more of this lineage is the classic Philadelphia Pepper Pot. Folklore insists that this thick soup was invented on the spot when provisions were at their lowest during the Continental army's desperate winter at Valley Forge, in Pennsylvania Dutchland. As Louis De Gouy once fantasized: ". . . General Washington's soldiers were in rags, shoes had worn thin; misery came unrelentingly; food was ever lacking. Cooks made ends meet where there were nothing but ends, and they met just over the starvation line. Soldiers began to think of home. Why stay to starve and die at Valley Forge? Desertions were frequent. The story is that General Washington took matters into his own hands and called for the head chef of all the Revolutionary armed forces. He explained the seriousness of the hour. He demanded a great dish. The chef protested: 'There is nothing, my general, but scraps in the kitchens. There is only tripe—a few hundred pounds, the gift of a nearby butcher. And there are peppercorns, a gift from a Germantown patriot. All the rest is scraps and more scraps.'

"'. . . From nothing,' said General Washington, 'you must create a great dish.' The chef experimented. The tripe was scrubbed, it was simmered tender. Additions went into the big kettles, all the odds and ends of the kitchens. The peppercorns were ground to add fire to the stew. The early darkness came. Great kettles sent up their heart-warming, belly-comforting fragrance to the miserable men. The call of the bugle, and men ate their fill of this fortifying dish. Men laughed again . . . they joked: '. . . Bring on the Red Coats!'

"The general called for the chef: '. . . This dish is the stuff of heroes! What is its name?' 'General, I have conceived it but not called it,' the chef replied, 'but pepper pot would be my humble suggestion, sir.' 'Call it Philadelphia Pepper Pot,' said Washington, 'in honor of your home town.'"

No matter whether or not George Washington had anything to do with it, this American peppery stew has never had another home town, even

though it no longer is sold from carts pushed by women through Philadelphia's once narrow streets, their cries piercing the hoary winter cold:

All hot! All hot!
Pepper pot! Pepper pot!
Makes backs strong,
Makes lives long,
All hot! Pepper pot!

Even in the centrally heated twentieth century the aromatic flavor of Philadelphia Pepper Pot insures this thick ragout a hearty welcome—psychologically, at least—when the winter seems long. It is a dish to line the ribs and soothe any spirit. It may well derive from another dish, "Dutch Goose," which is tripe that has been stuffed and which retains its popularity among modern Pennsylvania Dutchmen. Farm cooks still prepare Dutch Goose by packing a pig's stomach with ground pork or pork sausage mixed with potatoes and the savory herbs of the kitchen garden, or with shredded cabbage mixed with onions, potatoes, and a spice or two like caraway or cardamom.

J. George Frederick, who had a scholarly interest in American gastronomy, once pointed out that the average Pennsylvania Dutch farm was more isolated than most and therefore had to be more independent of general stores than other rural homes ever were. "For this reason," he wrote in 1935, "the Pennsylvania Dutch farm from 1700 to 1900—two full centuries . . . was made into a food factory of amazing scope and

Philadelphia Pepper Pot

Wash 2 pounds fresh tripe under running water, then put in pot with water to cover, bring to boil and simmer 7–8 hours, adding boiling water as necessary to keep meat covered, and 1 tsp. salt. Put a meaty veal knuckle in another pot with a bay leaf, 4 or 5 sprigs of parsley, 1 stalk celery with leaves, a green pepper chopped, 1 onion chopped, and 2 carrots sliced; cover with water, bring to boil and simmer 1 hour. Add ½ tsp. salt with ½ teaspoon each of allspice, marjoram, savory, thyme, and crushed whole peppercorns, and continue simmering 1 hour, until veal falls away from bone. Strain, chill, and remove grease. Remove tripe from its broth, adding broth to clear veal stock. Cut tripe in ½ inch squares and add with veal meat to combined stocks. Add 1½ cups diced potatoes, bring to simmering point, and cook until potatoes are tender.

range." Frederick's own boyhood in the state persuaded him that German farmers like his grandparents could not stop at mere self-sufficiency; the Pennsylvania *hausfrau* mastered "a phenomenally wide range of food manufacturing arts" to such an extent that each farm produced a great surplus of prepared food and transported it to markets as far as fifty miles away . . . "wagonloads of it to sell each week, winter and summer. . . ." Describing what he believed to be his grandmother's "genius with food," he boasted that "no conjurer ever pulled rabbits out of a hat with the facility that she exercised with food from May until December, in preparing and producing an endless variety of things to eat."

Her way of life, still followed by many Pennsylvania women who haven't succumbed to convenience foods, helps to explain why so much that is good in American culinary achievement was developed in this region. It is the cooking of artisans, artisans devoted to their craft of making the most of ingredients rather than to epicurean finesse. It is not, however, a kind of cooking to suit everyone's taste. Indeed, it has been said that one must be Pennsylvania Dutch to appreciate all of this regional cuisine. Yet there are dozens of dishes that awaken nostalgia when they are mentioned—or when they are served by cooks with Amish, Moravian, or other German or Middle European backgrounds who live in other parts of the country.

A Sufficiency of Soups

I first had chicken and corn soup when visiting a Midwest farm as a youngster, but many people think one must go to the source to taste the real flavor of this all-American pottage. This is a thick gallimaufry that combines pungent bits of simmered chicken with tender kernels from freshly picked corn and egg noodles rolled out while the saffron-flavored broth is brewing; and it brings tourists from far and near to Lancaster County and other parts of Pennsylvania Dutchland for church suppers and outdoor food festivals. The legendary pepper pot of Valley Forge is simply the best known of a parade of soups, thin and thick, that have become a part of culinary lore in many parts of the country. In Virginia cooks make a simple stew they also call pepper pot in which potatoes and butter balls are all that are added to the simmering tripe and veal knuckle. In Newton, North Carolina, the chicken corn soup that has brought fame to the annual women's guild supper derives from a recipe members are pledged to keep secret; in this Carolina town veal is simmered along with the chicken, and rice is also added.

Perhaps the Pennsylvania Dutch have more affinity for soups than others whose work has taken them outdoors, or who, in the days before central heating, had hearty need of food to help them withstand the cold. The so-called "Amish Preaching Soup" is just such a rib-sticking mélange which belongs to the Old Order of House Amish who hold their religious services in various homes and serve this mixture of beans and ham or smoked pork butts between their two Sunday preachings. A recipe for

Mock Oyster or Salsify (oyster plant) Soup comes from Salisbury, Pennsylvania, and the German version of eel soup in this part of the country is a fragrant purée of eel fillets, small sweet shrimp, veal, parsley and parsley root, carrots, celery, shallots, mushrooms, and accents of cayenne, thyme, laurel, mace, and basil.

There are other soups of the region that are delicate, and one of the best is Cream of Clam Soup, as prepared at a cooking club, formally organized in 1732 (it calls itself the oldest club in the world), that is officially known as the State in Schuykill. The circle of gentlemen chefs is referred to most familiarly now as the Fish House, from whence sprang the punch that carries that name. The edifice of the "fish house" is a castle on the Delaware, urban sprawl having driven the club to abandon the river whose name it bears,[2] and it is the gathering place of members who pretend that the State in Schuykill (originally the Colony) is an independent government complete with governor, counsellors, sheriff, and even a coroner. Never having accepted the Constitution, although it went on record as joining the union in 1781, the club was never troubled by the Prohibition that inhibited other states.

Aside from the Schuykill club's highly alcoholic punch—a mixture of rum, cognac, peach brandy, lemon, and sugar—there is no limit to the kind of cooking done by members when they don their white aprons and mandarin straw boaters. The club's version of pepper pot is made with meat dumplings that combine bread crumbs with minced veal and salt pork flavored with sherry, marjoram, thyme, cloves, and red and black pepper. Fish House terrapin is flavored with Madeira. The Fish House Cream of Clam Soup, as it was prepared by Chef John Wagner, gets its distinctive flavor from celery seed. Seeming never to tire of kitchens, most of the "citizens" of the State in Schuykill also are members of a junior cooking club known as the Rabbit—not because Welsh Rabbit is a specialty but because the original club house was on Rabbit Lane on the Main Line.

Another group, the Farmers' Club, spent years discussing the proper diet for farmers and debating ways to promote agriculture. Questions raised by members may seem effete. Should the farmer take sweet or dry champagne with him to the fields? Not infrequently one club entertains

Dutch Chicken Corn Soup

Boil chicken until tender, remove bones and shred meat; make a smooth dough of one egg and one and one-half cups of flour; roll out and cut into dice; score and cut off corn from six ears; put all into the chicken broth and boil together till corn is soft. Serve with popcorn floating on the soup.

—George Frederick

[2] Dr. Charles Browne, who served in Congress and as mayor of Princeton, New Jersey, wrote in 1930: "The dining-room or 'Castle' was floated down the Schuykill on barges and up the Delaware to the new club site, just below Eddington. The deal dining tables, built in 1748, are still in use and have silver plates in them marking the places where Washington and Lafayette dined. . . ." Browne himself presided over Princeton's Gun Club whose members, he said, were not stalkers of game and eaters of wild flesh but only shooters of clay birds who loved to cook and eat. In *The Gun Club Book*, which Browne compiled, he noted: "If an army fights upon its stomach (as Napoleon or someone else has said) the arts of peace also depend upon a well-fed nation." His book, he wrote, eschewed any attempt "to describe the alluring confections of the French cuisine . . ."; it deals, in fact, in many things, including "the great American standby, more fixed than the Constitution and less subject to amendments, 'ham and eggs.' "

another. Notes of a gathering of Farmers at the State in Schuykill indicate that the guests were greeted by the high sheriff and served with aprons and straw hats "of a pattern brought back by a citizen from China in the last century." One of the guests was assigned to cook the clam soup, one the boiled potatoes, one the lima beans, one to make tomato salad, etc. "Pursuant to the custom followed for 192 years," say these notes, "each person by whom the dish was prepared served it with the assistance of the apprentices"—stand-bys of forty or fifty with hopes of becoming active "citizens." When dinner was ready and a bell rung by one of the apprentices, the high sheriff called guests to the table by raising his baton crowned by a carved fish tipped with silver. At the end of the dinner the governor proposed the first toast, as always "to the memory of Washington."

As Smooth as Creamed Oysters

Philadelphia food is by no means, of course, exclusively Pennsylvania Dutch, but much emphasis remains on such things as scrapple and cinnamon buns; the city's fare has been described by Nathaniel Burt in *The Perennial Philadelphians* as "rich and smooth, as in creamed oysters, chicken or seafood croquettes, white mountain cake and Philadelphia ice cream." Menus are accented by Jerusalem artichokes cooked in milk then battered and fried in deep hot fat, by sauerkraut simmered with salt pork and caraway seeds, or by goose stuffed with apples, prunes, and slivered almonds. The custom of accompanying each meal of consequence with a multiplicity of relishes and preserved fruits—referred to as "seven sweets and seven sours"—prevails in certain Philadelphia quarters just as it does in Pittsburgh and, of course, in the "Dutch" cities of Reading, Lancaster, Allentown, and Bethlehem.

Wherever served, such food cannot be taken lightly. Indeed, it has been pointedly said that the average Pennsylvania Dutch menu is so satisfying and generous that "it has little need for some of the time-killers that are used to clutter menus elsewhere." The regional aphorism, "Fill yourself up, clean your plate," expresses a way of life. From beginning to end, from thick soup through meats, pies, cakes, and sweet desserts, dining in Pennsylvania Dutch tradition requires full commitment and an unreluctant appetite.

The pig in all its forms plays a large part in the cookery shaped by this tradition. Pigs' knuckles and sauerkraut with Moravian egg dumplings may not sound like a repast for every man, but when tenderly prepared and lovingly seasoned, the combination rouses appetites in Bethlehem and many parts of Pennsylvania. The richly jellied souse is made with pigs' feet, or sometimes a mixture of veal shin and pork shoulder. Cooks of this region are also justly renowned for their head cheese, and for the variety of their sausage recipes.

Sausage-making is so much a part of the American culinary tradition that even the recipe used by Martha Washington is a matter of record. The craft, as practiced by Germanic cooks, was an important function of

Dutch Jerusalem Fritters

Boil and mash 10 Jerusalem artichokes, let cool, and then add the yolk of 1 egg. Mold into cakes, dip in flour and fry in butter on a hot griddle.

—Tulpehocken farmwife

the "food factory" described by George Frederick. "With meat grinders, large mixing bowls and sausage stuffing machines," he wrote, "my grandparents would produce, before my astounded young eyes, a wide variety of foods; fresh pork sausage, smoked beef and beef sausage, Lebanon style bologna, highly spiced; liverwurst, and a half a dozen other wursts. They would smoke hams and slabs of bacon, tongues and other pieces of meat. . . . The bologna, five inches in diameter, [from the Pennsylvania town of that name] is probably over-spiced for most tastes, but it is surely appetizing."

Sausage stuffer

True Lebanon sausage, now as then, is made of nothing but coarsely ground beef precured and aged in barrels, then seasoned with sweet herbs and assertive spices, forced into airtight casings, and smoked over smoldering sawdust for a matter of days. Those who applaud the pungent flavor frequently dip pieces of Lebanon sausage in batter, or in egg and bread crumbs, fry, and serve them with sauerkraut and mashed potatoes, or in a white sauce to accompany flannel cakes. In recent years, as Pennsylvanians have come to absorb the Italian influence on American cooking, these sausages are sometimes diced, mixed with ground beef and tomato sauce, and served over spaghetti or German noodles. Some fans, I was astounded to learn, slice Lebanon sausage as they would cheese and eat it with apple pie.

Yet this idea is not strange at all to the Pennsylvania Dutch. Every one of the dishes in their multicourse meals is put on the table before the diners first sit down, for it is the custom to enjoy a piece of pie with one of the meat courses. And there is almost always more than one meat course. In the old days a Pennsylvania Dutch hotel dining room or restaurant habitually had forty or fifty dishes set out at mealtime; in private homes the tables are laden with a dozen or more, three times a day. It's no accident that the kitchen is almost always the largest room in the house. Of few people on this earth can the platitude be so accurately applied as to these citizens of the Keystone state: They eat to live, and live to eat. "Probably," one of their historians wrote, "it is the superabundance of pork and pie the Dutch have been eating for generations that turns so many of them into walking mountains of flesh." Rudyard Kipling, at the end of the nineteenth century, was enchanted by Pennsylvania Dutch farmers and their "fat cattle, fat women. . . ." The way these Americans lived, he wrote, was "as peacefull as Heaven might be if they farmed there."

A Meal without Pie May Be No Meal at All

Some social chroniclers seem convinced that fruit pies as Americans now know them were invented by the Pennsylvania Dutch. Let's just admit that it's possible.[3] Potters in the southeastern counties of the state

[3] However, the case for New England cooks may be just as probable. The history of one of the earliest ventures in wholesale pie-making was described in a 1963 issue of the New Haven *Register*. Amos Munson opened a factory in New Haven in 1844 to make and ship "Connecticut pies" via steamboat to New York where, he

Shoo-fly Pie

Have 2 pie tins lined with preferred pastry dough. Pour 1½ cups boiling water into a mixing bowl containing 1 teaspoon baking soda and stir 1 cup molasses into it. When well mixed pour half into one pie shell and half into the other. Mix 4 cups sifted flour, 2 cups brown sugar, 1 cup vegetable shortening and ¼ teaspoon salt until it forms crumbs, then divide the mixture evenly by sprinkling on top of molasses: the layer should be thick. Put pies in oven and bake 30–40 minutes at 350° until golden brown.

Pennsylvania Spiced Cantaloupe

Six pounds of cantaloupe cut as nearly one size as possible, 4 quarts water, 1 ounce alum; bring to boiling point, drop in your fruit, cook 15 minutes, lift and drain a short while. Then take 1 quart of vinegar, 3 pounds white sugar, 3 tsps. yellow mustard seed, 1 tsp. black mustard seed, 1 tsp. whole mace, 8-inch stick of cinnamon, 9 whole cloves, about a dozen whole allspice. Place the fruit in it and slowly cook until clear; requires about 2 hours.

were making pie plates early in the eighteenth century, and cooks had begun to envelop with crisp crusts every fruit that grew in the region. "It may be . . ." Frederic Klees asserted, "that during the Revolution men from other colonies came to know this dish in Pennsylvania and carried that knowledge back home to establish pie as the great American dessert. Why not?" Why else would there be no fewer than fifty kinds of dessert pies made today by various Pennsylvania Dutch cooks? Along with standard American apple, berry, butterscotch, chocolate, custard, lemon, mince, pumpkin, rhubarb, *et al.,* the Pennsylvania Dutch certainly originated shoo-fly pie, really a molasses sponge cake baked in a crust. They also make *rosina,* which is a lemony raisin affair that is always baked when someone dies and therefore is called "funeral pie." They make Amish half-moon pies whose other name is "preaching pies," because they are used to thwart the restlessness of children at long Sunday services.

No matter how many such pies are on the table, other sweet things are always served with a Dutch meal. Applesauce, of course, is a standard accompaniment for many pork dishes, and apple butter, claimed as a Pennsylvania invention, is an everyday spread for bread and toast. Perhaps the most famous of all is the dish still known as *schnitz und knepp.* Dried apples soaked until they regain their original size, and then cooked with highly-flavored ham, are accompanied by steamed dumplings. Smoked or otherwise, pork is seldom considered complete without a cooked fruit to lend contrast to its bland texture and taste.[4]

Chief accents—indeed, the rhetoric—of this eating style are found in that ancient custom known as "seven sweets and seven sours." Meals are not considered authentic unless meats and vegetables are complemented by jellies, jams, honey, ginger pears, spiced peaches, quince chips (to name a few "sweets"), and by briny pepper cabbage, pickled beets, chow-chow, Jerusalem artichokes in cider vinegar, pickled eggs, and green tomatoes (to name a few "sours"). Once no table was properly representative of a family's hospitality unless it had fourteen such preserves and condiments to pass from diner to diner. A great many herbs and spices were essential in the pantry.

Perhaps the early settlers of William Penn's colony had no greater

---

had been told by his own homesick son, there were many people who longed for "old-fashioned pies." Within five years Munson's cooks were producing a thousand pies a day, and his steamboat costs were so high that he opened a plant in New York. The market for New England pies was so great that one of Munson's employees set himself up in competition in New Haven, another in Providence, and a third went all the way to Chicago to further the influence of New England's way with pies.

[4] "By the by," wrote the British Captain Marryat in his *Diary in America,* "we laugh at the notion of pork and molasses. In the first place, the American pork is far superior to any that we ever salted down; and, in the next, it eats uncommonly well with molasses. I have tasted it, and *'it is a fact.'* After all, why should we eat currant jelly with venison and not allow the Americans the humble imitation of pork and molasses?"

access to spices from abroad than their neighbors, but they seem to have had a greater penchant for cinnamon in all kinds of cooking—with the use of ginger, nutmeg, cloves, allspice, even cardamom not far behind. Cinnamon buns are as much a part of Philadelphia's culinary folklore as is pepper pot. Gingerbread and ginger snaps and ginger cake and spiced pot roast that has languished in a bath scented with ginger and other aromatics are all characteristic of the cuisine of the Pennsylvania Dutch.

Much of the American appetite for sweet rolls and cakes comes from these specific Germans as well as from the Holland settlements that had so much early influence on New York, New Jersey, and Delaware. All of these early cooks made cinnamon-flavored breakfast- or coffee-cakes from recipes that vary only slightly, if at all, from methods in use in the twentieth century. All of them also share some of the responsibility for the national zest for doughnuts—as, in fact, do New Englanders who may, as some historians maintain, derive their proprietary interest in fried cakes from the years the Mayflower colonists spent in Holland before their landing at Plymouth. There have been previous admissions of the Down East claim. In *The Virginia Housewife* Mary Randolph captions her instructions: "Dough Nuts—a Yankee Cake."[5]

The Shape of Things to Come

Once there was a time when no American kitchen was deemed well equipped unless it had metal forms to shape doughnuts and cookies. Even before the use of metal stamps emigrants from Europe brought with them rolling pins and boards whose surfaces were divided into squares with carved indentations in the shapes of birds, animals, flowers, and human figures; cookies so shaped are still known as *springerles* ("little jumper") and are still made by Pennsylvania Dutch as well as many other Americans of German lineage. The word cookie itself is an American distortion of the Dutch word *koekje,* which means "little cake"; but the concept of small flat cakes the British still call biscuits has developed so greatly on this side of the Atlantic that cookies as we know them are generic to the U.S. cuisine.

So, in a way, is the dessert we call cake, which has changed in dozens of ways since the first Pennsylvania Dutch mixed stone-ground flour and molasses and sugar and eggs and ginger, and baked a *kuchen.* Early settlers from Moravia, Switzerland, and various parts of the old Austro-

Dutch Doughnuts, 1740

About twelve o'clock set a little yeast to rise, so as to be ready at five P.M. to mix with the following ingredients: 3¾ pounds of flour, 1 pound of sugar, ½ pound of butter and lard mixed, 1½ pints of milk, 6 eggs, 1 pint raised yeast. Warm the butter, sugar, and milk together, grate a nutmeg in flour, add eggs last. Place in a warm place to rise. If quite light at bedtime, work them down by pressing with the hand. At nine next morning make into small balls with the hand, and place in the centre of each a bit of raisin, citron, and apple chopped fine. Lay on a well-floured pie-board and allow them to rise again. They are frequently ready to boil at two o'clock. In removing them from the board use a knife, well-floured, and just give them a little roll with the hand to make them round. Have the fat boiling, and boil each one five minutes. When cool roll in sifted sugar.

[5] Louis P. De Gouy wrote in 1947: "The National Doughnut Dunking Association has always credited the invention of its pet provender to a Maine sea captain named Hanson Gregory. It was Gregory who, according to the story, objecting to the soggy center in his mother's fried cakes, is said to have remarked, 'Why don't you cut a hole in the middle where it doesn't cook?' That was 1847.

"But now [an even century later] a Cape Cod historian places the great event earlier by a good two hundred years. It seems that one day back in the seventeenth century a Nauset Indian playfully shot an arrow through a fried cake his squaw was making. The squaw, frightened, dropped the perforated patty in a kettle of boiling grease—and the result was the doughnut."

Hungarian empire had inherited a proclivity for cooking with spices from generations back when Crusaders brought exotic condiments from the east and when more than one ruler in Central Europe married a Byzantine princess who made cooking with aromatics fashionable. German-speaking cooks developed a deft hand, so to speak, at combining spices with nuts and fruits and, in Pennsylvania particularly, they came upon a richly endowed land. Their men often chose the acres upon which they settled on the sighting of a stand of black walnut trees, knowing that such woods indicated limestone soil that would guarantee rich harvests; they planted orchards of many kinds of fruit along with their other crops. Cakes and other desserts reflected this bounty.

There are Americans in the twentieth century who have yet to be enchanted by the flavor of black walnuts, but throughout Pennsylvania Dutchland—and in Virginia, West Virginia, Tennessee, the Carolinas, and the Middle West especially—lavish black walnut cakes are perennial favorites. Black John Cake is of two layers made from dough that blends brown sugar, molasses, eggs, butter, flour, ginger, cinnamon, buttermilk, and baking soda and has a filling accented by raisins, coconut, and black walnuts. The Magnolia Cake of the Moravian community in North Carolina is made with black walnuts in the dough, instead of the frosting, as is also Alyse Kistler's version of Pennsylvania Dutch Black Walnut Christmas Cake.

Nut cakes and nut breads have been common in American cooking in all periods and in all regions. But the so-called "fancy cakes" that evolved beginning with the first use of pearl ash (pearly-hued potassium carbonate) as a leavener added a new quality to New World cooking. Recipes for sponge cakes, which appeared about the same time, go back to the turn of the eighteenth century, and angel (or angel food) cakes, which some believe evolved as the result of numerous egg whites left over after the making of noodles, may or may not be the brain child of thrifty Pennsylvania cooks who considered it sinful to waste anything.

Mary Emma Showalter, who received her master's degree for a study of Mennonite cooking in America, gathered material from more than a hundred communities scattered across the country, and she came to the conclusion that cake recipes held first place in the "old hand-written notebooks that bear dates prior to the Civil War. . . . These cake recipes were not only the first ones recorded in [the average] book but they occupied the greatest number of pages." Baking powder had become available in this period and it undoubtedly added impetus to the urge to succeed at cake-baking.

For the Lock-up

One of the cakes that appeared in the study, and a recipe that is still popular, came from the Mennonite community in Rockingham County, Virginia; it is called Marble Cake—because of the swirling contrast of colors in its interior—and the recipe ends with the admonishment: "This cake will not keep unless it is put under lock and key!" Molasses was called for as the darkening agent in the documentary instructions, but most twentieth-century cooks use chocolate to get a similar effect and they have similar problems keeping a remnant of the cake once it has been tasted.

Although chocolate was first used in cooking by pre-Columbian chefs south of the Rio Grande, it was a Dutchman who developed powdered cocoa and a century later a Swiss who worked out the formula for milk chocolate. Trading vessels from the West Indies brought the cacao bean to American ports not long after the arrival of emigrants from Holland and Middle Europe. Although the earliest colonial use was almost exclusively in hot drinks, the making of desserts that were chocolate-flavored followed the establishment of the first American chocolate mill in 1765. The production of chocolate in various forms began soon thereafter in Pennsylvania.

Much candy, including fudge, with chocolate as the predominating flavor, is made by housewives, and there is a piquant chocolate sauce from Lansdale, Pennsylvania, that combines unsweetened chocolate with sugar and cornstarch to dress up desserts. Chocolate sauce over ice cream has become ubiquitous in America, and in Strathmore, a Philadelphia commuters' town, a chocolate sauce, accented with coarsely chopped butternuts, combines eight ounces of butter and twelve ounces of semi-sweet chocolate bits, simmered over boiling water, to serve warm over vanilla ice cream.

It's true that no German in Pennsylvania had anything to do with the invention of ice cream, but the record indicates that Philadelphians were among the first Americans to serve a frozen dessert, and that "Philadelphia ice cream" became a standard of excellence. There were vociferous partisans of the Philadelphia recipe in opposition to New York's method, or even to French ice cream with its base of beaten eggs. Writing early in the twentieth century Cornelius Weygandt, a gallant flag waver for the Germanic influences on American food, said flatly that the best ice cream was to be had in the Germantown section and in Philadelphia proper; he nominated Sauter's Ice Cream Parlor on Locust Street opposite the Academy of Music as setting a standard not to be trifled with, and pointed to other sources in Bristol, just up the Delaware, Norristown on the Schuykill, and one among the hex-marked barns of Bucks County.

"The Dutch Cupboard" in Coatesville serves a dessert of Pennsylvania origin which combines a number of flavors. Layers of vanilla cake with chocolate filling are topped by ice cream and butterscotch sauce, an example of gilding the lily in all-too-characteristic American fashion, but the ice cream itself is not to be faulted if it is the genuine old-fashioned Philadelphia kind.

That kind, according to Sarah T. Rorer who ran a distinguished cooking school and wrote *Mrs. Rorer's Philadelphia Cook Book*, could be made only one way: "To make good Philadelphia ice cream, use only the

Spiced Chocolate

Grate 2 squares of chocolate. Boil 1 quart of milk, reserving a little cold to moisten the chocolate, which must be mixed perfectly smooth to a thin paste. When the milk boils (in which the cinnamon must be put when cold, and boil in it), stir in the chocolate, and let it boil up quickly, then pour into a pitcher, and grate on a little nutmeg. Rich cream added to the milk, will improve it.

—*Miss Beecher's Domestic Receipt Book*, 1848

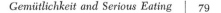

best materials. Avoid gelatine, arrowroot, or any other thickening substance. Good, pure cream, ripe fruit, or the best canned in winter, and granulated sugar, make a perfect ice cream. Next, get a good freezer, one working with a crank, and double revolving dasher, making a triple motion." She offered details for every step in a careful process of scalding the cream ("when raw cream is frozen . . . [it] has a frozen, snowy taste . . ."), packing the freezer and ripening the ice cream to blend the flavors. Mrs. Rorer's firmly worded instructions have been modified over the years, but Philadelphia-style ice cream, without eggs, as opposed to that called French which has a custard base, is still commercially made, with no compromise on the quality of ingredients, including the use of vanilla beans. And Bassett's in the city of its origin is an old-fashioned ice cream parlor serving a product that draws addicts toward it as if it were a minor mecca.

The Final Course

In Pennsylvania Dutch homes, where pie is served with the meat and at least one cake dresses the table, the final course—for which any hostess would expect one to make room—is a cooked dessert, a pudding, for instance, or sugar dumplings known as "Comforts." Fruit dumplings also are served, made with peaches, apples, prunes, or rhubarb, and frequently topped with vanilla sauce. Dutch Puffs, another common dessert, are made of a yeast dough that rises for four hours before being deep-fried and flavored with orange. Dumplings, disguised as slumps and grunts in New England parlance, and puddings with British pedigrees are common enough to Yankee cooks, and the cuisine of the South is plentifully supplied with custards. It takes a German-influenced hostess, however, to make a man feel he hasn't really eaten until he's topped off a meal of a dozen separate items with a rich and—let's face it—heavy dessert.

To put it as succinctly as possible, *Gemütlichkeit* came to American cooking when the first emigrants from Holland opened food shops and shared their baking and sausage-making with English-speaking neighbors in New York and New Jersey. Over the centuries there has been persistent migration from countries where the language is basically German. Richard Hofstadter pointed out that the path of German settlement during the colonial period can still be traced from Waldoboro, Maine, southward through the New York towns of Herkimer (once the best known of the cheese-making centers), Mannheim, Newburgh, down through Kutztown, Bethlehem, Emmaus, Ephrata, Gettysburg, and Hanover in Pennsylvania, through Hagerstown, Maryland, and Fredericksburg, Virginia, to New Bern in North Carolina, Orangeburg in South Carolina and New Ebenezer, just north of Savannah, Georgia. In New Amsterdam pork and cabbage was spoken of as *Speck ende kool*, in Pennsylvania as *sauerkraut und shpeck*; roast ducks in colonial New Netherlands were served with pork liver dumplings, in Pennsylvania

Dutchland liver dumplings still turn a soup into a meal in itself, and roast duck nests in a bed of sauerkraut. German cooks in Old Salem, North Carolina, also are known for their liver dumpling soup. And the Moravian Slaw "served routinely at suppers at Calvary Church in Winston-Salem as well as in Moravian homes" is made from a recipe virtually identical to others known variously as Pennsylvania Pepper Cabbage, or Pepper Hash—or Dixie Relish, as it is labeled by a Maryland Mennonite community. Under any name it is an almost exotic pickled cabbage to which New World peppers have added an indigenous piquancy in various American kitchens.

Growing up in the Middle West, I spent my first year away from home as a boarder with two German sisters who offered nothing but German food. Like thousands of others I fell in love with Hot Potato Salad. Neither my wife nor I has yet perfected a recipe to measure up to my young and impossible memories of how that early taste experience comforted my sensibilities. Yet that knack with potatoes and seasonings points up a central truth: one way to eat well is to have respect for simple ingredients, but to enhance their natural flavor with contrasting seasoning.

Dutch Slaw

Add sugar to vinegar to make sweet sour taste and heat along with a few celery seeds, stirring to dissolve sugar. Do not dilute vinegar. Remove from heat and cool.

Add chopped green pepper and pimiento as desired to chopped or shredded cabbage in a glass jar. Cover with vinegar solution. Put on lid and let it stand. It may be eaten right away but it is better after a day or so.

—Old Salem Cookery

Chapter 5

Body
and
Soul

I

T IS EASY ENOUGH to find Americans with great nostalgia for the food of their childhood. Mark Twain—in Europe and homesick in 1878—said it had been many months since he had had a proper meal, and he wrote out a menu of more than sixty dishes culled from his memory of American kitchens. Fifty years later Thomas Wolfe sprinkled his novels with his own hunger for good food—any food—but most often for the unpretentious fare of the Carolina hills.

No one, however, has written more eloquently than Ralph Ellison, describing a black youth, recently arrived from the South, chancing upon a street vendor in Harlem whose specialty is roasted yams: "At home we'd bake them in the hot coals of the fireplace . . . had carried them cold to school for lunch; . . . Yes, and we'd loved them candied, or baked in a cobbler, deep-fat fried in a pocket of dough, or roasted with pork and glazed with well-browned fat. . . . I took a bite, finding it as sweet and hot as any I'd ever had, and was overcome by such a surge of homesickness that I turned away to keep my control. . . ."

As Ellison's narrator walks along, eating his yam, "the sugary pulp steaming in the cold," his imagination is ignited by thoughts of chitterlings, mustard greens, racks of pigs' ears, pork chops, black-eyed peas, hot sweet potato fried pies, and he comes to the realization that he no longer needs to be ashamed of food he loves.

Twenty years or so after Ellison's book was published, there were few people ashamed to eat the food of the poverty-stricken South. A vogue developed for a distinct branch of American cookery called soul food. It became possible, even outside black-dominated areas, to order a soul food meal in a public place, and cookbooks limited to the subject were made available in large printings by publishers sensitive to the new interest. While soul food may not have made as deep a mark on the nation's consciousness as did the music that bore the same label, there were at least the beginnings of a realization that soul food was as much a factor to be reckoned with in American regional cookery as any other.

There is no dictionary definition of the term that is wholly satisfactory. "Soul" is considered by black people to imply a naturalness of expression, an openness to life and to one's fellows, a sharing of common sorrows, common joys. As there is a lack of inhibition in soul music, there is an absence of snobbishness about the ingredients that make up soul food. Some of the favorite dishes of American blacks are natural foods like collards and kale and turnip tops (and the wild greens that all American pioneers ate), as well as the remains of pig meat considered not choice enough for the "big house" on plantations. The percentage of slaves who were taught to cook in a European style is slight compared to the numbers of black women who learned to make do for their families—especially in the economic debacle that followed the defeat of the Confederacy—with roots, beans, fish, and an occasional 'possum.

"Soul food, black folk cooking," wrote Princess Pamela Strobel, who presides over the kitchen of her own Greenwich Village restaurant, "is compassion food." It requires the application of culinary genius to overlooked odds and ends and leftovers; and the act of eating "soul" is, she went on, "still close enough to honest-to-God hunger, to impart to food a savor deep enough for joy and solace."

Thrifty as the Dutch

There are those who say that soul food has evolved with little or no European influence. In fact it differs less from other styles of cooking than does jazz from its African and European roots. The black musician has not been stopped from appropriating (as does all music) the best of certain previous styles, but black women have been inhibited first by lack of access to a wide range of ingredients and second by impecunious budgets. Cooking for themselves, all black cooks have had to be even more thrifty than the thrifty Pennsylvania Dutch. Indeed, their appreciation of beans and other vegetables and their ways with offal—scorned by some more affluent kitchens—is akin to that of Germanic cooks who moved south through the Valley of Virginia. Again like jazz which has borrowed rhythmic influences from middle-European gypsy tempos, soul food has echoed Central Europe's way with pigs' feet and sauerkraut, adding accents of African heritage.

Soul food has traveled throughout North America, maintaining its basic integrity. Even in urban areas where there are no gardens and no wild vegetation within many leagues, supermarkets provide frozen greens, canned black-eyed peas, pork ribs and backbones, hocks and chitterlings.[1] Home-cooked food in Watts is identical to that in the South Bronx

[1] In 1972 James A. Beard, dean of American food authorities, wrote: "Chitterlings are the small intestines of the pig and are considered a great delicacy in the South

or Washington, D.C. In Maya Angelou's memoir of childhood in the Negro section of Stamps, Arkansas, the Sunday morning breakfast—a periodic feast—consisted of, among other things, "yellow hominy and crisp perch fried so hard we would pop them in our mouths and chew bones, fins and all."

Crisp fried fish has been far more significant in the diet of America's black people than is generally recognized. Slaves who lived along the coastlines of the South were familiar enough with the seafood that distin-

---

when cooked and served with turnip greens or black-eyed peas. . . . However they are done, they are a welcome change and resemble many European dishes made with the same ingredient. They are as old as history and not entirely exclusive to the South. . . . Recently I stopped at a huge shop in Los Angeles advertising 'Buckets of Chitlins.' They were wonderful. You can eat them there in the garden or you can literally carry away paper buckets of them."

guished their masters' cuisines, even though the field hands got little taste of it. But in antebellum times, and especially after emancipation, fresh-water fish, caught in stolen moments of free time, sometimes offered the only relief from a steady fare of corn and pork leavings.[2] Because pigs provided an excess of fat, the Negro cook for generations acquired and maintained a great knack for deep-fat frying.

Catfish, butterfish, mackerel, haddock, trout—the catch brought home from the nearest fishing waters—was scaled and gutted, lightly coated (head and tail) with cornmeal, lowered gently into a heavy pot filled to within three inches of the top with fat hot enough to brown a cube of bread in half a minute. Lifted out and drained on paper after a few minutes, such crunchy morsels of fish were often served in slave huts with cider vinegar. In plantation days Negro cooks sending dinner in to white diners would accompany the fish course with lemon, at the very least, and in Virginia they made an anchovy sauce to go with deep-fried perch. Or for those white masters who disdained catfish when fried they devised a stew highly flavored with curry powder.

The Importance of Using Pepper

Although such sophisticated combinations of spices were not available to any but house blacks, any palate conditioned in Africa or the West Indies had a tolerance for hot spices. An Alabama catfish sandwich calls for toasted scooped-out rolls spread with a mixture of Tabasco sauce, mustard, tomato catsup and onion to encase deep-fried catfish fillets still sizzling from the heat. A proper catfish stew—one with soul, that is—is seasoned judiciously with Tabasco or sprinklings of cayenne or crushed red pepper, and tame English-oriented codfish cakes were long ago transformed by Negro cooks when the bland basic mixture was lifted out of its rut by accents of vinegar, two kinds of peppercorns, and available herbs.

When soul cooks make their versions of souse, or jellied pork, they add red pepper with a generous hand; they boil pigs' feet until the meat is very tender, pulling it away from the bones and chopping it before forming it into a gelatinous loaf. Their sage-heady sausage is teeming with minced hot pepper pods or seeds. One of their ways with lamb kidneys is to slice and sauté them with onions and deck them with a red-peppery gravy in which dumplings are simmered. They make a hog maw salad flavored with celery and green pepper that is so esoteric it is some-times taken for chicken salad. The spicy touch may have developed as an antidote for the blues, but it certainly also is a vestige of cooking indigenous to western Africa.

[2] Lillian Britt Heinsohn, in a book describing twentieth-century plantation life, said she learned "that not only did our colored people love to fish, but that along about March or April an absolute compulsion for fishing seems to seize them. It's almost like a disease . . . 'catfish fever.' It occurs with unfailing regularity as soon as spring arrives, and it's useless to resist it."

Fried Fish

Wash 6 whole small fish under running cold water. Fill deep, heavy pot with vegetable oil or fat to within 3 inches of top; heat until temperature reaches 375°F. Meanwhile prepare 1 cup of dry ingredients (cornmeal alone or combined with flour, oatmeal flakes or other mixture), adding 1 teaspoon salt and ¼ teaspoon ground black pepper. Beat 2 egg yolks lightly with about 2 tablespoons cold water. Dredge each fish in dry mixture, then in egg mixture, and once more in dry mixture. Shake off excess but be sure coating is even and smooth. Put on foil or plate in refrigerator to chill. When oil is hot, lower fish carefully into hot fat and fry until brown, about 3½ minutes. Remove and drain on paper toweling in 200° oven.

Hog Maw Salad

Cook 4 pounds hog maws in salted boiling water about 4 hours, until tender. Remove fat and chop finely. Mix with 1½ cups chopped celery, 1 green pepper chopped, 2 medium onions chopped and 2 cups mayonnaise and season to taste with salt and pepper.

Tuskegee Soup

Sauté 4 or 5 minced scallions in fat 2–3 minutes, then stir in ½ cup of peanut butter and 3 tablespoons of flour, blending until smooth. Off heat, blend in 2 cups of chicken stock, return to heat and let mixture thicken. Add ½ cup cream and juice from 1 quart of oysters. Season with salt, cayenne and savory, and 2–3 Tbs sherry. Add oysters and let them get hot. Sprinkle each bowl with parsley.

Some of the same sea lanes that brought slave ships to America were followed by traders who returned to the New World food plants that had earlier been discovered by Columbus and others and had since become important in Europe and Africa. Thus peanuts went from Peru to the Guinea Coast and the Congo, and for a hundred years or more before the United States was colonized, black cooks had used peanuts in their cooking. One of the characteristic dishes on both sides of the Atlantic is chicken served with a peanut sauce.

Long before George Washington Carver, the Tuskegee Institute scientist, began his experiments with peanuts, as well as sweet potatoes,[3] peanuts had developed culinary importance in Africa, and soup made of ground-nuts, or goobers (to cite two names for the same plant), was brewed in colonial American kitchens soon after the first slaves were domesticated. Unfortunately no documentation exists for this kind of gastronomical history, but those early Virginians who planted peanuts as fodder for pigs helped to develop what has become famous as Smithfield ham. In the same colonial period Negro cooks began to "borrow" some of this animal food to supplement slave cabin diets. And the resulting dishes made of peanuts were soon adapted to plantation dining tables. Twentieth-century chroniclers have said that peanut soup is to Virginia what bean soup is to Boston. The nuts are most often blended with chicken stock and thick cream to make a bisque that seems ineffable to uninitiated diners. A combination equally imaginative and one popular long before the Civil War was the soup that resulted from blending ground peanuts with oyster liquor seasoned with black and red pepper on whose surface floated steaming plumped-up oysters.

Peanut butter and jelly sandwiches are made in millions of homes. Variations include peanut butter with crumbled bacon or slices of fresh garden tomatoes or both. But the inventiveness of soul cooks goes far beyond the use of peanuts in sandwiches or as snacks, far beyond the substitution of peanuts for pecans in the Southland's favorite of all pies. One of these fertile minds created a dish called "Kay's Yam Peanut Thing" in which equal parts of chopped peanuts and mashed yams are mixed with eggs, crumbs, and seasonings, formed into small cakes and stippled with shredded coconut, then fried in deep fat. In Africa, peanuts fresh from the garden are served as a vegetable, and in this country, soul cooks often prepare dried peanuts in a cream sauce. Another cream sauce, into which peanut butter is mixed, has devotees who use it to garnish cauliflower, cabbage or onions. Aficionados of the peanut recognize few limits. "The fillip of peanut butter spread on barbecued fresh green corn," an affluent hunter wrote after a stint in the Carolina mountains, "is a touch of genius." Peanut-flavored boiled dressings are used on fruit salads. Crisp double roasted peanuts mixed with onions, corn bread, melted butter, and wine accent just one of the inven-

[3] From peanuts Carver made cheese, milk, coffee, flour; from sweet potatoes flour, vinegar, and molasses. A man whose parents had been born slaves, Carver introduced to the dining hall at Tuskegee dandelion greens, watercress, pepper grass.

tive stuffings for goose, duck, or other poultry devised by black cooks. They also make peanut butter bread, biscuits, muffins, and a tasty vegetarian loaf that combines carrots, tomatoes, and peanuts in equal parts. Peanut candies, cakes, and other desserts are too numerous to mention.

Like Arabian Nights

Sesame seeds were not unknown to cooks with European backgrounds, yet South Carolina, and Charleston in particular, developed a proprietary interest because of a local tradition that slaves brought the seeds (in the Mandingo country on the upper Niger River the plant is known as *benne*) and used them in their native cooking. The same mystic power invoked by Ali Baba to open the cave of jewels was attached to benne seeds by old Negroes who planted sesame in their gardens and sprinkled their doorsteps with seeds to bring luck to the house and to ward off ants.

A story that may be apocryphal makes a poignant picture: Slaves hoeing cotton dropped benne seeds at the end of each row of their masters' crops, thus making a border of their own plants from the grains they had smuggled away from Africa.

As Middle Eastern cooks do to make *tahina*, slaves in the Carolina Low Country pounded benne into a paste and mixed it into hominy, knowing instinctively that it added nourishment, because it is high in protein. They combined oysters and benne seeds, instead of peanuts, to make a cream soup. In Charleston's twentieth-century cuisine one of the subtly spirited ways of serving chicken combines the flavors of benne seeds, orange peel, and orange juice; another South Carolina recipe from the days of slavery coats chicken breasts with grape preserves accented with cayenne, then sprinkled with benne seeds. Oozing with juices after grilling in the broiler, this is served with wedges of hot corn bread.

The most common soul food ways with benne seeds, however, include various recipes for cookies, and one or two for candy, and they come close to serving as a trademark for Charleston. Benne seed cookies (called good luck cookies up the coast at Myrtle Beach) are wafer thin and the result of combining brown sugar with flour, eggs, butter, and seasonings. In Mount Pleasant, just across the bridge from Charleston, cooks devised an icebox version. And a recipe that found its final details as far north as Winston-Salem uses no eggs but tempers the granulated sugar content with corn syrup. Benne seed candy, as made in Savannah (and as it was peddled once on the streets by bandanaed vendors) is based on equally simple formulas requiring no flour.

In most Negro kitchens candy of any kind was made for sale to whites, rather than for home consumption. In Charlottesville, Virginia, one day in conversation, a native housewife named Annie Hale told of having candy only when her father paid his bill at the country store. Each month he'd buy a bag for the children and, as it worked out, there would be one piece a night for a week for each child. Growing up on a small farm in

Soul Puddin'

Sift 2 cups cake flour, 2 tsps. baking powder, ½ teaspoon salt. Cream 3 Tbs. margarine, gradually adding 1 cup sugar to make a very smooth mixture. Add alternately flour and 1 cup milk, a little at a time; beat after each addition until smooth, adding ½ teaspoon vanilla with last of milk. Pour into 8 by 8-inch rectangular pan and bake at 350° about 1 hour. Serve hot with chocolate sauce.

the Piedmont, Annie nurtured her sweet tooth on fruits, wild and domestic, fresh from the branches or transformed into cobblers "from all the fruits you could name." From small dark wild grapes called coon grapes because, Annie said, "you had to reach so high to get them," the family made both a sweet wine and the wine jelly so characteristic of the South. And they cooked up preserves from blackberries, huckleberries, apples—and peaches that grew from the seed her father had planted.

Owning a farm made little difference in the soul food character of the family's diet. From the garden came butter beans, pinto beans, black-eyed peas—to be eaten fresh, and canned for winter. Cabbages and turnips were cooked all day, Annie said, with a piece of salted side meat, or shoulder. "The turnips would turn real brown," she remembered, "and we'd thicken the stew with flour so it was like gravy." Long slow cooking was the secret. "We boiled chitlins three hours, then dipped them in flour batter and fried them. We boiled pigs' ears until they were tender. We boiled down our own lard, and with the cracklings that were left we made crackling bread." When sheep were killed anywhere in that part of the Piedmont Annie's family sometimes got head and neck bones; it made a welcome change from pork and chicken. Raising their own poultry, the family sometimes had fried chicken and gravy, with rolls, for Sunday breakfast, and fried chicken again the same evening. They made their own sausage—"with sage," Annie said, "black and red pepper, salt—the crumbly kind. They were kept by wrapping the sausage in corn husks, packing them in cheesecloth bags, and hanging them. They'd get a little moldy but they never spoiled."

Food as Celebration

There were, she told me, "nine kids. Everybody chipped in and we loved doing that. I saw my mother doing things and I figured I could do it, too." She learned to make pancakes with cornmeal to eat with fried sausage meat. Her mother, she remembered, made batter bread with buttermilk in a hot oven and "would cut it up like brownies." Buckwheat cakes were made up the night before. "They rise in the bowl like something spoiled, but you just pushed it down and when they fried—my goodness, they was good. Sometimes there was sorghum molasses to go with." Naturally the biggest meal of the year was on Christmas day, the only time ham appeared on the table. With it would be baked spareribs that had been salted down, sliced sweet potatoes that gave off a great scent of nutmeg, yeast rolls made with precious white flour; there also invariably would be four cakes: caramel, chocolate, plain, and coconut, not just for the family but for the neighbors who stopped in for a taste, and for a drop of homemade wine.

There are fewer such self-sufficient farms left in the South than in the rest of the country, and most soul food cooking has become dependent on the distribution policies of supermarkets. Yet pork is still the basic meat, and greens or beans steaming in a pot are as likely as not to be among the

numerous dishes at weekend soul food parties that continue to demonstrate the Negro penchant for hospitality. It is a custom that comes,
according to Ruth Gaskins, a local food historian of Alexandria, Virginia,
"from back in the days when we were slaves. For over two hundred years
we were told where to live and where to work. We were given husbands,
and we made children, and all these things could be taken away from us.
The only real comfort came at the end of the day, when we took either the
food that we were given, or the food we raised, or the food we had
caught, and we put it in the pot, and we sat with our own kind and
talked and sang and ate."

Often the cooking could be started only when darkness had come and
the day's work in the fields had been finished. Instead of collapsing from
fatigue, black women found new strength when they poked up the fire, or
in later years of tenant farming turned on kerosene or primitive gas
stoves. To be able to cook and feed children and friends was more often
than not one of the few real pleasures that black families could share. It
was also a way to exercise creative urges, uninspiring as the material
available might seem. Mostly, it was a way of feeling free.

A black woman in one southern community gained fame locally for
celebrating the year-end holidays by crowding a buffet table with every
dish she possessed that would hold food. All those dishes were kept filled
from Christmas Eve until New Year's Day with corn-bread-stuffed turkey
and giblet gravy, country ham, fried chicken, collard greens, sweet peas,
sweet potatoes, corn pudding, potato salad, lettuce and tomatoes, biscuits, rolls, corn bread, cranberry sauce, pickles, homemade relish, apple,
pumpkin and sweet potato pies, caramel and chocolate cake, fruit cakes
and pound cakes, cookies, and egg nogs. Through her house, during
those days, there was always a constant stream of friends and strangers.

There must be very few black people who think a formal excuse is

needed for an open-house gathering. "No matter what his age," Ruth Gaskins wrote without too much exaggeration, "every Negro gives himself a birthday party. It usually starts at nine and ends when someone happens to notice the sun is coming up." It actually begins with a decision about food, she said. "If my birthday falls on a weekend I could spend the day cooking and cleaning chitterlings. If it comes on a week night I could spend the night before frying chicken." It seems apparent that the important thing is to invest the occasion with enough soul to make a lot of people happy. Soul food cooks say that the table for a Saturday night party or for a Sunday dinner is distinguished not so much by what things cost, or how fancy the recipes are, but by the bounty of simple food. "In fact," one of them said, "the foods that are typical of soul food are especially suitable for cooking in quantity—one-pot meals of soups, stews, gumbos, and beans."

The Soul of Brunswick Stew

Catfish stew with a strong accent of onions, tomatoes, and hot red pepper sauce for centuries was as popular among southern blacks as was catfish briskly fried in cornmeal. Many cooks preferred a version of Brunswick stew in which a pig's head, or tails, ears, feet, and hocks simmer with beans, tomatoes, hot peppers, and corn. Others, however, insisted upon what they considered to be authenticity. "One thing about Brunswick stew," a woman told her daughter who was collecting recipes, "it's a pretty pale imitation if it hasn't got squirrel. In other words, if it ain't got squirrel, it ain't got soul."

Squirrel pie has got soul in good measure when the meat is simmered with celery, onions, seasoned with both black and red pepper, then baked between layers of hard-boiled eggs in a pie shell. Squirrel is sometimes fricasseed and is considered a festive meal when served with grits, hot biscuits and honey. For frying, a good cook would prefer rabbit to squirrel, and the result is apt to be as tender and delicate as southern fried chicken.

Well into the twentieth century in the rural South, a possum hunt remained a favorite cold-weather sport, and roast possum and sweet potatoes was always cause for celebration. Sometimes the cleaned and dressed possum simmered with garlic, thyme, allspice, cloves, laurel, parsley, celery, salt, and red pepper until very tender, then went into the oven with the potatoes or yams cut in slices and flavored with lemon.

A soul food cook could always do similar things to raccoon, and in South Carolina and Georgia particularly some of the soul brothers who hunt bring back from an autumn trek along coastal creeks and inlets braces of marsh hens that seek the sky when high tides lash the land. These birds are traditionally skinned rather than picked and are kept under refrigeration for a couple of days before cooking, sometimes in deep fat. "Marsh rabbit" is an Eastern Shore euphemism for muskrat, a fine flavored meat which, after marinating overnight, is coated with flour and fried, then served up with currant jelly and beaten biscuits so hot they burn the fingers.

Perhaps no Americans know more than skilled Negroes about barbecuing wild game or, for that matter, meat of any kind. "When we think of barbecue and soul together," Pearl Bowser and Joan Eckstein wrote in their book entitled *A Pinch of Soul*, "ribs are what come to mind." Seldom able to get their hands on so-called luxury meats, "few of our grandparents indulged in a whole pig or side of beef cooked on an open fire," these writers pointed out. Yet techniques were perfected when slaves did the indoor and outdoor cooking for their masters. Small black boys kept the spits turning in the enormous fireplaces of colonial houses, and some of them became specialists at outdoor cooking when they grew up.

Bob Jeffries, who began cooking on an Alabama farm and who became a caterer and *chef de cuisine* in New York, put on paper his memory of what he called a "true" barbecue: "Back home we used hickory logs . . . and when the coals were just right to lay the chicken or ribs on, you could smell the fragrance for miles around." The meats, he said, were carefully arranged, "close together on the grill so that the smoke was trapped under them and not lost in the air. The fats will drip down into the hot ash and steam back up into the meat which also adds flavor."

The Jeffries instructions for barbecuing T-bone steaks begin: "Rub each steak with confectioner's sugar (no, you are not going to be eating a sweet steak, so read on before you decide this is not for you)." He made gashes close to the bone to insert garlic slivers and let the meat absorb room temperature until the dissolved sugar glistened on the surface. At six inches from very hot coals the surface was turned into a dark crust in about one minute for each side; the juices were sealed in while the steaks continued to cook.

Most barbecue sauces which permeate the surfaces of soul food spare-ribs, beef, or chicken are devised with a base of tomato catsup; they're really not much different from commercial sauces. Princess Pamela, however, puts together a sweet and sour mixture she calls Sauce Beautiful that includes peach preserves, sugar, lemon, vinegar, paprika, oil, and steak sauce.[4] Patrons of her restaurant eat ribs that have been baked in this sauce, or spoon the mixture over chicken that has been dipped in egg and a seasoned coating of flour and corn meal. In somewhat the same vein, the black cook at a plantation on the Georgia-Florida border seasoned her fried chicken with a touch of cinnamon and spiced peaches instead of a cooked peach accompaniment.

Perhaps it is obvious that there should be likenesses between soul food and that of the more affluent South. There are records to indicate that many recipes were written down by mistresses of plantations in an era when slaves who had not been taught to read or write were nevertheless inventive. The authors of *A Pinch of Soul* touched the heart of the matter when they wrote, "We had to rely on momma's and grandma's experience and what we could learn by watching as they went about their chores in the kitchen. The advantage of learning at grandmother's elbow is discovering things which are not in any book." Their conclusion was that the unsung, unrecorded soul food cook deserved as much praise as did any of her creations.

Soul in the Southern Repertoire

Just as it has been true that much of the soul food knack was never written down, there are also some records that prove that dishes now considered standard in the southern repertoire evolved from the black cook's skill at improvising. Marion Brown in her *Southern Cookbook* published a recipe she copied verbatim, she reported, from "a faded little copybook of penciled recipes" which she found on a Raleigh, N.C. plantation: "7 cup chicken, 2 quort creem. Make creem dressing 1 tablespoon to each cup, 5 pound mushroomes, 2½ cup celery, 1 green pepper, 1 tablespoon salt in creem dressing, 1 stick butter in creem dressing, I stick in mushroomes." Mrs. Brown offered this, she said, because "I have discovered some rich old recipes created by Negro cooks."[5]

[4] In his *Food Is a Four Letter Word* Eliot Elisofon wrote, "I have had two kinds of spareribs, the Chinese sweet and sour style, then the hot barbecued ribs served in Dixie. I decided to combine the two styles into one. I used honey instead of sugar, which the Chinese prefer, because of its more exciting texture and flavor. The Pickapeppa sauce is a hot sauce from Jamaica. . . . it also contains the flavor of tropical fruits . . . . there is no intention of making a really hot barbecued rib, but only a suggestion of it. . . ." His combination of soy sauce, vinegar, honey, cayenne, prepared hot sauce, pineapple, and Cointreau is reason enough for consulting his book.

[5] Their general ability to excel at cooking has not gone unnoticed, even by writers in the past who condescended to consult them about recipes and who often found

Other documentary examples are not hard to find. Slave cooks adapted the tradition of simmering turnip and other greens with hog jowl, developing variations drawn from their African backgrounds. One of these, called "herb gumbo," is the recipe of a woman who served as cook for forty years in the same family. As recorded by her mistress, it incorporates fresh spinach, beet tops, radish leaves, mustard greens, a head of lettuce, and the wild greens known as patience or spinach dock. The directions call for boiling the vegetables and chopping them "altogether on a nice clean board. . . . Fry a dozen small pieces of ham cut in pieces an inch long and half an inch wide, and also half a chicken cut in pieces, or a piece of veal, say half a pound. Add a cup of water [to the meat] and let it simmer three quarters of an hour or until all are soft. Then add your herbs. Let them simmer together for a quarter of an hour. If it looks too thick add a few tablespoons of water. It must have the consistency of a thick purée. To be served hot, and eaten with dry rice."

Lacking okra or sassafras, this is really not a gumbo but is a "mess o' greens" as slaves contrived the dish under the influence of the vegetables found in antebellum Louisiana. With the choice of greens skillfully balanced, so that the taste is neither too aciduous nor too bland, this can be a delectable concoction. In most of the twentieth-century South it is known simply as greens and pot likker, and no soul food restaurant bill of fare would be considered complete without it.

"A type of cooking made necessary by the environment in which southern blacks lived" is the phrase one soul food restaurateur used to describe his cuisine. In 1969, Bob Jeffries put it this way: "To begin with, soul food is honest. It is easy to cook but does not adapt well to 'Let's-get-out-of-the-kitchen-fast' shortcuts. It is delicious food, but does not allow for any frills. Sauces, for example, are used only because they taste good, never just to dress up a dish. Finally, it is sincere—because the good cooks who traditionally prepared it always worked with their whole heart, doing the best they could with what they had on hand to make sure that their dishes would be enjoyed by all who sat down to eat. . . . In addition, Negroes have always had an understanding and knowledge of herbs, spices, and seasonings and have known how to use them. It is only recently that soul food is being discovered, and I consider that good news."

---

them imprecise. In her book on Savannah cookery Harriet Ross Colquitt asserted that black cooks "are extremely modest about their accomplishments, and they cannot believe that the everyday dishes which they turn out with so simple a twist of the wrist, can be what we really admire, so they invariably add a few superfluous embellishments, by way of making them sound more imposing for the 'company.'"

Chapter 6

The Harvest Century

THE GOOD NEWS of the nineteenth century was the prevailing bounty. Out of this came gastronomical chauvinism. Native food, like every other American thing, was considered finer in quality and quantity than that of any other part of the world.

European visitors who criticized were dismissed as snobbish and pretentious. Easterners who showed empathy for foreign manners and tastes were considered by provincial Americans to be misguided if not disloyal. With field and garden crops so abundant no need existed (so the prevailing attitude seemed to make clear) for fancy ways in the kitchen. While the backwoodsman became transformed, as the public saw it, into homesteader, the cooking of the average nineteenth-century farmwife went through many changes for the better as a new American style evolved that was based on plenty—plenty of meat and fish, plenty of good things direct from the good earth, plenty of eggs and cream.

There was an innocence, perhaps a naïveté, in this jingoish culinary stance that ignored the future. Nineteenth-century Americans believed that the bounty was unending, inexhaustible. There was little reason to scrimp and scamp in the many farming regions where it seemed there was no end to good eating. That good eating depended, of course, on simplicity and the skill of the cook. Appreciations of such good eating make many old cookbooks a delight to read, and they have marked many memoirs with a thread of wistfulness.

Sometimes the wistfulness was more declamatory than affectionate. "My family dumplings are sleek and seductive, yet stout and masculine," Robert P. Tristram Coffin wrote on his Maine saltwater farm. "They taste of meat, yet of flour. They are wet, yet they are dry. They have weight, but are light. Airy, yet substantial. Earth, air, fire, water; velvet and elastic! Meat, wheat, and magic! They are our family glory!" Food like this, in a Maine man's view, was without doubt one of the items in those Olympic feasts which gave rise to the phrase "foods for the gods."

Pie Crust to Melt in One's Mouth

There are almost always intimations of Olympus. "My grandmother," a man born at the end of the century remembered, "was celebrated for her homemade sausage meat, her root and spruce and ginger beer, her mead and her currant, grape and gooseberry wines, made according to the recipes of her mother, my great-grandmother." He said that his mother "was admitted to be, in the local language of understatement, 'a good cook' of baked beans and brown bread and Injun pudding, of chicken and veal pot pies with feathery dumplings." And he couldn't resist adding that "Her chicken pies with a crust melted in one's mouth."

Meals that included any—and sometimes all—of a cook's repertoire of dishes with ingredients undisguised were dominant in the nineteenth century when friends and family gathered. Nostalgia brings back visions of tables stretching, as a Wisconsin writer recalled, "vast and white, crammed with two or three roasts and a dozen relishes and vegetables for an ordinary supper—and yet Aunt Dell moaning that she had nothing in the house." Bounty, clearly, has governed the cooking of American women more often than any urge for finesse.

Nostalgia for food of this sort was just what overcame Mark Twain while in Europe in 1878, and he wrote, only slightly tongue-in-cheek, toward the end of *A Tramp Abroad,* that after the long months since he had eaten what he called a nourishing meal, he was soon to have one—"a modest, private affair, all to myself. I have selected a few dishes, and made out a bill of fare, which will go home in the steamer that precedes me [across the Atlantic], and be hot when I arrive—as follows:

Radishes. Baked apples, with
   cream.
Fried oysters; stewed oysters.
   Frogs.
American coffee, with real cream.
American butter.
Porter-house steak.
Saratoga potatoes.
Broiled chicken, American style.
Hot biscuits, Southern style.
Hot wheat-bread, Southern style.
Hot buckwheat cakes.
American toast. Clear maple
   syrup.
Virginia bacon, broiled.
Blue points, on the half shell.
Cherry-stone clams.
San Francisco mussels, steamed.

Oyster soup. Clam soup.
Philadelphia Terrapin soup.
Bacon and greens, Southern style.
Hominy. Boiled onions. Turnips.
Pumpkin. Squash. Asparagus.
Butter beans. Sweet potatoes.
Lettuce. Succotash. String beans.
Mashed potatoes. Catsup.
Oysters roasted in shell—
   Northern style.
Soft-shell crabs. Connecticut
   shad.
Baltimore perch.
Brook trout, from Sierra Nevadas.
Lake trout, from Tahoe.
Sheep-head and croakers, from
   New Orleans.
Black bass from the Mississippi.

Small Cucumber Pickles

Wash and wipe one hundred small cucumbers and place them in jars. Cover them with boiling brine, strong enough to bear an egg; let stand twenty-four hours. Then take them out, wipe, place in clean jars, and cover with hot vinegar, spiced with an onion, twelve whole cloves, one ounce of mustard seed, and three blades of mace. They will be ready to use in two weeks.
   —Mrs. S. T. Rorer, 1886.

American roast beef.
Roast turkey, Thanksgiving style.
Cranberry sauce. Celery.
Roast wild turkey. Woodcock.
Canvas-back-duck, from Baltimore.
Prairie hens, from Illinois.
Missouri partridges, broiled.
'Possum. Coon.
Boston bacon and beans.
Green corn, on the ear.
Hot corn-pone, with chitlings,
    Southern style.
Hot hoe-cake, Southern style.
Hot egg-bread, Southern style.
Hot light-bread, Southern style.
Buttermilk. Iced sweet milk.

Boiled potatoes, in their skins.
New potatoes, minus the skins.
Early rose potatoes, roasted in
    the ashes, Southern style,
    served hot.
Sliced tomatoes, with sugar or
    vinegar. Stewed tomatoes.
Green corn, cut from the ear and
    served with butter and pepper.
Apple dumplings, with real cream.
Apple pie. Apple fritters.
Apple puffs, Southern style.
Peach cobbler, Southern style.
Peach pie. American mince pie.
Pumpkin pie. Squash pie.
All sorts of American pastry.

Cream and Butter without Sham

Mark Twain ran a gamut, from Boston beans to southern-style peach cobbler, from steamed San Francisco mussels to Lake Tahoe trout to Connecticut River shad, and mentions no adornments or sauces except "real cream," "clear maple syrup," and "American butter," which he said was not the "sham" that Europe's was because it is properly salted. He added a postscript that points up a philosophy he shared with his contemporaries: "Fresh American fruits of all sorts [should be added to the list], including strawberries which are not to be doled out as if they were jewelry, but in a more liberal way."

No more liberal way to show the bounty of America existed than to prepare food straightforwardly with cream or butter to add richness, and many women took just such refuge in quality, without regard to what might be considered *haute cuisine* in Newport, New York, or San Francisco.[1] That was what Mark Twain was after, and it is what armies of Americans thought about in the twentieth century when they were moved to describe traditional American food.

Nothing is more American than strawberries freshly picked and drenched in thick cream skimmed from the morning's milk unless it is strawberry shortcake. There are variations—sometimes this earthy Americanism has been gussied up by the employment of layers of airy white cake, or a bread dough enriched with sugar and eggs, as in old Nantucket kitchens—but an unimpeachable strawberry shortcake needs a baking powder biscuit dough lavishly mixed with butter and cream. Baked to

[1] The nostalgia is clear in these excerpts from an early twentieth-century letter: "Cream was used by my grandmother as we would use milk. Creamed codfish was just that, creamed with real cream, as well as potatoes cooked down on the back of the stove in cream and butter. . . . And a real cream pie, too. Not a custard, although they made that, with four or five eggs. . . . Their ice cream was also made of real cream, with no milk at all. . . . Homemade doughnuts, made with sour cream. Such Johnny cake, too, brown and with a cream taste. . . ."

flaky perfection, this is carefully split into two layers, the lower of which is usually slathered with butter before accepting its burden of berries with sugar to make a filling that drips in rivulets down the sides. The top half is buttered, still hot, and covers the crushed berries and in its turn is capped with more berries. Some cooks put their strawberry shortcakes back in the oven to ripen for a minute or two and then served the dessert with a pitcher of cream. In the twentieth century whipped cream (or, alas, a factory-made substitute) is often dolloped on the top.

Centers of Family Life

The unassuming honesty of such confections still conjures up kitchens in farmhouses or in frame houses with porches opening to elm-shaded streets. What we tend to think of as typical American cooking reached its zenith in those nineteenth-century kitchens. They were centers of family life, often doubling as dining rooms three times a day, as a place to sew by the fire, to whittle a new household gadget, to do homework, or just to hang around in while food was produced to suit seemingly insatiable appetites.

The Wisconsin novelist Edward Harris Heth wrote of his mother's kitchen: ". . . it was a kind of holy place from which she ministered lavishly to her family via stove and sink and cupboards and flour bins. There were rag rugs on the floor; usually wild white daisies or goldenrod stuck in a milk bottle, or garden flowers (her favorite bunch was of snow-on-the-mountain and small deep red dahlias); and almost always a rolling pin or flour sifter or earthenware mixing bowl was in sight. . . . She would have looked with smiling placidity, but inward scorn and despair for her sex, at today's housewives, who are helpless without packaged pie crust and canned potato salad and precooked rice and who deem it a chore to simmer day-long an honest soup, depriving themselves of its aromatic pleasure. Good cooking," Heth continued, "was a way of life and enjoyment. You did not save time but spent it recklessly, proudly, and with a full reward inside these four spotless walls."

In those years before central heating, there were radical changes in

Grandma's Muffins

(A hand-written recipe pinned into a page of *Miss Beecher's Receipt Book*, published by Harper & Brothers in 1848.)

" 4 Eggs
  2 Pints sweet milk
  1 Table spoon full of butter melted. A little salt
  4½ Pints of flour
  4½ Tea spoons full of Yeast Powder.

Bake in rings that have been well greased.

May 29 1874"

Cherry Pie

Seed the cherries first, then scald them in their own juice. Sweeten liberally and pour into a deep pie plate lined with a rich paste. Dredge with flour, cover with a top crust and bake. Scarlet or short-stem cherries are best. It is necessary to scald most fruits, as otherwise the pastry will burn before the fruit is thoroughly done.

—*Housekeeping in Old Virginia,* 1879

methods of storing and preserving food as well as the addition to the kitchen of the black iron cook stove. But people continued to eat greedily to stoke their bodies against the cold, or even, among women especially, to follow the fashion for abundant figures. Cook stove and icebox began to appear in urban kitchens about the same time, soon to be followed by a burgeoning canning industry that was to have a remarkable effect on the American kitchen. The availability of canned goods helped to minimize regional differences in American cooking at the very time many Yankees and Southerners were heading into the hinterlands of the West, taking with them recipes that had distinguished the food cooked by the mothers and grandmothers they were leaving behind.

Commercial canners made some kitchens less dependent on seasonal fruits and vegetables of a particular region; yet the basic style of cooking that had developed in colonial areas remained closely related to ingredients that could be grown in backyard gardens, on farms, or provided by local markets to which meat, fish, vegetables and fruit were brought from nearby suppliers. Given the choice, any cook who took pride in her ability—as did the majority in the nineteenth century—opted for the freshest possible ingredients. Any novice was sure to find helpful directions in the best of the professionally written cookbooks.

Away with Dead Vegetables

Mrs. N.K.M. Lee, who signed herself "a Boston housekeeper" when she published *A Cook's Own Book,* stressed that vegetables "should be brought in from the garden early in the morning; they will then have a fragrant freshness, which they lose by keeping. . . . Freshness is their chief value and excellence, and I should as soon think of roasting an animal alive, as of boiling a vegetable after it is dead." Sarah Rorer, in her *Philadelphia Cook Book,* spoke of "canned mushrooms, which are convenient and cheap, but tough and indigestible, and we caution those who eat them to masticate diligently."

No good nineteenth-century cook was willing to give up what she considered her right to the best available materials, and from the countryside she might habitually gather wild morels (known as "sponge mushrooms") to serve with fried chicken, or Fox grapes to make into a pie; or blueberries, blackberries, dewberries, growing unattended beside a creek, to stain muffins with purple splotches or to provide the molten foundation for an exclusively American dessert known as a cobbler. This last was a Midwest countrywoman's unwitting answer to the French provincial *clafouti,* and no country man living between the Atlantic and the Pacific would give the Gallic confection a second look were he forced to a choice.

Cakes, pies, and sweet puddings have remained the most popular American desserts. They gained popularity not only because they pleased the palate but also because they satisfied voracious hunger and provided energy for hardworking people—grown males certainly not the least of them. Sugar is a replacement food, one of the best and speediest sources of energy. Cooks in early America recognized the fact, and their inventive talents often substituted fruits of the wilderness for sugar that was hard to get.

"The Preference of Every True American"

Wherever sugar maple trees grow, farmers slash the bark along about Washington's Birthday to encourage sap to drip, and then settle into the arduous procedure of boiling nature's product into the liquid sugar that *The Old Farmer's Almanac* in 1798 predicted, too optimistically, "will ever have the preference of every true American." It became, in fact, a luxury product which all too often has been robbed of its true wild excellence by dilution at the rate of 90 percent cane syrup to 10 percent maple.[2] In its pure state it invests food with a unique flavor, and its uses are surprisingly diverse. Outside the United States and Canada, cooks have developed few recipes, for only in Germany and Japan have the trees been planted in appreciable numbers, and it takes forty years before a sugar maple can be tapped.

But American cooks have devised such combinations as cream cheese softened with sour cream and flavored with maple syrup, served with a topping of mashed strawberries accented by a drop or so of applejack. New Englanders, including the late John F. Kennedy, have preferred maple sugar over any other kind on cinnamon toast; some of them have considered buckwheat cakes unauthentic without maple syrup. There are dozens of variations of maple pies, cookies, cakes, and puddings, and early nineteenth-century cooks in Kentucky developed a maple salad dressing recommended for Bibb lettuce (which Kentuckians claim to have been propagated in the Blue Grass country by John B. Bibb of Frankfort). This sweet dressing is spicier than most of its kind, and it adds a purely American zest to fruit salads.

Maple syrup gives a distinctive flavor to country ham when it is added to the liquid in which the meat is boiled, just as it does when used in sauces to serve after the ham is cooked. Maine cooks mix two tablespoons of vinegar with a couple of teaspoons of dry mustard and about three-quarters of a cup of syrup to blanket a thick slice of cob-smoked ham while baking. In the South, maple flavor attaches a little mystery to a superlative combination of fried chicken and broiled Virginia ham on crisp waffles that is served with a thin but rich sauce of fresh cream.

When many nineteenth-century Wisconsin farmers tapped sugar maples, one or another farm wife modified a traditional pot roast by incorporating syrup in the broth, and the result is a tempting flavor at which guests usually can only guess. In the maple festivals of Chardon,

How to Sugar-Off for Maple Syrup

Use a caldron deeper than it is wide and never fill it more than half full to allow room for boiling up. Prepare a thick bed of faggots for fast, hot kindling. Since few people have the new sugaring-off houses, pile some brush to break the wind. He who figures to get more than one gallon of syrup from less than 35 gallons of sap is not good at figuring nor at making maple syrup.

[2] Pure maple sap contains much iron and phosphorus and is considered a good tonic. In northern Michigan, where U. P. Hedrick grew up, "Our syrup was dark brown. Its flavor was not delicate but robust; darkened by smoke . . . [with] a smoky taste like Irish bacon, Scotch whisky or Souchong tea. . . ."

1832 "Apple Fraze"

Cut Apples into thick slices, and fry them a clear light brown; take them from the pan, and lay them to drain; they may be pared or not; then make a batter. Take five eggs, leaving out two whites, beat them up with cream or flour, and a little white wine, make it of the consistency of pancake batter; pour in a little melted butter, mixed with nutmeg and sugar. Let the batter be hot, and drop in the fritters, laying on every one a slice of apple, and then a spoonful of batter on each. Fry them of a pale brown, when taken up, strew double-refined sugar all over them.

Ohio, the barbecued spareribs are maple-flavored. Maple sugar sprinkled generously on tart apple slices distributed evenly over a pastry shell and covered in heavy farm-fresh cream produces an indisputably New World apple pie.

A Scattering across the Nation

Without help from various quarters, however, apple pie might never have become the legendary American dessert that it is. It took a man named John Chapman to scatter apple seeds—perhaps a little like the scattering of colonial recipes—as he moved westward in the Ohio Valley. "Among the pioneers," a regional historian wrote in 1864, "was an oddity called Johnny Appleseed. . . . The trees from his nursery are bearing fruit in a dozen different counties in Indiana, and thousands are enjoying the fruit who never heard of Johnny Appleseed."

The seeds retrieved from cider mills by this early ecologist were planted and grew into small orchards to which John Chapman returned again and again to care for the trees that offered "pie timber"—as nineteenth-century cooks referred to ingredients for fillings—for many generations to come after him. He was a vegetarian whose preferred food, they said, was buttermilk and beebread (the pollen substance in honeycombs upon which bees feed); but, for all the nonconformism in his own diet, he helped to bring apples to pioneer kitchens from the Alleghenies to the Mississippi, and seeds from trees he had nurtured went further west when women accompanied their men on the Oregon Trail.[3] East of the Mississippi and in the Pacific West, wild crab apples provide an indigenous, if sour crop, and they make the best of jellies; but Johnny Appleseed did more, in his eccentric way, than anyone else to make most of America apple country.

Varieties of U.S. apples now are almost numberless, and some of the older types have been so pushed to the background that an orchard "museum" was established in North Grafton, Massachusetts, where one hundred old-time apples like Sterlings, Yellow Newtowns, and Roxbury Russets are tenderly encouraged to continue producing. Twenty-five percent of the nation's crop continues to come from large highly organized orchards in Washington state, but there are still rugged individualists among apple growers. Some family orchards, like that of Pine Tree farm in Minnesota, have harvested as many as fifteen varieties annually. In western Michigan, where orchardists have concentrated on McIntosh,

[3] Narcissa Whitman, the first of these, wrote her family in 1836 of sumptuous meals she had at Dr. John McLoughlin's Columbia River trading post that ended in "a nice pudding or an apple pie," made with fruit from a tree McLoughlin grew after he received seeds from a sea captain who, when requested to dress for dinner as was McLoughlin's habit, found in his long unused pocket the pits from a dessert apple given him by a young lady at a farewell dinner in London. McLoughlin had the tree so well attended that it not only forecast the arboricultural future of the Northwest but it thrived for more than a hundred years and was still alive at this writing.

Northern Spy, Jonathan, Delicious, and Wealthy, the wives of fruit growers in the 1950s toted up one hundred and twenty different apple dishes made with local apples, including apple salad, apple meatloaf, apple bread, relishes, desserts, apple punch, apple fritters fried in deep fat and dusted with sugar, candied caramel apples, apple butterhorns, apple potato salad, sweet potatoes baked with apples, and an uncounted number of apple pie variants.

Seventy-five percent of America's McIntoshes are grown in the New York–New England area. How much of this crop goes into pie is anyone's guess. But the way a McIntosh pie is seasoned is a matter of debate. Some insist the fruit must be pure, unadulterated by spices to insure a pervasive taste of apple. In Kent's Corners, Vermont (and many other places, too), cinnamon, nutmeg, and the zest of lemon accent the juicy McIntosh essence.

"My mother's pie was beyond description," Della Lutes' memoir of nineteenth-century Michigan says. "The crust was flaky, crisp, and tender. She used lard, and she mixed this with flour until it 'felt right.' She poured in water with a teacup, or the dipper, or whatever was at hand, but she never poured too much or too little. She laid on to the lower crust a bed of sliced apples to exactly the right height for proper thickness when the pie was done. It was never so thick that it felt like biting into a feather bed, nor so thin that your teeth clicked. It never ran over, and it had just the proper amount of juice. She sprinkled sugar over it with neither mete nor measure, and allspice and cinnamon from a can. But when the pie was done (crimped around the edges and golden brown on the humps, with an 'A' slashed in the top crust) it was a masterpiece of culinary art. With the edge of the oven's heat taken off, but never allowed to chill, and a goodly piece of cheese from the neighboring factory alongside, here was a dish which the average citizen of any country rarely meets."

From the Cuisine of New England Indians

Surely that Lutes masterpiece was an apple pie for Mark Twain, and just as surely it was a glowing example of the nineteenth-century gastronomy that depended equally on the love and skill of the cook and the simple quality of readily available ingredients. For such an apple-pie ending, a formal meal of the period might have begun with watercress and Jerusalem artichoke soup, made from the cress to be gathered at the farm spring and the artichoke that is really the delicately flavorful root of one of the members of the sunflower family, first noted by Samuel Champlain when he explored Indian gardens on Cape Cod in 1605. This is an elegant soup, rich with butter, a little flour, homemade chicken stock, milk, cream, egg yolks, and the fragrance of nutmeg, the verdant tartness of parsley, to perfect the combined flavors of watercress and the American sunflower root from the cuisine of Narragansett Indians.

In Europe Mark Twain pined for a porterhouse steak that might have

Warren, R.I. Apple Fritters

Sift together 3 cups of flour, ½ teaspoon of nutmeg, 1 cup of sugar and ½ teaspoon of salt. Dissolve ½ teaspoon of soda in ½ cup of milk and stir into sifted flour. Beat 2 eggs, adding ½ cup of milk, and stir into batter, blending until very smooth. Peel and core 6 tart apples, then slice them about ¼ inch thick and fold into batter so apple rings are completely covered. With long-handled fork carefully dip rings into deep fat (370°F.). Brown lightly, drain on absorbent paper, and sprinkle with mixture of sugar and cinnamon. Serve with maple syrup or honey.

been the *pièce de résistance* of a meal with this beginning and this ending. Although, once back in New York, the writer might have ordered such a steak at a chop house that specialized in them, the average housewife more often than not had to make do with beef as tough as saddle leather.[4] Very little beef was raised for meat alone until late in the century, and butchers dealt mostly with cuts that came from animals that had worked hard, rather than lazily grazing the plains before final weeks of eating corn to enrich the flavor and tenderness of the meat. Cooks learned to solve the problems of toughness, sometimes by simply marinating a steak for a dozen hours in clarified butter and pounding it flat before frying in a cast-iron skillet; sometimes a sirloin was soaked in a mixture of highly spiced vinegar and wine, then rolled up around a stuffing of suet and seasoned bread crumbs to be roasted on a spit. A man with a twentieth-century palate and a lifelong indulgence of the world's best beef pales at the thought, and is even more appalled at one sirloin recipe's title: "Rolled Beef That Equals Hare."

The Unyielding Appetite for Beef

Many twentieth-century cooks have looked askance at rabbit or hare, not realizing how good that meat tastes when skillfully prepared, and their way of treating tender porterhouse or T-bone, which is the smaller version of tenderloin steak, calls for the simplicity of broiling, by indoor or outdoor means. A good beef roast is likely to be cooked at home in the oven rather than on a fireplace spit, but it still comes to the table accompanied by a sizzling, egg-rich Yorkshire pudding as often as it did when English colonists saluted Hanoverian princes. The first published recipe appeared in a cookbook, issued in Manchester by a Yorkshire woman in 1762, which was bought by a number of Virginia homemakers before the Revolution. An old New England collection of recipes cautions that "Rare done is the taste of this age" when it comes to beef, and it directs that a roast be accompanied by cranberry sauce as well as Yorkshire pudding.[5] Beef, adorned and otherwise, has always been central to the notions most Americans have of a meal uninhibited by cost—or, for that matter, by Continental kickshaws.

Still, the nineteenth-century economy that limited the availability of top-grade beef widened the horizons of inventive cooks. A four-pound piece of chuck might be browned in bacon fat, salted, peppered, its top spread with prepared mustard and the juice of half a lemon, then covered with thin onion slices and five or six branches of dill and allowed to

[4] Porterhouse steak takes its name from the saloons that once specialized in dark brown malt beer for neighborhood porters and the cut of beef that comes between sirloin steaks and those called tenderloin.

[5] Settlers from Maine who founded Portland, Oregon, Americanized the pudding from Yorkshire by cooking the batter in custard cups lubricated with drippings from the roasting beef (or sometimes pork); another modification was the use of garlic and, frequently, herbs. The result is called "Portland Popover Pudding," individual balloons of crusty meat-flavored pastry.

simmer several hours in a small amount of red wine under a very tight cover. Or in the spring of the year a housewife might turn to veal, which only in that season was available—or to fresh-water fish.

Not the So-Called Baby Beef

As is true of most food in the twentieth century, there is no longer a limited season for veal, but traditionally the best meat from calves was available in the spring of the year. The youngest and most delicate was called "milk veal" and came from animals born late in the winter; "grass veal," found in butcher shops during the summer, came from animals that had left their mothers to feed in pastures during summer months. In spite of the fact that veal (not the so-called baby beef that has gone from milk-feeding to corn) is the flesh of calves from three to twelve weeks old and therefore tender, this young meat has for years been considered indigestible by many Americans who failed to understand how to cook it.[6] But there was a time on southern plantations and midwestern farms when, during the annual season, veal was so abundant that keeping the meat was a problem because of lack of ice machines and freezing equipment; as a result much imagination was exercised by willing cooks to create a great variety of veal dishes.

In Delaware a recipe for veal pot roast calls for the very slow simmering of a good-sized piece of rump with garden vegetables, the meat to be served in slices with a sauce made by puréeing the vegetables. Some New Englanders cut veal in collops, cook them gently, and dress them with a sauce that is a simple mixture of young cucumbers and rich cream. California's veal rolls are stuffed, flavored with onion, green pepper, and fresh herbs, topped with a sauce dominated by sliced black olives from orchards begun when Father Serra arrived in 1769. Some Floridians use olives and lime juice to accent veal served with a tuna fish sauce, and in some Louisiana kitchens veal steaks are cut in pieces, marinated in rum and fruit juice, braised in olive oil and embellished with a combination of pineapple juice, raisins, and ripe olives over which capers are sprinkled when this veal dish is served atop boiled rice. But at least as genuinely rural-American as any of these is a stew using a thick slice of veal from the leg that is simmered in stock with chestnuts.

When such dishes were commonly cooked, the chestnuts came from trees that grew on the home place, and the vegetables which added their separate flavors to the stew were from seeds planted by the cook herself, most likely, or by a member of her family. The combination of imaginative cooking and products of one's own farm made it easy to eat affluently at the cost of almost no cash at all. In other countries few "common people" possessed farms of their own and few had as various a horn of plenty from which to choose.

[6] "Veal stands lowest among the heat-producing meats," according to Mrs. D. A. Lincoln's cookbook first issued in Boston in 1887; veal should be, Mrs. Lincoln wrote, "eaten with potatoes or rice, which stand highest, or with bacon and jelly."

1832 Veal Pie

Take two pounds of veal cutlets, cut them in middling-size pieces, season with pepper and a very little salt; likewise one of raw or dressed ham cut in slices, lay it alternately in the dish, and put some forced or sausage meat at the top, with some stewed mushrooms, and the yolks of three eggs boiled hard, and a gill of water; then proceed as with rump-steak pie.

N.B.—The best end of a neck is the fine part for a pie, cut in chops, and the chine bone taken away.

Hands to Work, and Mouths to Feed

In this country, the operation of farms—before the late-nineteenth-century arrival of mechanization—required the help of many hands, and most farmers had many children. Their wives, thereby, had many mouths to feed. As their share in earning the food they ate, young boys did chores without question, and young girls helped in the cooking, gardening, dairying. Not long ago I read a childhood memory of a former airline stewardess who had retired to run a restaurant. "All of the Nortons old enough to read," she said of her family, "had sugar to measure and spice bags to assemble. All of the Nortons old enough to be careful with a knife had cutting and peeling chores to do. This was 'togetherness' before it became a magazine fad. We all felt we were part of our winter provisions, and we all knew this was the economy that made bicycles and doll carriages and patent leather Mary Janes a possibility." It was the nineteenth-century home economy that had carried over into pre-World War II days, surviving even into the age of flight, and reflecting a time when as many as a dozen heads might be counted around the table daily.

Cooking for so many on a regular basis, cooking for even larger appetites when the harvest season brought in helpful neighbors and hired hands to be fed as a part of the cost of bringing in the crops—these occasions were not only challenges in terms of logistics, but times of rivalry when good cooks showed how really good they were. When hungry threshers sat down at a harvest table they found it burdened with good things: relishes, cottage cheese, pickles, beets, hot baking powder biscuits, sliced fresh bread, two or three roast meats, fried chicken, a platter laden with pork chops, steaming greens, several kinds of potatoes, fried green tomatoes, sliced red tomatoes in oil and vinegar, assorted pies, and, yes, very likely, a cake or two as well.[7]

The plenty burdening a farmhouse table for harvesters is, I suppose, symbolic of the period. The land was fertile, much of it never tilled by any other than the resident family. Providence smiled. In years of church-going, of candles and oil lamps and no electronic distractions, no easy travel to far places, home was a place where contentment prevailed, or at least was encouraged. What better way of encouraging it than by serving bountiful meals that reflected the success of the home place? The holiday rhyme that recalls the pleasure of going "over the hills to Grandma's house" is implicit with the promise of a family gathering and abundant good food, a table laden (throughout the year, not just at harvest time) with relishes, preserves, condiments, fragrant roasts, every vegetable grown in the garden, desserts, hot coffee, homemade bread, and nuts to

Fried Green Tomatoes

Slice ¼ inch thick firm large tomatoes, green throughout. Sprinkle with salt, pepper and sugar. Dip in cornmeal and fry in a skillet containing enough bacon drippings to cover skillet ¼ inch deep. Have fat hot when tomatoes are added, then reduce heat and brown on one side. Turn with pancake turner and brown on the other side. Serve with hot homemade chili sauce.

—Old Kentucky recipe

[7] A twentieth-century Indiana menu for ten, recorded after a corn harvest, included "roast guinea, fried fish, roasting ears, potato salad, baked macaroni and cheese, baked beans, glazed sweet potatoes, green beans, celery, sliced onions in vinegar, sliced tomatoes red and yellow, homemade rolls with butter and blackberry jam, three kinds of cookies, pumpkin pie, milk, iced tea, coffee with endless cream and sugar."

eat at hearthside later.[8] It brings memories of coming home from church to be met by the smells of chicken baking in the iron stove's oven, of family reunions in days before calorie counts when many Americans lightened their spirits with food far more often than they did with alcohol.

Wines Preserved the Bounty

Although the temperance movement was steadily gaining momentum during the nineteenth century, cooks on farms and in small towns annually bottled a good deal of homemade wine. Early colonists had made many gallons of cider and wine because they were convinced that all human ills could be traced to drinking water. But in the nineteenth century fruit wines and vegetable beers were important because they comprised another way of preserving the bounty of the land. Wine was sometimes made after gathering bushels of blossoms from dandelions or elderberries, which had no other nutritive use; more often than not, however, the berries remaining after all the jams and jellies had been put up were mashed and their juices fermented, to serve medicinal or celebratory purposes. Gooseberries, raspberries, cherries, and currants were turned into popular wines, as were wild and domestic grapes of which there were many varieties. A recipe for blackberry wine, as made by Mrs. Robert E. Lee in the kitchen at Arlington, overlooking the national capital, was preserved by her daughter just as the general's lady wrote it down, and the instructions are very much like those used in humbler kitchens.

In virtually every region delicious and potable beers were brewed at home with roots or bark or buds as a base. Homemade root beer in the twentieth century has been a simple matter of using a factory-made extract, but the real thing, which was one of the pleasures of the nine-

Robert E. Lee Blackberry Wine

Fill a large stone jar with ripe fruit and cover it with water. Tie a cloth over the jar and let them stand three or four days to ferment; then mash and press them through a cloth. To every gallon of juice add three pounds of brown sugar. Return the mixture to the jar and cover closely. Skim it every morning for more than a week, until it clears from the second fermentation. When clear, pour it carefully from the sediment into the demijohn. Cork it tightly, set it in a cool place. When two months old it will be fit for use.

—Mrs. Lee in *Housekeeping in Old Virginia*

[8] Itemizing her baking for the year 1877, a Vermont housewife counted 152 cakes, 421 pies, 1,038 loaves of bread, 2,140 doughnuts.

Mary Randolph's Tomato Catsup

Gather a peck of tomatos, pick out the stems, and wash them; put them on the fire without water, sprinkle on a few spoonsful of salt, let them boil steadily an hour, stirring them frequently; strain them through a colander, and then through a sieve; put the liquid on the fire with half a pint of chopped onions, half a quarter of an ounce of mace broke in small pieces; and if not sufficiently salty, add a little more—one table-spoonful of whole black pepper; boil all together until just enough to fill two bottles; cork it tight. Make it in August, in dry weather.

—*The Virginia Housewife,* 1831

teenth century, was brewed from sarsaparilla roots, sometimes sassafras bark, molasses, and maybe some wintergreen leaves. Ginger beer is a compound based on ginger root or powdered ginger, and the spruce brew gets its distinction from essence of spruce or from boiling outer sprigs of the spruce fir.

Edward Everett Hale described the street sale of these forerunners of modern soft drinks: "Ginger beer and spruce beer were sold from funny little wheelbarrows, which had attractive pictures of the bottles throwing out their corks. . . . You might have a glass of spruce beer for two cents, and, to boys as impecunious as most of us were, the dealers would sell half a glass for one cent." In fact, the word pop derives from the effervescent quality of these drinks; a New England aphorism describes a clever man "as full of wit as a ginger-beer bottle is of pop."

New World roots like Jerusalem artichokes did not make their way into the wine cellar, but were instead pickled, as were so many other vegetables and fruits, in one of the many processes employed for making use of—i.e., not wasting—any of the plenty that came from the good earth. Methods of producing ketchup, which English cooks had adapted from a sauce brought back from Asia, were borrowed and changed by American cooks (some of them changed the spelling of the word, too) to create walnut catsups first, then cranberry, elderberry, gooseberry and grape catsups when sugar became plentiful. The earliest of these sauces, based sometimes on nuts, sometimes on mushrooms, had been made without sugar, resulting in spicy and tart concoctions in somewhat the manner of Worcestershire sauce. Early tomato catsup recipes are similarly tart: Mrs. Randolph's specifies only onions, mace, and black pepper as seasonings; a generation later Catherine Beecher, the sister of Mrs. Stowe, in her *Domestic Economy and Receipt Book* gave a tomato catsup recipe that required only cloves and nutmegs, pepper, and a little wine as seasonings.

I suspect the evolution of catsup may help to explain a rather important national characteristic. The writer and historian Kenneth Roberts wrote that Maine sea captains "brought tomato seeds from Spain and Cuba, their wives planted them, and the good cooks in the families experimented with variants of the ubiquitous and somewhat characterless tomato sauce of Spain and Cuba." Without resorting to the use of sugar, those Maine essays in making catsup, Mr. Roberts said, were so successful that the new tomato mixture came to be "considered indispensable with hash, fish cakes and baked beans. . . ." He himself became, he added, "almost a ketchup drunkard; for when I couldn't get it, I yearned for it. Because of that yearning I begged the recipe from my grandmother when I went away from home; and since that day I have made many and many a batch . . ." none of which was sugary, for a sweetened catsup "is regarded as an offense against God and man, against nature and good taste." The Roberts family catsup recipe had the tang of red and black pepper, allspice, mustard, cloves, and "sharp vinegar." Sharpness also distinguished the taste of tomato catsup in antebellum Charleston, that regional gastronomical capital where *bon gout* was more than an epigram. But soon, across the country, the American appetite for sugar had its way.

In the period immediately after the Civil War Joshua Davenport was manufacturing and selling vinegar, pickles, and catsup in the Berkshire Hills of Massachusetts. According to the recipe handed down (the story goes) in the Davenport family, Joshua added two cups of sugar to a mixture of a gallon of tomato stock and a half pint of vinegar flavored with cinnamon, cayenne, and salt. Chances are he was not the first man to sweeten the pot, but by the time Mrs. Rorer's cookbook began to influence a wide public in 1886 the sugary tomato sauce was firmly established. Catsup began to vie with mustard as the acceptable condiment for frankfurters and hamburgers—even for french fries and mashed potatoes —and before the nation was two hundred years old it had gone from having a president who believed in a cuisine of high standards for the United States, as did Jefferson, to one whose taste ran to cottage cheese and sweetened red catsup for lunch, according to White House reports.

In the twentieth century, weight-consciousness helped to explain some gustatory aberrations, but a hundred years earlier most Americans ate as much or more for lunch as they did for breakfast or supper; dinner was, of course, properly served at midday when, in town or city, a man came home from his job. Like the farmer, the urban male knew a lot about food, and many of them were more familiar with the stalls in their local market buildings than were their wives.[9]

"My grandfather," wrote Margaret Rudkin, who earned fame with her Pepperidge Farm bread, "often did a bit of shopping on his way home, and when he stopped at the slaughterhouse on First Avenue where the United Nations building now stands, he would bring home a treat—'the liver and lights.' That meant calves were being killed that day and he bought fresh calf's liver and sweetbreads. . . . The calf's liver was left whole, larded with thin strips of salt pork, sprinkled with herbs and spices, covered with strips of bacon, and roasted, being basted often with the bacon fat and plenty of melted butter. It was heavenly," Mrs. Rudkin remembered almost a half-century later, adding that the accompaniment for the baked liver was a purée of dried peas, and that it was often served cold next day with rye bread and mustard pickles.

Produce Direct from the Farm

The variety and quality of meals produced in urban kitchens, like those of rural cooks, were directly related to easy accessibility to food freshly delivered from local farms; and towns and cities throughout the nation provided great market buildings and sheltered outdoor areas to which

Fannie Farmer's Sweetbreads and Asparagus

Parboil a sweetbread, split, and cut in pieces shaped like a small cutlet, or cut in circular pieces. Sprinkle with salt and pepper, dip in crumbs, egg, and crumbs, and saute in butter. Arrange in a circle around Creamed Asparagus Tips.
  —*The Boston Cooking-School Cook Book,* 1896

---

[9] Daniel Webster, in Washington, found surcease from the demands of statesmanship—and a great variety of provender—on his early-morning market tours to make his choice of Maine salmon, New Jersey oysters, Florida shad, Kentucky beef, Delaware canvas-backs, Virginia terrapin, South Carolina rice-birds, as well as the best of the fruits and vegetables brought into the District.

farmers could bring their produce. The Philadelphia market, a half-mile long, was considered by some to be the best in the world. The average market, however, paid less attention to imported provisions and more to regional bounty. Seattle's Pike Place Market (now listed in the Department of Interior's Register of Historic Places) was established by the city expressly to help farmers from the Kent Valley, just south of Seattle, sell directly to the public. Pike Place is fighting the tide of urban renewal as this is written—much the way Olympia oysters are threatened by pollution in Puget Sound—but when a shopper finds the tiny Pacific oysters on sale in the sprawling Seattle market he can bring them home to make what Seattle cooks call Olympia pepper pot. The tiny oysters are combined with green peppers, tomatoes, catsup, and lemon, and served on buttered toast made, one hopes, from homemade bread as in the nineteenth century. Or the shopper can find in that market the Washington blackberries that good cooks often demand for a blackberry dessert in which sugared berries comprise the filling for sweetened baking powder biscuit dough "rolled like a jelly roll," then quickly baked and served warm with heavy cream.

When I was a child, my mother cooked in ways that she had learned before the turn of the century, and she maintained the best of those ways as her repertoire widened with travel and a developing taste. Like many of her generation, she never submitted to so-called convenience foods as a way of life. She believed in the best of ingredients. On one of the end papers of one of her numerous volumes of recipes there appears this way of using fresh fruit, with comment, in her handwriting:

RASPBERRY SHERBET
(I originated. June 1931, 102°)
2 c. raspberries, mashed
with 2 c. sugar.
1 qt. milk (whole)
juice of 1 orange
Partly freeze, then stir in 2 stiffly beaten egg whites,
finish freezing & pack. Best if left packed several hours.

It is a simple recipe, typical of many "originated" by women in every part of the country where there were cooks respectful of the quality of the materials at hand. It proves, if anything, that there was a time when nothing, not even the hottest day of a Midwest summer, was permitted by earnest cooks to interfere with the serving of good food.

Chapter 7

Shakers, Bakers, Breakfast Food Makers

AMERICAN FOOD STYLES changed unalterably as a result (indirect if you will) of a chain of events that began early in the nineteenth century. It might be said, in fact, that there is a traceable line from early Shaker cooking through the preachments of a man whose name is now coupled with whole wheat flour to the breakfast menus of most twentieth-century American homes. It is doubtful that the sounds of cornflakes ever would have been heard in the land had it not been for cooks who became convinced that good health is just as important as good food.

By the middle of the last century there was a massive reaction to a prevailing malaise that was usually described as dyspepsia but was aptly rechristened "Americanitis" by Marion Harland, a Virginia novelist who discovered a wider audience when she turned to writing books about food and household management. Thousands were in need of guidance. Those sedentary city dwellers who indulged in breakfasts of steak and pie, and greasy foods at every meal, belonged to a segment of the citizenry only too willing to listen to miraculous cure-alls.

An era of reform and revival had settled on the country—there was almost incessant talk of utopia, and many societies were formed to make the concept a reality, some in religious ways and some as socialistic panaceas. One of the earliest was the United Society of Believers in Christ's Second Coming, a spin-off from the Society of Friends whose members became known (there was a great deal of movement in their services) as the Shaking Quakers.

Shaker Haying Water

Put 4 cups sugar or 3 cups maple syrup, 2 cups molasses, 2 teaspoons powdered ginger, and 2 gallons cold water together and stir until thoroughly blended. Pour into large jug, and chill. Serves 30.

—North Union Shaker Village

As a celibate sect believing in the millennium, the Shakers established isolated communities dedicated to regular and simple living habits. Plain, wholesome food eaten in moderation was, they said, a preventative against indigestion and was central to the Shaker faith. Shakers were among the first to advocate greater use of vegetables and fruit, the use of whole grain in making flour. They considered their communities "Heavens on earth" in which they devoted themselves to thrift yet at the same time to standards of living far above the average. They created their own excellent architecture, designed furniture that is much coveted in the twentieth century, devised methods to increase productivity of soil and livestock, and became superior mechanics, responsible for inventions that helped improve the lives of many outsiders.

When outsiders had to be put up in a Shaker village because there was no nearby hostelry, they were fed cheerfully enough in a separate dining room but admonished to "eat hearty and clean out the plate," for Shakers could not tolerate waste of any kind. They stopped short of so dividing their visitors that men and women dined at different tables, as was required of themselves, but cards were placed in visitors' bedrooms asking that marital privileges be foresworn during the stay in the community.[1]

Vegetarianism was not strictly enforced among the Shakers, but because the sect's leadership believed in a future in which all mankind would accept a meatless diet, the women who cooked together in the large community kitchens perfected recipes that were often published in the Shaker *Manifesto*, a periodical that circulated in each of the separate

Cucumber Salad

Select 2 tender young cucumbers; peel one but leave the other unpeeled. Slice very fine. Sprinkle with salt and let stand just three minutes, thus removing any bitter taste of the skin. Mince ½ onion and add to cucumbers. Mix dressing of ½ cup sour cream, ½ cup vinegar, ½ teaspoon salt, ¼ teaspoon pepper, 2 tablespoons sugar, and ¼ teaspoon mustard; pour over cucumbers. Serve at once for full flavor.

—Amelia's Shaker Recipes

[1] A sample of Shaker versifying given to dining room guests: "We found of these bounties / Which heaven does give, / That some live to eat, / And that some eat to live— / That some think of nothing / But pleasing the taste, / And care very little / How much they do waste." Outsiders can still visit Shaker communities at Sabbathlake, Maine, and Canterbury, New Hampshire, as well as museums open at defunct villages near Hancock, Massachusetts, and Old Chatham, New York, and the Shaker Historical Society in Cleveland.

Shaker compounds. "It does not seem to be generally known that the cucumber is one of the most valuable vegetables we raise," announced one issue of the *Manifesto*. "It can be dressed in more palatable and suitable ways than most any other vegetable except tomatoes. It is far better than squash and more delicate than eggplant . . . and is most delicious when made into fritters in a dainty batter. . . ."

Another issue admonished: "One of the first signs of spring is the tiny sawlike leaf of the dandelion sticking its leaves above the thawing earth. Before they have a chance to burst into bloom, have the children gather these succulent plants. This furnishes you with a tasty dish and at the same time rids your dooryard of weeds."

The Doing of Inventive Things

While Shaker men found time to invent an apple parer, a pea sheller, a water-powered butter churn, an automatic cheese press, a superior wood-burning stove, matches, and a revolving oven for baking dozens of pies at a time, the women charged with the community cooking did inventive things with all kinds of ingredients. Shakers perfected a way to produce dried corn—and thereby helped provide Americans generally with year-round supplies that would not spoil easily. They made of the normal growing season "a rotation of crops of beans, peas, spinach, beets and turnips . . . in order to have crisp, fresh vegetables almost until the snow flies."

Shakers used herbs more profusely in all kinds of cooking—"Cucumbers want herbs!" cried the *Manifesto*—than did any other early American cooks, and growing them, drying, grinding, and packaging them provided some communities their chief source of income. They also were among the first to gather and market wild roots and other herbaceous plants that grew naturally on the frontiers. They may have been the first to use advertising to guide other cooks toward improving the flavor of the food served in average homes, pointing out in leaflets that herbs "stimulate appetite, they give character to food and add charm and variety to ordinary dishes."

Bread was very much the staff of life. There are surviving recipes for Sister Lisset's tea loaf, Sister Jennie's potato bread, a "Dyspeptic loaf," whey, rye, brown bread, a Boston loaf, and a buttermilk bread called Rutland loaf, for each of which their Shaker originators believed natural whole wheat flour was necessary. Shakers were among the first to insist on the whole of the wheat kernel being ground for flour. They were in the forefront of the struggle against millers who removed "the live germ" from wheat, and the Shaker *Manifesto* protested that "what had been for countless ages the staff of life has now become but a weak crutch!"

Their protestations reached the susceptible mind of a young man from Connecticut in search of a cause. Labeled a "mad enthusiast" in his college days at Amherst, Sylvester Graham had been expelled on a charge trumped up by his classmates, had had a nervous breakdown and

Shaker Herbade

Combine ½ cup lemon balm, cut fine, ½ cup mint, chopped fine, ½ cup regular sugar syrup, and ½ cup lemon juice, and let stand 1 hour. Then add 4 quarts of Shaker gingerade or ginger ale. Serves 16.
—Canterbury Shaker Village

Maple Wheaten Bread

Scald 1 cup milk and add 1 tablespoon salt, 4 tablespoons maple syrup (or honey), and 3 tablespoons butter, and ¾ cup warm water and stir well. Let cool to lukewarm. Dissolve 1 cake of yeast in ¼ cup warm water and add to other liquid mixture. Add 2 cups of flour and 4 cups of whole wheat flour gradually and knead into a smooth ball. Proceed as usual in kneading. When well risen in loaf pans, bake in moderate (350°) oven for 50 to 60 minutes. Yields one very substantial loaf of extremely wholesome bread.

—Eldress Clymena Miner, North Union

suffered from incipient tuberculosis. But he was determined to be a leader and to emblazon his name—as he saw things—in the skies of posterity. He became a Presbyterian minister in New Jersey, and then, after appointment as general agent for the Pennsylvania State Society for the Suppression of the Use of Ardent Spirits, he came into contact with members of a vegetarian church in Philadelphia. As with Shakers, the emphasis of this group was on a puritan life sustained by plain, wholesome food.

After such exposures, Graham studied the physiological aspects of the vegetarian church doctrines and became convinced that a great many Americans abused their bodies with bad food as well as with the evils of drink, and other excesses. On the lecture platform he inveighed against salt, condiments, pork, hot mince pie, heavy clothing, corsets, and feather beds on the grounds that the latter led to behavior to be considered less than puritan. He seems to have convinced himself that the fall from grace resulted when men "began to put asunder what God joined together"—specifically, to mill the bran out of wheat flour. One of his publications, *The Graham Journal of Health and Longevity*, asserted: "Every farmer knows that if his horse has straw cut with his grain, or hay in abundance, he does well enough. Just so it is with the human species. Man needs bran in his bread."

While a vegetarian leader of the Shakers was asking, in the forthright rhetoric of the sect, "Why make a graveyard of your stomach, when there are so many good, wholesome things to eat?" the Reverend Mr. Graham told a friend, "I *feel* I know the mind of God." To Graham it was clear that the only good bread was that made from the whole kernel of the wheat. Further, he preached that all bread should be made in home kitchens, and only by the wife and mother, not by any servant, for in his belief the least a housewife owed her family was the shaping—with her own hands—of dough made from whole kernel flour, investing it with all the love and care she gave to nursing a child when sick.

His accusations against commercially made bread (and against the slovenly practices of butchers in unsanitary abattoirs) aroused so much animosity in Boston that the mayor refused police protection for a Graham meeting, hoping to persuade the health food leader's followers not to appear. Instead, some of them waited until the protesting butchers and bakers had gathered, then set about routing them; they flung shovelfuls of lime on the bakers, refusing to be deterred until the enemy was as white and unappetizing-looking as the Grahamites considered the factory-made bread to be.

The Grahamite Courtship of Mr. Greeley

Graham's platform eloquence in the interest of a better national diet so aroused some cooks and their families that Grahamite societies were organized, and there were grocery stores that specialized in items recommended by the master. Some temperance hotels, which had been content

Catherine Beecher's Rice Gruel

Take two tablespoonfuls of ground rice, and a pinch of salt, and mix it with milk enough for a thin batter. Stir it with a pint of boiling water, or boiling milk, and flavor with sugar and spice.

—*Miss Beecher's Domestic Receipts*

to attract clients who were teetotalers, turned themselves into Graham hotels with strictly regulated dining rooms.[2] At one, Horace Greeley paid court—while consuming meals limited to Graham bread, baked beans, rice, and the blandest of puddings—to his future wife. Bronson Alcott, the father of Louisa May and other little women, may not formally have been a Grahamite, but he went even further than the strictest Shakers when he and Charles Lane established the colony called Fruitlands (on a farm not far from a Massachusetts Shaker village) where he ordered his seventeen resident adherents to put their bodies under "utter subjugation"; they were to live on native grains, fruits, herbs and roots—no fish, fowl, flesh, butter, eggs, milk, cheese, nor any drink but spring water to pass their lips.

More fanatic even than Graham in submitting to the charm of his own ideas, Bronson Alcott had gone too far in setting the rules for Fruitlands. The regime was too much for a young woman who was an assistant to Mrs. Alcott in preparing the spartan diet in the commune's kitchen. She admitted, upon discovery, to having eaten fish once at the house of a neighbor and to have hidden cheese in her trunk. Summarily, she was drummed out of the house of idyll.

Dr. Kellogg and the U.S. Diet

Neither the Grahamites nor the Shakers carried matters of diet to the extreme espoused by a woman leader of the Seventh Day Adventists whose world headquarters had been established at Battle Creek, Michigan. She was Ellen White, wife of Elder James White, who had adopted Graham ideas about food; Mrs. White was constantly receiving spiritual messages, and on Christmas Day, 1865, she became convinced that the

[2] Graham said his diet of unsifted flour and vegetables would cure alcoholism. A century later, the redoubtable Vrest Orton of Weston, Vt., reported in his treatise on whole grains that he received much mail from those who benefited from products of his gristmill. One letter that pleased him, he wrote, was from a young lady who began eating whole grains twice and sometimes three times a day after remaining childless five years. Ten months later she wrote Orton to announce the birth of twin sons.

Salt Rising Bread

To set rising overnight, take two-thirds of a cup of hot water (not scalding), a pinch of salt, a pinch of soda, and thicken with graham flour or corn meal. This must be kept warm and will ferment and become light in twelve hours or less. In the morning scald one pint of milk and put it into the bread pan or mixer, also one pint of cold water, one teaspoon salt, pinch of soda. Thicken with bread flour and add the cup of rising, stirring thoroughly. Keep in a warm place until doubled in bulk. Stir down, adding a little more salt and a bit of soda and flour to make out. This will make about three loaves. Put into tins and keep very warm until light. Bake forty-five minutes. This bread will sour very easily if allowed to become chilled at any stage, or if any of the utensils or dishes used are not immaculately clean.

—Grace Goodspeed,
1915, Pen Yan, N.Y.

Toll House Shredded Wheat Pudding

Crumble in baking dish 2 shredded wheat biscuits.

Mix in a bowl 2 eggs, slightly beaten, 2 cups milk, ¾ cup dark molasses, 1 teaspoon cinnamon, ¼ teaspoon salt.

Pour mixture over shredded wheat. Dot with butter. Bake in 350° oven for 45 minutes. Serve with Hard Sauce or whipped cream. Serves 4.
—Toll House Inn,
Whitman, Mass.

Mrs. Kellogg's Cereal Crust
(for 9-inch pie plate)

Blend 1 to 3 tablespoons sugar into 1½ cups cereal crumbs, then add 6 tablespoons melted butter. Mix thoroughly. Use your fingers if necessary. Turn out into a pie plate and press firmly against sides and bottoms. Place in warm oven (325°) and bake for 5 to 8 minutes.

Adventists, who were frequently troubled by dyspepsia, should be treated in a sanitarium of their own. Not long after her vision became a reality, Mrs. White and her husband awarded a medical scholarship to a young Seventh Day Adventist named John Harvey Kellogg and the influence of Battle Creek on the American diet was set in motion.

While pursuing his medical studies in New York, young J. H. Kellogg breakfasted daily on seven graham crackers and an apple—once a week allowing himself a coconut as well, and occasionally including potatoes or oatmeal in the menu. Kellogg did his own cooking and the chore increased his interest in developing a healthier diet for the patients he was being trained to serve back in Battle Creek.

"The breakfast food idea," he once recalled, "made its appearance in a little third-story room on the corner of 28th Street and Third Avenue, New York City. . . . My cooking facilities were very limited, [making it] very difficult to prepare cereals. It often occurred to me that it should be possible to purchase cereals at groceries already cooked and ready to eat, and I considered different ways in which this might be done." But it was two years later, after he had been put in charge of the Seventh Day Adventist health sanitarium, that he hit upon a workable formula and, as he put it, "prepared the first Battle Creek health food which I called Granola." In the following years, Kellogg told an interviewer, "I invented nearly sixty other foods to meet purely dietetic needs."

Granola may have been the first of the Battle Creek products that led to such twentieth-century breakfast items as "Kellogg's Special K," but it was only one of the experimental precooked cereal products flooding the market before the turn of the century. Shredded wheat resulted from work done by Henry Perky, a dyspeptic who became an apostle of the wheat berry as the perfect food. He ran a vegetarian restaurant in Denver as well. His heart, however, was in the cooked grain product he developed and made famous as Shredded Wheat.

Corn flakes are two words even better known internationally, and they acquired their specific meaning at the end of the century when Dr. Kellogg and his brother Will perfected a method of flaking which they first used on wheat kernels. Grape nuts, so christened because the dextrose contained in the kernels was called grape sugar and because the new product had a nutty flavor, were developed by C. W. Post, who had come to the Battle Creek sanitarium as a patient of Dr. Kellogg.

In all their great variety, dry precooked breakfast foods revolutionized menus for the morning meal. They helped to increase the consumption of milk and to minimize the high cost of living. Ironically, products that originated in the interest of improving health have undergone so many modifications to provide sweetness and other pleasant flavors that their once vaunted nutritional values have been all but lost. A study conducted in 1970 indicated that forty out of sixty dry cereals may "fatten but do little to prevent malnutrition."

Still, many other uses have been found for breakfast foods since Mrs. J. H. Kellogg, author of *Science in the Kitchen* and *Every-Day Dishes*, published her recipe for "Cereal Pie Crust" made from her husband's products. Commenting on the "dietetic evils of Pastries," she said that "the very name had become almost synonymous with indigestion and dyspepsia," and she worked out her recipe for a crumb crust not so much to increase sales as to steer cooks away from butter and lard.

Dr. Kellogg had said that the "original purpose in making the toasted flaked cereal was to replace the half-cooked, pasty, dyspepsia-producing breakfast mush." In the considerable writing his wife did, she agreed, and recommended that the new-fangled flakes would provide "the very best capital upon which people who have real work to do in the world can begin the day." She, too, advocated temperate eating in general. "A great variety of foods at one meal," she wrote, "creates a love of eating as a source of pleasure merely, and likewise furnishes temptation to overeat. Let us have well-cooked, nutritious, palatable food, and plenty of it," she added, "but not too great a variety at each meal."

With the nineteenth century drawing to a close, Mrs. Kellogg's appeal turned out to be prophetic—even though the more limited meals of the future were brought about by the absence of servants in the kitchen rather than because of sheer good sense on the part of menu-planners. But the doctor's wife may have helped to encourage people to get over the debilitating hunger for heavy dessert pastries that had sugar-coated the harvest years. While Kellogg competitors entered the market briefly with such products as Mapl-Flakes and wheat bits sprayed with apple jelly, Mrs. Kellogg prescribed real fruit to her cookbook readers. She was among the first to suggest ways to cook bananas as a substitute for potatoes or other starchy vegetables.

And through her experimental cooking in the Kellogg factory, Ella Kellogg developed great enthusiasm for cornmeal, devising many ways to make use of it in a well-balanced diet, including a recipe for corn puffs that can be served, like popovers, with the main course of dinner. Her husband said of her contribution to the diet revolution: "Without the help derived from this fertile incubator of ideas, the great food industries of Battle Creek would never have existed. They are all direct or indirect outgrowths of Mrs. Kellogg's experimental kitchen. . . ."

A Doctor's Name for Wheat

There were parallel developments in cities far from Battle Creek. In Baltimore the Ralston Club, founded by a local physician, blossomed into a national membership in 1898 of 800,000 persons. It was so influential that manufacturers of various food products sought the endorsement of Dr. Ralston who—for a small fee—would recommend that his members use the selections he approved. The story is that when the product known as Purina Wheat was developed in St. Louis it so pleased the Baltimore health man that he endowed the Purina company with his name.

The name of Horace Fletcher became at least as immortal when it found its way into dictionaries as "Fletcherism." A man who late in life

Mrs. Kellogg's Corn Puffs

Add ⅞ cup of milk and 1 teaspoon melted butter to 2 beaten eggs; then stir gradually into ½ cup flour, 4 level tablespoons yellow cornmeal, and ¼ teaspoon salt, which have been sifted together. Beat the batter with an egg-beater until full of bubbles. Fill well-buttered hot muffin pans two-thirds full. Bake 15 minutes at 450°; reduce heat to 375° and bake for another 15 to 20 minutes. This quantity will make 10 popovers in 2½-inch muffin tins. Be sure tins are preheated.

Stillwater Corn-Flake Pancakes

Put together 1 cup corn-flakes (preferably Post Toasties), 1½ cups white flour, ½ teaspoon salt, ½ teaspoon soda, and 1½ teaspoons baking powder, and sift over corn-flakes in mixing bowl. Add 1 egg, beaten light, 1 cup sour milk or buttermilk, 1 tablespoon melted shortening, and mix thoroughly. Bake a try-cake, and if too thick, thin with a little sweet milk. These are delicious if you use sour cream and no shortening.

—Parish Guild, Ascension Church, May, 1923

did a double back somersault into the Battle Creek sanitarium pool, Horace Fletcher was a friend of the Kelloggs who wrote such tomes as *The ABC of Nutrition, Glutton or Epicure,* and *Fletcherism: What It Is.* What it was was a businessman's theory that the more one chews, the less he needs to eat. "Nature will castigate those who don't masticate," he wrote, making a palatable rhyme of his instructions for what he termed "mouth thoroughness." It was this thoroughness that threw philosopher William James for a loss. "I had to give it up," he said after chewing assiduously for three months. "It nearly killed me."

Lethal or not, Fletcherism wasn't really so very new. Prime Minister William Gladstone, who had died before Fletcher's first book was published, had already put himself on record: "I have made it a rule to give every tooth of mine a chance, and when I eat, to chew every bite thirty-two times. To this rule," Gladstone wrote, "I owe much of my success in life." Nevertheless, the same theory was called Fletcherism when practiced by John D. Rockefeller, Upton Sinclair, Thomas A. Edison, and the cadets of West Point.

The possibility of charlatanism was ever-present, but at Battle Creek the initial belief in whole grains and mastication for improved nutrition was sincere—in spite of the fact that it made money. Not nearly so much money would have flowed in, however, had it not been for the promotion and sales genius demonstrated by W. K. Kellogg and C. W. Post particularly. Both died immensely rich, and Post said frequently, "All I have I owe to advertising." The same could be said for the whole breakfast food industry and its impact on American eating and cooking habits. The advertising slogan, "breakfast of champions," is not such a far cry from the precepts of the Shakers; to insure the superiority of their lives and their contributions to the world over those of outsiders they stuck to diets so healthful that they set records for longevity.

Cults that satisfy cravings to be in fashion, to attract attention, to be different, to be better . . . zealotry attached to any such desire happens all the time in all countries. But only in America, perhaps, could the yearnings of several generations of dissatisfied eaters be turned into a vast commercial success that has endowed every little eater and his parent with a new kind of meal altogether—in flavor, texture, and sound.

Chapter 8

Melting Pot?

BY THE 1950s few Americans were still aware that only a generation previously the style of cooking a bride might bring to her new house could represent ethnic differences. For some it seemed hard to believe that a girl from several generations of American background might once have had to learn to cook all over again if she married a demanding man with—for instance—Mediterranean antecedents.

Of almost countless examples, I know of one such marriage in which the lady sprang from a line of Yankees, her husband from an Italian metropolis. Only as she set up housekeeping did this young wife of the years before the Great Depression face the fact that her heirloom recipes—which ignored garlic and scarcely admitted the existence of olive oil—needed drastic overhauling if she were to feed her new husband in the style to which he was accustomed. Happily, she managed the trick, and along with others whose spouses had been reared on the cuisines of Middle Europe, Scandinavia, Greece, or one of the other Americas, her horizons widened as did those of the rest of gastronomical U.S.A.

This happened—there is no doubt about it. But other things were happening, too, some of them in direct opposition to infusions of new tastes. As many immigrant names were Anglicized to help their bearers blend more easily into the New World landscape, the menus of some immigrant families—those who could afford it—were also Anglicized, ridding kitchens of fragrances that ranged from the puckery atmosphere created by boiled cabbage or fried onions to the scented air thrown off by dishes in which herbs exercised their ineffable spells. Much was lost as new families, striving to be accepted, determined to make their meals as bland as those of neighbors who had lived longer in America.

However, the unavoidable fact is that much good food survived to become a part of an American cuisine because many people were too poor to have neighbors to keep up with. There were Dutchtowns, Jewish ghettos, and Little Italys in large cities, and in the unsettled west fledgling communities sprang up that were sometimes almost entirely populated by newcomers from, say, Scandinavia, Bohemia, or Holland. In neighborhoods dominated by one or another group from Europe the meals eaten by even the most economically depressed were, in any general assessment, more edible, more appetizing than those of middle-class families who felt themselves more directly related to Johnny cake and red meat.

The Italian Revolution

What everybody learned early about families arriving from Italy was that they seldom had a meal that failed to include spaghetti, a kind of food that, for some reason, seemed more exotic (read foreign!) than the noodles of the Pennsylvania Dutch or the macaroni that had been common enough—at least as a part of the American vocabulary—since it first had been imported by Thomas Jefferson.

Indeed, certain things about Italian meals had sturdy, if somewhat snobbish, champions. "Macaroni, as an article of food," Mrs. Rorer wrote in 1886, "is rather more valuable than bread, as it contains a larger proportion of gluten. It is the bread of the Italian laborer. In this country, it is a sort of luxury among the upper classes; but there is no good reason, considering its price, why it should not enter more extensively into the food of our working classes." Mrs. Rorer recommended Italian "spi-ghetti," as she spelled it, as "the most delicate form of macaroni that comes to this country."

And there were other noticeable influences. Italians were in evidence as restaurant proprietors and cooks as early as the Gold Rush of 1849, when every California mining town had at least one hostelry dealing in tomatoey sauces. It was also about this time that a Genoan sailor named Giuseppe Buzzaro, as San Francisco legends say, "invented" a fish stew that later became known as *cioppino*—perhaps a distorted version of *ciupin*, a Ligurian mariner's gallimaufry found by twentieth-century travelers on menus in Genoa. A delicious and "genuinely Californian" cioppino may include every fish found in San Francisco waters along with tomatoes, green peppers, and several herbs, but pasta is one thing it does not include.

Spaghetti, nevertheless, became as "naturalized" as did any Italo-American between the end of the nineteenth century and the beginning of World War II. It became a repast first accepted by nonconformists. Certainly its bohemian reputation was solidified by proximity: Greenwich Village's art colony (and this was true in San Francisco and other cities) was next door to New York's Little Italy, where a spaghetti dinner was cheap, filling, and redolent of good flavors not to be found elsewhere. The good word spread. American bohemians joined Italians in preparing

spaghetti in their own kitchens, buying the pasta from immigrant grocers in whose solidly stocked shops they also found imported cheeses and ingredients for sauces.

Two facts brought about the making of pasta in myriad forms by Italians in the United States. Dr. Mark Carleton, a Department of Agriculture agronomist, got farmers in Kansas and other plains states to grow durum wheat that had the necessary hard quality for good pasta dough; and World War I cut off imports and pushed the manufacture in this country that led gradually to distribution regionally and finally on a national scale. At about the same time, canning companies began to seal tomatoes hermetically, then developed canned tomato sauces that housewives had only to heat before serving a meal. Soon there were ready-to-eat products like meat- or cheese-filled ravioli put up in glass jars filled with sauce.

By the middle of the twentieth century dry pasta was being manufactured in 150 shapes and sizes, according to the National Macaroni Manufacturers' Institute. And for those Americans who had become *fanatici* there were portable machines for cranking out doughy ribbons of linguine and fettucine, as well as forms in which to make ravioli pouches at home.

Changing the Character of U.S. Cookery

Italian specialty food shops no longer catered exclusively to immigrants and their offspring. The shoppers who had first started coming in search of imported pasta also had found for the first time in their experience not only such dry sausages as *coppa* and *mortadella* but also salamis and bologna. (The latter became so standard in American life that it doubles, in its Anglicized spelling, as one of the sturdiest words in American slang.) The new Italian accent to American food was due to newcomers who clannishly had refused to abandon the delicacies of their native tables even though they lived far from Atlantic ports. They had seen to it that no tiny frontier village where Italians settled was too remote from a mail order house through which they could purchase olive oil, Parmesan and other cheeses, and various kinds of pasta.

The West Coast attracted many Italians with an extraordinary talent for making the soil produce, and they introduced fruits and vegetables that did much to change the character of American cookery. Californians sometimes say that artichokes, which came to cover so many acres around Half Moon Bay, were rejected as too much trouble to *eat* until Italians not only grew them better but showed how tastily they could be cooked. They trace the commercial growing of bell peppers, eggplants, broccoli, Savoy cabbage, fava beans, and many other vegetables to Italians; the western tomato industry began with Camillo Pregno, who improved growing techniques and opened a factory for canning tomato purée to appease the burgeoning demand for pasta sauces outside the Italian communities.

Although a Hungarian, Agoston Haraszthy, is still sometimes referred

to as "the father of California's modern wine industry," and Spanish vintners, well established in the eighteenth century, were joined by French, Alsatian, German, and other European winemakers, thousands of Italians worked the vineyards and some of their countrymen set up large, now famous wineries of their own. In addition, newly arrived *contadini* grew almonds and lemons in California, apples and peaches on the slopes of the Ozarks, watermelon, sugar cane, rice, and cotton in the southwestern states. They husbanded gardens that thrived in cities and sold their produce from door to door in non-immigrant neighborhoods.

They did more, perhaps, than any other ethnic group to expand the American cuisine. Even the *antipasto,* the vegetable-studded introduction to an Italian meal, has been blamed for the American habit of serving a garden or fruit salad before the entrée instead of as a light punctuation mark to cleanse the palate between one course and another.[1] Unlike the course of empire, the salad-as-appetizer syndrome has moved inexorably east from the Pacific Coast, bringing with it the fruit concoctions and gelatines and sweet salad dressings that are peculiar to the United States. In another wave from the same shore has come a national craze for the pizza, which has yet to catch up with the hamburger generally, but was charted by a 1970 Gallup poll as the favorite snack of Americans over twenty-one and under thirty-four.

A wedge of tomato-covered bread dough with the savor of orégano misting upward along with a briny anchovy tang, or the texture and taste of mushrooms nestled in one or more kinds of bubbling cheese, can be marvelous informal food; but neither the best of pizzas nor the average Italian restaurant meal (most of which have become Americanized) accounts for the permanence of the Italian accent on American gastronomy. The strongest influence—aside from Neapolitan sauces—has come

Camarillo Salad

Peel the largest ripe tomatoes that can be found, and slice them rather thick. Arrange flat or just slightly over-lapping on a large platter or tray, and sprinkle with salt. Now take orégano and, rubbing it between your hands, powder it in a thin dust over the tomatoes. A drizzle of olive oil will finish this salad. Vinegar is *not* neces-sary because of the acid in the to-matoes, and the orégano eliminates the need for pepper. Serve very cold.
—*Crumbs from Everybody's Table,* 1910

[1] Rather than blame the Italians, it should be noted that U.S. eating places prepare salads in advance and offer them as a stopgap for impatient diners while they await their steaks—or whatever entrée they may order.

from somewhat more elegant dishes. In California, for instance, those fields of artichokes were put to good use when cooks from Italy combined artichokes with tomatoes, orégano, Livermore sherry, and pounded veal cutlets. By the 1970s *scallopine*, the word for such pale pink pieces of calves' meat, had entered the language and even U.S. dictionaries. And cold *vitello tonnato* had been translated as veal with tuna fish sauce to become the rage for summer meals across the country.

Not the least of the reasons for the gradual increase in dishes of Italian origin on American menus lies in the fact that Italian butchers have prided themselves on being among the best. More than most others, they built reputations for knowing a good deal about the art of cooking and, equally important, how to transform leftover and inexpensive cuts of meat into dishes seldom duplicated in other ethnic kitchens. Some Italian butchers made it a habit to pass along recipes. In Barre, Vermont, for instance—where a lot of northern Italian stone quarriers settled—it became common to order a roast preseasoned with herbs by the butcher. Almost unconsciously many American cooks adopted Italian ways with meat and poultry; results seemed equally good whether they simmered marrow bones with tomatoes and called it *ossi buci*, or uttered Tuscan incantations when making one of the many variations of hunter-style chicken in a sauce fragrant with garlic and mushrooms.

Some time after World War II risotto, rice cooked in stock with the addition of meat or vegetables, became as acceptably American as San Francisco's Ghirardelli Square; a similarly popular one-dish meal, eagerly admired by mothers with a kitchen full of children and no domestic help, combined rice and sweet Italian sausage. Something called "Italian seasoning" was packaged commercially to seduce cooks whose herb shelves were otherwise bare. In American kitchens the gastronomy that had originated in southern Italy seemed simpler than either Paris's *haute cuisine* or the best provincial recipes of France; savory, colorful dishes like many splendored, many layered lasagne became widely accepted party fare among young people and in those middle-class circles where dieting was not the norm.

I learned some fine points about one of the simplest foods of this kind—the egg dish called *frittata*—in the Seattle kitchen of Angelo Pellegrini, a distinguished university teacher who is also, Tuscan that he is, an authority on food and on wine, which he makes himself, as do many Italo-Americans. His backyard garden is hedged in by berry vines, a thicket of tall artichokes, and a bushy row of hydrangeas and dahlias. The city plot furnishes the Pellegrini family with fruit, herbs, and vegetables from early spring to the end of the following winter. Fresh from this garden, the dominant ingredients of one of the family's favorite *frittate* are diced zucchini braised with zucchini blossoms.[2]

---

[2] The Yankee bride mentioned earlier who married a culinarily demanding Italian developed a recipe for a *frittata* of asparagus tips that marshaled onion, garlic, marjoram, and thyme to persuade her husband that American kitchens could rival those of the Mediterranean.

An Italian Butcher's Way with Marrow Bones

Wash 4 veal knuckles (1 for each person) in water to which you have added a little lemon juice. Dry them and dredge in seasoned flour. Melt 2 tablespoons of butter and 2 of olive oil in a heavy stewing pan or kettle and sear the veal knuckles. Remove them from the pan and set aside. Now add to the fat in the pan 2 onions, 2 carrots, 2 stalks of celery, 2 strips of bacon, and 2 slices of prosciutto (Italian ham), all finely chopped. Cook slowly for 10 minutes, then add a bay leaf, some chopped Italian parsley, a little basil and a little thyme. Return the veal knuckles to the pot and add enough liquid to just cover them; the liquid should be chicken bouillon, tomato juice, and dry white wine in equal parts. Cover the pan and cook slowly for 2½ to 3 hours. When done put the veal knuckles on a hot platter, strain the sauce, pour it over the meat, sprinkle with chopped parsley and a little grated lemon rind. Serve with risotto.

—Luigi Trianni, New York meatman

Like French omelets, a *frittata* can be made with many kinds of vegetables, meats, or fish, to add texture, flavor, and body. In fact, it is so plausible a way to combine eggs with other foods that we, at our house, had been duplicating Angelo's virtuosity with these flat, thick omelets without knowing they had an Italian name. Our "egg pie," cooked on top of the stove and finished under the broiler, long ago became a favorite way of proving the worth of the refrigerator's cache of leftovers. And neither I nor any of my relatives by blood or law have any Italian heritage.

It is easy to forget that all so-called American food has some foreign influence (British or otherwise) and that many dishes that bear titles in English fail to honor the place of their origin. In the past when demographers assured the world that the melting pot theory would prevail, that all traces of ethnic differences could be homogenized, names and regions of origin were often dropped along with many distinguishing flavors—in cookery as well as other customs. The formality of giving credit was easily overlooked. A contemporary cookbook includes a recipe for lamb patties with lemon sauce without admitting that the initial conceit was Greek; indeed, Italy's macaroni is widely considered as indigenous to America as Yankee Doodle.

Greeks à la Grecque

The difference between the Greeks and the Italians is that the latter opened restaurants to serve the kind of food they themselves preferred. The Greeks, for many decades, foreswore their own culinary tradition in the ubiquitous "Greek restaurants" that sprang up in every city; the food served in these places dominated by overhead fans was largely characterless. Not until air travel had given millions a chance to sample the best of Greek food in its native habitat did such delights as shish kebabs begin to turn up on American barbecue menus. And when that happened some of these food styles "discovered" abroad were accepted quickly and widely, just as cola drinks have become ingrained in the folkways of other countries.

Greeks first came to the east coast of Florida in the eighteenth century, and on the west coast of the peninsula, at Tarpon Springs, a colony of sponge fishermen in the 1880s began to adapt New World ingredients to ancient Hellenic methods. The "cioppino" of Tarpon Springs is an oil-based soup dominated by red snapper from the Gulf that is seasoned with wild marjoram, onions, green peppers, tomatoes, and lemons; beaten eggs are added at the end, along with fine strands of pasta. In Tarpon Springs tradition remained strong. Celebrating Greeks continued to stuff spring lamb with pecans and rice; their recipe for garden salad combined briny *feta* cheese, lettuce, celery, cucumbers, tomatoes, onions, green peppers, and avocados with the flavors of anchovies, olives, and orégano. The Florida version of the classic Greek *avogolemono*, or lemon soup, differed from that of the home islanders only in using beef broth instead of chicken broth.

Greek cooks did as much as those of Italy or any other Mediterranean country to increase the number of uses of eggplant in American kitchens. For instance, when chopped and combined with garlic, onion, herbs, spices, oil, and lemon it was transformed into something Americans call eggplant caviar.[3] Eggplant layered with minced lamb and seasonings under a blanket of baked custard—known as *moussaka* throughout the Middle East—became an American buffet supper treat. In a fifty-year period after the first edition of Fannie Farmer's cookbook was published in 1886 the number of eggplant recipes jumped from two bland suggestions to more than a dozen in the seventh edition; included was a prevalent Mediterranean way of mixing the pulp of eggplants with rice and highly aromatic seasonings that once were considered by some snobs fit only for immigrants who had learned no more about proper food than they had learned about the proper way to speak English.

One of the things that helped to chase away such disdain was the effort of immigrant offspring to preserve the best of their ethnic backgrounds by putting on annual folk festivals at which were offered samples of food as well as demonstrations of native song, dance, and costume. Often these celebrations in U.S. cities seemed to combine the atmosphere of a village market day abroad and the midway of an American county fair. In their purest form they gave a sampling of the folk arts of a single country. But in the period immediately after World War II especially, international festivals were staged annually in cities as far apart as Rochester, New York, Cleveland, Ohio, and Saint Paul, Minnesota. In New York's Little Italy members of the San Gennaro Society for several decades have held a street fair lining the length of Mulberry Street with

Andover Egg Plant

Take fresh purple ones, and pull out the stem; parboil them and cut them in slices about an inch thick. Dip them in a beaten egg, and then in a plate of bread or cracker crumbs, with salt and pepper, and fry them in drippings until they are nicely browned.
  —*The Young Housekeeper's Friend*, 1859

---

[3] Closer to real caviar is the Mediterranean *taramasalata*, a paste made from the roe of gray mullet or carp, now popular among some U.S. hostesses. When asked why the best caviar was so expensive, Chicago innkeeper Ernie Byfield once replied, "After all, it's a year's work for the sturgeon."

booths and the aroma of Italian sausages and barbecued sweetbreads. Because the San Gennaroans were not exclusive, the fair offered almost equal opportunities to nibble such Greek food as *chawarma*, the barbecued slices of lamb pared from a vertical spit. Or for other palates, Cantonese delicacies were served by Little Italy's neighbors from adjacent Chinatown.

A Symbol of the Blood of Life

There once was an effort to establish a Little Poland, not as a ghetto in a large city, but as a large geopolitical area in the Middle West, and though this dream of certain Poles proved unavailing it did encourage a wave of immigration that, incidentally, brought more subtle accents to the food of America. Few Polish contributions are as elegant as the dish that combines fish with lobster and cheese sauce, known as sole *à la Waleska,* but generally speaking many of the recipes that account for the abundant use of sour cream in the twentieth century—originally characterized as in the style of *Smetana*—were developed by Poles.

Perhaps borscht is the best known of them all. This luxuriantly red soup, a French chef said, "is national in Russia and in Poland, and in Russia you must swear on your life that it's Russian, but in Poland you must salute it as a symbol of Poland's life blood." In America many cooks consider borscht to be kosher, brought here by Jews from both countries. No matter—when it is spelled *barszcz* it is as authentic as any memory of the Vistula River.

"Borscht Polonaise," as some menus would have it, can be brewed from a broth of one whole duck, a large beef bone, and a chunk of bacon flavored with beets and carrots and leeks, laurel, thyme, parsley, celery, onions, garlic, and a grating of nutmeg. It takes hours. It is skimmed, sieved through cheesecloth, beaten with egg whites and their crushed shells, sieved again, and served very hot or very cold—always with plenty of sour cream to make a topping for an ideal soup to soothe a summer day.

With borscht available in cans and jars, few Americans continue to make the soup from scratch, but those of Polish extraction have helped to popularize another mélange they call *chłodnik*—a cold cucumber soup, based on sour cream, of course, with the flavor of beets, dill, onion, and sometimes hard-cooked eggs. In the twentieth century all kinds of Americans have gone overboard for sour cream on baked potatoes and as the basis for many sauces, to be used for desserts or otherwise. Sour cream provides the sauce for meat balls simmered with onions and mushrooms, in a recipe again attributed to both Russian and Polish immigrants, and known as *bitki*.

The recipes of Hungarian-Americans are perhaps at least as lavish in the use of sour cream. Goulash is an American cookbook term borrowed from Austria where, in turn, it is a Teutonic spelling of the Hungarian *gulyás*. As a kind of generic stew it became popular in the Middle West at the time of the great immigration from Central Europe. By 1969 when,

Northern Pike with Polish Sauce

Place one Minnesota Northern pike in saucepan with 2 cups white wine, 1 cup vinegar, a generous pinch of saffron and ½ cup seedless raisins; simmer slowly ½ hour. Blend 1 tablespoon flour with 1 tablespoon butter and stir into sauce, cooking until it thickens.
—Polanie Club, Minneapolis

according to a Gallup poll, Americans numbered it among their five favorite meat dishes, it had lost much of its original definition and was considered satisfactorily prepared as long as it was adorned with paprika and, for preference, sour cream.[4] Among purists, George Lang insisted in *The Cuisine of Hungary* that only in Transylvania was sour cream considered an authentic goulash ingredient. But all things appear to change in American kitchens, and an appetite for sour cream increased enormously after the mid-century introduction of the cultured product. The low calorie count of manufactured sour cream added many new culinary uses and boosted the popularity of salads dressed with the new product instead of mayonnaise or other dressings. Chicken paprika, another internationally accepted Hungarian ragout, requires an abundance of sour cream and is a mainstay of many American menus, including those of Hungarian steelworkers in such places as Gary, Indiana, and East Chicago.

A Nod from Escoffier

Paprika, as the powdered form of the New World *capsicum* plant is known, became associated with Hungary after chicken paprika was accepted as a national dish by the Magyars in 1844, when it first appeared on the menu of the exclusive parliamentary dining room. Thirty-five years later the French chef Auguste Escoffier, visiting the city of Szeged, tasted paprika-flavored *gulyás* and chicken in a rosy sour cream sauce, and soon thereafter he introduced *Gulyás Hongrois* and *Poulet au Paprika* to international travelers who ate his classic food at Monte Carlo. The recipes traveled with Escoffier when he joined César Ritz, as he and the chefs he trained set up kitchens on both sides of the Atlantic.

Aside from loyalty to paprika, Hungarian-American cooks also preserved old traditions by using tomatoes and green peppers as creatively as Italo-Americans, or the cooks of the Southwest and the Gulf Coast. Dozens of Hungarian stuffings for peppers continued to be used in American kitchens, and wonderful mixtures were concocted of sliced smoked sausage, onions, green peppers, and boiled eggs—layered in a casserole to provide one of the meals-in-a-dish that Americans like. Another Hungarian recipe puts fresh mackerel on a layer of potato slices in a buttered baking dish, calling for diagonal slashes in the fish into which to put juliennes of green pepper, tomatoes, onions, and bacon. Covered with sour cream or yoghurt, the fish is baked just long enough to be beautifully flaky and for the vegetables to maintain both tang and texture.

Like all the cooks of Central Europe, Hungarians spurred Americans to outdo even Vienna in emphasizing desserts. Joseph Wechsberg, who

[4] Something of the same thing happened to "Beef Stroganoff," which had a slightly more elegant popularity after World War II. *Boeuf à la Stroganoff,* a combination of tenderloin juliennes, shallots, mustard, broth, and sour cream, was created in a Paris restaurant for Count Paul Stroganoff, a nineteenth-century Russian diplomat. In the United States, every modish cook, professional or amateur, developed his or her own "refinements."

Grandma's Debricina Goulash

Dice 4 pounds of well aged round steak. Peel and cut up enough onions to make half as much as beef. Brown the meat in a deep, heavy metal pot. Push the meat aside; add the onions and cook, stirring, until golden brown. Add salt, pepper, and 2 tablespoons paprika. Mix well, cover and simmer for about 30 minutes. Cover with one No. 2½ can sauerkraut, being careful to keep meat and kraut in separate layers. Spread one cup sour cream over the kraut, being careful to keep this, too, separate. Cover and cook over low heat (at a simmer) for one hour. In the inns around St. Louis, this was served right from the pot, at the table.

—Mrs. Estelle Umbright, St. Louis

grew up in what had been the Austro-Hungarian empire, once wrote that he never heard of a dessertless meal, even among the very poor. That tradition was reinforced in the United States when immigrant women assuaged lean days by adding something sweet to their menus. The availability of cream of tartar in the 1850s, to be followed later by baking powder, made lighter, better cakes possible, but the lists of them in cookbooks remained largely confined to such colonial recipes as Shrewsbury cake and sponge cake and Boston cream until late in the nineteenth century. Newly arrived cooks helped to change the picture. It may have required a near-professional to turn out a copy of Vienna's Dobostorte (chocolate filled with a caramel frosting created by Josef Dobos, a great Hungarian pastry master), but an anonymous Midwest housewife made up for this by devising the five-egg, three-layer cake that achieved a little mystery by the use of red food coloring and became known as Minnesota Fudge Cake. In similar tradition, Wisconsin cooks bake a seven-layer cake and put a filling of different flavor at each level of their monumental creation.

"Cake sales" sponsored by women's church groups, or schools, or other efforts for one or another worthy cause, encouraged the competition that once put American women among the best dessert makers in the world. So did agricultural fairs at which their husbands showed off crops and livestock in pursuit of blue ribbons; similar awards were handed out to cooks who in many cases were demonstrating the worth of recipes their mothers or grandmothers had brought from abroad.

As the historian Arthur M. Schlesinger put it after a half-century of scholarly attention: "The European newcomer, although ever the chief gainer in the matter of food, atoned in some degree by enriching the national menu with his own traditional dishes. In this sense the melting pot was also the cooking pot." In the Midwest and far Northwest especially, menus were enriched by Scandinavian cooks whose cuisine may not have been as rich as that of the old Austro-Hungarian empire but was distinguished by variety that helped make the style of eating known as smorgasbord a part of the gustatory experience of many Americans.

Eye-Appeal for Informal Dining

In her *West Coast Cook Book*, the definitive treatise on gastronomical mores between the Rockies and the Pacific, Helen Evans Brown pointed out that "the smorgasbord, that fabulous feast of good food, has won the complete and enthusiastic approval of the entire West Coast. It's really a natural for us," she wrote in the 1950s "—it's perfectly adapted to informal entertaining, which is what most of us go in for. . . . " Smorgasbord dining also came naturally to several midwestern states, like Minnesota, where Scandinavians outnumbered all other immigrants. It was introduced to other Americans at Scandinavian church suppers, and it became so modified by various informalities that a committee of women of the Swedish Institute in Minneapolis was moved in the middle of the twentieth century to issue a brief dissertation cautioning Ameri-

Smorgasbord Meat Balls

Soak ½ cup fine dry bread crumbs in ½ cup cream. Grind ½ pound beef, ¼ pound veal, and ¼ pound pork three times, using fine blade. Mix crumbs and meats thoroughly; add ½ cup milk, 2 egg yolks, beaten slightly, 2 tablespoons minced onion, 3 teaspoons salt, ⅛ teaspoon pepper, ½ teaspoon allspice. Blend well, form into tiny balls and brown on all sides in 4 tablespoons fat. Keep warm over hot water.
—Swedish Institute,
Minneapolis

cans on the proper approach to serving a smorgasbord. "It should be noted that every effort is made toward an attractive and well-balanced effect. 'Eye-appeal' is stressed, rather than a mere attempt to serve the largest assortment of foods," the ladies said.

They stipulated the possibility of assembling on the table as many as twenty-five cold dishes and a dozen or more hot ones that might include pickled and smoked fish, jellied meats, roasts with fruit, sausages, hot meat balls, escalloped herring, sweetbread omelet, vegetables, cheeses, stewed fruit. "The smorgasbord can be the most simple form," it was emphasized, "or it can be an elaborate culinary masterpiece." In its simplest form it provided (along with the old-time saloon "free lunch") inspiration for the array of appetizers, canapes, or hors d'oeuvre served at cocktail parties or with preprandial drinks.

Most Swedes, Norwegians, and Danes who came to America chose parts of the country where the weather was similar to the subarctic climate of their homelands, and the meat and fish dishes that bolstered the traditional smorgasbord supplied—along with aquavit with which to wash them down—energy and warmth that helped to mollify winter temperatures. But Scandinavian cooks are also gifted artists who create decorative open-face sandwiches, skewered combinations of cold meats and cheese and fruits, and many other jewel-like tidbits, as well as the more filling dishes that have, for generations, made a smorgasbord a square meal in itself.

More than that, Scandinavians were perhaps more responsible than anyone else for making America as coffee-break-conscious as it is, and for perfecting the kind of food that goes well with coffee. German women already had brought the *kaffee klatsch* to their frontier communities, but it was in the kitchens where there was always a pot brewing on the back of the stove that Scandinavian hospitality and coffee became synonymous. There, also, began the average American's habit of having coffee with or without food, at virtually any hour of the day. The term "coffee klatch" became part of the language, and its original meaning—a moment that combined gossip with coffee-drinking—was changed to define the American version of England's tea, a mid-morning or afternoon gathering at which to imbibe and ingest. From these social hours in homes evolved the "coffee break," an office ritual so firmly established that it became in many cases a matter of union contract or of law.

"Coffee and a Danish"

Like the cooks from Central Europe, most Scandinavian cooks have prided themselves on the simple forms of pastry-making that include so-called coffee breads, coffee cakes, coffee rings, sweet rolls, and buns. Danish pastries became so popular that no more was needed than the single word "Danish," in any short-order eating place, to order any of a number of light, bready confections. Of a richness somewhere between coffee cake and fine pastry, they might be either Danish, Swedish, or Norwegian in origin, but they have become as authentically a fixture on

Montana Coffee Cake

Use a basic recipe roll dough. Roll out a thin crust (about ½-inch). Place in cake pans, making sure crust fits smoothly without stretching the dough. Fill the crust with cream filling and bake at 375° F. until well done. Filling: Beat 2 eggs until light, and ½ cup sugar, ½ teaspoon cinnamon, little salt, 1 cup cottage cheese, light cream. To this you may add prunes, apples, peaches, raisins or whatever your favorite fruit may be.

—Florence Weist, Havre

American breakfast menus as French toast. A Danish can be a fat envelope of pastry containing sugary spices or something fruity; it can be crescent-shaped or molded like a comb with tines the thickness of a thumb. Its chief characteristic is the flakiness of the superbly light crumb. After World War II it became almost as popular at stool-and-counter breakfasts as the doughnut.

The Scandinavians brought their own versions of cooked-food shops to America, but it was in the German delicatessens, which cropped up in cities large and small toward the end of the nineteenth century, that many German foods began the process of Americanization. There one could find pumpernickel, zwieback, bauernbrot, sauerkraut, sauerbraten, leberwurst (which became liverwurst), wienerwurst (which brought about the corruption of the name of Austria's capital to weenie), and *lager* and *bok* as two kinds of beer. It was H. L. Mencken who pointed out that such words "mirror the profound effect of German migration upon American drinking habits and the American cuisine." He also said in *The American Language* that as late as 1921 he had found *sourbraten* [*sic*] on the menu at Delmonico's and, "more surprising still, '*braten* with potato salad.'" Another German-Americanism, the hot dog, was mated with a roll shaped to fit a Frankfurt-style *wurst* at the St. Louis World's Fair of 1904, but its nickname came along when a sports cartoonist created a dachshund with a body the shape of a sausage.

By the last third of the twentieth century the delicatessens which once sold a good many frankfurters had changed as had most other food emporiums; most were run by Jews who were not necessarily of German background. By that time a "hot pastrami on rye" had become a favorite sandwich of Americans, few of whom knew that pastrami was a Romanian word for beef that had been pickled and smoked and made popular by New York kosher delicatessens.[5] A Reuben sandwich, another New York Jewish creation that joined corned beef, sauerkraut, and cheese under a broiler, could be successfully ordered at eating places across the country, and had been miniaturized for serving as a cocktail snack. Chopped liver also lost little time in leaving the ghetto. It so captured the hearts of the Jews' fellow Americans that a Methodist woman in a North Carolina town won a cooking competition with her non-kosher recipe and earned lengthy comment from Harry Golden, editor of the *Carolina Israelite*.

Golden wanted a statue erected in Washington to the Jewish immigrant mother whose talent for turning meager ingredients into food made her, he thought, unique. Throughout his writing, this former New Yorker cites his mother's cooking, mentioning "Mother's potato latkes (pancakes) and holishkas (chopped beef and spices rolled in cabbage leaves

Sweet Potato Tzimmes

Put 4 unpeeled sweet potatoes and 4 carrots in boiling water, cook until tender. Drain and peel, then put in bowl and mash until smooth. Cook 1 cup prunes in water to cover 15 minutes; drain, reserving 1 cup liquid. Pit and chop prunes and add to potato mixture with reserved liquid, ¼ cup honey, salt and pepper to taste. Place in baking pan in oven preheated to 350° F. for 15 minutes.

[5] So popular that *New York* magazine conducted its "First Pastrami Olympics" early in 1973, lining up a jury of experts to taste and test sandwiches from eighteen delicatessens. Prices ranged from a $2.45 high to a low of $1.50 per sandwich; the amount of meat in each varied from three ounces to six ounces. The winner chosen by the six jurors weighed 3.75 ounces, cost $1.75, and was judged on the quality, flavor, and texture of the smoked beef. The most expensive of the lot also had the most meat, but its general quality rated it no better than sixteenth place.

and cooked in a sweet-and-sour raisin sauce). . . ." He referred those who said Jewish food is nothing more than German, or Romanian, or Russian, to the Declaration of Independence. Jefferson knew about Magna Carta, didn't he? In other words, Golden argued that Jewish food may have links to someone else's past, but it becomes different as it becomes a part of the Jewish experience. The same logic applies to the whole of American gastronomy.

Kreplach in the San Hsien T'ang

There are interesting duplications among many ethnic cuisines. Jews for centuries have spoken reverently of their own kreplach, which are small airy pouches of dough, usually filled with minced meat and put into chicken soup. When many Jews—in the United States particularly—became addicted to dining out in Chinese restaurants, they found won ton soup "with kreplach," as some of them said in surprise; actually the soup contained the Oriental version of tiny envelopes laden with meat. Similarly, those Jews who lived in Italy in the Middle Ages might have been equally nonplussed at their first encounters with ravioli, or with *agnolotti*, the meaty Italian pasta plumped with minced ham, sausage, and sweetbreads that are also served in soup. It is not true, however, that the Western world, including makers of kreplach, had to wait until Marco Polo returned from Cathay with the first "spaghetti." Ravioli, the pasta dumpling usually filled with cheese, was a popular Roman dish before the Italian trader headed toward the Orient; ravioli was served then, as in the twentieth century, as a dish by itself, the way many Bronx and Brooklyn housewives often served kreplach after browning it in hot fat.

Had Jews or Italians gone after culinary secrets in China they might have come back with many. Chinese cooking ranks with the cuisine of France at the top of international gastronomy. It is because it is different—rather than because of a few look-alikes such as kreplach and won ton—that Oriental food in general was slow in finding acceptance among most Americans. But there were Chinese dishes that were exceptions, of course. Some of the simplest, like eggs foo yung, spareribs, fried shrimp, and fried rice were considered indigenous to the West Coast before half of the twentieth century had slipped away.

A century earlier, in 1847, the first Chinese immigrants settled in San Francisco and were followed by thousands who helped to build the transcontinental railways. Some of them were cooks for the work gangs, and one of these, I once read, invented the sandwich that is called a "Western" in states east of the Mississippi and a "Denver" in most of the rest of the country.[6] When a hungry cowboy asked for a sandwich

[6] The meals of hundreds of California families were influenced by cooks who were Chinese and had been hired as housemen in middle-class homes. They seldom were permitted to prepare Oriental meals, but they held to their art of serving vegetables that do not lose their crispness or color. Perhaps a modest contribution, but it eliminated English overcooking that had been habitual among Americans of British heritage. Vegetable cooking on the West Coast never again was categorically as bad as in some other regions.

between meals, the story goes, the Chinese cook prepared eggs foo yung by making the traditional Oriental omelet from vegetables and meats at hand—in this case the green pepper that was grown by early Spanish in the west, along with onions and some chopped ham. Put between slices of bread, this hasty Chinese creation became the prototype of one of the most American of all sandwiches.

There are similar stories about the origin of chop suey—which translates ignominiously as "miscellaneous odds and ends"—first served, some say, to a party of non-Oriental Americans who liked it enough to return to the same Cantonese eating place repeatedly. Chow mein, a term often confused with chop suey, is an admitted part of the Chinese food lexicon and means, literally, soft-fried noodles; it is a dish utterly different from the chow mein noodles invented to please occidental tastes and sold in retail food stores everywhere. In the early California Chinese restaurants there was a beginning of this willingness to cater to customers—some proprietors served their non-Chinese clients only what they thought those diners wanted, i.e., chop suey and fried steak.

Better restaurants gained fame on San Francisco's Grant Avenue, on or near New York's Mott Street, in Los Angeles, and every other American city of consequence, and the developing taste for genuine Chinese food resulted in a vogue for home delivery of easily portable items like egg rolls and chicken chow mein in paper buckets. But it wasn't until after World War II that Americans began consciously to augment their Oriental kitchen repertoires by attending classes in Chinese cooking and avidly sampling new tastes that became available in restaurants specializing in Mandarin, Hunan, Fukien, and Szechwan dishes in addition to those from Canton. (On August 18, 1974, in the *New York Times*, John L. Hess, that publication's former restaurant critic, said that "the best food in America is found in Chinatown, New York.")

This influence on American eating habits came after new political relationships encouraged interest in largely unknown regions of the People's Republic, and many more Chinese entrepreneurs arrived to join what had been essentially a Cantonese population in the United States. Increased interest in Japanese food, on the other hand, was due to air travel that took thousands of Americans on vacations that heightened their appreciation of the food they ate in cities like Tokyo and Kyoto. Recipes for sukiyaki had already entered American cookbooks, and the Japanese ceremony in which guests could share in the table-top cooking of beef, mushrooms, bamboo shoots, and other more colorful vegetables had become as much the raison d'être for a party as had the Swiss fondue.

Tastes of the Fiftieth State

Much earlier, the Japanese had had a tremendous effect on food in the Hawaiian Islands, but it did not take Hawaii's statehood to make mainland Americans practitioners of Island cookery. Bananas and pineapples had become important in the kitchens of New England women whose seafaring men had brought the tropical fruits back from various ports of

130 | Melting Pot?

call. They were much favored in Charleston's market square in the early nineteenth century. But the Spanish-American War and the consequent exploitation of the tropical fruit canning business did as much as anything to embellish meals in every state with fruit salads, upsidedown cakes, and baked hams adorned with pineapple slices.

The fiftieth state acquired a cuisine as international as any of its sisters. Hawaii was characteristically Polynesian until the nineteenth century, and its diet of flesh and fruit remained unmodified until the coming of the missionaries and clipper ships from New England. Dried meat and salted fish had fed American sailors, and these foods became a part of Hawaiian tradition—like *pipikaula*, the jerked beef that is broiled in tiny pieces and served with a sweet-sour sauce, and like *lomo lomo,* a kind of salted salmon which some New Yorkers have described as better, in its own way, than the lox (smoked salmon) from their favorite delicatessens. Fish chowder, made in a basic Yankee fashion, is at least as common as on the mainland, and Scots who came to the islands as technicians and plantation overseers added scones and shortbreads to the daily fare of thousands of Hawaiians.

Corn meal and red bean soup, both brought by Portuguese immigrants, have been accepted as Hawaiian by people of all ethnic roots. But the striking factor is that Island cooks have not submitted to one style or another; they have, instead, incorporated European dishes, along with many from Chinese, Japanese, and Korean sources, into a culinary tradition that may be among the most festive in the world.

The *luau* is the ultimate of American picnics, cookouts, and barbecues; it has added much to the colorfulness of outdoor feasting on the West Coast. Yet the great Hawaiian influence on American food may be forgotten in the haze of too many cocktail parties. A chunk of pineapple broiled in a wrapping of bacon is properly known in Honolulu as a *pupu.* It is closely related to *rumaki,* the Hawaiian bacon-wrapped kebabs of skewered chicken livers and water chestnuts that turn up at parties in Charleston, St. Louis, or Pasadena, blessed by the *New York Times* as "almost as popular as pizza pie in metropolitan America. . . ."

In urban and rural areas as well, many Americans in the 1970s began to be interested in the nation's inherent cookery. Natives who traced their ancestry back to the Old Dominion or whose pedigrees were rich with Mayflower stock had learned to embrace the onion, to dally even with garlic. Anyone who loved good food had become aware that in the eclectic style that had developed there was included—although often in modified form—a bill of fare with origins of the highest order.

The Yankee bride had learned a lot from her Italian husband. "The culinary arts of all countries were our birthright," she wrote, adding, "England, Holland, Italy, France, Spain, Scandinavia, Germany, and other lands, both Occidental and Oriental, merged their kitchen secrets within our borders to give us richer, fuller food consciousness than any other single people." She thought that added up as "a legacy to treasure."[7]

[7] Irma Goodrich Mazza, *Herbs for the Kitchen* (Boston, 1937).

Hawaiian Pipikaula

Combine 1 cup soy sauce, juice of ½ lemon, 1–2 tablespoons of rock salt, freshly ground pepper and 1 teaspoon of sugar. Have 2–3 pounds of steak cut 1–1½ inches thick. Cut beef into strips about 1½ inches wide, and pound strips slightly before marinating them in soy mixture; run the sauce into meat and let stand 1 hour. Then dry in hot sun about two days (be sure not to let it stay out in the night air). Broil, turning until nicely browned. It is delicious with poi or baked sweet potato.

—Hilo Woman's Club

Chapter 9

Beginnings Revisited

GUSTAVE W. SWIFT took his wife and six children to Chicago's freight yards one day in 1877 to witness a family triumph. As a train began to move, he is reported to have turned to his wife with a smile. "There are gigantic days in every man's life, Annie," Swift's biographers tell us he said. "This," he added with obvious pleasure, "is one of mine."

The day was also a big one for everyone interested in American food because the Swift family had been gathered to watch the first train equipped with effectively refrigerated cars head east with tons of freshly butchered meat that was virtually guaranteed against spoilage. After years of persistence Swift had devised the system that was to make beef, veal, pork—all kinds of perishables—available to Americans regardless of season and without dependence on local conditions.

A half-century later, Clarence Birdseye, a Department of Agriculture naturalist, quit the government to try to prove that a method of food preservation he had learned from the Eskimos could revolutionize the marketing of many kinds of food. Birdseye worked out fast-freezing techniques to attain the solid effect caused in an instant by Labrador winter weather. His methods and equipment, later perfected to preserve vegetables, fruit, meat, and poultry, as well as fish, did more than Swift's refrigerated cars to change the American attitude toward food.

Most of what is bad and much of what is good about American cookery has been governed by industrial enterprise. The fifty states might never have evolved into a nation of steak-eaters had not refrigerated transportation become important so early in the history of the fledgling country. Railroads did much to revolutionize the supply system for fruits and vegetables, as well. Gustave Swift's competitor, Philip D. Armour, also invested heavily in refrigerator cars and, in order to use them fully, looked for products other than meat to carry. He encouraged southern farmers to grow large quantities of perishable fruits and berries that would require refrigerated shipping to cities in the North.

Railroad promoters imported green peas from Louisiana to Chicago, and others ran a special train, known as the "Pea Line," to bring produce across the Hudson from New Jersey's garden region to New York. Vegetables and fruits were shipped north from the rail center established at Norfolk, Virginia. The new transportation ended the era in which New Yorkers had to pay $1.50 for strawberries while housewives in Baltimore, for instance, could have all the berries they wanted for $.10 a quart. Food seasons got longer in metropolitan areas, for vegetables like tomatoes became available, as the result of the new efficiency, all year round instead of being limited to the old season of four months.

In the rest of the world cooking styles that developed because of regional limitations retain their principal characteristics through the maintenance of market days on which farmers gather at appointed places in villages and towns to sell the raw materials that are indigenous to the region. In the United States, even before World War I, lettuce, asparagus, watermelons, cantaloupes, and tomatoes grown in irrigated fields of California's Imperial Valley were transported three thousand miles by refrigerated cars to markets across the continent. By the 1930s the average distance between the fields where fruits and vegetables were grown and the markets in which they were sold was fifteen hundred miles. Fresh fruits and vegetables no longer were considered a luxury in off seasons for the average American family.

At the same time, the commercial process of canning various foods had been introduced in France, and the system was applied in the United States to such an extent that larger amounts, and many more different

kinds, of food were being packed in American plants than in all other countries combined. The effects on American menus were such that one historian of the canning industry felt entitled to wax lyrical:

> Canning gives the American family—especially in cities and factory towns—a kitchen garden where all good things grow, and where it is always harvest time. There are more tomatoes in a ten-cent can than could be bought in city markets for that sum when tomatoes are at their cheapest, and this is true of most other tinned foods. A regular Arabian Nights garden, where raspberries, apricots, olives, and pineapples, always ripe, grow side by side with peas, pumpkins, spinach; a garden with baked beans, vines and spaghetti bushes, and sauerkraut beds, and great caldrons of hot soup, and through it running a branch of the ocean in which one can catch salmon, lobsters, crabs and shrimp, and dig oysters and clams.[1]

Like the frozen food industry that followed it, commercial canning had advanced the process of turning American women into short-order cooks. So did the food departments of women's magazines whose pages were loaded with luring appeals for the use of factory-packaged and manufactured foods—advertisements and recipes replete with simplified methods of cooking that included such shortcuts as substitution of various canned creamed soups for freshly made sauces. And national advertising created national rather than regional appetites and tastes.

The Oranging of America

Skillful affluent advertising, for instance, transformed Americans from a population that occasionally ate oranges as fresh fruit to one more apt than not to begin the day with a glass of orange juice. The technical factor that made the market almost universal was the perfection of a process to condense and freeze juice; as a result, a consumer who added water to orange concentrate could have a fresh-tasting, mellow drink, free of seeds, pulp, and bitter oil. The idea was one whose time had come in 1948, but it needed financial backing as well as advertising and promotion.

John Hay Whitney, having invested heavily in the company that had developed the frozen concentrate process, one day offered a glass of Minute Maid orange juice to his golf partner, who happened to be Bing Crosby. The singer liked what he tasted. He bought twenty thousand shares and began to exploit frozen orange juice on his radio shows and later in television commercials. The business of reducing fruit juices to frozen-concentrate form skyrocketed, and the demand for Florida oranges increased four-fold. Floridians themselves became so partial to frozen juice that there were times when a traveler could not buy a glass of orange juice freshly squeezed. The state that produced more oranges than even California succumbed to the argument that natural juice might be either too sweet or too sour; reconstituted frozen orange concentrate, on the other hand, could be so well blended after a good harvest, it was thought, that it produced a beverage like wine—so good, some orangemen said, that it had vintage years that reflected the seasonal climate.

[1] James H. Collins, *The Story of Canned Foods* (New York, 1924).

Many of the advertising approaches that helped to put frozen juice in virtually every active kitchen had been used earlier in the promotion of a patented mixture of powdered gelatine, sugar, and fruit flavors that was packaged with recipe folders suggesting scores of desserts to be easily made by the addition of such ingredients as fresh berries or chunks of pineapple. In addition, advertising depicted gelatine salads that were misleadingly luscious-looking, and the saturation publication in periodicals that touched every American home resulted in meals designed around sweet salads in a culinary style that was, to put it mildly, different from any other.

"The Six-Year-Old Palate"

To measure the influence of advertising, one had only to travel the country to experience the blandness of public food that was one of the results of skillful commercial persuasion. National advertising and standardization combined to reduce quality. The Iowa novelist Vance Bourjaily once told an interviewer that "people in the United States don't eat for pleasure. To them, eating is just something done in response to advertising." And James Beard, author of a score of cookbooks and the dominant culinary influence on thousands of home cooks in the decades after World War II, succinctly defined the lowest common denominator of public feeding as "the six-year-old palate," a mass market unattracted —regardless of age—by the adventure implicit in trying food that is new and different.

Advertising combined with television productions to make an instant success of "TV dinners" accurately aimed at the six-year-old palate. At the same time, those meals-in-a-lap did terrible things to the reputation of good American cooks whose abilities seemed to have been forgotten in the push to sell precooked foods that needed nothing but heating before they were served. The only good thing to be said about many such foods was that they were labor-saving. And in many cases advertising compounded deception. Hams, for example, were promoted as "tenderized" when in actuality they had been put through a steaming process that filled them with water to add to the weight for which the consumer must pay. They were "ready to eat," as the ads said, but they robbed home cooking of the tang, texture, and honesty of smokehouse products.[2]

Away from home, advertising and its allied arts were combined to produce the unprecedented success of a food chain known as McDonald's, "a great machine [in the words of James Beard] that belches forth hamburgers." McDonald's is also a brain trust of exploitation prac-

[2] At the same time, the number of cooks unwilling to accept the "tenderized" hams increased—and so did the availability of country hams cured in old-fashioned ways that brought on bouts of nostalgia when their flavor was tasted by gastronomes who had felt deprived for years. New smokehouses cropped up in hill-country regions to make traditional hams easy to order by mail. Some of these reflected the proverbial urge of the city man to return to simple rural life: in Wolftown, Virginia, a former New York Yankees player, Jim Kite, Jr., settled down to turn out what food authority Craig Claiborne called "conceivably the finest ham produced in America."

tices. The string of hamburger emporiums that has been spun in the last third of the twentieth century promises the public that each of its licensees or operators is a graduate of "Hamburger University," and it set up an inspection system to insure that its graduate hamburger-makers pursued the corporate policies. (The computerized recipe stipulates ten hamburgers to the pound of meat.) Its gimmickry proved so successful that it did more than had been done before to establish American "fast-food" tactics abroad. McDonald's hypnotized many traveling European youths. But a Parisian friend who tried a "Big Mac" for lunch in New York said cheerfully to my wife and me, "This is not food—this is a vector for communication." And as if to prove himself a genuine Parisian, he added that he found in the McDonald atmosphere "a *complaisance* that might be considered a national myth."

The myth had long before become an overbearing reality. The hamburger originally was a nineteenth-century import from Germany, a meat dish of chopped beef known as a Hamburg steak, after the teeming port on the Elbe River. In America the broiled patty went through several changes.[3] Like the hot dog, the hamburger was accepted as a classic American sandwich after being introduced at world's fairs around the turn of the century. But it was the automobile and a nation constantly in motion that made the hamburger an institution.

Charles Kuralt, sent forth by the Columbia Broadcasting System to shed light on American foibles—including eating habits—appeared on home screens with his hamburger report in the fall of 1970. Against a changing tapestry of scenes showing carhop service along highways and city streets in many parts of the country, Kuralt delivered himself of the following observations on the great American snack:

> Americans ate forty billion hamburgers last year, give or take a few hundred million, and on the road you tend to eat more than your share. You can find your way across this country using burger joints the way a navigator uses stars. . . . We have munched bridge burgers in the shadow of Brooklyn Bridge and Cable burgers hard by the Golden Gate, Dixie burgers in the sunny South and Yankee Doodle burgers in the North. The Civil War must be over—they taste exactly alike. . . . We had a Capitol burger—guess where. And so help us, in the inner courtyard of the Pentagon, a Penta burger. . . . And then there was the night in New Mexico when the lady was just closing up and we had to decide in a hurry. "What'll it be," she said, "a whoppa burger or a bitta burger?" Hard to decide. . . .

[3] Prescribed for his British patients by Dr. J. S. Salisbury, the chopped meat that went under the broiler was known in the late nineteenth century (indeed the name still clings) as a Salisbury steak. In the twentieth century the American hamburger became known throughout England as the Wimpy, sold by a chain bearing the same name—which originated in "Popeye," the American comic strip drawn by Segar. That cartoon strip could not "be credited with the popularity of the hamburg sandwich," etymologist Arnold Williams wrote, but he added that the cartoon endowed hamburger "in the character of Wimpy . . . with a mythos." Perhaps a more descriptive euphemism was that of a young Midwest mother who referred to the diet on which her children survived as "The Daily Grind."

But this is not merely a local phenomenon. The smell of fried onions is abroad in the land, and if the French chefs among us will avert their eyes, we will finish reciting our menu of the last few weeks on the highways of America. We've had grabba burgers, kinga burgers, lotta burgers, castle burgers, country burgers, bronco burgers, Broadway burgers, broiled burgers, beefnut burgers, bell burgers, plush burgers, prime burgers, flame burgers . . . dude burgers, char burgers, tall boy burgers, golden burgers, 747 jet burgers, whiz burgers, nifty burgers, and thing burgers. . . .

Kuralt wound up as the camera showed a hamburger stand surrounded by nothing but endless desert, and said that he wondered, if the last American to survive the holocaust were to leave a single monument, whether or not it would be a shack with a blazing hamburger sign.

The Survival of Pop Food

He might have picked an equally frail edifice dedicated to production of fried chicken, an American "pop food" for which many entrepreneurs lay claim to sales equal to those for hamburgers. Colonel Sanders' Kentucky Fried Chicken combines "finger lickin' good" as an advertising slogan and a secret mixture of herbs that he said came from an old family recipe. He opened an international field of food-on-the-run that was soon entered by Chicken Delight, Kansas Fried ("with a touch of soul"), Chickin Lickin, and a Southwest chain called Church's that specializes in chicken pieces savored because of their crispness—a quality unattributable to other chains, either national or regional.

Pop food, like pop art, scorns many of the traditions of creativity, but its survival has been assured by the disappearance of "help" in the home kitchen and an economy in which affluence has become persuasive. For middle-income families it is easier and almost as inexpensive to feed the children at the local hamburger joint; a bonus came in the fact that the jaunt was also considered entertainment. Among average women who have children—and frequently a job as well—culinary creativity had narrowed down in the 1960s to such *chefs d'oeuvre* as casseroles made with preseasoned mixtures referred to as "hamburger helpers" and "homemade" desserts that might be conjured from packaged cake mixes and other processed ingredients sure to turn out exotic puddings in minutes.

The nation's cooking had become worse only to take a turn for the better. During the same time period at least a fraction of all those post–World War II travelers had been learning to take the act of eating as something more than stoking up. Unhappily the meaning of the word gourmet became distorted as it was misused, but the distortion signified, at least, a generally healthy respect for excellence in the kitchen. "What originally began as a gastronomic expedition of a few Idle Rich and Serious Epicureans has become a widespread phenomenon of mass travel," epicurean writer Joseph Wechsberg wrote in 1967.

Tourists who went on those gustatory romps multiplied alarmingly. Among them were some who once might have been considered "Idle

Rich" but were in the 1970s paying, instead, for the privilege of working as menials in *les hautes cuisines*. Women flocked to L'École de Cordon Bleu, then wrought wonders in their own kitchens with their new mastery of techniques, savoring their classic recipes like blue-chip stocks and bonds. Some of them managed to arrange stints of labor as apprentices in three-star restaurants. Some used their experience to serve better food than ever to their guests at home; others started cooking schools in their communities—not so much to provide their families with extra income as to establish themselves in careers of distinction.

Gastronomy and Revenge

Perhaps for the first time among middle-class Americans cooking was recognized as an art form, dining as a social grace to be taken seriously. General readership magazines in the United States went beyond the parameters to which women's monthlies had previously confined themselves by probing the mysteries of great cuisines and great chefs. The subject of food had been taken over by the cognoscenti. And wine—that, too, became a subject to be mastered by one and all. The whole spirit of the period may have been summed up one day in October 1973, when the weekly magazine called *New York* (itself a guidon in the prevailing winds) adapted an acerbic Spanish proverb by captioning its issue on food and drink that autumn: Eating Well Is the Best Revenge.

Food had become a central factor in living well, in pursuing a stylish life. Mastering the art of the cuisine had become more than a fad. To this end the return of Julia Child from years of living abroad had been fatefully timed. In France she had collaborated in the writing of a cookbook that changed the lives of many Americans after its publication in 1961. Mrs. Child's television performances as "The French Chef" persuaded thousands that the ability to turn out epicurean dinners could be achieved by all who were seriously intent upon cooking well. Her down-to-earth, unassuming demonstrations helped to make cooks out of men and women who had been afraid of the kitchen for much of their lives. Her message seemed to be that *haute cuisine* techniques could help to improve any cooking style, and that cooking could be fun. She so touched the mood of the country that she became a celebrity in small towns as well as cosmopolitan gathering places.

James Beard, without the regularity of television exposure, but whose column appeared in many newspapers and who criss-crossed the country making local appearances, became as recognizable as a homerun-hitter among baseball fans.[4] Conversely, Craig Claiborne, for more than a

[4] Frequently spotted when eating in restaurants, Beard was implored one day in Chicago to write a good luck message for his waitress to pass on to her son about to graduate from a school for chefs. Julia Child, strolling a Midwestern street with her husband, the painter Paul Child, was accosted by a woman who followed her television show and recognized Mrs. Child's distinctive voice. The admirer stopped her and asked, "What will we be having tonight, dearie?" Unlike most celebrities of the entertainment world, the "superstars" of food are seen by many admirers as members of their families.

decade the restaurant critic of the *New York Times* (as well as its food editor and the author of numerous cookbooks) considered himself lucky to have what he termed his "anonymous face." During the time he was the *Times'* critic of restaurants that face saved him from being easily spotted at lunches or dinners, eliminating the possibility of restaurateurs upgrading the food for his benefit—and theirs.

In the 1960s the character of the best American cookbooks changed from catch-all collections of recipes to skillfully written books that had themes, vibrancy, and eclecticism. Some of them became best sellers. Some, like *Simca's Cuisine* by Mrs. Child's French collaborator, Simone Beck, were personal testaments; Mme. Beck wrote a book especially for American cooks in an effort to show ways a family cook could adapt classic recipes by using her imagination and the materials available to her. Margaret Rudkin, who had proved that thousands would buy bread made from her farm-kitchen recipe—instead of the commercial loaves of questionable quality—also combined her personal testament with recipes that reflected her own philosophy of cooking. And among many women involved in collections of regional recipes, the gifted June Platt published her *New England Cook Book* in 1971 at the end of a series of volumes that made her, as James Beard has said, "undoubtedly one of the most important gastronomic authorities this country has produced."

Beard himself summed up a lifetime of kitchen mastery and accumulated knowledge of food in all the fifty states in his *American Cookery*. Three books by Michael Field delved into culinary styles in several countries and helped to stir interest in later works on one or another European or Asian cuisine. The twelfth edition of *The Joy of Cooking*, by Irma S. Rombauer and her daughter Marion Becker, expanded its command of the American kitchen by including such exotica as *couscous* and *rijsttafel*. For every taste there was a proliferation of books to be studied or used as guides in home kitchens. American publishers issued 49 cookbooks in 1960, and by 1972 the annual total had jumped to 385 new titles, according to *Publishers Weekly*. And a series of colorfully illustrated volumes published by Time-Life Books had used the mail order route to bring *The Foods of the World* to people miles away from book stores. In the five years beginning in 1967 the circulation of *Gourmet*, a monthly paean to the art of cooking and eating triumphantly, had increased from 250,000 to 550,000, and the mail received by the editors reflected the great increase in serious cooking among men, a noticeable proportion of them identifying themselves as doctors of medicine.

On every economic level, however, the interest among the young was most noticeable of all. There were in most American communities wives of servicemen who had lived abroad, and many had learned about foreign food by doing their own marketing in addition to mastering recipes that were new to them. The appreciations which they brought back and shared in suburban and small town "gourmet" clubs proved contagious. In places like Burlington, Vermont, where there is an air force base and where numerous young academics live, young women took turns planning and executing dinners for club members on a monthly schedule. Cosmopolitan cities like New York and New Orleans had their Chevaliers du Tastevins, but there were even more groups in such cities as Minneapolis and St. Paul, which organized as "societies of amateur chefs"—not simply gatherings of aficionados but of those who found more joy in the act of cooking than in spectator sports.

Cooking as a Life-Style

"The absolute status symbol of the New York apartment," a fashionable decorator told the *New York Times* in 1973, "is the kitchen." With few people hiring cooks or dining room maids, more and more festive meals are being served in kitchens transformed into rooms that echo an American past when the center of the house was a fireplace used for cooking as well as heating. Kitchen work tables, often made of laminated butcher-block wood, serve first in the preparation of a meal and are then rearranged to be used as dining tables in rooms no longer reminiscent of chemical laboratories. Utensils of copper and other decorative materials once again are recognized as suitable objets d'art to hang on walls; sometimes dry sausages, even country hams are hung from ceilings, and pendent baskets hold fruits and vegetables. Practical equipment receives even more attention, and there are an increasing number of stores specializing in high quality kitchen equipment. Some of them, indeed, have been turned into popular hangouts by kitchen buffs.

Host or hostess not only admits guests to the scene of his or her culinary activity—a new kind of party described as a "come-help-cook" dinner has become chic among young adults. This social wrinkle has thrived especially, I think, because of mounting interest in meals that include a large number of separate dishes. Any cooking style calling for the chopping of various spices, herbs and vegetables—like that of India, China, or any of the Middle Eastern countries—provides a good reason to enlist guests who like food to join in the preparation.

This exposure to other ways of life, which had inspired the cooks who enriched their American cuisine with herbs and spices and new ways of preparing common ingredients, transformed many others into vegetarians and even more into devotees of natural foods. Again there was an echo of the past as so-called health food stores sprang up throughout the country. In New England and the South especially waterwheels that had been still for generations began to turn again to grind whole grains into flour. Farms devoted to raising unadulterated foodstuffs increased as the demand for organic food mounted—such crops were raised by those who relied on age-old pest repellents like garlic, nasturtiums, praying mantises, tansy and yarrow plants instead of commercial pesticides and chemical fertilizers.

Thousands of people in the 1970s went back to preparing some of the same kind of food their ancestors had eaten, and others, wittingly or otherwise, seemed to emulate the food faddists of the nineteenth century by refusing to eat anything injected with antibiotics or hormones, or contained in packages on which the fine print accommodated government strictures to confess the use of synthetic sweeteners, preservatives, emulsifiers, dyes, and stabilizers.

Young people who had served in the Peace Corps had learned overseas that interesting and appetizing food need not be luxurious. They learned that no true Indian dish is made with ready mixed curry powder, but that flavor comes from the cook's initiative in blending spices like coriander, cumin, ginger, garlic, nutmeg, or turmeric. They learned what various foods taste like when they are grown naturally and turned into appealingly aromatic dishes when seasoned naturally and not embellished with synthetics. This trend was identified by Madhur Jaffrey in her superlative *Invitation to Indian Cooking*, published in 1973. Young Americans, she wrote, "seem to have a great desire to experience the 'real' thing, an authentic taste, a different life style. Anything fake is deplored, fake foods included."

For some the impetus to find a different life-style was rebellious. Many young Americans—reacting against adult life and everything "fake" it represented to them—discovered they didn't have to visit Asia or the Middle East to learn to appreciate the cracked wheat dishes that were known variously as kasha or burghul and were not so very different from the American Indian samp, once a mainstay of New England diets.[5] In their spiritual quests these young people gathered in communes not unlike Brook Farm, Fruitlands, and the Shaker villages of a century earlier, and those of them who cooked sometimes dished up fine things after simmering pots of groats to which mushrooms were added. In their rejection of ersatz values, they ate brown rice by the carloads, sat down to hearty meals composed of the earthy goodness to be tasted in dandelion soup, green peppers stuffed with lentils, braised Jerusalem artichokes, salads of carrots and raisins, herbal teas, or bread they made themselves from whole grain flour.

Not all of the communes (again paralleling the nineteenth century) have lasted. Some youths, leaving the land, or finding basic democracy an impossible dream, have moved into such places as the hill towns of Vermont and mountain communities in the Rockies where they have set up stores that specialize in retailing natural foods and elixirs. Others in many of the same localities have established restaurants where a bowl of

[5] The worth of a diet based on cereal has been proved again and again, of course. In her marvelous book, *How to Cook a Wolf*, M. F. K. Fisher tells of a California college student who lived for two years during the Depression on about seven cents a day. "He would buy whole ground wheat at a feed-and-grain store, cook it slowly in a big kettle with a lot of water until it was tender," Mrs. Fisher wrote, "and eat it three times a day with a weekly gallon of milk which he got from a cut-rate dairy. Almost every day he stole a piece of fruit from a Chinese pushcart near his room." Perhaps in contrast to the mores of the 1970s, Mrs. Fisher added: "After he graduated he sent the [pushcart] owner a ten-dollar bill, and got four dollars back, with an agreeable note inviting him to a New Year's party in Chinatown in San Francisco. He went."

soup is brewed in the kitchen instead of coming from a can, where the fish is caught the day it is served, and the home-grown vegetables not only look more lively but awaken the taste buds of oldsters who hadn't tasted organically nurtured food since their childhoods.

Aside from those who dropped out, however temporarily, or from those health faddists whose pattern had been set long before by such personages as Greta Garbo—indeed, aside from those whose pretensions might be lumped under the "gourmet" rubric—some cooks in the 1970s could thank inflation for their own realization that cooking could be fun in addition to being economical. Shortages in steaks and other high-priced cuts of various meats combined with rising food costs in general to persuade cooks with hungry families to try recipes long ignored as too taxing or complicated. Some heartily agreed when columnist Harriet Van Horne wrote during critical weeks in 1973, "Some of the best meals I have ever eaten have been savory blends of inexpensive meats, simmered gently with vegetables and herbs." That thought didn't convince the worshipers of red meat, of course, but it may have helped in varying the menus of others.

"The silent revolution of the American palate," as it has been called, occurred as a reaction to problems of ecology as well as of economy. Young people were specifically concerned about pollution that affected the availability of food. They worked to clean up dead rivers like the Hudson, a source for past generations of favorite American fish like shad and striped bass. Many who were not necessarily formal vegetarians were keenly interested in meat substitutes, but not in the commercial "analogs," the meatless meats analogous to beef, ham, chicken, and seafood that are served in some eating places to unwary customers.

The vanguard, instead, accepted soybeans without pretense. Their soybean croquettes may look like hamburgers but they are served without euphemism. Broiled patties are sometimes quite delicious mixtures of soybeans, wild rice, and vegetable seasonings; they make soybean chili, and festive combinations of the Oriental legume with tomatoes, squash, garlic, garden herbs and grated cheese. Not very different, really, from the South Union, Ohio, Shakers of a century ago who baked for dinner a meat-like loaf that combined succulent lentils, grated onions, and their own tangy cheese and served it with a sauce made from fresh tomatoes, garlic, and fragrant herbs.

There were, here and there, other signs of a return to beginnings. Rejecting the factory product that had lost any connection with traditional bread, thousands of women—and men, too—turned to baking their own. Young people in search of karma made dark and aromatic loaves while others, back from gastronomical travels, proved that Julia Child's recipe for French bread was, as one of them averred, infallible. *Beard on Bread*—a volume that brought together all the styles of baking contributed by Americans of every ethnic background—demonstrated the author's thesis that well-made bread "is the most fundamentally satisfying of all foods." There was no accurate tally of homemade breads in 1974, but twentieth-century cooks are proving that more efficient ovens are no deterrent to emulating their grandmothers. "The smell of good bread baking, like the sound of lightly flowing water," M.F.K. Fisher wrote in 1968, "is indescribable in its evocation of innocence and delight." The smell of good bread baking, evoking the past, is one of the compensations for Americans rediscovering the general satisfactions of the kitchen.

The United States, ending its second century, perhaps has no distinctive cuisine to call its own, but in many ways Americans with appreciative interest in food have looked back into the past to find inspiration and renewal. And the best of them might say, with Thomas Jefferson, "I too am an Epicurian. . . ."

Recipes

(in collaboration with Judith B. Jones)

A personal gathering of recipes
from various periods in
U.S. history, various regions, and
various ethnic influences.

Chapter 10

Appetizers and Hors d'Oeuvre

Avocado-Hazelnut Dip

1 large avocado	2 Tbs. finely chopped green pepper
⅓ cup cottage cheese	1 scallion, minced
lemon juice	2 Tbs. minced parsley
2 Tbs. chopped hazelnuts	shredded fresh basil
2 Tbs. finely chopped sweet red	dip-size tacos
pepper	

Peel and mash avocado and blend with cottage cheese and a few drops of lemon juice until smooth. Mix in nuts, peppers, minced scallion and parsley. Add salt and pepper only if needed. Serve in a mound garnished with strips of purple basil (if available), or parsley, and surrounded by tacos.

MAKES ABOUT 2 CUPS

Avocado-Clam Dip

1 large ripe avocado	¼ tsp. chili powder
1 garlic clove	1 tsp. lemon juice
½ tsp. salt	4 Tbs., or more, minced clams

Peel avocado and garlic, cutting latter into halves and rubbing it into mixing bowl. Mash avocado in mixing bowl, adding salt, chili powder, lemon juice, and minced clams. Chill for 1 hour.

MAKES ABOUT 1½ CUPS

Lake Michigan Blini

Whitefish caviar from Port Washington, Wisconsin, needs no comparison with Beluga, Sevruga or Osetra from the Caspian Sea. It has its own virtues—it is dense, salty, and tangy, and is particularly delicious as filling for buckwheat cakes served sometimes as a first course or, as in Nashville, on silver-dollar pancakes to eat at cocktail time. It's also good on broiled tilefish (p. 280).

1 recipe Buckwheat Pancakes (p. 170)
2 cups sour cream
½ cup caviar

Thin batter with ¼ cup warm water to make cakes about 5 inches in diameter. Mix half of sour cream with caviar and spread quickly on hot cakes; roll cakes and put a dollop of plain sour cream on top of each.

MAKES ABOUT 8 SERVINGS

Aunt Rose's Cheese and Pimiento Sandwich Spread

Devised in Durand, Wisconsin, and making use of the state's best Cheddar, this is a Welsh-American cook's variation on the ancient Cymric standby, Welsh Rabbit; it is also very good hot (Cambrian Baked Eggs with Cheese Sauce, p. 309).

2 Tbs. butter
1 cup shredded Wisconsin Cheddar
1 cup milk
3 eggs, well beaten
½ tsp. salt
¼ tsp. dry mustard
5 canned pimientos, chopped

In the top part of a double boiler, over simmering water, melt butter and blend in cheese, stirring until free of lumps. Stir in the milk and add well-beaten eggs, continuing to stir over low heat as mixture thickens; stir in salt and mustard. Do not let boil or eggs will tend to scramble. Remove from heat and stir in chopped pimientos. Cool in refrigerator overnight.

MAKES ABOUT 2 CUPS

Chiles Rellenos

Chiles rellenos, or stuffed chili peppers, were popular on California's Spanish ranchos before Yankees and Southerners arrived from the East, and they were so appreciated by the newcomers that they began to appear immediately in local cookbooks. They are often served with refried beans, with a salad, tortillas, or immersed in tomato sauce.

½ lb. Monterey Jack cheese
6 to 8 canned green chilies
4 eggs, separated

3 Tbs. flour
½ tsp. salt
corn oil

SAUCE:

1 onion, finely chopped
1 garlic clove, minced
2 Tbs. oil
2 cups tomato purée
2 cups chicken stock

1 tsp. salt
freshly ground pepper
¼ tsp. dried orégano
¼ tsp. dried basil

Cut cheese (use Cheddar if you prefer) into pieces to fit chilies. Remove seeds from chilies unless you like things very spicy-hot. Wrap chilies around cheese pieces. Beat egg yolks until fluffy, then gradually stir in flour and salt. Beat whites until peaks form, and fold into batter. Fill skillet to depth of 2 inches with corn oil and heat. Dip stuffed chilies into batter, one at a time, coating thoroughly. Slide into hot oil, turn immediately, cook for 5 minutes, then turn and cook other side for about the same time. Drain on paper. *Chiles rellenos* may be cooked any time ahead, if they are served with sauce.

Make the sauce: Sauté onion and garlic in oil, then add tomato purée and stock. Stir in salt, a few turns of pepper grinder, orégano, and basil; simmer for at least 30 minutes. Drop in stuffed cooked chilies and simmer just long enough to heat. If chilies are cold, continue simmering for 5 to 10 minutes. Serve piping hot.

MAKES 6 TO 8 SERVINGS

Hot Chili-Tomato Dip

2 to 3 Tbs. butter
2 large onions, finely chopped
2 garlic cloves, minced
3 Tbs. minced green chili peppers
1 Tbs. Worcestershire sauce

1 cup grated Monterey Jack cheese
2½ cups canned tomatoes, drained and chopped
1 Tbs. cornstarch
corn chips

Melt butter in a saucepan and sauté onions, garlic, and peppers for about 4 minutes; add Worcestershire sauce. Melt cheese in top part of double boiler over simmering water; stir in tomatoes and cooked onion mixture. When this begins to bubble stir in cornstarch mixed with a little water; stir until sauce thickens. Keep hot while serving with corn chips as dips.

MAKES ABOUT 4 CUPS

Coach House Crab with Prosciutto

A worthy American restaurant to which to take even a cosmopolitan citizen of Paris is New York's Coach House where this hors d'oeuvre combines the native crab meat of the Eastern Shore with thin slices of ham made by Italo-Americans in the traditional way.

24 thin slices of prosciutto
12 oz. fresh lump crab meat
6 oz. (1½ sticks) butter
1 tsp. Worcestershire sauce

½ tsp. Tabasco or Louisiana hot sauce
1 lemon
2 Tbs. minced parsley
   freshly ground black pepper

Arrange 4 slices of prosciutto on a flat surface, each slice slightly overlapping another. Place in the center a heaping tablespoon of crab. Roll ham slices over filling cigar style; repeat with remaining prosciutto and crab. Heat butter in large skillet; when it foams add the 6 rolls. (The ham will cling to crab when heated.) Turn rolls once and cook until ham starts to frizzle and crab is heated through; transfer to hot plate. Add Worcestershire and Tabasco to skillet and squeeze in juice of lemon. Heat for about 30 seconds and pour over ham. Sprinkle each roll with minced parsley and freshly ground pepper.

MAKES 6 SERVINGS

Individual Crab Soufflés Baked in Shells

3 Tbs. butter
3 Tbs. flour
¾ cup milk
2 egg yolks
½ tsp. salt
½ tsp. minced chives
½ tsp. minced parsley
½ tsp. dried savory
   Tabasco

⅔ cup grated Wisconsin Asiago
   cheese
2 Tbs. Madeira
12 oz. crab meat
1 tsp. lemon juice
1 Tbs. softened butter
5 egg whites

Preheat oven to 425°

Melt butter in a saucepan over low heat, then stir in flour, eliminating lumps. Let mixture bubble for about 1 minute, then remove from heat and stir in milk with a wire whisk, mixing briskly. Return to heat and keep stirring constantly until sauce thickens to a pastelike consistency. Off heat, beat in egg yolks, one at a time, then add salt, chives, parsley, savory, a dash or two of Tabasco, ¼ cup grated cheese, and the Madeira.

Remove any hard bits from crab meat and sprinkle it with lemon juice. Butter 4 scallop shells. Beat egg whites until they form peaks, then fold into cooled sauce. Put a spoonful of soufflé mixture into each shell, then gently distribute one quarter of crab meat over each one. Divide remaining soufflé mixture among the shells, making a neat mound on top, but do not let them overflow. Sprinkle with remaining cheese. Bake for 10 minutes; turn heat down to 375° and bake for 10 minutes more.

MAKES 4 SERVINGS

Cold Crab in Basil Sauce

6 to 7 oz. crab meat
4 water chestnuts
12 large basil leaves, minced
2 Tbs. minced parsley
1 whole egg
½ tsp. salt
1 Tbs. wine vinegar

½ tsp. Dijon mustard, or ¼ tsp. dry
    mustard
½ cup olive oil
½ cup vegetable oil, or walnut or
    peanut oil
lemon juice

Remove any bits of bone in crab meat. Drain water chestnuts, and slice thin. Spin basil and parsley with egg, salt, vinegar, mustard in a blender for about 50 seconds, then slowly pour in both oils mixed together while continuing to blend. If mixture becomes stiff before using all of oil add a few drops of lemon juice. When sauce is thoroughly blended and oil is completely used, taste for seasoning and add a few drops more of lemon juice. Mix this sauce into crab meat and stir in sliced water chestnuts. Serve with tomato and cucumber slices as an hors d'oeuvre. Or serve as lunch for 4 in avocado halves.

MAKES 6 HORS D'OEUVRE SERVINGS

Cocktail Frankfurters in Pastry

1 recipe pie dough (p. 349)
¾ lb. cocktail-size frankfurters

1 to 2 Tbs. mustard (old-fashioned
    whole seed preferred)
1 egg beaten with 1 Tbs. water

Preheat oven to 450°

Divide pie dough into 2 pieces. Roll out thin. Arrange half of frankfurters on one sheet of dough so that each sausage has enough dough to wrap around sides and ends; cut dough accordingly. Brush each frankfurter on all sides with mustard, then pull sides and ends of dough upward, painting inner seams with egg wash. Tuck in ends and seal main seam, pressing edges firmly together. Arrange packages seam side down about 1 inch apart on a buttered cookie sheet. Repeat with second half of franks and remaining dough. Brush all tops and sides with remaining egg wash, then prick tops with a fork. Chill for 10 minutes before putting in oven. Bake for 10 minutes, or until golden.

MAKES 12 OR MORE

All-American Hot Hors d'Oeuvre

Crisp bacon-wrapped hot mouthfuls are made in American kitchens in every state. Angels on Horseback, oysters wrapped in bacon, have been known as *ostras ángeles* in Spanish California, and they become "Angelenos" when an anchovy fillet encircles the oyster underneath the wrapping of bacon. Broiled bacon also encircles chicken livers, cocktail sausages, lobster chunks, mushrooms, scallops, shad roe, shrimps, water chestnuts. Put them under the broiler and keep turning until done.

Bacon pinwheels are made by trimming the crust from an unsliced loaf of fresh white bread, then cutting it into ¼-inch lengthwise slices. Each slice is spread with cream cheese softened at room temperature and rolled like a jelly roll. Cut the rolls into 2 or 3 pieces and wrap each in sliced bacon, fastening with a toothpick. Toast under moderate broiler heat, turning often until bacon is cooked.

Liver Spread

1 to 1½ cups cooked beef, veal, or chicken liver	3 to 4 Tbs. soft butter freshly ground pepper
2 hard-cooked eggs, sieved	3 Tbs. heavy cream
1 small onion, very finely minced	¼ cup minced parsley
8 anchovy fillets, mashed to a paste	

Put the liver through the fine blade of a meat grinder, then mash through a sieve. Mix in the eggs, onion, anchovies, and butter. Add freshly ground pepper to taste and stir in the cream a little at a time, using more or less according to desired consistency. Shape mixture into a mound on a suitable serving dish and sprinkle with minced parsley, or use as a sandwich spread.

MAKES 8 SERVINGS OR MORE

As a cold first course for a St. David's Day dinner, this is a Welsh-American answer to the French *coquille St. Jacques,* originally made with cockles and mussels, a-live, a-live, o! Welsh from Minnesota and Wisconsin have been known to use the crayfish once common in fresh running streams (they are native to Washington, Oregon, and of course Louisiana also) when canned cockles are hard to come by. But tiny canned shrimps do nicely in this combination of seafoods.

½ bunch of watercress, blanched for
    1 minute
3 sprigs parsley
1 whole scallion
1 egg
½ tsp. prepared mustard
¼ tsp. salt
1 lime

½ cup olive oil
½ cup peanut oil
1 can (12 oz.) mussels
1 can (6 oz.) tiny shrimps
3 shallots, finely minced
1 Tbs. minced parsley
1 Tbs. minced chives

Make green sauce by spinning in blender the watercress, parsley, scallion, egg, mustard, salt, and ½ Tbs. lime juice; save half of lime to slice for garnish. Add oil, a little at a time, to achieve mayonnaise consistency; if too thick add a little more lime juice, as spinning continues. Drain mussels and shrimps and mix with minced shallots; fold in one third of green sauce, then divide to fill 8 scallop shells. Top with remaining green sauce, and sprinkle with parsley and chives.

MAKES ABOUT 2 CUPS

1 lb. uncooked shrimps
4 Tbs. butter
⅓ lb. fresh mushrooms, sliced
1 cup sour cream at room temperature
½ tsp. salt

freshly ground white pepper
1 tsp. soy sauce
paprika
¼ cup grated Parmesan cheese

Shell and clean shrimps. Melt butter in a skillet and stir in sliced mushrooms; sauté for 5 or 6 minutes, then stir in shrimps and sauté until they turn pink, about 3 minutes. Put sour cream in saucepan and heat slowly, stirring in salt, pepper, soy sauce, and enough paprika to make sauce pink; do not let boil. Stir into shrimps and mushrooms and cook just long enough so sauce is thick and well blended. Spoon into 4 scallop shells and sprinkle cheese over tops. Put under broiler until cheese turns golden.

MAKES 4 SERVINGS

Hot Oyster Cocktail

24 large oysters, drained
½ cup chili sauce
½ cup tomato catsup
¼ cup finely chopped celery

1 tsp. Tabasco
½ tsp. lemon juice
2 Tbs. butter

Make sure oysters are very fresh. Mix chili sauce, catsup, celery, Tabasco, and lemon juice. Melt butter in a saucepan, add mixture, and stir while it heats; do not let it boil. Stir in oysters and let them plump up.

MAKES 6 SERVINGS

Shrimps de Jonghe

Years ago when we first tasted this or a dish very similar to it, it was called Shrimps Boveri and served in a Chicago restaurant of that name. Versions which vary in the number of herbs used are popular in St. Paul, many parts of the Midwest and the South. In Louisville not long after World War II Marion Flexner reported that this hors d'oeuvre had been the specialty of a Belgian couple named de Jonghe who ran a Chicago restaurant, that their nephew had taken over the business "although he refuses to divulge the secret family recipe. However, he does insist that his version has 12 herbs in it. . . ." In that respect it is somewhat like oysters Rockefeller: the recipe is under lock and key and outsiders can only trust their taste memories.

2 garlic cloves, minced
½ tsp. each of finely minced parsley,
    scallions, shallots, chives, chervil
    tarragon, thyme
¼ lb. butter
1 cup fresh bread crumbs
¼ cup dry sherry

Tabasco
nutmeg
mace
salt
freshly ground pepper
1 lb. uncooked shrimps

Preheat oven to 400°

Stir minced garlic and minced fresh herbs together, then work into butter until evenly distributed. Add bread crumbs, sherry, a dash of Tabasco, and a pinch each of grated nutmeg and mace. Taste, adding salt if necessary and several turns of pepper grinder. This will improve if left to mature in refrigerator. Shell and clean shrimps and cook in boiling salted water for 3 minutes, then divide into 4 piles. Put a layer of herbed butter-crumb mixture in the bottom of each of 4 scallop shells. Arrange shrimps spoon fashion in a single layer, pressing into butter-crumb mixture. Divide remaining butter into 4 parts and spread over tops of shrimp. Bake for 10 to 15 minutes, or bake for 10 minutes, then put under broiler until tops brown.

MAKES 4 SERVINGS

Cocktail Popcorn

½ cup popcorn
⅔ cup butter, or ⅓ cup butter and
    ⅓ cup corn oil

1½ tsp. salt
1 small garlic clove, minced
¼ cup minced chives

Use a skillet large enough so corn kernels can spread over bottom in one uncrowded layer. Put empty skillet over low heat and melt ⅓ cup butter or heat oil; after 2 minutes test by dropping in 1 kernel. If kernel pops immediately, add remaining corn and cover skillet. Shake back and forth to keep kernels moving. In a separate pan melt remaining butter; add salt, garlic, and chives; pour over popped corn and toss.

MAKES 3 QUARTS

Salmon-Caviar Hors d'Oeuvre

2 cups flaked cooked salmon
4 cup-shaped lettuce leaves
½ cup red caviar, chilled

½ cup fresh mayonnaise
½ cup whipped cream

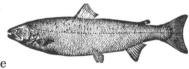

Arrange flaked salmon in lettuce cups. Carefully fold caviar into freshly made mayonnaise, then fold in stiffly whipped cream. Spoon this sauce over salmon.

MAKES 4 SERVINGS

Louisiana Shallot Pie

In some regions, especially the South, the word shallot is used for scallions (or tiny green onions) instead of for the somewhat garlic-shaped cloven brown onion that in France is known as *échalote*. Although the flavors are quite different, scallions and shallots are often used interchangeably. In this ham-flavored pie, as in a Bayou cornmeal pie, the subtlety is the result of mincing both white and green parts of scallions. In the latter, 2 cups of minced scallions and the same amount of grated cheese are cooked in butter to make a filling between 2 layers of cornmeal mush, then baked in a hot oven for 30 minutes. Because it is so rich and tasty we have found the scallion-ham-cream filling particularly delicious in bite-size pastry shells served piping hot as a cocktail snack.

3 egg yolks, beaten
½ tsp. salt
   cayenne
1 tsp. flour
   freshly ground white pepper
1 cup sour cream

3 Tbs. butter
1 cup minced scallions
½ cup minced ham
16 to 20 prebaked small pastry shells
   (see page 349)

Preheat oven to 350°

Mix beaten egg yolks with salt, a pinch of cayenne, the flour, one or two turns of white pepper, and sour cream. Cook in top part of double boiler over simmering water for about 20 minutes, until thick; let cool. Melt butter and sauté scallions for 2 or 3 minutes. Stir in ham and cook for 1 minute more, then mix well with custard. Pour into prebaked pastry shells and bake for 7 to 8 minutes.

MAKES 8 TO 10 SERVINGS

Broiled Mushrooms with Ham Stuffing

12 medium-size mushrooms
¼ cup olive oil
1 Tbs. lemon juice
1 garlic clove, minced
2 Tbs. butter
1 medium-size green pepper, finely
   chopped

2 large shallots, finely chopped
½ tsp. dried chervil
½ tsp. dried orégano
½ cup minced ham
   toast points

Remove stems from mushrooms and set aside. Use sharp knife to slash mushroom caps and put in a bowl with oil, lemon juice and garlic for 30 minutes. Meanwhile melt butter and sauté green pepper, shallots, and herbs. Chop mushroom stems very fine, mix with ham, and stir into green-pepper mixture, cooking over very low heat for about 10 minutes; add marinade from mushroom caps. Broil caps for 3 minutes on each side. Put on toast points and spoon stuffing over.

MAKES 4 HORS D'OEUVRE SERVINGS

Jerusalem Artichoke and Celery-Root Salad

1 large celery root
¾ lb. Jerusalem artichokes
⅔ cup country ham cut in matchsticks

1 cup Lemony Mustard Sauce
   (p. 329)
lettuce cups
¼ cup minced parsley

Peel celery root, cut into halves, then parboil for 7 minutes. Wash artichokes very thoroughly but do not peel; boil for about 10 minutes. Cut blanched celery root into match-size strips. Trim all hard knotty areas from cooked Jerusalem artichokes along with a little of skin, although some skin should be left for texture and flavor; slice lengthwise, then into 3 or 4 strips. Toss ham and vegetable strips gently with mustard sauce. Distribute equal portions over lettuce leaves and top with parsley. Serve as first course.

MAKES 4 SERVINGS

Little Canada Rabbit Terrine

MARINADE FOR RABBIT:

1½ cups red wine
¾ cup wine vinegar
1 onion roughly chopped
1 carrot cut in chunks
2 stalks celery in short pieces

1 garlic clove, crushed
½ tsp. dried dill weed
½ tsp. mustard seed
½ tsp. coriander, bruised
½ tsp. peppercorns, bruised

Mix and add about ¾ cup of water or enough to cover meat. Marinate 24 hours or more, turning occasionally.

1 rabbit (3 lbs.), marinated for several
   days
1 lb. lean pork, ground
1 lb. pork fat, ground
2 medium-size onions, finely chopped
3 Tbs. lard
2 garlic cloves, finely minced
½ cup applejack or other brandy or
   Madeira
2 eggs

2 to 3 tsp. salt
   freshly ground pepper
2 Tbs. minced fresh parsley
1 tsp. dried savory
½ tsp. dried thyme
2 or 3 whole allspice, mulled
½ lb. salt pork, sliced thin
1 lb. country ham, cut into ⅓-inch-
   thick strips
1 large bay leaf

Preheat oven to 350°*

Strip well-marinated rabbit meat from bones. Use best pieces (about half of total) to cut into long strips ½- to ¼-inch thick. Grind less-tender pieces and scraps of rabbit and mix with ground pork and ground fat. Sauté onions in lard until translucent, then stir into ground meat; add garlic, applejack, eggs, and seasonings. Test flavor by frying a small sample of mixture; it should be heartily seasoned, but not oversalted if the country ham is as tangy as it should be.

Blanch salt-pork strips in 2 quarts of water; drain and pat dry, then use them to line 2-quart terrine, letting edges just meet. Spread one third of ground meat over bottom, then lay over it alternating strips of rabbit meat and ham, using half of total. Repeat layer of ground meat and use remaining half of meat strips; cover with final layer of ground meat. * Put bay leaf in the center, then cover top with salt-pork pieces, tucking down into sides so mixture is well wrapped. Cover. Set terrine in pan with hot water that comes about halfway up outside of terrine; bake for 2½ hours. Remove to cool, weighting top surface with an old flatiron or other heavy object. When cool, chill for several days. Serve from the terrine.

MAKES 12 SERVINGS

Smoked Whitefish Cocktail Appetizer

The availability of smoked whitefish from the Great Lakes led to the development of this party tidbit. Members of the Society of Amateur Chefs in Minneapolis found it so popular that they received hundreds of requests for the recipe after it was described on a television program.

2 lbs. smoked whitefish or other smoked fish
1 cup Homemade Mayonnaise (p. 294)
1 Tbs. dry mustard

1 Tbs. minced chives
1 large tomato, peeled, seeded and diced
1 Tbs. dry sherry
freshly ground black pepper

Several hours ahead, bone and flake fish and refrigerate. Mix mayonnaise with mustard, chives, and tomato dice. Fold in flaked chilled fish, then blend with sherry and add several turns of pepper grinder. Salt should not be necessary but it may be added if fish is bland. Serve on Melba rounds.

MAKES 12 SERVINGS

Chapter II

Breads and Pancakes

Buttermilk Biscuits

2 cups flour
⅜ tsp. baking soda
¾ tsp. salt

¼ cup vegetable shortening
¾ cup cultured buttermilk

Preheat oven to 450°

Sift flour, baking soda, and salt together 3 times. Cut in shortening until mixture is crumbly, then gradually add buttermilk, mixing until smooth. Knead dough lightly on floured surface. Roll to ⅛ inch thick and cut into circles. Bake 10 to 12 minutes.

MAKES ABOUT 2 DOZEN SMALL BISCUITS

Apple-Cheese Muffins

4 Tbs. softened butter
½ cup sugar
2 large eggs
1½ cups sifted flour
1 tsp. baking powder
1 tsp. baking soda
½ tsp. salt
¾ cup rolled oats

1 large tart apple, cored and peeled
⅔ cup grated Cheddar cheese
½ cup chopped walnuts
¾ cup milk
  thin slices of large apples
4 Tbs. melted butter
2 Tbs. sugar mixed with
  1 Tbs. cinnamon

159

Preheat oven to 400°

Cream softened butter and sugar. Add eggs and beat well. Sift together flour, baking powder, baking soda, and salt, then stir into butter-sugar mixture; stir in oats. Chop apple into ⅛-inch dice; add dice to mixture with grated cheese and chopped walnuts. Gradually stir in milk, mixing lightly. Fill 12 well-buttered muffin tins two thirds full. Cut thin slices of apples the same diameter as muffin tins; brush slices with melted butter and coat with cinnamon-sugar mixture, then top batter in each muffin tin with 1 apple slice. Sprinkle remaining cinnamon-sugar mixture evenly on muffins. Bake for about 25 minutes.

MAKES 12

Bacon and Peanut-Butter Muffins

2 cups sifted flour
1 Tbs. baking powder
2 Tbs. sugar
1 tsp. salt
2 Tbs. melted bacon fat or butter

1 egg, beaten
1 cup milk
3 uncooked bacon strips, finely chopped
about ¼ cup peanut butter

Preheat oven to 400°

Sift flour, baking powder, sugar, and salt together. Blend melted fat, well-beaten egg, milk, and finely chopped bacon, then stir in flour mixture, but do not beat; mixture should be just moistened. Pour a little batter into each well-greased muffin tin, then drop in about ⅛ teaspoon of peanut butter before filling tins three-fourths full. Bake for 20 to 25 minutes.

MAKES 12

Blueberry Muffins

2 cups flour, sifted twice
1 brimming cup blueberries, washed and hulled
2 Tbs. sugar
½ tsp. salt

1 Tbs. baking powder
2 Tbs. melted butter
1 egg, well beaten
¾ cup milk

Preheat oven to 375°

Be sure flour measures 2 cups after sifting; mix ½ cup with blueberries and set aside. Add sugar, salt, and baking powder to remaining flour and sift 3 times. Stir together melted butter, well-beaten egg, and milk, then add this mixture alternately with berries to flour mixture, tossing lightly, just enough to moisten flour. Do not overmix. Grease a cast-iron gem pan. Pour batter to three-quarter point in 10 cups of gem pan and half-fill remaining cups with water (this keeps muffins from scorching). Bake for 25 minutes.

MAKES 10

Bran and Ham Muffins

1 cup bran	½ tsp. salt
1¼ cups milk	2½ tsp. baking powder
1 egg, beaten	1 cup ground ham
2 Tbs. melted butter	1 scallion, finely minced
1 cup flour	1 to 2 Tbs. minced parsley
1 Tbs. sugar	freshly ground black pepper

Preheat oven to 400°

Let bran soak in milk for about 5 minutes, then stir in beaten egg and melted butter. Sift together flour, sugar, salt, and baking powder; blend this lightly into milk mixture, just enough to dampen the flour. Stir in ham (country-cured ham will give muffins real character), scallion, parsley and 3 or 4 turns of pepper grinder. Divide among 12 well-buttered muffin tins and bake for 25 to 40 minutes.

MAKES 12

Hominy Muffins

3 Tbs. hominy	1 Tbs. sugar
salt	½ cup scalded milk
2 tsp. dry yeast	1½ to 1¾ cups flour
4 Tbs. butter	

Preheat oven to 375° ❋

Cook hominy by sprinkling it into 1 cup boiling water. Add ⅛ teaspoon salt, turn down heat, cover, and let simmer, stirring occasionally, for 25 minutes; it should make about ½ cup cooked. Dissolve the yeast in 2 tablespoons warm water. In a larger bowl mix cooked, still warm hominy with the butter, sugar, milk, and ½ teaspoon salt, making sure to break up any lumps. When cool, add dissolved yeast and flour, mixing well. Turn out on a floured board and knead for a few minutes, adding a little more flour if necessary, although dough should be moist. Cover and let rise in a warm place until the dough has doubled in bulk. Punch down. Butter gem pans for 12 muffins, fill two-thirds full, and let rise uncovered for 1 hour. ° Bake in top third of the oven for 25 to 30 minutes.

MAKES 12

Everyday Corn Bread

1 cup flour
1 Tbs. sugar
¾ tsp. salt
5 tsp. baking powder

1 cup yellow cornmeal
3 Tbs. butter, melted and cooled
1 cup milk
1 egg, lightly beaten

Preheat oven to 425°

Sift together twice flour, sugar, salt, and baking powder, and stir in cornmeal. Mix melted butter, milk, and lightly beaten egg. Combine with dry ingredients, and beat for about 1 minute. Pour into buttered 8-inch-square baking pan and bake for 25 minutes. Cool on cake rack.

MAKES 8 SERVINGS

Soft-as-Pie Texas Corn Bread

1 thin bacon slice
¾ cup coarsely ground yellow
    cornmeal
1 cup boiling water
2 Tbs. melted butter mixed with
    2 Tbs. sausage or bacon fat

3 medium-size eggs, beaten
2 tsp. baking powder
1 cup buttermilk
1 Tbs. molasses
    optional: 1 or 2 chili peppers,
    chopped

Preheat oven to 350°

Put 7- or 8-inch iron skillet containing the bacon slice in preheated oven and let bacon sizzle while preparing remaining ingredients. Scald cornmeal with boiling water and let it steep for 5 minutes. Then add melted butter and fat and mix well; stir in beaten eggs, baking powder, buttermilk, and molasses. (If you are serving this as a kind of spoon bread with meats, you might add ¾ cup cooked corn kernels and about 4 tablespoons more of butter.) Add chili peppers to give a hot accent. When well blended, pour mixture on top of bacon in skillet and bake for about 30 minutes.

MAKES 6 SERVINGS

Spoon bread, sometimes called batter bread, has distinguished American tables since colonial times, and it has been a common twentieth-century substitute in the South for mashed potatoes. The recipe below belongs to Edna Lewis who presided over the kitchen of a New York restaurant known as Nicholson's at which the bill of fare had southern overtones. Edna Lewis' family still lives in the Virginia region in which their forebears once were slaves and where the style of cooking, she believes, still shows the influence of Jefferson's commitment to *haute cuisine*. Spoon bread isn't French—it is sometimes accented with fresh corn kernels, whole hominy, or rice—but it was prepared regularly in the Monticello kitchens.

1 cup white water-ground cornmeal	1 tsp. baking powder
¼ tsp. salt	3 medium-size eggs, beaten
2 tsp. granulated sugar	2 Tbs. butter
⅛ tsp. baking soda	2 cups buttermilk

Preheat oven to 400°

"Use an 8-inch-square baking pan, or a 1½-quart soufflé dish. Sift the cornmeal, salt, sugar, soda, and baking powder together in a mixing bowl, making a well in the center. Pour in beaten eggs. At this point, set baking pan in oven with 2 tablespoons butter to heat. Stir the eggs into meal vigorously. Pour in the buttermilk and stir well again. Remove hot pan from oven, tilt it around to butter surface of pan, pour excess butter into meal batter, stirring quickly, then pour batter into hot baking dish. Bake for 35 minutes. Serve right from oven with loads of fresh butter."

MAKES 8 SERVINGS

Boston Brown Bread

½ cup rye flour	½ tsp. salt
½ cup whole-wheat flour	1½ cups buttermilk
½ cup yellow cornmeal	½ cup warm molasses
½ tsp. baking soda	butter
½ tsp. baking powder	

Preheat oven to 300° *

To make pouring easier, put container of molasses in warm water while measuring the flour and cornmeal. Sift flour with baking soda, baking powder, and salt into a large bowl. Add cornmeal. Make hollow in sifted ingredients, then mix buttermilk and warm molasses and pour into hollow; beat mixture thoroughly. Butter a 1-quart melon mold, including inside of lid, and pour in mixture. See that it is covered tightly, then set on a rack in a kettle and pour in boiling water to a point about halfway up mold. Cover kettle and steam for 3 hours. * After 2¾ hours, preheat oven to 300°. Take lid from mold and put bread in oven to dry for 6 or 7 minutes.

MAKES 6 SERVINGS

Grandma McLeod's Gingerbread

¼ cup shortening
½ cup sugar
¾ tsp. baking soda
½ cup molasses
1½ cups flour
¾ tsp. baking powder

1 tsp. cinnamon
1 tsp. ginger
¼ tsp. ground cloves
pinch of salt
¾ cup boiling water
1 egg, beaten

Preheat oven to 325°

Cream together shortening and sugar. Beat ½ teaspoon of the baking soda into molasses until fluffy and light; add to shortening and sugar. Sift flour, baking powder, cinnamon, ginger, cloves, and salt; mix boiling water and remaining ¼ teaspoon baking soda, then gradually add liquid, alternately with dry ingredients, to molasses mixture. Stir until well mixed, then stir in beaten egg. Grease and flour an 8-inch-square baking pan and pour in gingerbread mixture. Bake for about 20 minutes.

MAKES 8 SERVINGS

Pumpkin Bread

3½ cups flour, sifted before measuring
1 tsp. salt
2½ cups sugar
2 tsp. baking soda
2 cups pumpkin purée
1 cup vegetable oil

½ cup water
4 eggs, beaten
¾ tsp. cinnamon
½ tsp. nutmeg
optional: 1 cup chopped nut meats

Preheat oven to 350°

Sift all the dry ingredients together. Mix pumpkin, oil, water, eggs, and spices together and combine with dry ingredients, but do not overmix. Add nuts if desired. Bake in 2 well-buttered loaf pans (9 x 5 x 3 inches) for 45 minutes to 1 hour, or until straw comes out clean. Turn out and cool on cake racks.

MAKES 2 LOAVES

At Rockport, on Cape Ann, they used to tell a story that gave this New England bread its name: Anna was a lazy wife whose bread was so much like her character that her Yankee husband devised his own recipe while he muttered "Anna, damn 'er!"

1 pkg. dry yeast
½ cup warm water
2 Tbs. butter or other shortening
½ cup molasses

2 cups hot water
about 5 cups unbleached flour
½ cup cornmeal
2 tsp. salt

Preheat oven to 400° ✱

Dissolve yeast in warm water. Melt butter and molasses in hot water. Cool to lukewarm and stir in yeast mixture, then mix 4 cups of flour with cornmeal and salt; blend with yeast-molasses liquid, 1 cup at a time. Continue to add flour until dough is stiff. Turn out on floured board and knead for 10 minutes, adding more flour as necessary. When dough is smooth and elastic and springs back, place in well-buttered bowl and turn to coat with butter all over; cover with a cloth and set in a warm place until dough has doubled in bulk. Punch down, knead again for a minute or so, then form into 2 loaves. Put loaves in 2 buttered 8-inch bread pans. Cover and let rise again in warm place until dough has risen over tops of pans by about ½ inch. ✱ Bake loaves for 15 minutes, then reduce heat to 350° and bake for 35 to 40 minutes longer.

MAKES 2 LOAVES

Challah (Jewish Egg Bread)

This light, airy yeast bread is common in Jewish delicatessens and is even more delicious when made at home every week for the Sabbath. Gertrude Berg, who created the famous radio heroine, Molly Goldberg, wrote that in making challah when her children were small "I would always make enough dough so that they could each make their own loaves," according to the child's size. She added, "Before you knew it they were making loaves of challah as big as mine." The chief bread maker at our house said: "Until you've made your own, you have little idea of how delicious, tender and spectacular looking challah can be, to say nothing of how much fun to make."

1¼ pkg. dry yeast
¾ cup warm water
1 Tbs. sugar
2 tsp. kosher salt
2 eggs, lightly beaten

2 Tbs. vegetable oil
3½ to 3¾ cups flour
1 egg yolk mixed with ½ tsp. water
poppy seeds

*Preheat oven to 400°**

Dissolve yeast in warm water in a large bowl. When dissolved, add sugar, salt, eggs, oil and, 1 cup at a time, as much flour as can be stirred into liquid. Turn out onto floured board and knead for at least 10 minutes, adding more flour as wanted, until dough is smooth and elastic. Put in oiled bowl, cover, and leave in warm place until doubled in bulk. Punch down, knead in a little more flour if too moist to handle, then divide into 2 portions. Portion 1: cut into 3 equal parts, rolling each into ropes about 10 inches long. Pinch one end of each rope together, then braid and pinch together other ends, to make one braided piece. Portion 2: divide into 2 pieces, one larger than the other; make braids of each piece in same manner as with portion 1. Now take first large braid and place on oiled cookie sheet; place next largest braid on top of first; then the smallest on top. Pinch here and there where the three portions touch to help them sit firmly in place. Cover and let rise at room temperature until double in bulk. * Brush loaf with egg-yolk mixture, covering surfaces thoroughly, and sprinkle liberally with poppy seeds. Bake for 10 minutes, then reduce heat to 375° and bake for 35 to 40 minutes more. Remove and cool on rack.

MAKES 1 LARGE LOAF

Good Earth Bread

2¼ cups boiling water	2 pkg. dry yeast, or 2 cakes fresh yeast
2 cups rolled oats	1 cup warm milk
½ cup cracked wheat	1 tsp. sugar
¼ cup wheat germ	3 cups stone-ground whole-wheat flour
¾ cup blackstrap molasses	2 to 3 cups unbleached flour
2 Tbs. melted butter	1 egg white
1½ Tbs. salt	

*Preheat oven to 375°**

Pour boiling water over rolled oats, cracked wheat, and wheat germ. Add molasses, butter and salt; mix well, let cool to body temperature. Meanwhile dissolve yeast in warm milk, add sugar, and let mixture bubble up. Now mix the yeast with whole-wheat flour and 1 cup unbleached flour, then add steeped oats and mix well. Turn out onto a floured surface. Let rest for a few minutes, then start kneading, adding some of the rest of the flour to achieve a firm, pliable consistency; it will be sticky so don't do much kneading at this time. Butter a large bowl and put dough in it; cover and let rise in warm place until double in bulk. Turn out on floured surface and knead well this time—for 8 to

10 minutes—adding more flour as necessary. Divide into halves and form 2 loaves; place in buttered bread tins (9 x 5 x 3 inches); dough should fill tins about two thirds. Let rise again until almost doubled; dough should swell over tops of tins. * Brush with egg white mixed with 1 teaspoon water. Bake for 15 minutes, then reduce heat to 350° and continue baking for 40 to 45 minutes, until bread sounds hollow when tapped. Remove loaves from pans and return them to oven. Turn off heat and let bread cool in oven. Remove and place on racks.

MAKES 2 LOAVES

Whole-Wheat Bread

1½ pkg. dry yeast
¼ cup warm water
2 cups skim milk
3 Tbs. butter
2 Tbs. molasses

2 tsp. salt
2 to 3 cups unbleached flour
3 cups stone-ground whole-wheat flour
½ cup wheat germ

Preheat oven to 425° *

Dissolve yeast in warm water. Meanwhile warm milk just enough to dissolve 1 tablespoon butter, the molasses and salt. In a large bowl mix 2 cups unbleached flour with all the whole-wheat flour and wheat germ. Stir in yeast and warm milk mixture, blending thoroughly. Turn out on floured board or marble and knead, adding as much unbleached flour as necessary to keep dough from sticking as you knead. After about 10 minutes, dough should be smooth and elastic; turn into buttered bowl and let rise in warm place, covered with a towel, until double in bulk. Punch down, knead for a few seconds, then shape into 2 loaves and place in buttered bread pans (9 x 5 x 3 inches). Cover loaves and let rise under towel until dough has swelled over tops of pans. * Bake for 10 minutes, then reduce heat to 400° and bake for approximately 25 minutes longer, or until loaves sound hollow when tapped. Cool on racks.

MAKES 2 LOAVES

Cinnamon Buns

1 pkg. dry yeast
¼ cup sugar
1 cup scalded milk, cooled to
    lukewarm
4 cups flour

4 Tbs. vegetable shortening
¼ lb. butter, softened
1 cup brown sugar
¾ tsp. ground cinnamon

Preheat oven to 375° *

Dissolve yeast cake in a little warm water in a large mixing bowl. When yeast is a milky liquid, add sugar and lukewarm milk; stir until smooth, then stir in flour. Melt shortening and blend into dough. Put dough in a bowl, cover with a cloth, and let dough rise in warm place for 1 hour; it should double in size. Turn out on floured board and roll flat to about ¼-inch thickness; spread with half of the softened butter. Mix brown sugar and cinnamon and sprinkle half over buttered dough, then roll dough like a jelly roll and slice into 1½-inch sections. Mix remaining butter with remaining brown sugar and cinnamon and scatter over surface of baking pans; put rolls in pans and let rise to double their size. * Bake for 25 to 30 minutes.

MAKES ABOUT 20

Herb Wheat Bread

1 cup scalded milk
2 Tbs. sugar
1 Tbs. salt
2 pkg. dry yeast
1 cup warm water
3 Tbs. chopped fresh parsley
2 Tbs. chopped fresh basil, or
    1 Tbs. dried

1 Tbs. chopped chives
1 tsp. dried orégano
¼ tsp. dried thyme
3½ cups unbleached flour
1 cup stone-ground whole-wheat
    flour
    butter

Preheat oven to 375° *

Put scalded milk in a bowl with sugar and salt and let cool. Empty yeast into large bowl and cover with warm water, letting yeast dissolve completely. Stir in milk mixture, herbs, 3 cups of unbleached flour and all the whole-wheat flour. Mix well and beat with a wooden spoon for about 1 minute. Let rest, then turn out on floured surface and knead, working in remaining ½ cup of unbleached flour; dough is ready when it is smooth and shiny. Rinse out bowl with warm water, butter it, and return dough, moving it so it picks up butter and is coated all over. Cover with towel and let rise in warm place.

In about 1 hour, when dough has doubled in bulk, turn out of bowl and knead briefly. Butter a shallow 1½-quart casserole (this will make 1 large loaf; butter smaller casseroles to make 2 loaves), and put dough in it. Let rise for 45 minutes, until dough swells to make rounded dome on casserole. * Bake for about 1 hour for large loaf, 50 minutes for smaller loaves. Turn off oven, take out bread, and put on rack; return to oven for 10 minutes to give bread glorious crust.

MAKES 1 LARGE OR 2 SMALL LOAVES

Parker House Rolls

Harvey D. Parker opened the Boston hotel that bore his name in 1856, after several years of running a restaurant which may have been the first to serve food at any hour instead of at fixed times for breakfast, lunch, and dinner.

1 pkg. dry yeast or 1 cake fresh yeast	1 tsp. salt
¼ cup lukewarm water	2 cups milk, scalded
4 Tbs. butter	5½ to 6 cups unbleached flour
2 Tbs. sugar	¼ lb. butter, softened

Preheat oven to 375° *

Dissolve yeast in water. Stir 4 tablespoons butter, the sugar, and salt into scalded milk. When milk has cooled to lukewarm, mix in dissolved yeast. Sift the flour and stir enough of it into milk mixture to make dough just stiff enough to handle. Butter a large bowl. Knead dough for 5 to 10 minutes on floured board, then put in buttered bowl. Melt half of softened butter and butter top of dough lightly; cover and put in a warm place to rise to double its bulk, about 2 hours. Dust your hands with flour and shape risen dough into 2½-inch balls. Flatten slightly and crease top with floured rubber spatula. Brush half of top with softened butter and fold other half over it. Set on buttered baking sheets, cover, and let rise in warm place about 45 minutes. * Brush tops with melted butter and bake for about 25 minutes.

MAKES 4 DOZEN

Buckwheat Pancakes

Wrote Mrs. Rorer: "This grain is inferior to wheat in nutritive value, containing more heat-producing food, and not half the muscle or brain-food." The source of this prejudice is unknown, and the truth is that buckwheat—aside from its wonderful flavor—is rich in B vitamins.

BASIC YEAST BATTER:

1 pkg. dry yeast, or 1 cake fresh
   yeast
2 cups warm water
1 cup buckwheat flour

1 cup unbleached flour
1 tsp. salt
1 Tbs. butter, melted
¼ tsp. baking soda

FOR SWEET CAKES:

2 Tbs. molasses

About 12 hours before cooking time, dissolve yeast in warm water in a large
bowl, then stir in both flours and salt. Cover and set in warm place. Just before
using, add melted butter and baking soda (and, if you are making sweet pancakes, the molasses). You may need to thin batter with up to ⅛ cup more warm
water. For blini and stuffed pancakes, omit molasses and add enough water to
give batter about the consistency of heavy cream. To bake, brush a large heavy
skillet with softened butter. Heat until almost smoking, then pour in 2 tablespoons of batter, to form 3 or 4 cakes, not touching. Turn when bubbles appear
on the surface and bake until lightly browned on the other side. For stuffed
pancakes, use a 6- or 8-inch skillet and fill completely with a thin layer of
batter.
      MAKES ABOUT 20 SMALL CAKES, OR 10 LARGE CAKES

Buttermilk Pancakes

2 cups sifted flour
¾ tsp. baking soda
1 tsp. salt
2 eggs, separated

2½ cups buttermilk
2 Tbs. melted butter
   grated cheese

Sift together flour and baking soda and stir in salt. Beat egg yolks, then add to
flour mixture with buttermilk and melted butter and beat until smooth. Beat
egg whites stiff enough to form peaks and fold into batter. Drop spoonfuls of
batter onto a hot griddle, making 12 pancakes; turn and brown on other side.

Cornmeal Griddle Cakes

3 cups milk
2 eggs
1 cup yellow cornmeal
½ cup all-purpose flour
1½ tsp. sugar

1 tsp. baking powder
½ tsp. salt
½ cup melted lard
   bacon fat or butter

Pour milk into a large mixing bowl and beat in eggs until well blended. Mix cornmeal, flour, sugar, baking powder, and salt in another bowl, then gradually stir this dry mixture into milk and eggs. Add melted lard and blend until a smooth batter is formed. Heat an iron griddle and brush it with bacon or other fat. Drop batter, 2 tablespoons at a time, onto hot griddle and cook until bubbles break in center and edges are slightly crusty. Turn cakes and brown for about 1 minute on other side. Hold in oven or in covered warm dish until serving.

MAKES ABOUT 16–18 SMALL CAKES

Wild Rice and Cornmeal Cakes

6 Tbs. cornmeal, white or yellow
2 cups water
1 tsp. salt
2 cups cooked wild rice

coarse salt
freshly ground black pepper
1 cup bacon fat

Dribble cornmeal into 2 cups rapidly boiling salted water. Stir constantly until smooth, then lower heat and cook, stirring occasionally. After about 10 minutes, when mixture is very thick, remove from heat and cool. Stir in cooked wild rice, salt to taste, and several turns of pepper grinder. Form into 4 large cakes or 8 smaller ones. Chill for 20 to 30 minutes. Heat bacon fat to sizzling point and fry cakes, turning after 3 or 4 minutes to brown on both sides. Egg-cream sauce makes a good accompaniment.

MAKES 4 SERVINGS

171

Chapter 12

Soups

Cold Artichoke Soup

1 pkg. (9 oz.) frozen artichokes
1 medium-size white onion, chopped
1 medium-size potato, peeled and
    diced
2 Tbs. butter

3 cups chicken stock
1 cup heavy cream
1 Tbs. mixed chopped parsley and
    fresh basil

Thaw artichokes enough to chop coarsely, then put in a heavy saucepan with onion, potato, and butter, and sauté for about 5 minutes. Add stock, cover, and simmer for 40 minutes. Purée in a blender, then refrigerate for about 3 hours. Beat in cream and serve soup in chilled bowls, garnished with chopped herbs.
MAKES 4 SERVINGS

Helen's Avocado Soup

Helen Corbitt, a transplanted Pennsylvanian, created one of Texas' great cuisines at the Neiman-Marcus Zodiac Room in Dallas; she also created this soup and gave us the recipe* during a pleasant afternoon talking about food.

4 Tbs. butter
4 Tbs. flour
2 cups milk
2 cups light cream

3 avocados
¼ tsp. ground ginger (optional)
    grated rind of 1 orange
    salt

* It appears in *Helen Corbitt's Potluck* by Helen Corbitt, Houghton-Mifflin, Boston, 1962.

172

Melt butter, stir in flour, and cook until bubbly. Off heat, add milk and cream, then cook until thickened and smooth; cool. Peel and mash avocados, reserving enough to make 1 cup of avocado cubes for garnish. Stir mashed avocado into cream sauce with ginger and grated orange rind, then spin in a blender until smooth as velvet. Add salt to taste. Chill for several hours. Serve very cold with garnish of avocado cubes.

MAKES 8 OR 10 SERVINGS

Cream of Barley Soup

2 Tbs. butter
1 carrot, finely chopped
1 medium-size onion, finely chopped
1 leek, finely chopped
2 stalks celery, finely chopped
5 cups veal, lamb, or chicken stock
½ cup uncooked pearl barley

½ tsp. dried thyme
1 tsp. salt
freshly ground pepper
1 cup thinly sliced mushrooms
lemon juice
½ cup heavy cream
2 Tbs. minced chives

Melt 1 tablespoon of butter, reserving remainder. Sauté vegetables in it for 5 or 6 minutes, stirring occasionally. Add stock, barley, and seasonings and simmer, uncovered, over low heat for 1 hour. Meanwhile melt remaining butter in skillet, add mushrooms and a sprinkling of lemon juice, and sauté until mushrooms are tender. When ready to serve, stir heavy cream into mushrooms, heat without boiling, then mix mushroom-cream into barley soup. Sprinkle with minced chives.

MAKES 6 SERVINGS

Baked Bean Soup

3 cups baked beans
4 cups water or stock
2 Tbs. minced onion
2 to 3 Tbs. finely chopped celery
1 tsp. instant coffee (optional)

4 cooked frankfurters, or ¼ cup cooked
  diced salt pork or hard sausage
2 Tbs. sherry
1 lemon, sliced
2 hard-cooked eggs, finely chopped

Divide into 3 or 4 batches beans, water or stock, onion, and celery, and spin each batch in a blender until smooth. Simmer this resulting purée over low heat for about 30 minutes, adding a little liquid only if it seems too thick. (One Vermont cook adds a teaspoon of instant coffee to give her soup a deeper color; the flavor blends to the point of mystery.) Cook the frankfurters, or fry salt pork until crisp; if using sausage cut into small dice. Add meat to soup and heat; add sherry just before ladling soup into hot dishes. Put a lemon slice in each serving and sprinkle in bits of chopped egg.

MAKES 6 SERVINGS

Black Bean Soup

1 lb. dried black beans
1 lb. veal, cubed
1 veal knucklebone
3 onions, chopped
1 lemon, quartered
4 whole cloves

¼ tsp. ground allspice
freshly ground black pepper
3 Tbs. salt
½ to 1 cup dry sherry
lemon slices

Cover beans with cold water and soak overnight. Put about 3 quarts water in a soup kettle with drained beans, veal, knucklebone, onions, lemon quarters, spices, and salt. Bring to a boil and simmer for about 5 hours, until beans are very soft. Take out meat and bones and set aside. Discard lemon and cloves. Put 2 or 3 cups of beans in a blender and spin until smooth; repeat until all beans are puréed. Return to kettle and shred veal into purée; stir in sherry gradually, according to taste. Simmer for 5 minutes. Center a lemon slice in each bowl when serving.

MAKES 8 SERVINGS

Lancaster Red Bean Soup

1 cup dried kidney beans
1 ham bone with some meat
1 leek
1 large carrot
2 onions, unpeeled
2 Tbs. bacon fat

½ cup chopped celery
1 medium-size onion, chopped
2 tomatoes, chopped (about 1 cup)
1 tsp. dried basil
Tabasco
½ cup cooked rice

Put beans in a bowl and pour over enough water to cover by about 1½ inches; soak overnight. Put ham bone, leek, carrot and whole onions in pot and add 4 quarts of water; bring to a boil and simmer for about 4 hours. In another large pot melt bacon fat and sauté celery and chopped onion. When ham stock has reduced by about one third, strain it over celery and onion. Add the soaked beans and their soaking liquid and bring to a boil; simmer for 3 hours. Add chopped tomatoes (canned will do), basil and Tabasco to taste and continue simmering for 15 minutes. Add cooked rice about 5 minutes before serving.

MAKES 6 TO 8 SERVINGS

Cantaloupe-Tomato Cold Soup

3 cups tomato juice
⅔ cup sour cream
1 small white onion, grated
1 Tbs. lemon juice
1 tsp. grated lemon rind
  salt

freshly ground white pepper
4 bacon slices
⅔ cup diced peeled cucumber
1½ to 2 cups cantaloupe balls
4 tsp. minced fresh basil
1 Tbs. minced fresh rosemary

Pour tomato juice into a mixing bowl and stir in sour cream, grated onion, lemon juice and rind; add a little salt and freshly ground pepper to taste. Cover and refrigerate for 3 to 4 hours. Meanwhile sauté bacon until crisp and crumble into small bits. Lightly mix cucumber dice and melon balls and refrigerate for 3 hours or longer. Chill soup bowls. Immediately before serving combine tomato and sour-cream mixture with cucumber and melon balls. Divide among 4 chilled soup bowls and scatter crumbled bacon over each.

MAKES 4 SERVINGS

Cold Carrot Soup

3 Tbs. butter
2 Tbs. grated onion
1 lb. carrots, ground
1 cup ground almonds
2 tsp. puréed chervil, or ½ tsp. dried
¼ tsp. grated nutmeg
  salt

Creole or cayenne pepper
2½ cups chicken broth
½ cup buttermilk
1 hard-cooked egg, minced
1½ to 2 Tbs. minced parsley

Melt butter in a saucepan and in it cook grated onion over very low heat for 1 minute. Stir in ground carrots and almonds, cover, and braise for 20 minutes. Stir in chervil, nutmeg, a little salt, a dash or two of hot pepper and the broth. Simmer for 15 minutes. Stir in buttermilk and chill. Sprinkle with chopped egg and minced parsley before serving.

MAKES 6 SERVINGS

Jerusalem Artichoke Bisque

Lately the French term *bisque* has been narrowly used in *haute cuisine* to identify creamy shellfish soups, but it really has a wider meaning and American cooks have been making vegetable bisques at least since Fannie Farmer published her first book in 1896. This recipe, and the one that follows, richly deserve to be included among the best of bisques.

½ lb. Jerusalem artichokes
1 small onion
2 Tbs. butter
2½ cups chicken broth
1 cup heavy cream
  salt

freshly ground pepper
2 Tbs. mixed chopped parsley and
  watercress
dusting of paprika

Scrub and peel the Jerusalem artichokes; peel and slice the onion. In a heavy pot melt the butter and sauté the vegetables slowly for about 5 minutes. Add the chicken broth and simmer for 30 to 40 minutes, until vegetables are soft. Put through a vegetable mill or spin in a blender for just a few seconds. Return to the pot, add cream and salt and pepper to taste. Serve with chopped greens on top and a dusting of paprika.

MAKES 4 SERVINGS

Celery–Fennel Bisque

2 Tbs. butter
1 cup finely chopped celery
1 cup finely chopped fennel
1 medium-size onion, chopped
4 cups beef stock

½ tsp. salt
¼ tsp. cayenne pepper
  sour cream
2 to 3 Tbs. minced chives

Melt butter and sauté celery, fennel, and onion for about 3 minutes. Add stock, bring to a boil, and simmer over low heat for about 4 minutes, until vegetables are soft. Put in a blender and spin for 30 seconds, then strain; or put through a food mill. Return to pan and reheat; add salt and cayenne. Divide soup among 4 soup bowls, top each with dollop of sour cream, and sprinkle with minced chives.

MAKES 4 SERVINGS

Fishy Cream of Celery Soup

American cooks traditionally have been inventive about leftovers, and many good soups have resulted from the use of a fish carcass in making stock. Keeping fish stock in the freezer is highly recommended as a base for such soups as this.

1 Tbs. butter
1 cup chopped celery
1 medium-size onion, chopped
2 cups fish or seafood stock

1½ Tbs. cornstarch
2 cups milk
  minced parsley

Melt butter in a saucepan and stir in chopped celery and onion; cook over low heat for 3 or 4 minutes. Add half of fish stock, bring to a boil, and simmer for 10 to 12 minutes. Cool. Spin in a blender until smooth. Return to saucepan with remaining stock and simmer. Stir cornstarch into ½ cup of milk until it is smooth, then blend into soup. Cook slowly until soup thickens. Off the heat add remaining milk; return to heat and cook for 5 minutes. Serve with minced parsley sprinkled over each serving.

MAKES 4 SERVINGS

Chestnut Soup

None of us likes to peel chestnuts; it's one of the world's more tortuous chores. However, this potage has made such a splendid beginning to some of our Thanksgiving feasts that it seems worth that initial effort.

1 lb. chestnuts	½ tsp. salt
vegetable oil	½ tsp. sugar
4 Tbs. butter	cayenne pepper
4½ cups chicken stock	2 egg yolks
1½ cups heavy cream	minced parsley

Preheat oven to 350°

Use a very sharp knife to make a large X on rounded side of each chestnut. Put them in a shallow pan with enough oil to coat them and shake well. Put in oven until shells and skins split; then peel off. Melt butter and sauté nuts for 4 or 5 minutes, until soft. Add some of stock and simmer for 1 minute; cool before puréeing nuts and stock in a blender. Stir purée into remaining stock, add cream, salt, sugar, and a few grains of cayenne. Simmer for a few minutes. Beat egg yolks, then add some hot soup, a little at a time; when beaten eggs are warm and very fluid, stir into soup and heat for 2 minutes without boiling. Add a dash of cayenne and sprinkle with minced parsley.

MAKES 6 SERVINGS

Chicken Soup with Matzoh Balls

1 chicken (5 to 6 lbs.) with giblets	4 celery ribs
(also feet and neck, if possible)	1 parsnip, scraped
1 Tbs. salt	1 bay leaf
1 large onion	4 parsley sprigs
2 carrots, scraped	½ tsp. dillweed

Cut up chicken, put it in a large pot, and cover with 3 quarts cold water. Sprinkle in salt and bring to a boil, then simmer, covered, skimming as necessary. In 30 minutes add vegetables and herbs, continuing to cook for 2 to 2½ hours, until chicken is tender. Strain and chill. Skim off fat, reheat, and serve with matzoh balls (or kreplach).

MATZOH BALLS:

4 eggs, separated
1 cup matzoh meal
1 tsp. salt
   freshly ground pepper

⅛ tsp. grated nutmeg
1 Tbs. minced parsley
2 Tbs. melted chicken fat

Beat egg yolks and stir in matzoh meal with 3 or 4 tablespoons of the soup, the seasonings, and chicken fat. When thoroughly mixed, fold in stiffly beaten egg whites. Chill for about 40 minutes. Wet hands to shape chilled mixture into walnut-size balls. Drop into boiling soup, cover, and simmer for about 15 minutes.

MAKES 8 SERVINGS

Sage and Pimiento Chicken Soup

¼ cup minced fresh sage
¼ cup chopped canned pimiento
2 cups diced cooked chicken
4 cups chicken stock

2 Tbs. lemon juice
salt
freshly ground pepper

Combine fresh sage, pimiento, chicken, and stock in a saucepan; add lemon juice and salt and pepper to taste. Simmer for 10 minutes.

MAKES 6 SERVINGS

Pennsylvania Chicken-Corn Soup with Noodles

This has been described as the favorite summer soup in Lancaster County and for generations the *pièce de résistance* of Sunday school picnic suppers and other outdoor gatherings.

1 chicken (5 to 6 lbs.)
4 qts. water
1 Tbs. salt
1 medium-size onion
½ tsp. saffron shreds
2 eggs

noodles (see below)
freshly ground pepper
2 pkgs. (10 oz. each) frozen corn
   kernels, thawed
¼ cup minced parsley
¼ cup minced celery leaves

Cover chicken with water, add salt and onion, and bring to a boil; cover and simmer over low heat for about 2 hours, or until tender. Remove chicken and let it cool. Skin chicken, remove meat from bones, and cut meat into small dice; return meat to broth. Stir in saffron. Beat 2 eggs and set aside.

NOODLES:

2 eggs
1½ cups flour, more or less
¼ tsp. salt

Beat eggs in a large bowl; stir in flour and ½ eggshell of water to make a stiff dough; season with salt. Knead for 10 to 15 minutes, until smooth and elastic. Roll out on floured board, making dough as thin as possible. Cut into pieces ½ inch by 1½ inches. Bring chicken broth to boil, add noodles and several turns of pepper grinder, then cook for 5 minutes. Add corn (thawed or cut from ears), return broth to boil, and simmer for 3 minutes. Stir in reserved beaten eggs, then add minced parsley and celery leaves. Test noodles, which should now be firm but not too chewy.

MAKES 10 TO 12 SERVINGS

Cream of Clam Soup

½ cup white wine
4 dozen clams, well scrubbed
1 small onion, minced
3 Tbs. chopped celery
1 Tbs. minced parsley
1 tsp. dried sage
¼ tsp. dried chervil
¼ tsp. dried thyme
¼ tsp. peppercorns
6 whole allspice

2 cups heavy cream
1 cup half-and-half
1 cup milk
¼ tsp. baking soda
1 Tbs. cornstarch
   freshly ground black pepper
   cayenne pepper
1 egg yolk
3 Tbs. dry sherry
   minced parsley

Put white wine in a large pot and add enough water to cover bottom to depth of 1 inch; add well-scrubbed clams, cover tightly, and steam for about 10 minutes, until all are open. Strain out clams, reserving liquid, and put clam meat through medium blade of meat grinder. Combine vegetables, herbs, and spices with clams and their liquid and simmer very gently for about 1 hour. Allow broth to settle, then draw off broth from sediment very carefully, and add enough water to make 1 quart. Heat cream, half-and-half and milk together; add clam broth, and stir in baking soda. Mix cornstarch with enough water to make a thin paste and stir into soup; watch carefully so that soup thickens without boiling. Season with several turns of pepper grinder and a sprinkling of cayenne. Beat egg yolk until creamy, then add some of hot soup, a little at a time, stirring continuously; when this mixture is warm stir it carefully into rest of soup and heat gently for 4 or 5 minutes without letting it boil. Add sherry when soup has thickened. Serve in heated bowls with sprinkling of parsley.

MAKES 8 TO 10 SERVINGS

Polish Cucumber and Beet Soup

This is an immigrant soup called *chłodnik* that was Americanized by Polish women of Minnesota who adapted recipes from their mothers.

1 cup finely diced, peeled cucumber
1 cup finely diced cooked beets
2 cups commercial sour cream
1 cup yoghurt
1 Tbs. finely minced fresh dill

1 Tbs. finely minced fresh scallion
2 hard-cooked eggs, minced
4 bacon slices, cooked crisp and crumbled
2 Tbs. minced parsley

Scald cucumber dice with boiling water, rinse in cold water, then chill for at least 3 hours. Chill all other ingredients, drain beets if necessary, and stir together everything except eggs, bacon, and parsley; return to refrigerator until just before serving. Stir in bacon bits and sprinkle each serving with chopped eggs and minced parsley.

MAKES 4 SERVINGS

Chicken-Squash Soup with Oysters

3 Tbs. butter
½ cup minced celery
½ cup minced onion
6 Tbs. flour
1½ cups mashed cooked squash

½ tsp. salt
freshly grated pepper
3 cups chicken stock
1 cup heavy cream
1 cup fresh oysters with juice

Melt 2 tablespoons butter and stir in celery and onion; simmer for 10 minutes. Stir in remaining butter and the flour, a little at a time, blending well with vegetables. Add mashed squash, salt and pepper. Off heat, gradually blend in stock. When perfectly smooth, return to heat and add cream, cooking until soup thickens to desired consistency. Add oysters with their liquor and continue cooking only until oysters are hot.

MAKES 6 SERVINGS

Chilled Cucumber-Yoghurt Soup

3 cucumbers
4 cups chicken stock
2 Tbs. minced scallion
½ cup chopped celery
½ tsp. dried dillweed

½ tsp. dried mint leaves
1 tsp. grated lemon rind
2 cups yoghurt
minced parsley

Peel cucumbers, cut into halves, and remove seeds; dice enough to make 3 cups. Bring chicken stock to a boil, add cucumbers, scallion, celery, dillweed, and mint, and simmer for 10 minutes. Cool; spin in a blender until smooth, or put through a food mill. Add lemon rind and stir in yoghurt. Chill for 3 to 4 hours. Sprinkle each serving with parsley.

MAKES 6 TO 8 SERVINGS

Pennsylvania Dutch Eel-Shrimp Soup

3 lbs. eel, filleted
4 Tbs. butter
cayenne pepper
salt
lemon juice
2 Tbs. minced parsley leaves
½ cup sherry
1½ cups chopped carrots
1 medium-size celery rib, chopped
2 shallots, minced
2 scallions, minced

¼ cup minced parsley stems
1 cup chopped mushrooms
½ tsp. dried thyme
½ tsp. dried basil
½ tsp. mace
freshly ground pepper
1½ qts. chicken stock
1½ lbs. raw shrimps, peeled
8 egg yolks
minced parsley

Cut filleted eel into 1½- by 2-inch pieces. Melt 2 tablespoons butter in a large saucepan, add eel, a liberal sprinkling of cayenne, about 1 teaspoon salt, 1 teaspoon lemon juice, and the minced parsley leaves. Cook over low heat for about 20 minutes, stirring frequently. Add sherry, bring to a boil, simmer for 2 minutes, and set aside. In another saucepan melt 2 tablespoons butter, stir in chopped vegetables, herbs and spices and sauté for 5 minutes. Add chicken stock and simmer for 30 minutes. Meanwhile, return eel mixture to heat, stir in shrimps, and cook for about 5 minutes, until shrimps turn color. Combine fish with vegetable broth and cook for about 3 minutes; add a few turns of pepper grinder. Beat egg yolks and stir into them a little at a time enough hot broth to raise temperature without curdling eggs; stir immediately into soup. Serve with sprinkling of minced parsley leaves.

MAKES 6 TO 8 SERVINGS

Cold Gumbo Bisque

This beautiful summer soup developed when we had in the freezer a stock made of the skeleton of a pike and about a cup of crab claws from which crab meat had been extracted. Lacking such a stock, a base for the bisque can be made by simmering for at least an hour 1 quart of chicken bouillon, ¼ cup of cider, and the remnant claws of one 13-ounce can of crab claws. But for best results save your next large fish skeleton.

1 can (13 oz.) fresh crab claws
    (remove meat and reserve)
1 fish skeleton with head (from baked
    pike or other large fish)
¼ cup cider
1 celery rib

1 medium-size onion
1 carrot, scraped
1 bay leaf
½ tsp. dried thyme
3 qts. water

Combine above ingredients in a large saucepan and simmer until liquid is reduced by about half.

GUMBO:

3 Tbs. butter
1 cup diced celery
1 cup chopped onion
¼ cup chopped green pepper
1½ cups fresh okra, tips removed, cut
    into slices

2 cups canned tomatoes, chopped
½ cup uncooked rice
    salt and pepper
    flaked crab meat

Melt butter in a large pot and cook celery, onion, and green pepper until onion is transparent; add sliced okra and chopped tomatoes and bring to a boil. Strain fish stock and stir into vegetables, then add rice. Cover the pot and simmer, stirring frequently, for about 1½ hours. Taste, adding salt and pepper only if needed. Spin about 1 cup at a time in a blender until soup is very smooth. Refrigerate overnight to meld flavors. Serve in chilled soup bowls garnished with meat reserved from crab claws.

MAKES 6 TO 8 SERVINGS

Double Mushroom Soup

Gatherers of wild mushrooms, and there are growing numbers of them in America, often combine 2 kinds in a soup when the day's hunt has been particularly good, using one variety for the purée and a rarer, fine-textured kind for the garnish. The inventive Michael Field put this trick to work with the commercially grown species that appear in supermarkets. In our kitchen, double mushroom soup is made as follows:

5 or 6 scallions, including some of
 green part, minced
3 Tbs. butter
1 Tbs. flour
2½ cups stock (chicken, turkey or
 goose)

1 lb. mushrooms
¾ cup heavy cream
 salt
 freshly ground pepper

Sauté minced scallions in butter over very low heat for about 15 minutes. Stir in flour and cook for several minutes. Remove from heat and slowly stir in stock, eliminating all lumps. Set aside 4 large mushrooms of uniform size and mince remainder very fine. Stir minced mushrooms into soup; bring to a boil, and simmer gently for 10 minutes. Put soup through a vegetable mill or strainer. Return to stove, add cream, and heat. Season to taste. Meanwhile slice reserved mushrooms very thin, and put them in a warm soup tureen or individual soup dishes. Pour in hot soup and serve.

MAKES 4 SERVINGS

Lobster Bisque

1 small live lobster (about 1¼ lbs.)
¼ lb. butter
1 large carrot, diced
2 heaping Tbs. chopped onion
½ cup white wine
6 cups fish or chicken stock
 bouquet garni

¼ cup uncooked rice
 salt
 freshly ground pepper
 cayenne
½ cup heavy cream
¼ cup brandy
 minced parsley

Cut live lobster into large pieces, reserving coral (lobster roe) and liver. Melt half of butter in a skillet and simmer carrot and onion until they begin to look golden. Add lobster with its shell and cook until it turns bright red, about 5 minutes. Add wine, boiling until liquid is reduced to half; add enough stock to cover lobster pieces and simmer for 5 minutes. Remove lobster, reserving meat, and put shells in a large saucepan; cover with wine-stock in which lobster cooked, including carrot and onion. Add remainder of fish or chicken stock, the *bouquet garni*, and the rice. Cook for 20 minutes, then remove lobster shells and herbs. Put through a food mill or spin in a blender remaining butter, the coral, liver, contents of saucepan, and reserved lobster meat, reserving 1 or 2 pieces for garnishing tureen. Strain to remove any particle of shell. Wash saucepan and return soup to it; reheat. Sprinkle with salt, freshly ground pepper, and cayenne, then stir in cream and brandy; cut reserved lobster pieces into neat slices and float in the bisque, which must be served very hot, with a sprinkling of parsley in each soup dish.

MAKES 6 TO 8 SERVINGS

Kansas Hazelnut Soup

½ lb. butter
2 carrots, peeled and chopped
2 celery ribs, chopped
1 leek, chopped
1 garlic clove, minced
1½ cups finely chopped hazelnuts
2 qts. chicken stock

2 Tbs. flour
grated nutmeg
cayenne
2 bay leaves
1 cup heavy cream
salt
freshly ground pepper

Melt ¼ pound of the butter in a saucepan and sauté chopped vegetables, minced garlic, and ⅔ cup of the hazelnuts; turn heat very low, cover, and cook for about 30 minutes. When vegetables are softened, let cool and purée in a blender using a little of the stock if necessary. Return to saucepan, sprinkle in flour, and blend thoroughly. Cook for about 2 minutes and stir in stock; season with several gratings of nutmeg, a dash of cayenne, and the bay leaves. Simmer for about 1 hour. Just before serving add cream, remaining butter in small bits, and remaining hazelnuts. Add salt and pepper to taste. Heat soup but don't let it boil.

MAKES 8 SERVINGS

Joe Tilden's San Francisco Cream of Onion Soup

A *bon vivant* famous in the Bay area at the turn of the century, Major Tilden perfected his own versions of many dishes, American and otherwise. In our kitchen, we make his creamy soup this way:

3 to 4 Tbs. butter
4 medium-size onions, sliced thin
2 cups beef broth
2 cups milk

1 tsp. dried chervil
1 tsp. dried savory
4 egg yolks, well beaten
½ cup grated Monterey Jack cheese

Melt butter in a heavy iron pot and stir in onion slices over low heat; cook slowly for at least 15 minutes, stirring often. Onions should be rich brown in color, without burning. Stir in broth and milk and add herbs. Cook for at least 5 minutes to marry flavors. Just before serving, add soup, a spoonful at a time, to beaten egg yolks; when this mixture is warm and well blended stir into soup and cook for 3 or 4 minutes to thicken. Cheese may be added just before ladling out soup, or served separately.

MAKES 4 SERVINGS

Onion Soup with Hamburger and Mozzarella

2 Tbs. butter
4 small onions, thinly sliced
½ tsp. sugar
½ lb. beef round, ground
6 cups boiling water
¼ tsp. dried orégano

¼ tsp. dried basil
½ tsp. salt
  freshly ground pepper
4 slices of rye bread
2 Tbs. corn oil
4 thin slices of mozzarella cheese

Preheat oven to 375°

Melt butter in a saucepan and sauté onion slices over low heat for about 20 minutes, stirring occasionally, until they turn brownish. Stir in sugar and let it caramelize before adding beef; continue stirring and scrape up bits from pan bottom until meat has lost its redness. Pour in boiling water, add seasonings, and simmer covered for 10 minutes. Fry bread slices quickly in sizzling oil, then put them in bottom of 4 heatproof individual casseroles. Put a large slice of cheese on top of bread, pressing down to make it adhere to bread. Pour piping hot soup into each casserole; cheese and bread will rise to surface. Put in preheated oven for 20 minutes. Finish, if preferred, by putting casseroles close to broiler heat to melt cheese.

MAKES 4 SERVINGS

East Craftsbury Pumpkin or Squash Soup

1 pumpkin or winter squash (about
    8 inches in diameter and 6 to 8
    inches high)
2 Tbs. softened butter
  coarse salt

GARNISH:

4 bacon strips, cooked crisp and
    crumbled, and
2 Tbs. grated mozzarella cheese

  freshly ground pepper
1 medium-size onion, sliced thin
¼ cup uncooked rice
4 cups chicken broth, boiling
    pinch of freshly grated nutmeg

or:
½ cup heavy cream and
1 tsp. minced chives

Preheat oven to 375°

Cut a lid out of pumpkin or squash, as if making a jack-o'-lantern, then scrape out all the seeds and fibers. Rub walls with butter, coarse salt, and grind in a few turns of pepper. Sprinkle onion slices and rice on bottom, then pour in boiling broth. Put pumpkin lid back on, put pumpkin in pan, and bake for 2 hours. Before serving, scrape some of the tender pumpkin pulp from walls into broth. Correct seasoning, add nutmeg, and serve. Garnish either with crumbled bacon and cheese on top, or with warm cream floated on top of broth, then sprinkled with chives. Be sure each serving gets a generous portion of scraped pumpkin pulp.

MAKES 4 SERVINGS

Bisque of Frozen Peas and Corn

1 pkg. (10 oz.) frozen kernel corn	1 cup chicken stock
1 pkg. (10 oz.) frozen peas	¾ cup heavy cream
1 medium-size onion, chopped	salt
2 Tbs. butter	freshly ground pepper

Cook corn and peas separately according to package directions. In 1½-quart saucepan, sauté onion in butter until soft. Put corn through a food mill, squeezing out hard skins, or spin in a blender, then strain out skins. Put peas in blender, add sautéed onion, using rubber spatula to scrape out all of butter, then spin until very smooth. Return to saucepan and stir in puréed corn, chicken stock, and cream; simmer for 3 or 4 minutes. Add salt and several turns of pepper grinder, to taste.

MAKES 6 SERVINGS

Southern Scallion Vichyssoise

Louis Diat, chef of New York's Ritz-Carlton, is said to have served the first *crème vichyssoise glacé* in 1910, having chilled the kind of leek and potato soup his mother had made and named it in honor of the fashionable French watering place. By then French-speaking Louisianans had been making "shallot porridge" for generations, combining potatoes with sautéed scallions instead of leeks. In Louisville a version similar to the one below is made with eggs instead of potatoes as a thickener. Diat's creation, at one time as popular a party dish as beef Stroganoff is now, just missed entering history as *"crème gauloise"* in 1941 when a group of chefs in America voted to change the name because they were offended by the wartime Vichy government. Too many people, however, were addicted to the original term which is now ingrained in the American language.

8 large scallions	freshly ground white pepper
1 qt. chicken stock	3 egg yolks
¼ tsp. dried tarragon	2 cups heavy cream
4 to 5 Tbs. chopped celery leaves	minced chives
salt	

Cut scallions into thin rings, including all of the green part that is fresh. Add to chicken stock with tarragon and celery leaves and simmer for 20 to 25 minutes. Taste and sprinkle in salt and white pepper as necessary. While soup cools, beat egg yolks with cream. Strain soup and combine with cream mixture in top part of double boiler; stir constantly while soup cooks until it will coat a spoon. It must not boil. Chill in refrigerator for several hours. Sprinkle each serving with minced chives.

MAKES 6 SERVINGS

Scallop Soup

2 bottles (8 oz. each) clam juice
1 Tbs. butter
½ tsp. Worcestershire sauce
½ tsp. dry mustard
1 Tbs. minced celery leaves
   salt

freshly ground white pepper
¾ lb. scallops
2 egg yolks
1 cup heavy cream
¼ cup dry white wine
   minced parsley

Put clam juice and butter in a saucepan and simmer, adding Worcestershire, mustard, celery leaves, a little salt if needed, and a turn or two of pepper grinder. When just about to boil add scallops; tiny bay scallops are in order, but sea scallops can be used—cut them into small pieces. Simmer for 3 or 4 minutes. Meanwhile beat egg yolks with cream, and stir into them a little hot broth; then stir egg mixture into the soup and continue simmering for 1 or 2 minutes more. Add wine, bring to boiling point, and serve with minced parsley sprinkled into each bowl.

MAKES 4 LARGE SERVINGS

Sweet Potato Soup

2 cups diced raw sweet potatoes
1 cup mixed chopped onions and leeks
   or shallots
½ cup chopped carrots
½ cup chopped celery
¼ cup roughly chopped parsley

2 Tbs. butter
4 cups chicken stock
½ tsp. dried tarragon
½ to ¾ cup cream
2 Tbs. finely minced parsley

In a heavy 2-quart saucepan sauté chopped vegetables in butter for 5 minutes, stirring occasionally. Add chicken stock and tarragon, bring to a boil, and simmer for about 1 hour, covered. Put through a vegetable mill, return to saucepan with cream, blend well, and season to taste. Serve sprinkled with minced parsley.

MAKES 4 TO 6 SERVINGS

Eastern Shore Terrapin Soup

4 Tbs. butter
1 Tbs. flour
2 cups milk
   salt and pepper
3 hard-cooked eggs

2 lbs. cooked terrapin meat, cubed
½ cup heavy cream
¼ cup dry sherry
   cayenne

Melt butter in a good-size saucepan and blend in flour; off heat gradually stir in milk; add salt and pepper to taste. Chop whites of hard-cooked eggs very fine; mash yolks. Stir chopped egg whites and terrapin into white sauce, add mashed yolks, and simmer for 5 minutes. Stir in cream as soup cooks for 5 minutes more. Blend in sherry; dust each bowl with cayenne before serving.

MAKES 6 SERVINGS

Jellied Watercress Soup

4 cups rich chicken or other poultry
   stock
½ tsp. unflavored gelatin, if needed
1 Tbs. Madeira
1 bunch of watercress, finely chopped

salt
freshly ground white pepper
lemon juice
lemon slices

If stock is not quite firm enough to jell, blend gelatin with Madeira and add to heated stock (otherwise simply add wine). If you choose not to chop watercress in favor of the blender, shred the sprigs coarsely and spin with 1 cup of stock for a couple of seconds, just enough to mince but not mash. Add watercress to heated stock and season with a little salt, freshly ground pepper, and lemon juice to taste. Divide among 4 soup dishes and chill until firmly set. Serve with thinly sliced lemon.

MAKES 4 SERVINGS

Zucchini Soup

4 medium-size zucchini
6 cups chicken or turkey stock
1 medium-size onion, sliced
¼ tsp. dried chervil
   salt

freshly ground pepper
½ cup young fresh or frozen peas
   fresh herbs (see below)
¼ to ½ cup sour cream

Cut washed zucchini into chunks and set aside. Heat stock in a saucepan; add onion and chervil, and a little salt and pepper depending on taste of stock.

Bring to a boil, add zucchini, and simmer for 20 minutes. Add peas, return to a boil, and simmer for 5 minutes. Put one third of soup at a time in a blender and spin for 2 or 3 seconds, retaining some of vegetable texture. If available, mince 2 to 3 tablespoons of fresh basil and tarragon; or substitute parsley and chives. Garnish soup with sour cream and sprinkling of fresh herbs.

MAKES 6 SERVINGS

Chapter 13

Vegetables

Braised Artichokes

4 medium-to-small artichokes
½ lemon
½ cup olive oil
1 large onion, finely chopped
2 garlic cloves, peeled and finely chopped
1 carrot, peeled and finely chopped

1 large tomato, peeled, seeded, and finely chopped
1 cup chicken broth
salt and freshly ground pepper
2 to 3 Tbs. mixed chopped parsley and basil

Trim the tops and stems from the artichokes, snip the thorny tips from the leaves, and remove small, tough outermost leaves. Split into halves and with a sharp knife cut out the chokes. Rub all the cut surfaces with lemon. Coat the bottom of a heavy pan with oil and arrange the artichokes in one layer, cut side up. Spoon chopped vegetables over, filling up the scooped-out centers. Pour broth around, season well with salt (about ½ teaspoon) and freshly ground pepper, and cover the pan tightly. Let simmer for about 45 minutes, or until flesh pierces easily. Remove the artichokes with a slotted spoon, and distribute chopped vegetables on top. Pour remaining oil over and sprinkle with lemon juice and a garnish of chopped parsley and basil. Serve tepid or chilled.

MAKES 4 SERVINGS

Artichokes Stuffed with Peas

4 artichokes
1 can (10½ oz.) condensed beef bouillon
1 lemon
salt and freshly ground pepper

½ cup cooked small peas
2 Tbs. minced chives
4 thin slices of mozzarella cheese
4 tsp. bread crumbs
4 thin squares of butter

190

Cut artichoke stems off evenly, so vegetables will sit nicely. Level off the tops and cut away the thorny tips of leaves. Remove small, tough outermost leaves. Cook the artichokes in boiling bouillon diluted with equal amount of water, plus the juice of 1 lemon and about ½ teaspoon salt, for about 25 minutes, or until a leaf pulls out easily. When done, remove the small leaves in the center and then with a teaspoon scoop out the fuzzy part (the choke) over the heart. Mix the peas with the chives and salt and pepper to taste, and fill each artichoke with equal amounts. Place a slice of mozzarella on top and cover with bread crumbs, then with a square of butter. Broil for 10 minutes.

MAKES 4 SERVINGS

Jerusalem Artichokes in Lemon Sauce

1 lb. Jerusalem artichokes
6 to 8 Tbs. vinegar
1 lemon
4 Tbs. butter

3 Tbs. minced parsley
salt
freshly ground white pepper

Wash and peel artichokes, dropping them into 2 quarts of water to which vinegar has been added to prevent vegetable darkening. Drain, then cook in boiling water for about 25 minutes, until soft. Meanwhile grate rind of lemon, then squeeze out all juice. Melt butter in a saucepan, stir in juice, rind, parsley, very little salt and freshly ground white pepper. Drain artichokes and serve covered with lemon sauce.

MAKES 4 SERVINGS

Barley Baked with Mushrooms and Green Pepper

½ pound mushrooms
3 to 4 Tbs. bacon fat
¼ cup chopped green pepper
1 cup uncooked barley

2 beef bouillon cubes
1 qt. boiling water
1 tsp. salt

Preheat oven to 350°

Wipe mushrooms with a damp cloth, trim tough ends of stems, and slice. Melt the fat in a flameproof 1½- to 2-quart casserole and sauté the mushrooms with the green pepper for about 5 minutes. Stir in the barley, coating it with the fat, then add bouillon cubes dissolved in the boiling water, and the salt. Bake uncovered for 1½ hours, stirring occasionally, then cover the casserole and continue baking for 30 minutes longer.

MAKES 4 SERVINGS

Green Beans Baked with Cheese

1 lb. green beans
3 Tbs. butter
2 small onions, chopped
1½ cups milk
2 eggs, beaten
1½ cups ½-inch bread cubes

½ cup grated cheese, Parmesan or
    Cheddar
½ tsp. salt
    freshly ground pepper
½ tsp. each of dried basil, orégano
    and rosemary

Preheat oven to 350°

Trim beans and cut on bias; cook in boiling salted water for about 10 minutes. Butter a 1½-quart casserole while beans are draining. Melt remaining butter and sauté chopped onions for about 4 minutes. Off the heat, add milk, beaten eggs, bread cubes, cheese, salt, and several turns of pepper grinder; add herbs and stir well before adding drained beans. Transfer to buttered casserole. Bake for 40 minutes.

MAKES 4 SERVINGS

Pueblo Cauliflower with Pumpkin Seeds

Indians of the Southwest ate a lot of pumpkin seeds even if they didn't grow cauliflower until after white men took over the territory. Nobody knows what good New Mexico cook first arrived at this combination, or adapted the idea from Mexico.

1 head of cauliflower
½ cup toasted pumpkin seeds
¼ cup blanched almonds
½ tsp. cuminseeds
3 small green canned Tabasco peppers

1 large garlic clove, minced
4 Tbs. minced parsley
1 cup chicken stock
⅓ cup grated Monterey Jack cheese

Preheat oven to 350°

Put cauliflower in boiling salted water and cook for about 20 minutes. Drain, cool, and break into flowerets. Put pumpkin seeds, almonds, and cuminseeds in a blender; spin until gritty. Remove seeds from canned green peppers, add them to contents of blender with garlic and parsley and spin long enough to make a smooth paste. Put this in a saucepan and add stock, a little at a time, while bringing mixture to a boil. Simmer for about 5 minutes and add drained cauliflower. Mix well and turn into baking dish; top with grated cheese. Bake for 10 minutes, until cheese bubbles.

MAKES 4 SERVINGS

Arizona Baked Corn

1 Tbs. lard
1 onion, minced
1 Tbs. finely chopped celery
2 Tbs. butter
2 Tbs. chili powder

2 cups tomato purée
3 cups raw tender corn cut from cobs
  salt
  freshly ground pepper
¼ cup grated Monterey Jack cheese

Preheat oven to 350°

Heat the lard and sauté the minced onion without browning; then stir in celery
and cook for 5 minutes more. Add butter and stir in chili powder, then the
tomato purée and the corn. Season to taste with salt and pepper. Pour into a
casserole, top with grated cheese and bake, covered, for 45 minutes. Remove
the cover and continue baking for 15 minutes more.

MAKES 4 SERVINGS

Bruce Young's Corn Oysters

Not everybody can count on freshly picked ears from Bruce Young's Vermont
garden, but this recipe was developed with that head start. The important
thing is to have corn as fresh as possible.

4 large ears of fresh corn
2 eggs, separated
2 Tbs. flour
½ tsp. salt
  freshly ground pepper
  fat for deep-frying

optional:
1 tsp. finely chopped green pepper
½ tsp. chopped chives

Use a very sharp knife to cut kernels from cobs. Beat egg yolks and stir in
flour, salt, several turns of pepper grinder, and green pepper and/or chives if
you choose. Stir in corn. Beat egg whites with a pinch of salt until they form
soft peaks; fold into corn batter. In two batches, drop spoonfuls of batter,
about the size of oysters, into deep fat heated to 375°. Corn oysters brown
quickly. Turn once and remove to drain on paper, and serve immediately.

MAKES 4 SERVINGS

Corn on the Cob Poached in Milk

12 ears of sweet corn
2 qts. milk
2 qts. water

melted butter
salt
freshly ground pepper

Fill a good-sized pot with milk and water, add corn that has been shucked and freed of silk, then bring to boiling point. Remove from heat, leaving corn in liquid for 10 minutes if freshly picked, otherwise about 15 minutes. Serve with plenty of melted butter, salt, and freshly ground pepper.

MAKES 6 SERVINGS

Creamed Corn and Green Peppers

4 bacon slices	½ cup heavy cream
4 ears of corn	salt
2 medium-size green peppers, or	freshly ground black pepper
1 green and 1 sweet red pepper	1 Tbs. minced parsley
3 or 4 scallions	1 canned pimiento, cut into strips
4 Tbs. butter	

Cook bacon in medium-size skillet until crisp; drain on paper towel. Meanwhile cut kernels from corn cobs with a sharp knife. Cut peppers into ¾-inch squares. Mince scallions, including some of green leaves. Pour fat from skillet and melt butter in same pan to sauté vegetables. After cooking for about 1 minute add cream and a little salt and pepper, and cover skillet. Simmer for 30 minutes, until corn is tender. (Corn that is not very fresh will be tough and take longer to cook.) When the vegetables are done, the cream should be almost absorbed. If it cooks away in finishing the corn, add a little extra cream and let it cook down; the dish should be moist but not liquid. Just before serving, crumble bacon and sprinkle over top with a scattering of minced parsley and pimiento strips.

MAKES 4 SERVINGS

Virginia Corn Pudding

2 cups corn kernels	2 eggs, beaten
1 Tbs. flour	½ cup heavy cream
½ tsp. salt	¼ cup milk
cayenne	3 Tbs. butter
grated nutmeg	2 Tbs. minced parsley

Preheat oven to 350°

Drain corn if canned. Mix corn with flour, then add salt, a little cayenne, and a few gratings of nutmeg. Stir in well-beaten eggs, cream, and milk. Butter a baking dish and melt remaining butter, stirring it into corn mixture; pour corn into baking dish and sprinkle top with parsley. Set dish in a pan of hot water and bake for about 50 minutes.

MAKES 4 SERVINGS

Corn Sautéed with Walnuts

6 ears of corn
2 Tbs. walnut oil or other oil

¼ cup ground black walnuts
salt and pepper

Cook corn until just tender, then cut kernels from cobs with a sharp knife. Heat oil in a skillet, add corn and nuts, and sauté for about 5 minutes, stirring frequently. Add salt and freshly ground pepper to taste.

MAKES 4 SERVINGS

Pennsylvania Dutch Fried Cucumbers

2 cucumbers, 7 to 8 inches long
  salt
1 cup fresh loosely packed bread
  crumbs (see preparation)
1 egg
¼ tsp. dried savory

¼ tsp. dried thyme
  salt
  freshly ground pepper
6 Tbs. corn oil
  juice of ½ lemon

Peel the cucumbers and cut into ¼-inch slices. Sprinkle with salt and let them rest for about 20 minutes, then drain and pat dry. Prepare bread crumbs by removing crusts from a couple of slices of firm white bread, tearing bread into pieces, and spinning in a blender for a moment until you have 1 cup of quite fine crumbs. Dip the cucumber slices into egg, then into the crumbs seasoned with the herbs and salt and pepper. Fry the slices gently in oil for about 15 minutes, turning once to give even color. Sprinkle with lemon juice. Serve with flank steak and sautéed mushrooms or stuffed pork tenderloin.

MAKES 4 SERVINGS

Sautéed Cucumbers

2 medium-size cucumbers
2 tsp. coarse salt
1 tsp. vinegar
3 or 4 scallions
2 Tbs. butter

1 Tbs. vegetable oil
  salt and pepper
1 Tbs. each of minced parsley and
  dill or basil
  optional: 4 Tbs. heavy cream

Peel cucumbers, split lengthwise, and scoop out seeds; split lengthwise once or twice again and cut into pieces 1 inch long. Toss in a bowl with salt and sprinkle with vinegar. Let stand for at least 30 minutes, then drain and pat dry with paper towels. Chop white part of scallions, reserve tenderest part of green leaves. Heat butter and oil and sauté chopped scallions until they begin to take on color; add dried cucumbers and mix with scallions before covering pan to cook over very low heat for 20 to 30 minutes, depending on how crunchy you like cucumbers. Taste and add salt only if needed; sprinkle with freshly ground pepper, then toss with herbs. Mince reserved green scallion leaves and toss again. For a richer dish, add heavy cream and boil down slightly to thicken.

MAKES 4 SERVINGS

Eggplant and Corn in Skillet

1 medium-size eggplant	salt
3 ears of fresh corn	freshly ground black pepper
3 Tbs. oil	3 Tbs. minced fresh herbs (parsley,
12 to 15 cherry tomatoes	chives, basil)
3 Tbs. butter	

Do not peel eggplant, but cut into ¾-inch slices, then chop into neat cubes. Cut corn kernels away from cobs. In a good-size skillet with close-fitting lid, heat oil to almost smoking. Toss in eggplant and turn several times until cubes brown on all surfaces. Lower heat and add corn kernels. Cut tomatoes into halves and add. Break butter into small pieces and scatter over top of vegetables. Sprinkle with a little salt and a few turns of pepper grinder, then cover tightly and let cook over gentle heat for about 20 minutes; shake pan from time to time. Taste to see if eggplant is cooked but still firm and if corn is tender; cook for 5 minutes more if needed. Sprinkle with minced herbs before serving.

MAKES 6 TO 8 SERVINGS

Eggplant Kentucky Style

1 medium-size eggplant, or 2 or 3
   very small ones
1 Tbs. coarse salt
6 Tbs. vegetable oil
1 large onion, sliced
2 Tbs. minced parsley
   freshly ground pepper
½ cup heavy cream

1 egg
6 slices (1-inch thick) of French
   bread or dry rolls, soaked in
   enough milk to cover
1 Tbs. butter
1 Tbs. grated Parmesan or other sharp
   dry cheese

Preheat oven to 350°

Slice eggplant into ½-inch slices and toss in a bowl with coarse salt to let sweat for about 30 minutes. Heat some of the oil in a large skillet. Pat dry pieces of eggplant and fry in several batches, not crowding, until browned on both sides, adding more oil as necessary. Remove to brown paper or paper towels and then fry onion slices until translucent. Spread half of the eggplant on the bottom of a 1½-quart casserole, cover with the onions, sprinkle with parsley and pepper, then top with rest of eggplant. Beat cream and egg together and pour over all. Finally make a layer of the soaked bread. Dot the surface with butter and cheese. Bake for 30 minutes; increase heat to 450° for last 5 minutes to brown, or slip under the broiler.

MAKES 4 SERVINGS

Fiddleheads

Ferns with tips that curl like the head of a violin have been cooked and eaten by Americans since colonial days, and there are twentieth-century devotees in places like Maryland and in Maine where communities gather together to hunt them in the spring. Of three types, the most popular is the ostrich fern, which thrives in lowlands and comes to life when spring freshets recede. Faneuil Hall Market in Boston used to be famous for its shipments of fiddleheads; today the ferns are available in cans and they can be cooked in delicious ways when frozen. They have delicate flavor when boiled (below) and are sometimes used in a soufflé, in salads with oil and vinegar dressing, or served hot with a cheese sauce.

2 lbs. fresh fiddleheads
1 cup boiling water
2 Tbs. butter

1 tsp. lemon juice
½ tsp. salt
   freshly ground pepper

Cook fiddleheads in boiling water for 10 to 15 minutes, until easily pierced with sharp-tined fork. Drain well. Toss while hot with butter, lemon juice, and seasoning to taste; serve on toast.

MAKES 6 SERVINGS

Fennel Baked with Cheese

This vegetable is a member of the celery family, but it has the flavor of anise; it was not well known in America until after gardens were planted by Italian immigrants, but it became more and more popular after World War II both in cooked dishes and in salads.

3 medium-size heads of fennel	½ tsp. salt
4 Tbs. butter	freshly ground white pepper
2 Tbs. flour	¼ cup grated Parmesan cheese
2 cups milk	2 to 3 Tbs. fresh bread crumbs

Preheat oven to 350°

Trim leaves and tough outer ribs from fennel. Boil bulbs in salted water for about 20 minutes, until they feel barely tender when tested with a fork. Drain thoroughly, then cut into ½-inch slices. Melt butter in a skillet and sauté slices over brisk heat, turning to avoid burning. When just slightly colored, stir in flour, smoothing out all lumps. Off the heat, stir in milk, a little at a time, until mixture is smooth. Return to heat and stir while sauce thickens. Add salt and 2 or 3 turns of pepper grinder. Turn into baking dish, sprinkle top with cheese, then with bread crumbs. Bake for 15 minutes to brown bread crumbs.

MAKES 4 SERVINGS

Water Street Creamed Mushrooms

There are natural caves under the business district of St. Paul, Minnesota, where French frontiersmen, down from Quebec, began growing mushrooms a century ago. This is a Minnesota version of the classic recipe.

2 lbs. cultivated mushrooms	2 Tbs. puréed chervil
4 to 5 Tbs. butter	salt
½ cup heavy cream	freshly ground white pepper
2 Tbs. flour	

Wipe mushrooms with a damp cloth and trim stems close to underside of caps. Melt butter in a large skillet and stew mushrooms, uncovered, for 10 minutes. Put cream and flour in a jar with screw cap and shake until flour is absorbed. Pour into skillet with mushrooms and cook for several minutes to thicken sauce. Add puréed chervil (which can be bought in specialty food shops). Add salt and pepper to taste.

MAKES 6 TO 8 SERVINGS

2 cups cooked grits
¼ lb. butter
2 garlic cloves, minced
1½ cups grated Cheddar cheese, plus
    ¼ cup additional (optional)

1 cup milk
4 eggs, well beaten
  salt
  freshly ground pepper

Preheat oven to 350°

Break up cold grits with a fork. Melt butter with minced garlic. Add cheese, milk and beaten eggs; stir well and combine with cold grits until mixture is very smooth. Taste and add salt if needed and a few turns of pepper grinder. Pour into buttered 2-quart casserole and bake for about 45 minutes. If you like, sprinkle the top with additional ¼ cup of grated cheese and bake for 15 minutes more.

MAKES 4 SERVINGS

1 cup diced Cornhusker or Cheddar
    cheese
1 cup diced Monterey Jack cheese
1 pkg. (10 oz.) frozen cut-up okra
2 cups halved cherry tomatoes
1 cup chopped green pepper

2 cups cream-style corn, drained
3 or 4 scallions, green part chopped,
    white part minced
1 Tbs. butter
  salt
  freshly ground black pepper

Preheat oven to 350°

Assemble cheeses and vegetables to make layers in 2-quart casserole which has been well buttered. Cover bottom with one third of halved tomatoes, okra, green pepper, and corn. Sprinkle with one third of chopped green scallion leaves, a little salt, and several turns of pepper grinder. Add a layer of one third of each cheese. Repeat each layer twice. Strew minced scallion over top layer of cheese. Bake for about 40 minutes. Serve with boiled rice.

MAKES 6 TO 8 SERVINGS

Creole Baked Parsnips

This is very good as a separate dish and really first rate when baked in the same pan with roast pork.

6 medium-size parsnips, about 2 lbs.
1½ tsp. salt
¼ tsp. grated nutmeg
3 Tbs. sugar

4 eggs, lightly beaten
½ cup chopped green pepper
4 Tbs. butter
½ cup raisins

Preheat oven to 350°

Cook parsnips in boiling salted water for 40 minutes. Plunge into cold water, peel, and cut out hard fibers at core. Mash until smooth, adding salt, nutmeg, sugar, and beaten eggs. * Meanwhile sauté chopped green pepper in butter for about 6 minutes; stir with raisins into mashed parsnips. Bake in buttered casserole (or with pork) for about 15 minutes.

MAKES 4 TO 6 SERVINGS

Potato-Carrot Pudding

3 Tbs. butter
2 cups grated potatoes
1 cup grated carrots
1 cup minced scallions or grated onion

2 tsp. salt
freshly ground pepper
2 Tbs. cream

Preheat oven to 350°

Lightly butter a 1½-quart casserole and divide remaining butter into small dollops; mix these into combined vegetables with salt, freshly ground pepper, and cream. Cover casserole and bake for about 40 minutes; remove cover and continue baking for 5 to 10 minutes, until crisp on top.

MAKES 6 TO 8 SERVINGS

Braised Potatoes and Celery

4 medium-size potatoes
4 celery stalks
¼ cup olive oil

salt
2 Tbs. lemon juice
freshly ground black pepper

Peel potatoes, cut into ½-inch slabs, and cover with water. Clean and trim celery and cut into ½-inch semicircles, reserving leaves for other use. Put oil in a skillet with celery and ½ teaspoon salt and bring to a boil; cover and simmer over low heat for about 30 minutes. Add potato slabs, lemon juice, about 1 teaspoon salt, and a few turns of pepper grinder. Continue cooking for about 30 minutes, until celery and potatoes are soft but still firm. Remove with slotted spoon. Good with Cheese-Breaded Lamb Chops (p. 221–222).

MAKES 4 SERVINGS

Hashed Brown Potatoes

Hashed brown potatoes are a classic American side dish from Maine to San Diego County, California, and there was a time when short-order cooks in roadside eating places took great pride in their mastery of the techniques necessary to serving potatoes in this omelet form. Short-cut versions are commonly listed on breakfast menus in the West, and California cooks with more ornate notions sometimes mix in chopped almonds, filberts, walnuts, or sesame seeds.

8 medium-size potatoes, or 6 large	freshly ground black pepper
6 Tbs. bacon or other fat	parsley
coarse salt	

Boil potatoes in skins until just barely done. Cool and peel. Chop roughly. Heat half of fat in a large heavy skillet. Add potatoes, press down with spatula, and fry over medium heat. Salt and pepper liberally. Turn half of potatoes over on top of other half, then add more fat to empty side of pan; when sizzling turn potatoes over onto fat. Break up, mix around, add salt and pepper, and again press down with spatula. Repeat twice more. (This way you should get all pieces of potato really brown, which is secret of good hashed browns.) After last turn let potatoes get a good solid crust. Chop some parsley. Fold one side of potatoes over other, sprinkle with parsley, and serve like an omelet.

MAKES 8 SERVINGS

Rutabaga Soufflé

Often called yellow turnips, which they are not, rutabagas (or *Brassica campestris*) frequently were the first root vegetable to be planted in newly broken soil of Plains States homesteads, and they were cooked sometimes as a substitute for potatoes, sometimes in combination with them. Scandinavian-Americans are particularly adept at various rutabaga dishes.

4 cups diced peeled rutabaga	1 Tbs. minced onion
1 tsp. salt	3 eggs, separated
1 tsp. sugar	2 Tbs. grated Colby cheese
2 Tbs. butter	1 Tbs. minced parsley
freshly ground pepper	

Preheat oven to 325°

Put diced rutabaga, salt, and sugar in a large saucepan and add enough boiling water to cover by 1 inch. Boil for 3 minutes. Cover pan and reduce heat so water boils very gently while rutabaga cooks for about 15 minutes. Drain when soft, and whip until fluffy, adding butter, several turns of pepper grinder, and minced onion. Taste and add a little salt only if needed. Beat egg yolks until lemony and stir into vegetable mixture; beat whites until stiff, then carefully fold in. Pour mixture into greased 1½-quart casserole and bake for about 55 minutes. Sprinkle with grated cheese and bake for 5 to 8 minutes more, until cheese melts. Sprinkle with parsley.

MAKES 6 TO 8 SERVINGS

Sauerkraut and Apples

This is particularly good as an accompaniment to goose, wild or domestic, or roast pork or sausages.

1 lb. sauerkraut	3 large tart apples
3 Tbs. fat, preferably goose or	2 tsp. brown sugar
chicken fat	1 tsp. caraway seeds
1 cup cider or white wine	salt
½ cup chicken stock	freshly ground pepper
1 small onion, chopped	

Preheat oven to 350°

Drain the sauerkraut and rinse slightly; 1 cup of cold water poured over is sufficient. Melt 1 tablespoon of the fat in a heavy saucepan that can go into the oven; add the sauerkraut and stir well over medium heat to coat the kraut. Pour cider and chicken stock over and leave to simmer, covered, while preparing additional ingredients. Sauté chopped onion in remaining fat. Peel and core apples and chop into ¾-inch dice. Add to onion, turn, and brown slightly. Sprinkle on 1 teaspoon of the brown sugar to glaze. Add this mixture to the sauerkraut. Mix in caraway seeds, salt and pepper to taste, and sprinkle remaining brown sugar over the top. Bake for 30 to 40 minutes.

MAKES 4 SERVINGS

Baked Spinach and Tomatoes

2 pkgs. (10 oz. each) frozen spinach,
    cooked according to directions
1 Tbs. lemon juice
¼ cup sour cream
¼ lb. fresh mushrooms
2 Tbs. butter

2 large ripe tomatoes
5 to 6 Tbs. grated Cheddar cheese
1 tsp. salt
    freshly ground black pepper
    thin slices of mozzarella cheese

Preheat oven to 375°

Sprinkle cooked spinach with lemon juice and stir in sour cream; set aside. If mushrooms are very small leave them whole; if large remove stems and quarter heads. Melt butter in a skillet and sauté mushrooms for 5 minutes, just long enough to soften. Fold into spinach. Slice tomatoes about ¼ inch thick. Put spinach-mushroom mixture in a 1½-quart casserole. Sprinkle lightly with grated cheese. Cover with layer of tomato slices, half of the salt, a few gratings of pepper, and more grated cheese. Repeat, using all of tomatoes and all of remaining grated cheese. Top with enough thinly sliced mozzarella to seal. Bake for about 30 minutes, until vegetables bubble and mozzarella is golden.

MAKES 4 TO 6 SERVINGS

Baked Squash in Cinnamon and Cream

1 medium-size butternut squash
    butter
    cinnamon

    salt
    freshly ground pepper
1¼ to 1½ cups heavy cream

Preheat oven to 350°

Split squash and scoop out seeds; peel and grate or slice very thin with vegetable peeler. Butter a 1½-quart casserole; add a layer of squash, sprinkling it with cinnamon, salt, freshly ground pepper, and cream. Repeat until all squash is used. Dot with butter and bake for 1½ hours, until all cream is absorbed and top is slightly browned.

MAKES 4 SERVINGS

Acorn Squash Stuffed with Apples and Chutney

2 medium-size acorn squash
1 cup diced tart apple

½ cup chutney (mango, apricot, or
   green tomato)
2 Tbs. butter

Preheat oven to 350°

Cut squashes into halves and scoop out fibers and seeds. Fill each half with diced apple mixed with chutney in equal quantities; top with ½ tablespoon butter. Put in a shallow pan with about ½ inch water in bottom. Bake for about 1½ hours, until squash is tender.

MAKES 4 SERVINGS

Green Tomato Stew

4 bacon strips, cut into squares
1 small onion, chopped
½ cup chopped celery
6 large green tomatoes
¾ to 1 cup grated medium-sharp
   Cheddar cheese

salt
freshly ground black pepper
¼ cup shelled peas
hot buttered toast

Sauté bacon pieces until almost crisp, then add onion and celery and cook for 3 or 4 minutes more. Slice tomatoes, add, and cook for 15 minutes. Stir in cheese (the exact amount depending on how strong cheese is), salt to taste, a few turns of pepper grinder, and the peas. Continue to cook for about 5 minutes, or until peas are just tender. Serve on buttered toast.

MAKES 6 SERVINGS

Turnips Baked with Maple Syrup

1½ lbs. white turnips
3 Tbs. butter
2 Tbs. prepared mustard
3 Tbs. maple syrup

salt
freshly ground pepper
½ cup fresh bread crumbs

Preheat oven to 400°

Peel turnips and slice about ⅛ inch thick, then drop into boiling salted water and cook for about 8 minutes. Meanwhile melt butter in 1-quart shallow oven-proof dish. Stir in mustard, using less if mustard is hot (old-fashioned mustard with whole seeds is best). Drain turnips and pat dry; toss slices in butter-mustard mixture; add maple syrup, a sprinkling of salt, and a few turns of pepper grinder. Use whole-wheat bread crumbs if possible and sprinkle them over top. Bake for 10 minutes, or set dish 8 to 10 inches from broiler heat and broil until browned.

MAKES 4 SERVINGS

Mashed Turnips with Rice

2 medium-size white turnips
¾ cup chicken stock
2 cups cooked rice

½ tsp. dried chervil
salt and pepper

Peel and dice turnips, then cook in boiling water for about 15 minutes, until tender. Drain and spin in blender with stock just long enough to remove lumps. Combine with cooked rice and chervil and add salt and freshly ground pepper to taste. Return to heat and cook over brisk heat, stirring constantly, to reduce excess liquid and blend flavors.

MAKES 4 SERVINGS

Vermont Zucchini-Potato Casserole

4 medium-size zucchini
3 medium-size new potatoes
¼ cup minced parsley
4 or 5 large fresh basil leaves, minced
2 garlic cloves, minced
4 Tbs. butter

1 cup grated Vermont Cheddar cheese
1 cup fresh bread crumbs
salt
freshly ground pepper
1 Tbs. olive oil

Preheat oven to 350°

Wash zucchini and slice ⅛ inch thick. Peel and slice potatoes as thin as possible. Mash herbs and garlic to a paste. Butter a 1½- to 2-quart casserole. Make a layer of zucchini slices, sprinkle with some cheese, bread crumbs, dots of butter, and a little of garlic-herb mixture; add a little salt and pepper. Make a layer of sliced potatoes and sprinkle with cheese, bread crumbs, garlic-herb mixture, salt, and pepper. Continue in alternate layers until all is used up, ending with last of crumbs, cheese, and butter. Sprinkle with about 3 table-spoons water and dribble olive oil over top; cover and bake for 1½ hours, removing cover after 1 hour and 10 minutes so top browns.

MAKES 6 SERVINGS

Zucchini with Black Walnuts

1 lb. zucchini
1 large onion, sliced
3 to 4 Tbs. corn oil

1 cup chopped black walnuts
¼ cup Zinfandel wine
1 Tbs. lemon juice

Clean zucchini and cut into ½-inch slices. Sauté onion in oil for about 1 minute, then add sliced zucchini and nuts and cook over low heat for 15 minutes, turning occasionally. Add wine and lemon juice, bring to a boil, and simmer for 5 minutes longer.

MAKES 4 SERVINGS

Chapter 14

Meat

Flaming Beef Collops

MARINADE:

2 onions, thinly sliced
1 garlic clove, crushed
1 cup Burgundy wine
½ cup olive oil
2 Tbs. vinegar

2 tsp. salt
   freshly ground pepper
   pinch of cayenne
¼ tsp. dried orégano
1 bay leaf, crushed

SKEWERS:

1½ lbs. beef, sirloin, or prime chuck,
    cut into 1½-inch cubes
12 mushroom caps
 1 green pepper, seeded and cut into
    1-inch squares

12 cherry tomatoes, or 3 small
    tomatoes, quartered
 1 lemon, quartered
¼ cup brandy

Mix the marinade ingredients in a bowl and steep the meat for 3 to 4 hours or overnight. Drain, but reserve the marinade. Arrange meat cubes on 4 skewers, alternating with mushroom caps, pieces of green pepper, and tomatoes. Place a lemon quarter at the end of each skewer. Broil slowly, turning often and brushing several times with reserved marinade. Warm the brandy and soak 4 cotton balls in it. Test meat for doneness by slicing into a chunk; the sirloin can be as rare as desired but the chuck should be broiled a bit longer and moistened frequently while broiling. When the meat is ready, bring skewers to the table aflame by sticking a cotton ball on the end of each one and setting alight.

MAKES 4 SERVINGS

Braised Beef California

4 bacon strips, diced
1 large onion, chopped
2 lbs. beef chuck, cut into small cubes
  flour, seasoned with salt and freshly
  ground pepper
1 cup California red table wine

1 can (8 oz.) tomatoes
1 bay leaf, crumbled
⅛ tsp. dried thyme
½ tsp. dried marjoram
1 cup pitted ripe olives, halved
2 Tbs. chopped fresh parsley

Cook bacon and onion together in a heavy flameproof casserole or Dutch oven. Remove pieces with a slotted spoon and set aside. Dredge the meat with seasoned flour. Brown in 4 separate batches in the fat in the casserole; brown on all sides, taking care not to crowd. When the last batch is done, return all the meat, bacon and onion to the casserole; add the wine, tomatoes, and seasonings. Cover and simmer gently for 2½ hours, stirring now and then and thinning with a little water if the sauce gets too thick. Five minutes before serving add the olives, and at the last sprinkle parsley over all.

MAKES 4 SERVINGS

Marinated Beef Brisket

3½ to 4 lbs. beef brisket in one piece

MARINADE:

1 cup vinegar
1 cup water
8 whole cloves
6 parsley sprigs
2 bay leaves
2 celery ribs with leaves
½ tsp. dried thyme

½ tsp. dried rosemary
½ tsp. dried basil
2 juniper berries, crushed
1 medium-size onion, sliced
2 garlic cloves, minced
1 tsp. salt

SAUCE:

1 to 2 Tbs. bacon fat
1 cup tomato purée
1½ cups beef stock
1 Tbs. brown sugar
1 Tbs. lemon juice

1 tsp. thin slivers of lemon rind
8 gingersnaps, crushed
1 Tbs. Worcestershire sauce
2 beef bouillon cubes

Preheat oven to 325°

Put meat in an earthenware dish large enough so beef lies flat and fits snugly; pour vinegar and water over and add remaining marinade ingredients. Cover and put in lowest part of refrigerator, turning twice daily for 4 days.

At least 4 hours before meal time, drain meat thoroughly and reserve marinade. Put bacon fat in a large roasting pan and sear meat on all surfaces, over high heat. * When meat is brown pour marinade over it, then stir in tomato purée, stock, brown sugar, lemon juice and rind slivers, gingersnaps, Worcestershire, and bouillon cubes; mix well. Cover and cook for about 4 hours. When meat is very tender put it on a platter to rest. Strain sauce, reheat it, and serve it on sliced meat.

MAKES 6 TO 8 SERVINGS

Best Hamburger Ever

4 large mushrooms
4 Tbs. butter
4 scallions, including tender part of
    green, chopped
2 lbs. chuck, freshly ground
1 Tbs. good strong mustard

few drops of Worcestershire sauce
1 Tbs. kosher salt
    freshly ground pepper
3 Tbs. chopped parsley
⅓ cup dry red wine

Sauté mushroom caps in 1 tablespoon of the butter. Chop the stems and add. Remove with a slotted spoon when just cooked through, about 5 minutes. In the same skillet sauté the scallions gently in remaining butter until limp and translucent. Meanwhile spread out the ground meat, smear the mustard over, add Worcestershire, and season well with salt and pepper. Add the scallions and most of the butter they were cooked in, leaving only a thin film of fat in the skillet. Toss 2 tablespoons of the parsley into the meat and mix all gently with your fingers. Divide into quarters and shape 4 large hamburgers, keeping the meat light, *never* slapping it down. Heat the skillet and sauté the hamburgers over quite high heat for about 3 minutes on each side, more if you like them well done. Remove hamburgers and pour the wine into the skillet, cooking over high heat for about 1 minute and scraping up pan juices; add mushrooms and caps to heat through. Serve hamburgers topped with mushroom caps with winey pan juices poured over and sprinkled with remaining parsley.

MAKES 4 SERVINGS

Burgers with Ham and Cheese

1½ lbs. top round or chuck, ground
4 Tbs. minced country ham or
    prosciutto

½ cup grated sharp Cheddar cheese
    salt
    freshly ground pepper

Shape ground beef lightly into 4 hamburgers and broil for 4 to 6 minutes on each side. Remove from broiler and put 1 tablespoon country ham on top of each burger; top this with even amounts of Cheddar cheese spread evenly over the ham. Return to broiler and leave for 2 minutes when cheese will have melted and browned. Very little salt is needed because of salty ham. Serve freshly ground pepper at table along with mustard and pickles and other condiments.

MAKES 4 SERVINGS

Chinatown Meat Balls

1 lb. ground beef	½ cup soy sauce
½ cup chow mein noodles	¼ cup sherry
½ cup sour milk	1 Tbs. sugar
2 Tbs. roughly chopped onion	1 tsp. grated gingerroot
2 garlic cloves	2 Tbs. vegetable oil
freshly ground pepper	

Put ground beef in mixing bowl. In a blender spin the noodles, sour milk, onion, and garlic until you have a smooth paste, then mix this into the meat, adding freshly ground pepper. Shape meat mixture into 24 small balls, and put them in a large flat pan. Mix the soy sauce, sherry, sugar, and gingerroot and pour this over the meat balls. Let them marinate for about 1 hour, using a bulb baster to saturate the meat from time to time. Drain, reserving the sauce. Heat the oil in an electric skillet and sear meat balls at 300°. Add marinating sauce and cook for about 15 minutes, turning 2 or 3 times. Serve with sauce poured over.

MAKES 4 SERVINGS

Alfred Lunt's Pot Roast

During his long acting career with his wife Lynn Fontanne, one of Alfred Lunt's favorite relaxations was cooking, often done in the kitchen of his Swedish farmhouse near Genesee Depot, Wisconsin. His recipe for pot roast, given to many friends, reflects a Scandinavian influence common in the use of native bounty in the Midwest.

3½-lb. rolled rump of beef	16 peppercorns
fat from beef	12 allspice berries
4 Tbs. cider vinegar	2 bay leaves
2 Tbs. pure Wisconsin maple syrup	3 anchovy fillets
2 medium-size onions, finely chopped	2 cups beef stock
	arrowroot starch

Have butcher trim fat from meat and include it with roast. Try out the fat in an iron pot; brown the roast on all surfaces, then drain off all but 2 tablespoons of fat. Add vinegar, maple syrup, onions, spices, and anchovies. Pour in stock, bring to a boil, and simmer over low heat for 2½ hours, until roast is tender. Thicken the broth with a teaspoon or more of arrowroot mixed with a little water.

MAKES 6 SERVINGS

West River Colonial Beef and Kidney Pie

There was no starving time in colonial Maryland, and the rich food served in the homes of lords of manors on both sides of the Chesapeake was royalist in style. Stewed beef kidneys have remained a favorite Sunday breakfast throughout the twentieth century, and more than one house along the Severn River serves claret-braised lamb or veal kidneys with buttermilk rice waffles. This pie can also be topped with baking powder biscuits.

1 beef kidney (about 1 lb.)
2 lbs. lean beef chuck, cut into 1- to
    1½-inch cubes
    flour
6 Tbs. butter
1 medium-size onion, sliced very thin
½ lb. mushrooms, sliced
1 cup boiling water

2 tsp. salt
    freshly ground pepper
1 tsp. dried rosemary, mulled
1 cup red wine
2 Tbs. flour mixed with water to make
    thin paste
1 recipe pastry (p. 349)

Preheat oven to 350°

Soak the beef kidney in salted water for 1 hour. Trim any fat from beef chuck, then dredge with flour. Melt half of butter in a heavy skillet at least 12 inches in diameter; sauté onion over low heat for about 10 minutes, then push to one side. Sear beef cubes quickly, stirring in a few at a time and turning so surfaces are evenly browned. Drain kidney, trim away fat and gristle, cut into thin slices, and pat dry with paper toweling. In a large heatproof casserole, melt remaining 3 tablespoons butter and add sliced mushrooms and kidney, stirring over low heat for about 5 minutes. Turn seared beef cubes and onion into casserole. Rinse the skillet with some of the boiling water to get all the beef and onion juices and pour into casserole. Add remaining boiling water, salt, a few turns from pepper grinder, the rosemary, and the wine. Cover, bring to a boil on top of stove, and put in preheated oven for 1 hour. Stir in flour paste to thicken sauce. Replace cover with pastry rolled out to fit top of casserole. Return to the oven for 10 minutes. Or roll out pastry and cut to size and bake separately for about 15 minutes, to place over beef and kidney pie just before serving.

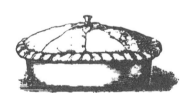

MAKES 6 SERVINGS

Beef Roast Marinated in Spiced Soy Sauce

A party dish. Serve it hot for dinner, or chill it overnight for a buffet, in which case you might like to have uniform, very thin slices cut on your friendly butcher's machine.

½ tsp. cardamom seeds
½ cup cracked black peppercorns
7-lb. eye of round, trimmed of fat
1 garlic clove, minced

1 cup soy sauce
2 Tbs. tomato catsup
¾ cup vinegar

Preheat oven to 300° *

Remove seeds from cardamom pods and measure, then grind in a mortar, or spin in a blender; combine with cracked pepper and rub well into meat on all surfaces. Stir garlic into soy sauce; add catsup and vinegar. Put roast in a bowl in which it fits snugly and over it pour spiced soy sauce. Leave in refrigerator overnight, or for 24 hours if possible. Bring to room temperature 1 hour before roasting. * Use one large piece of aluminum foil to wrap so meat juices will be contained; put on a rack in a shallow pan and roast between 2 and 3 hours, using meat thermometer to test for desired doneness. Open foil carefully and pour off juices to heat and serve separately. Increase oven heat to 450° and brown roast for about 10 minutes.

MAKES 12 SERVINGS

Beef Shank with Vegetables

1 beef shank, chopped into pieces
   about 2½ inches thick
½ cup flour
1 tsp. dried savory
1 tsp. dried rosemary
1 Tbs. salt
   freshly ground pepper
3 Tbs. bacon fat

2 celery ribs
12 allspice berries
1½ cups diced carrots
1½ cups diced turnips
2 cups peeled tiny onions
2 Tbs. softened butter
3 Tbs. port

Wash shank pieces and pat dry. Mix flour with herbs, salt, and pepper, and dredge meat pieces thoroughly; reserve remaining seasoned flour. Brown meat, a few pieces at a time, in hot bacon fat, then put in a large pot or casserole. Add enough water to cover meat by 1 inch; bring to a boil and skim the surface. Add celery and allspice, reduce heat, and cover. Let simmer very slowly for 2½ to 3 hours, until meat is tender. Remove meat pieces from pot and set liquid aside to cool until fat rises to top. When it can be easily skimmed off, remove it and strain the liquid. Return meat to the pot with liquid, add diced vegetables and onions, and cook until they are just tender, about 30 minutes. With your fingers mix 4 tablespoons of the reserved seasoned flour with the softened butter and add, in small bits, to the pot, stirring constantly over medium heat to incorporate; use just enough of the butter-flour to thicken to a gravylike consistency. Add port, correct seasoning, and simmer for another 5 minutes.

MAKES 4 SERVINGS

Short Ribs with Apricots

3 lbs. beef short ribs	6 allspice berries
5 to 6 Tbs. flour	6 cloves
1 tsp. kosher salt	¼ tsp. ground cinnamon
2 Tbs. goose fat or other flavorful shortening	1 cup dried apricots
	2 Tbs. brown sugar
1½ to 2 cups beef stock	2 Tbs. vinegar

Dredge meat with flour and salt thoroughly. Brown in hot fat in a heavy pan large enough to hold the ribs flat in one layer; don't crowd; brown only half at a time. When the ribs are crusted and brown, drain off the fat, return ribs to the pan, and cover them with the beef stock mixed with the spices. Bring to a boil on top of stove, then reduce heat so sauce barely simmers when pan is covered. Cook very slowly for 2½ hours. Add apricots, brown sugar, and vinegar, and simmer for another hour. Remove from heat and refrigerate until the fat congeals at the top and can be easily removed. Then reheat and serve.

MAKES 4 SERVINGS

Pennsylvania Short Ribs with Parsley Dumplings

2½ lbs. beef short ribs, cut up	1 Tbs. sugar
2 cups canned tomatoes	4 tsp. prepared horseradish
1½ cups water	2 Tbs. strong spicy mustard
1 Tbs. vinegar	dash of Tabasco
1 Tbs. Worcestershire sauce	1 tsp. salt
2 medium-size onions, sliced	freshly ground pepper
3 bay leaves	

For best results, make this a day ahead of serving. Put cut-up ribs in bottom of a large flat-bottomed bowl. Mix remaining ingredients and pour over meat, coating well; keep in refrigerator overnight. On the following morning, turn meat and marinade into a heavy iron pot. Cover tightly, bring to a boil, then simmer for about 2½ hours, until meat is very tender. Chill during afternoon, and skim off fat shortly before mealtime. Reheat short ribs in their sauce and serve with parsley dumplings (recipe follows).

MAKES 4 SERVINGS

Parsley Dumplings

2 cups sifted flour	nutmeg
4 tsp. baking powder	3 cloves, ground fine
1 tsp. salt	⅓ cup minced fresh parsley
thyme	1 Tbs. butter
sage	½ to 1 cup boiling water

Return sifted flour to a sifter and add baking powder, salt, a pinch each of dried thyme and ground sage, a liberal grating of nutmeg, and the cloves. Sift on top of minced parsley in a large bowl. Cut in the butter, then mix in the boiling water, using just enough to give a stiff consistency. Drop by teaspoons into short rib stew (preceding recipe), or soup, chowder or fricassee.

MAKES 4 SERVINGS

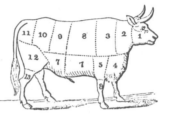

Short Ribs Ranch Style

3 lbs. short ribs of beef, or more	1 tsp. ground cuminseed
¼ cup flour seasoned with salt and pepper	½ tsp. chili powder
	1 cup chili sauce
3 to 4 Tbs. fat	1 cup red wine
½ cup chopped onion	½ cup brown sugar
½ cup chopped celery	1 cup beef consommé
½ cup chopped green pepper	salt
1 large garlic clove, minced	freshly ground pepper

Roll beef ribs in seasoned flour, then sear in hot fat in an iron pot. Add chopped vegetables and sauté for 5 minutes or so; sprinkle in cuminseed and chili powder. Add chili sauce and wine with brown sugar and stir well. Cover with consommé diluted with some water, just enough to cover, and simmer for 2½ to 3 hours, stirring from time to time and adding a little more consommé and water if sauce condenses too much; it should have the consistency of thick gravy. The dish is not done until meat is about to fall off bones. Correct seasoning, adding more salt and pepper if necessary. The final sauce should be a subtle blend of flavors with only a slight sweet-sour taste, and just fluid enough to pour over rice served as the accompaniment.

MAKES 4 SERVINGS

Club Steaks with Green Peppercorn Sauce

American cooks are apt to try the newest of anything, particularly if it has been featured as the latest rage in Paris. When the *New York Times* did a story on pickled green peppercorns and they became available here in small glass jars, there was a run on them and numerous new ways of cooking with them evolved. This recipe is one that came out of our kitchen.

4 individual club steaks, about ⅓ lb. each
2 tsp. green peppercorns, drained
3 Tbs. butter
    coarse salt
¼ cup dry red wine

¾ cup strong beef stock or leftover gravy (we used some from a beefsteak and kidney pie left over)
2 Tbs. chopped parsley

Trim steaks and melt fat to grease the bottom of a large skillet, big enough to hold the 4 steaks comfortably without crowding; otherwise use 2 skillets. Mash the peppercorns into the butter, crushing each one. Discard any extra fat from the skillet and sear the steaks in the hot fat, frying for 3 or 4 minutes on each side. Remove to a warm platter and sprinkle with coarse salt. Quickly pour the wine into the hot skillet; let it sizzle and reduce by more than half. Add the stock and continue to boil until reduced to about ⅓ cup, then swirl in the butter-peppercorn mixture. Spoon this sauce over the steaks, sprinkle on chopped parsley, and serve.

MAKES 4 SERVINGS

Donn Pierce's 50th Steak

The late Donn Pierce was a gentleman chef who developed his repertoire in many places, including a ten-year hitch in Hawaii where he adopted many an Island way with American ingredients. As we do, he believed that flank steak has the best of all beef flavors, and he left this admonishment: "Flank steaks should be treated gently. They can be completely wrecked by overcooking." It reminds one of the cowboy named Ray Pugh who was in London in 1885 with a Wild West show. When Ray ordered a rare beefsteak his waiter brought him one so rare it jerked about on the plate and Ray drew his piece and fired several shots into the flopping sirloin to kill it dead. The *Breeder's Gazette* reported to its American readers that 50 London bobbies were called to arrest Mr. Pugh who persuaded them to let him finish devouring the beef that by this time had had just enough exposure to fire.

1 flank steak, about 3 lbs.
1 cup soy sauce
½ cup sugar
½ cup sherry

1-inch piece gingerroot, peeled and finely grated
1 garlic clove, minced

Cover steak with soy sauce, sugar, sherry, gingerroot, and garlic and set aside to marinate for about 2 hours. Drain, reserving marinade for future use. Broil steak for 5 minutes; turn. Broil other side for about 3 minutes, depending on taste and thickness of meat.

MAKES 8 SERVINGS

Stuffed Marinated Flank Steak

1 flank steak, about 2 lbs.
2 medium-size tomatoes, peeled and chopped
1 medium-size onion, chopped
2 garlic cloves, minced
1 tsp. prepared mustard
1 tsp. Worcestershire sauce
½ tsp. dried thyme

1 bay leaf, crumbled
1 Tbs. minced parsley
salt
freshly ground pepper
1 cup beef stock (approximately)
1 cup dark beer (approximately)
melted butter
bread crumbs

Preheat oven to 400° *

Trim flank steak of excess fat. Mix tomatoes, onion, garlic, mustard, Worcestershire sauce, and herbs; add salt to taste and several turns of pepper grinder. Spread this mixture on side of meat; roll carefully and tie in 3 places. Put in a bowl just large enough to hold rolled steak, and pour over equal amounts of beer and stock. Marinate in refrigerator for at least 8 hours, turning several times.

Put roll and marinade in pot and simmer for about 2 hours, until meat is tender. * Lift out meat and brush with butter, then with bread crumbs. Bake in hot oven for 15 minutes to brown crumbs. Meanwhile boil down marinade to little more than 1 cup; serve as sauce for meat.

MAKES 4 TO 6 SERVINGS

Flank Steak Grillades with Orange Sauce

½ cup flour
1 Tbs. kosher salt
1 Tbs. paprika
freshly ground black pepper
1 flank steak (about 2 lbs.), cut into 4 equal pieces
3 Tbs. beef fat
½ cup chopped green pepper

1 cup chopped shallots or scallions
1 cup chopped tomatoes
½ cup orange juice
2 cups beef stock
¼ tsp. dried rosemary
¼ tsp. dried thyme
2 bay leaves

Mix flour with salt, paprika, and a dash of pepper. Pound it into the pieces of steak. Melt the fat in a heavy skillet large enough to hold the meat in one layer. Sear steaks, then add green pepper, shallots, tomatoes, orange juice, stock, and herbs. Bring to a boil, then simmer gently, covered, for 3 hours, or until meat is tender enough to cut with a spoon.

MAKES 4 SERVINGS

Pennsylvania Dutch Braised Round Steak

1 round steak, 2 lbs. or a little more
½ tsp. sugar
½ lemon
½ cup flour
1 Tbs. dry mustard
1 tsp. salt
  freshly ground pepper

4 Tbs. bacon fat
2 medium-size onions, chopped
2 large celery stalks, chopped
1 green pepper, chopped
¼ lb. mushrooms, chopped
1 cup beef stock

Preheat oven to 275°

Rub surface of steak with sugar, then squeeze a few drops of lemon over it and rub with cut side of lemon; repeat on other side. Mix flour, mustard, salt, and several grindings of pepper; sprinkle on meat and pound in, using the edge of a heavy plate or meat pounder; use as much of flour mixture as meat will absorb. Melt bacon fat in a large cast-iron pot (oval shape is best) and sear the meat over brisk heat for about 2 minutes on each side, tending carefully so flour does not burn. Lift out, letting fat drip back into pot; set meat aside. Sauté vegetables together in the same pot for 3 or 4 minutes, stirring constantly. Return meat to pot and scatter vegetables over. Pour in beef stock, cover tightly, and bring to a boil on top of stove. Then bake in low oven for 3 hours. Serve with Pennsylvania Dutch egg noodles.

MAKES 4 TO 6 SERVINGS

Southwest Round Steak

½ cup flour or masa harina
  salt
  freshly ground pepper
2½ lbs. beef round steak
2 Tbs. beef fat, oil, or lard
6 canned green chilies, chopped
1 Tbs. dried mint

1 green bird pepper, cut into strips
1 medium-size red onion, chopped
2 cups tomato juice
1 tsp. brown sugar
½ tsp. fennel seeds
½ cup dry red wine

Season the flour with salt and pepper and pound into the meat, using the edge of a plate. Heat fat in a heavy skillet or cocotte and brown meat on all sides. Add all the rest of the ingredients. Bring to a boil, then simmer, the barest burbling of liquid when covered, for 3 to 4 hours. Serve with chickpeas or grits.

MAKES 4 SERVINGS

Salisbury Steak

2 lbs. beef round, chopped	⅔ cup fresh bread crumbs
5 Tbs. onion, finely minced	freshly ground pepper
2½ Tbs. buttermilk	salt
2 Tbs. minced parsley	2 bacon slices, chopped

Bring chopped beef to room temperature. Add to it minced onion and buttermilk and mix lightly but thoroughly with hands. Mix minced parsley and bread crumbs. Shape meat into flat oval about 1¼ to 1½ inches thick, and sprinkle all surfaces evenly with parsley-crumb mixture and several turns of pepper grinder. Reserve salt. Put meat on aluminum foil or in shallow pan, and broil about 3 inches from heat for 3 minutes. Take out and salt cooked side, then turn over and press bacon bits into uncooked side; return and broil 4 inches from heat for about 5 minutes if you like it rare in the center. Season very lightly with salt on bacon side, along with a few turns of pepper grinder.

MAKES 4 TO 6 SERVINGS

East Chicago Beef Stew with Dill

4 Tbs. butter	freshly ground pepper
3 medium-size potatoes, peeled and cubed	⅔ cup beef stock, hot
	1 bay leaf
2 medium-size onions, cut into thin slices	⅓ cup dry red wine
	1 cup sour cream
2 Tbs. vegetable oil	1 Tbs. chopped fresh dill
1 lb. beef chuck, cut into ½-inch cubes	1 Tbs. chopped parsley
salt	

Preheat oven to 350°

In a large skillet melt 3 tablespoons of the butter and sauté the cubed potatoes, turning frequently, until they have turned golden brown. Remove with a slotted spoon and reserve. Add the rest of the butter and in the same pan sauté the onions until translucent and golden; remove them too, and reserve. Finally, add the oil to the skillet, increase the heat, and brown the meat cubes, a handful at a time, until nicely browned. Now arrange in a casserole first the meat, seasoning it well with salt and pepper, then the onions, then the potatoes. Pour hot beef stock over and add the bay leaf and the wine. Bake, covered, for 1 hour. Shortly before serving pour the sour cream over and top with chopped dill and parsley, mixed. Return to the oven long enough to warm through and serve from the casserole.

MAKES 4 SERVINGS

New England Boiled Dinner

3½ lbs. corned beef brisket	4 medium-size potatoes
6 turns of freshly ground pepper	½ cabbage
1 bay leaf	6 small beets, preboiled and peeled
1 parsnip	3 Tbs. horseradish
½ rutabaga	6 Tbs. sour cream
3 large carrots	5 or 6 dashes of Tabasco

Cover the corned brisket with fresh water, add pepper and bay leaf, and bring to a simmer over medium heat. Continue to simmer for a total of 4 hours. Before the last hour add the parsnip, rutabaga, carrots, and potatoes. Before the last 20 minutes add the cabbage, and before the last 10 minutes add the cooked beets. Remove the corned beef and slice thinly. Remove the vegetables with a slotted spoon and distribute around the beef slices, breaking the larger vegetables into 4 servings. Prepare accompanying sauce by mixing the horseradish, sour cream, and Tabasco together; serve sauce separately.

MAKES 4 SERVINGS (with some corned beef left over for red flannel hash)

Lamb Blanketed with Dill Sauce

1 large bunch of dill, about ¼ lb.	3 Tbs. butter
5 cups water	3 Tbs. flour
8 peppercorns	1½ Tbs. vinegar, preferably white
1½ bay leaves	wine
1 Tbs. salt	1½ tsp. sugar
3 lbs. shoulder of lamb, cut into	2 egg yolks
good-size pieces with bone left in	freshly ground black pepper
1 cup uncooked rice	

Preheat oven to 375°

Mince about 2 tablespoons of dill tips and set aside; simmer remainder in water with peppercorns and bay leaves and salt for about 20 minutes; let cool to lukewarm before adding lamb pieces to steep for 30 minutes. Bring to a boil, remove scum, and simmer for 1½ hours or a little more, until meat is tender. Meanwhile remove 2½ cups of hot broth and strain; put rice in heatproof dish, pour broth over rice, cover tightly, and bake for 20 to 25 minutes. Let the lamb cook for 10 minutes more; remove and keep warm. In a saucepan melt butter, stir in flour, and cook for 2 or 3 minutes. Stir in remaining lamb broth and add vinegar and sugar. Beat egg yolks lightly, then stir a little hot broth into them; blend this warm mixture into hot lamb sauce; add meat. Adjust seasoning. Serve on a hot platter; sprinkle with reserved minced dill with baked rice spooned around the meat.

MAKES 4 SERVINGS

Leg of Lamb, Butterflied and Barbecued

1 leg of lamb, about 6–7 lbs.	1 celery stalk with leaves
1 garlic clove	1 small bunch of parsley
1 tsp. dried rosemary	1 tarragon sprig with leaves
1 cup olive oil	

Have butcher remove bone from leg of lamb so meat opens out flat, in one piece. It will vary in thickness, giving the cook easy opportunity to serve well-done pieces to those who like them, rare pieces to others. Grill over very hot coals. Mince garlic and add with dried rosemary to oil; put this mixture in a wide, open-mouthed vessel. Find a suitable stick to use as handle and tie securely to one end the celery, parsley, and tarragon. Use this as a mop to brush meat at frequent intervals while grilling.

MAKES 8 SERVINGS

Mussel-Stuffed Spit-Roasted Lamb

3 lbs. fresh mussels	2 Tbs. minced fresh basil (purple leaf if available)
1½ cups cooked rice	
1½ cups cooked chopped spinach (10-oz. package frozen or 2 lbs. fresh)	1 tsp. minced fresh rosemary salt and pepper
1 medium-size onion or 4 scallions, finely chopped	1 leg of lamb, 6 to 7 lbs., with shin bone intact, but larger bone removed to leave pocket for stuffing
1 garlic clove, minced	
¼ cup minced parsley	

Scrub mussels under running water, then steam open over a small amount of water in a heavy pot with cover, for 2 or 3 minutes. Remove mussels from shells, mix with rice, cooked spinach, onion, garlic, herbs, salt to taste, and several turns of pepper grinder. Stuff mixture into pocket in lamb made by removal of bone; sew up, sprinkling salt and pepper over outside. Fix lamb on spit and roast close to source of heat for about 2 hours.

MAKES 8 SERVINGS

Puerto Rican Leg of Lamb

When Ponce de León abandoned his colony of Puerto Rico in 1513 to search for the fountain of youth he left behind a Spanish community that has maintained a strong gastronomical influence not only on the island but on mainland United States, especially in the lively herbal seasonings that make such dishes as this memorable dining experiences. In addition, although it must be marinated for 24 hours, this is one of the simpler ways of preparing roast lamb.

1 leg of lamb, 6 lbs. or smaller
2 large garlic cloves
1½ tsp. coarse salt

1 to 2 Tbs. dried orégano
1 tsp. freshly ground black pepper
3 Tbs. olive oil

*Preheat oven to 350°**

Use a sharp knife to score the fat side of the leg of lamb, forming a diamond pattern. The day before serving, mince garlic very fine and put in a mortar with coarse salt, orégano, pepper, and olive oil, and mix with a pestle, bearing down hard to bind ingredients into an oily paste. Spread this over all surfaces of meat. Put roast in a shallow container and cover with butcher paper, tucking edges down around meat (foil or plastic wrap may be used); put in lower part of refrigerator. Remove about 3 hours before roasting and let meat come to room temperature. * About 15 minutes before roasting, preheat oven to 350°. Put meat on a rack in a shallow roasting pan and roast for about 15 minutes per pound. Serve with lamb juices as sauce.

MAKES 8 SERVINGS

Cheese-Breaded Lamb Chops

4 lamb chops about 1 inch thick
2 lamb kidneys, halved
⅓ cup grated Parmesan cheese
1 egg, beaten

1 cup fresh bread crumbs
2 Tbs. vegetable oil
salt
freshly ground pepper

Trim excess fat from chops and wrap tail of meat around kidney halves, skewering securely. Put cheese on wax paper and press chops into it, covering all surfaces. Dip chops in beaten egg, then in crumbs. Cover bottom of skillet large enough to hold all chops flat with about ½ inch of oil; heat. Carefully place chops in hot oil and let them brown. Watch closely so they do not burn, and turn after about 4 minutes. Sprinkle top with salt and pepper and cook about 4 minutes. Turn down heat, cover skillet and cook 20 minutes. Drain and serve very hot.

MAKES 4 SERVINGS

Smithfield or Other Country Ham

Some country hams come with instructions attached but generally speaking they require little or no scrubbing while those bearing the Smithfield label should be well cleaned before cooking. It isn't necessary to bake a ham after it has been boiled, yet there is a certain festiveness in a decorated ham, and there is added flavor when the following recipe is used.

1 Smithfield ham	1 tsp. ground cloves
⅔ cup brown sugar	2 cups champagne, scuppernong or
⅛ cup prepared mustard	other white wine
1 Tbs. ground allspice	

Preheat oven to 350° *

Soak ham 24 hours if possible, no less than 12 hours, changing water at least 3 times. Scrub soaked ham in hot water with stiff brush, then wipe with a damp cloth. Put it in a kettle or boiler large enough so that it can be thoroughly covered with water. Simmer slowly 18 minutes to the pound, until the shank bone comes out easily. Skin and rub with some of the brown sugar. *Mix together remaining sugar, mustard, allspice, cloves and 1 cup champagne or other wine, and spread this paste over fatty surface of ham. Bake at 350° for 1 hour, pouring one more cup of wine into bottom of roasting pan. Cool and serve by slicing paper thin.

Ham Hocks and Greens

4 fresh pigs' knuckles	½ lb. kale, chopped
2 qts. cold water	½ lb. mustard greens, chopped
½ tsp. crushed red pepper	½ lb. turnip greens, chopped
1 tsp. salt	¼ lb. watercress, chopped
freshly ground black pepper	vinegar
½ lb. salt pork	2 hard-cooked eggs
1 lb. collards, chopped	4 scallions, minced

Put pigs' knuckles in a large pot with a cover and pour in the cold water; add crushed red pepper, salt, and a few turns of pepper grinder. Bring water to a boil, then simmer, covered, for about 30 minutes. Cut salt pork into dice, add to pot, and continue simmering under cover for about 30 minutes more, until meat is soft and beginning to fall away from bones. Add chopped greens, return to a boil, cover, and simmer for about 1 hour. Taste and add more salt and freshly ground pepper and a splash of vinegar if desired. Slice hard-cooked eggs. Use a slotted spoon to put greens and meat on a serving plate, topping with egg slices and minced scallions. Serve pot liquor in separate cups, and hot corn bread on the side.

MAKES 4 SERVINGS

Cumberland Ham Loaf

2 cups ground Tennessee country ham	freshly ground pepper
2 cups ground lean pork	1 cup milk
2 eggs, lightly beaten	¾ cup brown sugar
1 small onion, finely chopped	1 tsp. dry mustard
½ green pepper, finely chopped	¼ cup cider vinegar
½ tsp. dried chervil	3 slices of fresh pineapple
½ tsp. dried rosemary	1 Tbs. red currant jelly

Preheat oven to 375°

Combine ham, pork, eggs, chopped onion and green pepper, chervil, rosemary, a few turns of pepper grinder, and milk; mix well. Mix sugar, mustard, and vinegar and spread on bottom of a well-greased loaf pan. Trim pineapple slices, cutting out core, and press them into sugar mixture in loaf pan; fill holes with jelly. Fill pan with ham mixture. Bake for about 1½ hours; if loaf browns too fast, reduce heat to 350° and cover top of meat with greased paper. Turn upside down onto a platter to serve.

MAKES 4 SERVINGS

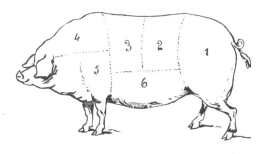

Dan Okrent's Stuffed Fresh Ham

1 fresh ham, 12 to 15 lbs., with bone in
¾ cup coarsely chopped pistachios, with some whole ones
¾ cup sultana raisins, presoaked in sherry

1 cup chopped Italian parsley
5 garlic cloves, minced
¼ cup coarse salt
  freshly ground black pepper
1 tsp. dried sage

Preheat oven to 325°

Wipe ham with damp cloth. Make stuffing by mixing pistachios, raisins, parsley, and garlic. Rub outside of ham with salt mixed with plenty of freshly ground pepper and sage, then use a sharp knife to cross-hatch fat on top of pork; stick knife into lean parts of meat, twisting and turning to open up deep holes; stuff these tightly with nut-raisin mixture. Bake for 25 minutes per pound, until interior temperature is 170°. Meanwhile make basting sauce:

⅓ cup melted butter
⅓ cup dry sherry
⅓ cup apple jelly

Blend above ingredients and baste meat frequently during the last hour of cooking.

MAKES 10–12 SERVINGS WITH LEFTOVERS

Ham Steak with Fried Apple Rings

1 center-cut thick slice of country ham
1 to 2 Tbs. applejack or hard cider
4 tart cooking apples
1 egg, well beaten
¾ cup milk

¼ tsp. salt
6 to 8 Tbs. flour
  brown sugar
  cinnamon

Trim fat from ham and render enough of it to film bottom of skillet; brown ham on both sides and pour the applejack over. Cover the skillet and cook over low heat for 30 minutes, turning several times. Core unpeeled apples and cut into horizontal slices about ⅓ inch thick. Beat together egg, milk, salt and enough flour to make a medium-thick batter. In another skillet melt enough ham or bacon fat to cover bottom about 1 inch deep and heat until almost smoking. Dip apple rings into batter and fry a few at a time until golden brown on each side. Arrange ham steak on a platter with a ring of apple slices sprinkled with brown sugar and cinnamon.

MAKES 4 SERVINGS

At Salley, South Carolina, near the South Fork of the Edisto River, travelers gather from all over on the late fall day when "Miss Chitlin Strut" is crowned, and they crowd in at long tables outdoors to devour platefuls of this tidbit that is considered a great delicacy by all kinds of people in the South. Chitlins (chitterlings) are boiled and eaten with greens, and sometimes dipped into batter and deep-fried. They are best when fresh, as they are at Salley's annual bash, but they can be bought year round cleaned and frozen.

10 lbs. chitlins, thawed
½ cup water
1 medium-size onion
2 celery ribs
3 Tbs. salt

6 whole peppercorns
2 whole garlic cloves
1 tsp. crushed red pepper
1 cup vinegar

Soak chitlins in running water and remove all bits of fat—a job that takes a couple of hours. Drain, then rinse again in fresh cold water. Put in a large pot; add ½ cup water and remaining ingredients; simmer for 3 to 4 hours, until very tender. Serve with potato salad, greens, corn bread, maybe a turnip pie made in squash or pumpkin pie style, beer and/or iced tea.

MAKES 8 SERVINGS

Creole Chitlins in Hot Sauce

10 lbs. chitlins, cooked, broth reserved
1 Tbs. butter or bacon fat
1 medium-size onion, chopped
1 medium-size green pepper, chopped
2 celery ribs, thinly sliced

1 garlic clove, minced
2 cups chitlin broth (above)
2 cups tomato sauce
¾ cup tomato paste
crushed red pepper or Tabasco
½ tsp. dried orégano

Cut cooked and drained chitlins into 1-inch pieces. Melt fat in a skillet and sauté onion, green pepper, celery, and garlic over low heat until celery is somewhat soft. Stir in reserved chitlin broth, tomato sauce, tomato paste, and as much red pepper or Tabasco as guests can stand; stir in orégano and simmer for 5 minutes. Add chitlins, cover, and continue simmering for about 1 hour.

MAKES 8 SERVINGS

Chinese-American Pork with Mushrooms

This easily prepared combination of meat and vegetables can be cooked either in a skillet or a wok, the efficient Oriental concave pan used for stir-frying. Few diners will guess that leftover pork may have been used.

3 Tbs. vegetable oil
3 or 4 scallions, finely sliced
1 garlic clove, whole
1 slice of fresh gingerroot
1 cup mushrooms cut into narrow strips, fresh or dried

3 cups julienne strips of cooked lean pork
½ tsp. salt
½ tsp. sugar
¼ cup soy sauce
¼ cup chicken stock
1 tsp. cornstarch

Heat oil and stir in scallions, the whole garlic clove, and slice of gingerroot; fry for about 1 minute. Add mushrooms (soaked for 20 minutes and drained, if you are using dried), pork, salt, sugar, soy sauce, and stock; cook for about 5 minutes. Stir in cornstarch mixed with a little water and heat mixture thoroughly. Serve on boiled rice.

MAKES 4 TO 6 SERVINGS

Roast Pork with Apples and Applejack

Some cooks in U.S. apple-growing regions began developing unique recipes flavored with applejack soon after this American version of apple brandy was first produced in New Jersey in the late seventeenth century. Pork lends itself well to variations, and this roast with apples and potatoes is a very successful main course at our house.

5-lb. pork loin roast, chops cracked
¾ cup applejack
1 Tbs. coarse salt
    freshly ground black pepper
    freshly grated nutmeg
¼ tsp. ground cloves

2 or 3 allspice berries, crushed
6 medium-size potatoes
6 large tart apples
½ cup brown sugar
¼ tsp. ground cinnamon

Preheat oven to 325° *

Marinate pork in applejack for at least 4 hours, or overnight, spooning liquid over meat several times. About 3 hours before dinner, drain and save marinade. * Rub pork on all surfaces with salt, a generous amount of freshly ground pepper, a liberal grating of nutmeg, the ground cloves, and allspice. Put the meat on a rack in a roasting pan and roast in oven for 2 hours. About 1 hour before serving, peel potatoes and boil in salted water for about 5 minutes.

Drain, cut into quarters, and pat dry. Pour off fat from roasting pork into a shallow metal pan, toss potatoes in fat, then spread them out in roasting pan and let them roast in oven beside pork. Peel and core apples, then slice. Remove pork from its pan and spread apples around bottom of pan; sprinkle them with brown sugar and cinnamon. Warm the marinade, add a little extra applejack if you choose, set it aflame, and pour over apples. Return pork to bed of apples and continue roasting for 45 minutes or more, until pork is very tender. If meat seems to be getting dry, cover with foil. Turn potatoes about 30 minutes after they begin to roast; if they are not really crisp, turn oven heat to 500°, remove tender roast and apples, and cook potatoes for about 5 minutes while pork rests.

MAKES 8 SERVINGS

Florida Pork Back Ribs

3 lbs. pork back ribs, cut into pieces	¾ cup orange juice
2 tsp. salt	½ cup water
¾ tsp. Tabasco	1 lemon, thinly sliced
½ cup finely minced onion	2 tsp. arrowroot starch

Preheat oven to 300°

Parboil meat for 15 minutes; cool. Rub salt and Tabasco into meat. Place fatty side down in skillet and cook over low heat to render some of fat; pour off all but 3 tablespoons fat. Add onion and continue cooking for 3 or 4 minutes. Transfer meat and onion to a shallow baking dish, add orange juice and water, and bake, uncovered, for 2 hours, basting frequently. Skim off fat (or drain most of juices into a shallow dish, put in freezing compartment of refrigerator, then skim when fat has congealed). Meanwhile put lemon slices on top of meat pieces and return to oven for 30 minutes. Blend the defatted juices with arrowroot by shaking together in a covered jar; mix this with meat juices in baking dish and let thicken in oven for 5 minutes more. Serve with baked tomatoes.

MAKES 4 SERVINGS

Roast Pork with Chili and Olive Sauce

3 garlic cloves, minced	2 cups tomato purée
2 tsp. salt	1 Tbs. chili powder
1 tsp. dried orégano	2 cups water
1 tsp. ground cuminseed	½ cup sliced ripe olives
3 lbs. loin of pork	½ cup raisins
4 Tbs. flour	½ cup chopped green chilies (optional)

Preheat oven to 350°

Mix garlic with salt, orégano and cuminseed, then rub over pork. Roast pork for 2 hours. Pour off all fat and return roast to oven. In a saucepan put 4 tablespoons of pork fat and stir in the flour to make a smooth paste; let it brown a bit, then stir into it the tomato purée, chili powder, water, sliced olives, raisins, and the green chilies if desired. When this is well blended, pour over roast and return to oven until internal temperature reaches 170°.

MAKES 6 SERVINGS

Rabbit with Ham and Herb Sauce

1 rabbit, about 2 lbs., cut up
2 Tbs. butter
2 Tbs. oil
1 medium-size onion, minced
1 garlic clove, minced
   rabbit liver, chopped
½ cup minced country ham or Italian-
   style ham
1 Tbs. flour

½ tsp. dried rosemary
½ tsp. dried thyme
½ tsp. grated lemon rind
1 cup chicken stock
½ to ¾ cup dry white wine
1 Tbs. chopped mint
   toast points for 4 persons
2 Tbs. minced parsley

Dry rabbit pieces with paper towels. Use skillet large enough to fit in meat side by side in one layer; melt butter in skillet and add 1 tablespoon of the oil. Brown meat, in several batches, on all surfaces; remove and keep in warm place. Add remaining oil to skillet and sauté onion and garlic for about 2 minutes. Stir in liver and minced ham, sprinkle in flour, and continue stirring over heat for about 2 minutes, sprinkling in herbs and lemon rind. Add stock and wine and stir until sauce is smooth and thickened. Now return rabbit pieces to skillet, turning pieces to cover well with sauce and regain heat. Cover skillet and simmer over very low heat for about 1½ hours, or bake in preheated 325° oven. About 15 minutes before serving stir mint into sauce. Make toast or fry bread triangles in butter. Top with rabbit pieces and their sauce, and sprinkle with parsley.

MAKES 4 SERVINGS

South St. Louis Rabbit Stew

Domestic rabbit tends to be a little bland, tasting more like chicken. Twenty-four hours, or a couple of days, in this bath gives the meat of rabbits raised as a crop a "gamey" flavor.

MARINADE:

1½ cups red wine

¾ cup wine vinegar

1 medium-size onion, coarsely
   chopped

1 carrot, cut into chunks

2 celery stalks

1 garlic clove, crushed

½ tsp. dillweed

½ tsp. mustard seeds

½ tsp. coriander berries, bruised

½ tsp. peppercorns, bruised

Mix in a large bowl, adding about ¾ cup of water, which should be enough to cover 4 pounds of rabbit cut in pieces. Turn rabbit occasionally so meat steeps evenly.

STEW:

1 rabbit, 3 to 4 lbs.

¼ lb. bacon, diced

1 Tbs. butter

½ lb. mushrooms, sliced

8 small white onions

2 Tbs. flour

1 cup beef stock

1 cup red wine

1 Tbs. minced parsley

2 carrots, sliced

1 small bay leaf

  salt

  freshly ground black pepper

In a heavy pot cook bacon and butter until bacon browns; then sauté drained rabbit pieces, browning all surfaces; stir in mushrooms and onions and sauté until onions brown. Add flour and blend into fat. Off heat, stir in stock and wine, parsley, carrots, and bay leaf. Return to heat and simmer over low heat for 2 hours, depending upon tenderness of rabbit.

MAKES 6 SERVINGS

Santa Cruz Veal Ragout with Artichokes and Tomatoes

6 Tbs. olive oil

3 lbs. veal shoulder with some bone,
   cut into 2-inch cubes

2 medium-size onions, chopped

4 garlic cloves, minced

2 bay leaves

2 tsp. dried rosemary

1 tsp. salt
   freshly ground pepper

¾ cup Pinot Chardonnay white wine

¼ cup minced parsley

2 pkgs. (9 oz. each) frozen artichokes

1 large can (28 oz.) Italian plum
   tomatoes, coarsely chopped

Heat oil in a large iron pot and brown veal on all surfaces. Stir in onions and garlic and cook for 5 minutes, scraping onions from bottom of pot. Add bay leaves, rosemary, salt, and several turns of pepper grinder; pour in wine. Cover tightly and simmer over very low heat for 1 hour. Add parsley, artichokes, and tomatoes and cook for 30 minutes or more, until veal is very tender.

MAKES 6 SERVINGS

Roast Veal with Kidney

In many parts of the country, especially St. Louis which began as a French outpost, then became American, and later acquired a very strong German character during the nineteenth century, a kidney-veal roast was a favorite of housewives who sometimes flavored it with nasturtium seeds.

4 to 5 lbs. veal roast with veal kidney	1¾ cups cider or white wine
1 large onion, unpeeled	2 carrots, peeled and sliced
12 to 15 canned anchovy fillets	2 medium-size onions, chopped
2 Tbs. butter or oil	salt
1 garlic clove, minced	freshly ground black pepper
¼ cup applejack	chopped parsley

Preheat oven to 375°

Spread out meat for stuffing. Put unpeeled onion in oven to bake for about 1 hour, until skin darkens and inside is soft. Place kidney on veal and distribute drained anchovies evenly; roll up and tie. Heat butter or oil in a large iron pot and in it brown all surfaces of roast; stir garlic into hot fat. Add applejack and cider or wine, and stir in sliced carrots and chopped onions. Cover pot and bake in oven for 2 to 2½ hours. After 1 hour reduce heat to 350° and add salt and pepper to taste. If charred onion is soft remove skin, mash soft interior, and add to veal and vegetable juices in pot. Continue cooking until meat can be cut with a spoon. Sprinkle finished roast with chopped parsley.

MAKES 8 SERVINGS

Veal Scallops with Crab Meat

It is not uncommon to find various cuts of veal served in combination with seafood in the Middle West. Veal steaks, encased in egg, minced mushrooms, and cornflake crumbs, sometimes go to the table with asparagus spears and a sherry-flavored lobster sauce. Veal chops are served with crab and asparagus. None is better than this way with thinly pounded scallops.

8 veal scallops	1 tsp. dried marjoram
flour	3 Tbs. vegetable oil
1½ tsp. salt	2 to 3 Tbs. minced parsley
freshly ground pepper	

Have veal pounded thin. Dust each piece thoroughly in seasoned flour, then sauté quickly over brisk heat for about 3 minutes to a side. Cover with crab-meat sauce and sprinkle with parsley.

CRAB-MEAT SAUCE:

3 Tbs. butter
2 Tbs. flour
1½ cups milk
1 tsp. salt
　cayenne pepper

½ to ¾ cup crab meat
1 tsp. lemon juice
2 Tbs. sherry
1 egg yolk

Melt butter and stir in flour until smooth, then gradually add milk off heat, stirring constantly to make a well-blended mixture; return to heat to thicken, adding salt and a dash of cayenne. Flake crab meat and stir into sauce. Just before serving add lemon juice, sherry, and egg yolk, stirring over low heat for about 1 minute.

MAKES 4 SERVINGS

Veal Collops with Cucumber Sauce

Earlier American cooks seem to have found many delicious ways to serve cooked cucumbers, as a single hot vegetable or as an integral accompaniment to meat or fish. One rule of thumb asserted cucumbers must be served "under meat and over fish." An affinity for veal was established long ago by New England cooks, and this recipe breaks the rule by topping the meat with cucumbers.

2 cucumbers, 6 to 7 inches long,
　peeled and thinly sliced
8 or 9 medium-size shallots
3 Tbs. butter

½ to ¾ cup sour cream
½ tsp. dried thyme
　salt
　freshly ground pepper

Cover sliced cucumbers with boiling water and parboil for 10 minutes; drain. Peel and slice shallots. Melt butter in a saucepan and sauté shallots over low heat for 10 minutes. Stir in sour cream, thyme, and salt and pepper to taste. Simmer over lowest possible heat for 10 minutes.

1½ lbs. leg of veal cut and pounded
　into thin collops about 2 by 3
　inches

3 Tbs. butter
1 tsp. salt
　freshly ground black pepper

Have veal at room temperature. Be sure no fat or gristle remains. Melt butter and sauté collops for about 4 minutes to each side. Season, and serve topped by cucumber sauce.

MAKES 6 SERVINGS

Baked Veal Stew with Chow Mein Noodles

Poet Louis Untermeyer and his wife for years had an Ohio farmwife named Clara as a cook. "Though she was never out of her county," Untermeyer once wrote, "Clara has learned to cook in any language; the more exotic, the more brilliant." Clara's wine-baked veal is another example of Americanism in the kitchen—a touch of *blanquette de veau*, a little *zöldpaprika*, and crisp so-called chow mein noodles invented by Chinese Americans. The combination of contrasting flavors and textures is unusual and a delight to the palate.

1½ lbs. lean veal (leg preferred), trimmed and cut into 1½-inch cubes
¼ lb. butter
1 Tbs. flour
1½ cups milk

¼ cup chopped green pepper
salt
freshly ground pepper
5 to 6 Tbs. California white wine
1 can (3 oz.) chow mein noodles

Preheat oven to 350°

Make sure veal cubes are free of gristle. In a heavy skillet melt butter, add meat, and cover tightly to steam over very low heat for about 20 minutes. After 10 minutes turn meat pieces so all sides are exposed to butter; increase heat, remove cover, and let moisture evaporate; then fry the veal, stirring frequently, so cubes brown lightly on all surfaces. Add flour and stir constantly, letting it brown lightly and scraping from bottom. Take pan from heat and continue stirring and scraping while adding milk. Return to heat and cook slowly until sauce thickens and is smooth. Stir in green pepper, ¼ teaspoon or a little more of salt, and a few turns of pepper grinder. Pour into a 1½-quart casserole, cover with foil, and bake for 45 minutes. Remove foil, add wine a little at a time, and spread noodles over top. Increase heat to 500° and leave dish in oven for 5 minutes to turn noodles very crisp, being careful not to burn them or boil sauce hard. Serve very hot.

MAKES 3 TO 4 SERVINGS

Venison in Cabbage Leaves

3 cups chopped or coarsely ground cooked venison (about 1 lb.)
2 cups cooked wild rice
2 to 3 Tbs. butter
salt
freshly ground black pepper

1 small head of cabbage
2 medium-size onions, chopped
3 to 4 cups meat stock (venison, chicken, beef, etc.)
1 Tbs. cornstarch
1 to 2 tsp. guava jelly

Preheat oven to 350°

In a large mixing bowl stir together meat and rice; add butter in small bits, season and set aside while preparing cabbage. Wash cabbage, remove and save outer leaves. Cook cabbage in boiling water for 10 to 12 minutes; drain and cool sufficiently to handle. Carefully peel off 8 perfect leaves without tearing. Chop reserved outer leaves, mix with chopped onions, season well with salt and pepper, and spread on bottom of shallow casserole large enough to hold 8 stuffed leaves snugly; pour over this bed 1 cup of stock. Put about 3 tablespoons of meat-rice mixture on each of prepared cabbage leaves, roll up, and place, flap side up, on vegetable bed in casserole. Cut aluminum foil to cover and seal cabbage rolls, pushing foil down around edges of casserole. Cover and bake for 1 hour, checking liquid and replenishing as necessary. Dissolve the cornstarch in ⅛ cup of water and blend into remaining stock to make a sauce; add guava jelly to taste; serve with the stuffed leaves.

MAKES 8 SERVINGS

Roast Loin of Venison

8-chop loin of venison, about 6 lbs.
2½ cups California Cabernet
    Sauvignon or other good red
    wine
1½ cups water
2 bay leaves
2 Tbs. minced fresh thyme, or
    ½ tsp. dried thyme

8 juniper berries, crushed
2 onions, sliced
2 garlic cloves, minced
    beef suet or fat to cover top of
    roast
4 or 5 bacon slices

Preheat oven to 450° ✱

Have butcher partially separate chops, leaving enough uncut to hold roast in one piece when tied. Combine wine, water, bay leaves, thyme, juniper, onions, and garlic; pour over meat and marinate under refrigeration for about 36 hours, but baste meat often during this period.

   ✱ Bring to room temperature; drain marinade and put venison in a roasting pan, spreading beef suet or fat and bacon slices on meaty top. Roast for about 18 minutes. Reduce heat to 350° and roast for about 15 minutes per pound, or until interior temperature reaches 140°. Remove from oven and let venison rest for about 10 minutes before carving. Serve with wild rice and baked tomatoes seasoned with fresh herbs.

Beef Liver Hilo Style

The Hawaiian way of combining livers, spices, soy sauce, and water chestnuts, then broiling them with bacon, is a favorite cocktail nibble in most of the fifty states. The version below is a meal, very rich and moist and not for those who like liver cooked dry.

1 lb. beef liver, in 4 slices	1 tsp. minced lemon peel
½ cup soy sauce	1 can (6 oz.) water chestnuts, sliced
½ cup peanut oil	4 bacon slices, cut into squares
½ cup applejack	4 Tbs. butter
2 Tbs. sugar	½ cup bread crumbs
¼ tsp. ground ginger	2 bananas, sliced

Preheat oven to 350° ❋

Wipe liver with a damp cloth. Stir together soy sauce, oil, applejack, sugar, ginger, and lemon peel. Marinate meat and sliced water chestnuts in the mixture for 2 hours. About 30 minutes before serving time, sauté bacon pieces, then drain on paper towel. ❋ In a saucepan melt most of butter and stir in bread crumbs. Butter a shallow baking dish lightly. Drain liver and water chestnuts thoroughly and put in a buttered baking dish; arrange banana slices on top and spread with buttered crumbs. Bake for 20 minutes.

MAKES 4 SERVINGS

Creole Calf's Brains

3 pairs calf's brains	2 to 3 Tbs. minced celery
1 Tbs. lemon juice	2 Tbs. minced parsley
salt	½ tsp. dried savory
4 Tbs. butter	½ cup heavy cream
½ lb. mushrooms, sliced	2 Tbs. Madeira
2 Tbs. minced shallots or scallions	freshly ground pepper
2 Tbs. flour	bread crumbs
1 cup chicken stock	

Preheat oven to 425° ❋

Soak brains in cold water for 30 minutes, changing water 2 or 3 times; drain. Put in a saucepan and cover with boiling water; add lemon juice and about 1 teaspoon salt. Simmer gently for 20 minutes. Drain and plunge into cold water. Meanwhile melt 2 tablespoons butter and sauté mushrooms and shallots for 5 minutes. Stir in flour, mixing well, and cook for another minute or two. Off heat pour in chicken stock, minced celery, and herbs, then return to heat and cook slowly, stirring constantly, until sauce is thick and smooth. Add the cream and Madeira, blend well, and season to taste with salt and pepper. ° Now remove the membrane from the cooled brains and slice them about ⅓ inch thick. Place them in a shallow casserole, pour the sauce over, and sprinkle bread crumbs on top, dribbling over them the remaining 2 tablespoons of butter. Bake the casserole just until it bubbles and has browned on top, about 5 minutes.

MAKES 4 SERVINGS

Beef Liver in Herbed Wine

1½ lbs. beef liver, in ½-inch slices	3 Tbs. dry sherry
3 Tbs. butter	2 Tbs. port
¾ tsp. dried rosemary	salt
½ tsp. dried sage	freshly ground pepper
2 large scallions, minced	

Cut sliced liver into rectangles 1 by 1½ inches. Melt butter in a skillet and stir in herbs and scallions; add liver pieces and sauté, turning to brown evenly on both sides. Add sherry and port over brisk heat to bring wine to just below boiling point. Season to taste. Serve immediately over hot rice.

MAKES 6 SERVINGS

Calf's Liver with Juniper-Buttermilk Sauce

4 slices of calf's liver	8 juniper berries, crushed
1½ cups buttermilk	1 Tbs. flour
¼ cup butter	1 tsp. salt
¼ cup bouillon	freshly ground pepper
½ cup fresh bread crumbs	

An hour before cooking time pour buttermilk over liver slices and set aside. Drain when liver has soaked for at least 1 hour; reserve buttermilk, which will have absorbed some of meat juices, and warm over very low heat. Melt 1 tablespoon butter in a skillet and brown liver carefully over moderate to high heat, then turn very low and cook for 10 minutes, basting with bouillon. In a small pan melt remaining butter and stir in crumbs and well-crushed juniper berries; stir in flour, salt, and several turns of pepper grinder. When flour has absorbed butter smoothly, remove pan from heat and stir in warmed buttermilk. Pour over liver slices and cook for 4 to 5 minutes, until sauce thickens slightly. Serve with sautéed mushrooms.

MAKES 4 SERVINGS

Carolina Low Country Oxtail Stew

2 lbs. oxtail, in 2-inch pieces
1 Tbs. butter
¼ lb. piece of bacon, cubed
16 small white onions
½ lb. mushrooms, sliced
2 to 3 Tbs. flour
2 cups boiling water
¾ cup Madeira wine
1 stalk celery, coarsely chopped

½ bay leaf
½ tsp. dried thyme
  salt
  freshly ground pepper
2 small white turnips
4 small carrots, quartered
1 Tbs. minced parsley
  fried hominy

In a large heavy pot put oxtail pieces, butter, bacon cubes, onions, and mushrooms. Stir constantly over brisk heat until meats are seared and vegetables take on color. Stir in flour and let it brown while stirring. Stir in boiling water and wine, then add celery, bay leaf, thyme, a little salt, and several turns of pepper grinder. Cover and simmer over low heat for 3 hours or more, until meat is tender. Meanwhile peel and quarter turnips and boil in salted water until tender. When oxtail has cooked for 2½ hours, add carrots; when they are tender add drained turnips and parsley. Serve on fried squares of cold cooked hominy grits.

MAKES 4 SERVINGS

Walnut-Stuffed Meat Loaf

1¼ lbs. lean beef, ground
½ lb. veal, ground
¼ lb. lean pork, ground
⅓ cup milk
1 egg

2 Tbs. minced shallots or scallions
1½ tsp. salt
  freshly ground pepper
½ tsp. dried sage leaves
1 cup beef bouillon

STUFFING:

2 cups fresh bread crumbs
2 Tbs. minced shallots or scallions
1 tsp. salt
  freshly ground pepper
1½ cups very finely chopped celery

¼ tsp. dried thyme
¼ tsp. dried basil
½ cup red wine
¾ cup chopped walnuts (black
  preferred)

Preheat oven to 375°

Mix meats in a large bowl if butcher has not ground them together; be sure they are well blended. Beat together milk and egg and stir into meat with shallots and seasonings. Reserve bouillon. Combine stuffing ingredients. Turn meat mixture out on wax paper and roll into a flat rectangle, about 12 by 15 inches and ¾ inch thick. Spoon stuffing along widest edge of meat, shaping into a smooth roll. Lift wax paper and roll meat over stuffing, joining two edges of meat rectangle and covering stuffing. Carefully slide rolled meat loaf off wax paper and into a shallow baking pan. Pour about ¼ cup bouillon over length of loaf. Bake for 1 hour, basting frequently with bouillon.

MAKES 6 SERVINGS

Three-Meat Paprika Stew

1 Tbs. butter
2 large onions, sliced thin
1 tsp. salt
1 Tbs. cider vinegar
½ lb. each of beef round, lean lamb, and pork shoulder, cut into strips ½ inch by 2 inches
1½ cups beef stock
1 medium-size carrot, cut into matchstick strips

1 leek, cut into matchstick strips
1 medium-size white turnip, cut into matchstick strips
3 medium-size potatoes, diced
1 Tbs. rose paprika
½ tsp. Worcestershire sauce
2 Tbs. red horseradish sauce
¼ tsp. dried marjoram
1 egg yolk
¼ tsp. cornstarch

Paprika

Melt butter in a large pot and sauté onions over low heat for about 5 minutes. Stir in salt, vinegar, and beef strips, then cover tightly and simmer over very low heat for 25 minutes, stirring occasionally. Add lamb and pork strips and beef stock, cover again, and simmer for about 1 hour. Add vegetables, paprika, Worcestershire, horseradish, and marjoram, and continue simmering for about 30 minutes, or until everything is tender. Remove pot from heat; stir egg yolk and cornstarch in a small bowl, adding some of liquid from stew little by little. Stir this mixture into stew and return to heat, letting stew liquid thicken for about 5 minutes. Do not let it boil.

MAKES 4 SERVINGS

Dried Beef and Sweetbreads

1 pair sweetbreads
lemon juice
3 oz. dried beef
½ lb. mushrooms
2 Tbs. butter
2 Tbs. flour

1 cup milk, warmed
1 tsp. chopped fresh rosemary, or ½ tsp. dried
salt
freshly ground pepper
lemon

Plunge sweetbreads into cold water and soak for 20 to 30 minutes. Run cold water between leaves of dried beef. Parboil sweetbreads in 1 quart of water with a few drops of lemon juice for 20 minutes. Cool, and remove membrane;

cut into 1-inch pieces. Slice the mushrooms; sauté in butter for 5 or 6 minutes, turning occasionally. Sprinkle in the flour and blend well. Then slowly add the milk, stirring constantly until the sauce thickens. Add the diced sweetbreads, dried beef, and rosemary. Season to taste with a little salt, freshly ground pepper, and a few drops of lemon.

MAKES 4 SERVINGS

Pickled Tongue with Sweet-Sour Sauce

1 pickled tongue, 4 lbs.	1 tsp. salt
1 large onion, sliced	6 peppercorns
2 cups canned tomatoes, coarsely chopped	4 whole cloves
2 lemons	1 garlic clove
5 Tbs. brown sugar	½ cup raisins

Put tongue in a heavy pot large enough to let it straighten out and deep enough so tongue can be immersed in water; pour enough boiling water over it to cover well, cover pot, and let water bubble for 10 minutes. Drain and remove hard skin. Put onion, tomatoes, juice of 1 lemon, and 4 tablespoons brown sugar into same pot, mixing well. Lay peeled tongue on top and cover with boiling water, cover pot, and simmer very gently for 1 hour. Add salt, peppercorns, cloves, and garlic, and continue gentle simmering for about 3 hours, turning tongue occasionally. In a saucepan cook raisins for a minute or so with vegetables strained from tongue broth. Add remaining lemon juice and sugar to make sauce sweet and sour to suit taste. Slice tongue and put on platter; cover with sweet and sour sauce. Serve on hot plates with Rutabaga Soufflé (pp. 201–202).

MAKES 6 TO 8 SERVINGS

Delicious Tripe Croquettes

1 lb. boiled tripe	1 tsp. lemon juice
1 egg	1 tsp. salt
½ cup bread crumbs	freshly ground black pepper
2 tsp. grated onion	

Grind tripe with finest blade of a food grinder and mix with other ingredients. Grease bottom of skillet with bacon fat or butter. Shape mixture into flat patties and sauté over medium heat until well browned.

MAKES 4 SERVINGS

Chapter 15

Poultry

Capon Breasts with Orange and Black-Walnut Sauce

breast of 5- to 6-lb. capon, or
   2 whole chicken breasts
3 Tbs. butter
   salt
   freshly ground pepper
4 thin slices of country ham or
   prosciutto

2 Tbs. flour
2 oranges, squeezed to make ¾ cup
   juice
¾ cup chicken stock
   julienne strips of orange peel
½ cup chopped black walnuts

Remove breast meat from bones in 4 uniform pieces. Melt butter in a large skillet, skim off foam, then sauté breast pieces in hot butter, being careful to keep butter from turning brown; use tongs to lift pieces when turning them, and cook on all surfaces, basting regularly with butter, for 12 to 15 minutes. Sprinkle all sides with salt and several turns of pepper grinder. Remove meat from skillet and keep warm. Put ham slices in skillet and warm them in remaining butter, then lift them out, letting butter drip off, and put 1 slice on each piece of breast. Stir flour into skillet to absorb remaining butter and cook for about 2 minutes before stirring in orange juice, a little at a time; stir in stock. When thickened add orange-peel strips and nuts. Spoon sauce over ham and breast pieces.

MAKES 4 SERVINGS

239

Capon with Wild Rice and Pecan Stuffing

1 capon, 6 to 7 lbs.
1 cup cooked wild rice
1 cup pecans, finely chopped
1 small onion, grated
1 egg, well beaten
1 tsp. salt
  freshly ground pepper

2 to 3 Tbs. melted chicken fat or
  butter
4 Tbs. chopped parsley
½ tsp. dried savory
4 Tbs. softened butter
1 cup heavy cream, scalded
2 to 3 tsp. flour

Preheat oven to 425°❋

Remove fat from inside capon and render. Mix cooked wild rice with pecans, grated onion, beaten egg, salt, a little freshly ground pepper, and enough chicken fat or butter to moisten; then stir in the herbs. ❋ Pack the stuffing loosely into the bird, sew up, and truss. Rub all over generously with softened butter, then place on a rack in roasting pan and roast for 15 minutes; reduce heat to 350° and continue roasting for another 1½ hours, basting at intervals with scalded cream. When done, remove bird and make gravy: sprinkle flour in bottom of roasting pan, scraping up all browned bits, and blend in any remaining cream and a little water if too thick. Serve in separate gravy boat.

MAKES 6 SERVINGS

Roast Capon with Pennsylvania Dutch Stuffing

1 capon, 6½ lbs., with giblets
  salt
3 medium-size potatoes
2 onions, chopped
½ cup chopped celery
2 to 3 Tbs. cider or white wine
1 egg, beaten

  freshly ground pepper
½ tsp. dried savory
½ tsp. dried thyme
½ tsp. dried sage
1 cup cubed stale bread
¼ cup melted butter

Preheat oven to 375°❋

Rinse capon inside and out and pat dry before rubbing salt into cavity and over skin; remove fat deposits around opening of cavity and render. Scrub potatoes and boil in salted water for 40 to 45 minutes, or until easily pierced by fork; cool. Cover capon neck, gizzard, and heart with water, bring to a boil, and simmer for about 1 hour. Break potatoes up with fork, tossing as lightly as possible. In rendered capon fat, sauté chopped onions and celery for about 5 minutes. Chop uncooked liver and add to vegetables, stirring just long enough for liver to change color. Toss this mixture with potatoes; deglaze pan with cider or wine, scraping up bits of liver, and add to stuffing. Stir in beaten egg, a little salt, several turns of pepper grinder, savory, thyme, and sage, and toss again with bread cubes. Remove gizzard, heart, and neck from broth. Chop the meat finely and stir lightly into stuffing. * Spoon stuffing into capon cavity without forcing; put any extra into a buttered casserole to bake with capon. Put capon on a rack in shallow roasting pan and bake for 25 minutes. Reduce heat to 325° and bake for about 1½ hours longer. Baste frequently with melted butter and pan juices.

MAKES 6 SERVINGS

Chicken Breasts with Oyster Stuffing

2 Tbs. butter
3 Tbs. minced scallions or shallots
4 slices of stale firm white bread, crusts removed, roughly diced or crumbled
¼ cup finely chopped celery
2 Tbs. chopped parsley
¼ tsp. salt
several grindings of fresh white pepper

½ tsp. paprika
⅛ tsp. grated nutmeg
1 pint oysters, drained, reserving liquor
4 whole chicken breasts, less than ¾ lb. each
salt and pepper
2 Tbs. soft butter
Oyster Sauce (p. 327)

Preheat oven to 375°

Heat the butter and sauté the scallions over gentle heat until they are soft. Meanwhile mix all the other stuffing ingredients except oysters and liquor. Toss with the butter and scallions, cooking for a few minutes until thoroughly coated; if too dry, add a little of the oyster liquor. Chop drained oysters into 3 or 4 pieces, depending on size, and fold into stuffing.

Split chicken breasts and flatten each half by opening up the area where there is a natural fold. Place each one between 2 pieces of wax paper, and pound to make a fairly thin scallop. Salt and pepper each piece. Place about ⅓ cup of stuffing in the center, fold chicken over, and roll, securing with a piece of string tied at each end and in the center if there is a loose flap. Butter a shallow pan that will hold the breasts comfortably (there should be a little space between), rub soft butter over the meat, cover loosely with foil. Bake for 30 minutes. Meanwhile prepare Oyster Sauce. Remove breasts with a slotted spoon, coat with a little of the oyster sauce, serving the rest in a sauceboat.

MAKES 4 SERVINGS

Chicken Breasts with Pears and Cider Cream Sauce

4 halves of chicken breasts
4 Tbs. butter
2 or 3 scallions, minced
1 large fresh pear
¾ cup cider or apple wine

¼ cup applejack or bourbon
salt
freshly ground pepper
1 cup heavy cream

Wipe chicken breasts with a damp cloth. Melt butter and sauté chicken and scallions over low heat for about 10 minutes. Meanwhile peel the pear and core, cutting uniform slices about ½ inch thick (try to get 8 slices in all). Cover slices with cider or apple wine and poach for about 20 minutes, until soft but not mushy. Pour applejack or whiskey over chicken and ignite, letting it burn out. Sprinkle with salt and pepper, then add cream and the cider or wine in which pears were poached; stir and let mixture cook down until reduced by almost half. Lift out chicken pieces and put on a heatproof platter with slices of pear on each piece; pour reduced sauce over and glaze under broiler for about 2 minutes, just long enough to brown. A very American delicacy (pears were among first fruits grown by colonists) when served with parboiled okra that has been fried with a coating of egg and fine soft bread crumbs.

MAKES 4 SERVINGS

Charleston Benne Chicken

1 frying chicken, 2½ to 3 lbs.
½ cup sesame seeds
½ cup flour
1 Tbs. salt
¼ tsp. cayenne
¼ tsp. black pepper

2 oranges
2 Tbs. bacon fat
2 Tbs. butter
½ cup cream
1½ cups chicken stock

Preheat oven to 325°

Have chicken cut into serving pieces. In a paper bag combine ¼ cup sesame seeds, the flour, salt, cayenne, and black pepper. Grate rind from oranges and add to flour-sesame mixture. Shake 1 piece of chicken at a time, coating thoroughly with contents of bag. Over low heat, brown chicken pieces in bacon fat. Meanwhile melt butter in a saucepan; stir in 2 tablespoons of the flour-sesame mixture remaining in the bag, then gradually add cream and stock, making sure no lumps form. Squeeze juice from the oranges and slowly add to sauce; when sauce is thick and smooth add remaining ¼ cup of sesame seeds. Transfer browned pieces of chicken to ovenproof casserole. Pour off all but 2 or 3 tablespoons of fat from skillet, then scrape up browned bits and add to them the orange sauce from saucepan; blend well before pouring over chicken. Cover and bake for 45 minutes; remove cover and bake for 15 minutes more.

MAKES 4 SERVINGS

Floridian Chicken Fricassee

The Spanish influence that has touched Florida ever since Ponce de León sought a fountain of youth may be stronger than ever in the twentieth century. There are many similar ways with chicken, but the method below can produce superb results.

1 chicken, about 3 lbs., cut up
½ cup flour, seasoned with salt and pepper
2 to 3 Tbs. bacon fat
2 medium-size onions, chopped
1 medium-size green pepper, trimmed and chopped
2 garlic cloves, minced
3 or 4 tomatoes, peeled and chopped
½ tsp. dried thyme

½ tsp. dried orégano
1 bay leaf
saffron
1 cup water
½ tsp. salt
freshly ground pepper
½ cup raisins
2 Tbs. capers, drained
½ cup slivered blanched almonds

Wipe chicken with damp cloth, dredge with seasoned flour, and brown all surfaces in some of the bacon fat; set aside and keep warm. Sauté onions and green pepper for about 4 minutes, using more bacon fat as needed, then add garlic, tomatoes, herbs, a large pinch of saffron, water, salt, and a few turns of the pepper grinder. Add chicken, cover, and simmer over very low heat for 1 hour, spooning sauce over chicken occasionally. Add raisins, capers, and almonds and cook for about 15 minutes more.

MAKES 4 SERVINGS

Southern Fried Chicken

1 frying chicken, 2 to 2½ lbs., with giblets
bacon fat

1 cup unbleached flour
1 Tbs. coarse salt
1 tsp. freshly ground black pepper

GRAVY:

1½ Tbs. flour
1½ cups milk

1 Tbs. minced parsley
salt and pepper

Divide chicken into pieces; separate thighs from legs, remove backbone, divide breast into 2 pieces, and detach wings. Use a skillet just large enough so pieces will lie flat and fit snugly. Heat enough bacon fat to cover bottom of skillet by 1 inch in depth. While fat is heating over moderate to high heat, put flour, salt, and freshly ground pepper in a sturdy brown bag, then drop in chicken pieces, one or two at a time, and give bag a good shake.

By that time, fat will be sizzling, but not quite at smoking point, so gently place a few floured chicken pieces, no more than four at a time, into skillet;

preferably use long-handled tongs because there is bound to be a good deal of splattering. Brown chicken quickly on all sides over high heat, then remove to platter. Repeat the process until all chicken pieces have been browned golden crisp on outside even though not cooked on inside.

Now turn down heat to moderate, and put back all chicken pieces, tucking them in snugly, which is the secret of keeping them from drying out during their interior cooking. Cook for 40 to 45 minutes; turn frequently with tongs, moving pieces around from center to edge and vice versa. About 10 minutes before they are finished add chicken heart, and then the liver for last 5 minutes. When done, chicken should be fork-tender and still crisp; put pieces in warm oven while making cream gravy.

To make gravy, chop cooked heart and liver and set aside. Pour off all but 1½ tablespoons of fat and remove some of the overly browned bits of flour that may have accumulated. Stir in 1½ tablespoons flour, mix well, and let brown. Then add the milk (more or less, depending upon how thick you prefer gravy) and chopped heart and liver. Stir mixture until it thickens, scraping up brown bits from pan, then simmer for about 10 minutes. Finally add minced parsley and salt and pepper to taste.

MAKES 4 SERVINGS

New England Chicken and Clam Pie

2 Tbs. butter	freshly ground white pepper
1 bunch of scallions, minced	½ tsp. dried summer savory
2 Tbs. flour	1½ cups diced cooked chicken
1 cup chicken stock	¾ cup diced cooked carrots
1 can (6½ oz.) clams with juice	1 recipe Buttermilk Biscuits
salt	(p. 159), unbaked

Preheat oven to 375°

Melt butter and sauté minced scallions for 2 or 3 minutes before stirring in flour; blend in chicken stock and juice drained from clams. Stir in a little salt, depending on saltiness of stock and clam juice, and a few turns of pepper grinder; add savory, cooked chicken and carrots, and the reserved clams. Line an 8-inch shallow baking dish with biscuit dough rolled about ⅛ inch thick. Into this dough pour the chicken-clam mixture; place an upturned cup in the center. Place remaining rolled-out dough across top, crimping edges and slashing to permit steam to escape. Bake for about 30 minutes.

MAKES 4 SERVINGS

1 chicken, 5 lbs.
  salt
1 garlic clove, split
2 oranges
1½ cups toasted bread cubes
1 cup thin celery slices
¼ cup melted butter
  freshly ground white pepper

3 sprigs each of fresh tarragon and
    rosemary, or ½ tsp. dried
¼ cup wine vinegar
3 Tbs. sugar
2 cups chicken stock
1 Tbs. cornstarch
  watercress for garnish

Preheat oven to 375° or use spit

Sprinkle inside of chicken with salt and rub garlic halves well into skin, then sprinkle outside with salt; secure wings at back. Use vegetable peeler to remove as thinly as possible the orange-colored rind from 1 orange only; cut these peelings into slivers and set aside, then squeeze peeled orange. Remove skin and pith from second orange and divide fruit into segments. Mix bread cubes, celery, butter, about ½ teaspoon salt, several turns of pepper grinder, and half of herbs, fresh or dried. Toss this mixture with orange segments, then spoon into cavity of chicken and tie legs. Roast on a spit, if you have one, for about 2 hours; if not, roast in oven for about 30 minutes per pound. Meanwhile put vinegar and sugar in a saucepan, bring to a boil, and stir until sugar dissolves. Stir in stock and remaining herbs and simmer for 10 minutes; stir in orange juice and simmer for 10 minutes more. Dissolve cornstarch in 2 tablespoons water and stir into sauce, cooking for 1 minute or so, then add slivered orange rind. Serve in sauceboat. Garnish the bird with watercress.

MAKES 4 TO 6 SERVINGS

Rio Grande Simmered Chicken

1 cup natural pumpkin seeds
1 cup fresh popped corn, preferably
    homemade and unsalted
6 cuminseeds
¼ tsp. ground coriander
1 Tbs. fresh chili powder

1 garlic clove, minced
1 frying chicken, 3½ lbs., cut into
    8 pieces, with giblets
2 medium-size tomatoes, peeled and
    chopped
  salt

Spin pumpkin seeds in blender until pulverized; do the same with popcorn, then combine and stir in cuminseeds, coriander, chili powder, and garlic. Pull chicken fat away from meat and render in a pot large enough to hold chicken; pour off all but about 2 tablespoons. Remove wing tips and tail and put them in a saucepan with heart, gizzard, and neck; cover with 4 cups of water and simmer for 1 hour or more, seasoning as desired. (Or have on hand 3 cups

canned chicken broth.) Brown chicken pieces in rendered fat. Spin chopped tomatoes in blender, and stir into seed mixture; add 3 cups of chicken broth, a little at a time, until a smooth sauce results. Pour this over browned chicken pieces and cook over low heat for about 30 minutes; sauce should barely bubble when pot is covered. Chicken will be ready to serve when fork easily penetrates drumstick. Watch out for commercial popcorn saltiness; taste and stir in salt only if needed, just before serving.

MAKES 4 SERVINGS

Steamed Chicken with Watercress Sauce

1 chicken, 3 to 4 lbs.	½ cup California dry vermouth
½ lemon	1 fresh tarragon sprig
1 tsp. salt	2 bunches of watercress
freshly ground pepper	1 cup heavy cream
2 cloves	2 egg yolks
1 celery rib, diced	1 tsp. capers, drained
½ cup water	

Carefully remove skin from chicken, chop skin very coarsely, and put in bottom of a heavy iron pot with tight-fitting lid. Rub flesh of chicken briskly with cut side of lemon, and sprinkle on salt and freshly ground pepper. Toss cloves and diced celery in on top of chopped skin, pour in water and vermouth, and bring to a boil. Twist wings to lock at back of chicken, and tie legs. Place a rack in pot over skin and broth and put chicken, breast side up, on rack. Cover breast with tarragon leaves. Cover pot tightly and simmer for about 30 minutes; time will depend on chicken, so watch carefully so as not to overcook. Cook watercress in 2 cups of boiling water for 20 minutes, keeping tightly covered; drain, and purée in a blender. When chicken is done, remove from pot and keep warm. Remove skin, celery, and cloves from broth with slotted spoon. Off heat stir in cream and beat in 1 egg yolk at a time; cook over very low heat until mixture thickens. Add capers and a few drops of lemon juice, and blend in puréed watercress. Garnish chicken with some of this sauce, and serve remainder in a sauceboat.

MAKES 6 SERVINGS

Country Captain

One of the earliest compilers of American recipes, Eliza Leslie, told her readers that "Country Captain" got its name from a British army officer stationed in the hinterlands of India who preserved this method of currying chicken or other fowl. But some Georgians assert it is a Savannah recipe developed when ships sailed the spice routes. Strangely, a twentieth-century Tar Heel historian believed it originated with a famous Columbus hostess for Franklin D. Roosevelt, and he added that General George S. Patton once sent word ahead when he was to visit Columbus briefly: "If you can't give me a party and have Country Captain, put some in a tin bucket and bring it to the train." It is usually made with uncooked chicken and belongs among the curry dishes brought to America by English colonists.

4 bacon slices
1 green pepper, chopped
1 medium-size onion, chopped
2 garlic cloves
¾ cup chopped celery
6 canned tomatoes with juice
1 cup orange juice

2 Tbs. curry powder
¼ to ½ tsp. dried thyme
8 slices of uncooked turkey breast
½ to 1 cup dried currants
½ cup toasted almonds
¼ cup minced parsley

Sauté bacon until crisp, set aside, and drain all but 2 tablespoons fat from pan. Stir in green pepper, onion, garlic, and celery and sauté for 5 minutes. Chop tomatoes coarsely and add with a little of their juice and the orange juice; season with curry powder and thyme. Bring to boil and simmer for 5 minutes. Put in pieces of turkey and spoon hot sauce over them; continue simmering, covered, for 30 minutes. Serve with rice; a scattering of crumbled bacon, currants, almonds, and parsley is the usual garnish.

MAKES 8 SERVINGS

Barbecued Duck in Soy Sauce

Summers in New York can be more tolerable if space to cook outdoors is available. This recipe developed on the terrace of a poor man's penthouse equipped with a charcoal-fired spit, and it works equally well with a kitchen rotisserie.

1 Long Island duckling, about 5 lbs.
    salt
1 small onion
½ lemon
4 Tbs. blackstrap molasses

½ cup sherry
½ cup soy sauce
2 Tbs. honey
1 garlic clove, minced

Wipe duck inside and out with damp cloth, sprinkle salt into opening, then drop in onion and lemon. Push wing tips into duck's spine and tie securely; tie legs together. Combine molasses, sherry, soy sauce, honey, and garlic in a saucepan, bring to the boiling point, and simmer gently for about 5 minutes. Insert spit rod so weight of duck is well balanced and prongs hold it firmly. Paint with warm barbecue sauce, as rotation begins. Roast for about 3 hours, depending upon quality of heat. Paint at least every 15 minutes with sauce to build glossy dark carapace over duck skin; delicious. Duck is done when thigh moves easily and juices run clear of blood.

MAKES 4 SERVINGS

Crusty Baked Duckling

1 Long Island duckling, about 5 lbs.
  salt
  freshly ground pepper
1 egg

2 Tbs. milk
2 cups fresh bread crumbs
½ tsp. dried savory
2 Tbs. flour

Preheat oven to 350°

Peel all skin from duck except on wings. Remove as much fat as possible and reserve. Use very sharp knife or poultry shears to cut out backbone and neck; put these pieces in pot with giblets, about 1 teaspoon salt, a few turns of pepper grinder, and water to cover amply. Simmer for a couple of hours to make stock for sauce. Remove legs, dividing into drumsticks and second joints; remove wings and divide breast into 4 pieces, easing meat away from ribs; add bones to stock pot. Cut skin and fat into small pieces and render over low heat. Beat egg with milk, 1 teaspoon salt, several turns of pepper grinder, and savory. Dip duck pieces into this mixture, then roll in seasoned bread crumbs, and brown in 2 or 3 tablespoons of duck fat. Transfer to shallow casserole in which all pieces can lie flat. Cover and bake for about 50 minutes. Meanwhile stir flour into 2 tablespoons duck fat in a saucepan and brown lightly, then blend in enough of the stock to make sauce. Season to taste and serve in sauceboat with the baked duck.

MAKES 4 SERVINGS

Long Island Duck Stew

1 duck, about 5 lbs.
1 Tbs. flour
1 cup water
1 medium-size onion, chopped
1 Tbs. minced mint

1 Tbs. minced sage
1½ tsp. salt
  freshly ground pepper
1 small rutabaga, peeled and diced

Pull away as much fat from duck as possible, and render fat. (You may pull off skin and layer of fat underneath it and discard.) Cut duck into serving pieces and brown in rendered fat in enameled iron pot with tight-fitting cover. Turn pieces occasionally, searing all surfaces. When well browned pour off all but about 2 tablespoons fat and stir in flour; off heat stir in the water, add onion, herbs, salt, and a few turns of pepper grinder. Cover and cook over low heat for 40 to 50 minutes. Stir in rutabaga dice, cover, and cook over low heat for 30 minutes more. Let cool; put in refrigerator and let fat congeal. Scrape off fat, then reheat stew to serve.

MAKES 4 SERVINGS

Rock Cornish Game Hen with Black-Walnut Sauce

4 Rock Cornish game birds, halved
  celery leaves
1 shallot or small onion
3 cups water
  salt
  freshly ground pepper

3 Tbs. butter
¼ cup broken black walnuts
1 Tbs. flour
1 cup sour cream
  paprika

Cut off wing tips and put with necks, gizzards, hearts, 1 sprig of celery leaves, and the shallot in a saucepan; add water and simmer for about 40 minutes, until stock is reduced to about 1½ to 2 cups; season to taste with salt and freshly ground pepper. Meanwhile wipe birds dry and rub with salt and pepper. Melt 2 tablespoons butter in a skillet large enough to hold birds without crowding; brown them as evenly as possible. When stock is ready, strain it, setting giblets aside; pour stock over browned birds and simmer, covered, for about 30 minutes. Spin nuts in blender until pulverized. Use a sharp knife to mince giblets very finely. Melt 1 tablespoon butter in a saucepan and stir in flour to make a roux. Pour broth from simmered chicken, a little at a time, into roux, stirring constantly while sauce thickens; stir in nuts and giblets, then sour cream, blending well without boiling. Pour over birds, cover pan, and heat very slowly for about 15 minutes. Sprinkle with paprika just before serving.

MAKES 4 SERVINGS

Goose Roasted with Apple-Onion Sauce, Corn-Bread Stuffing

1 goose, 10 to 12 lbs.
  salt
3 to 4 cups crumbled corn bread
1 Tbs. dried sage
12 juniper berries, bruised

1 medium-size apple, finely chopped
1 medium-size onion, sliced
1 Tbs. salt
  freshly ground pepper
1 egg, separated

SAUCE:

2 large apples, peeled, cored and
  chopped
½ cup good beer, ale, or stout
1 small onion, chopped
2 Tbs. sugar

2 tsp. vinegar
2 Tbs. bread crumbs
½ tsp. dry mustard
½ tsp. ground cinnamon
2 Tbs. flour

Preheat oven to 400°

Wipe goose with damp cloth and rub salt inside and out. Set aside liver and cook giblets and neck in water to cover, simmering for 30 to 40 minutes. Set giblet stock aside. Put crumbled corn bread in a large bowl and toss with sage, juniper berries, chopped apple and onion, 1 tablespoon salt, and a few turns of

pepper grinder. Chop liver and add with beaten egg yolk. Then beat white until frothy and fold into stuffing mixture. * Spoon into goose and sew up openings. Roast for 20 minutes, then reduce oven to 325° and roast for 20 minutes per pound, basting frequently with a little water and drawing off fat with bulb baster.

Make the sauce: Simmer chopped apples with beer, ale, or stout, chopped onion, sugar, vinegar, bread crumbs, mustard, and cinnamon for about 20 minutes. Meanwhile heat 3 tablespoons of fat drawn from goose and stir in flour. When smooth stir in reserved giblet stock to make thinnish gravy, then combine with apple-onion mixture.

MAKES 8 SERVINGS

Spit-Roasted Wild Canadian Goose with Fried Apples

1 Canada goose, 5 to 6 lbs.	4 Tbs. butter
coarse salt	2 to 3 Tbs. brown sugar
freshly ground pepper	3 Tbs. dried currants soaked in a
5 tart apples	little applejack
1 celery rib	¼ cup warm applejack
2 pieces of fresh pork fat, approximately 3 by 5 inches	

Rinse cavity of goose, dry with paper towel, and rub in coarse salt and fresh pepper. Stuff with 1 apple, quartered, and the celery rib; skewer or sew up vent. To roast, make sure the spit is under a good hot broiler or over very hot coals. Cover the breast with the pork fat, tying string around snugly. Place bird on spit, and roast for 1 hour. About 20 minutes before serving, prepare fried apples by coring and peeling remaining apples and slicing into fairly thick pieces. Fry in foaming butter, turning and adding the brown sugar after 5 minutes. Continue to fry until golden, then add currants. Place apples around goose on a platter and just before serving pour flaming applejack over all.

MAKES 4 SERVINGS

Breasts of Guinea Hen with Virginia Ham

2 guinea hen breasts, halved	1½ Tbs. sherry
1 to 2 Tbs. butter	4 mushroom caps, broiled
1½ Tbs. minced shallot	4 paper-thin slices of Virginia ham
8 medium-size mushrooms, chopped	4 slices of toast
2 cups cream	

Remove skin from guinea breasts, and sauté breasts in butter for about 10 minutes, turning to cook evenly. Remove from pan and keep warm. Add a little butter to the pan if necessary and sauté shallot and chopped mushrooms for 1 or 2 minutes; cover pan, lower heat, and simmer for 5 minutes. Add cream and sherry; when liquid is hot add meat and simmer for 10 minutes. Meanwhile broil mushroom caps, heat up ham slices, and make toast. Place 1 slice of ham on each slice of toast, top with a guinea hen breast, and pour mushroom-shallot sauce over all. Garnish each serving with 1 broiled mushroom cap.

MAKES 4 SERVINGS

Scallops of Turkey Breast with Cream and Sesame Seeds

At a time when milk-fed veal was generally almost impossible to find in supermarkets the idea of slicing turkey breasts in scallop-size pieces and freezing them proved a boon to adaptable cooks. This recipe and the one following suggest two of many imaginative American ways to make one of the so-called convenience foods palatable. Of course the same instructions can be applied to slices of fresh turkey—cut from the breast, or from the thigh.

12 frozen turkey breast scallops, about 1½ lbs. altogether	3 Tbs. vegetable oil
¼ cup flour	2 Tbs. minced shallots or scallions
salt	¼ cup dry white wine
freshly ground pepper	½ cup heavy cream
3 Tbs. butter	2 Tbs. sesame seeds
	¼ to ⅓ cup chicken broth

Defrost turkey scallops, pat dry, and dust with flour well seasoned with salt and freshly ground pepper. Place between pieces of wax paper and pound each 2 or 3 times. Heat butter and oil to sizzling; brown scallops, three or four at a time to avoid crowding, turning each once. Then return all scallops to pan and cook for 5 minutes. Set aside and keep warm. In same pan cook shallots until brown, add wine, and cook down quickly, scraping up braised bits, then add cream and boil it down to syrupy thickness. Turn down heat and return scallops to pan. Meanwhile, heat sesame seeds in a small heavy skillet, shaking pan until they are toast-colored; turn off heat. Thin sauce in scallop pan with broth, adding a little at a time to obtained desired consistency. Sprinkle turkey with toasted sesame seeds and serve.

MAKES 4 SERVINGS

Scallops of Turkey Breast Stuffed with Dried Beef

8 frozen turkey breast scallops, about 1 lb. altogether
½ lb. smoked dried beef, chopped
3 medium-size onions, finely chopped
2½ cups fresh bread crumbs
2 Tbs. minced parsley
2 Tbs. minced fresh basil

2 Tbs. minced fresh thyme
½ tsp. dried orégano
1 tsp. salt
    freshly ground black pepper
4 Tbs. grated Parmesan cheese
2 eggs, beaten
3 to 4 Tbs. butter

Bring turkey scallops to room temperature and put between pieces of wax paper; pound to increase their size about 1½ times. Mix chopped dried beef, onions, 1½ cups of bread crumbs, and the herbs. Beware of salt. If beef is very salty do not use any salt. Mix in several grindings of pepper and the cheese. Place about 2 tablespoons of this stuffing on top of each pounded scallop, then roll, turning in ends; lace each one together with a skewer. Dip rolls into beaten eggs, then into bread crumbs. Brown in butter, turning frequently. Cover pan, reduce heat as low as possible, and cook for about 30 minutes, checking frequently.

MAKES 4 SERVINGS

Thanksgiving Turkey

No Thanksgiving holiday arrives without much discussion of ways old and new to cook the American bird. Turkeys have changed greatly since ancestral family providers took a firing piece from the wall and went into the woods in search of a fowl large enough to feed a houseful of relatives. Nowadays many turkeys come with explicit cooking instructions attached. No treatise on American food, however, may seem complete without some thoughts on this very American subject.

10-lb. turkey
    stuffing (following)
    butter
1 large onion, sliced
2 medium-sized carrots, chopped

1 stalk celery, coarsely chopped
½ cup water
1 cup chicken or turkey stock
    salt
    freshly ground pepper

Preheat oven to 350°

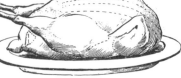

Fill turkey with prepared stuffing and close cavities with skewers. Rub all over with about 3 tablespoons of butter. Put vegetables and water in bottom of roasting pan. Sprinkle turkey with salt and pepper and place on rack in roasting pan. Cut a piece of cheesecloth large enough to drape over turkey and spread it liberally with butter before covering turkey. Put in preheated oven for 3¼ hours, basting frequently with juices in bottom of roasting pan. Be sure to lift off cheesecloth each time turkey is basted, and add stock as necessary to pan juices. Discard cheesecloth about 40 minutes before bird is done so it will brown on top, but continue basting.

Tennessee Country Sausage Stuffing for Turkey

1 lb. chestnuts
2 Tbs. butter
1½ cups chicken or beef stock
2 Tbs. Madeira
½ lb. Tennessee smoked country
    sausage, or other pork sausage,
    preferably but not necessarily
    smoked

4 onions, chopped
1 to 2 cups chopped celery
1 tsp. dried thyme
½ tsp. dried sage
¼ cup minced parsley
6 cups cubed stale bread
    salt
    freshly ground pepper

To prepare chestnuts: cut a cross in each, cover with cold water, and bring to a boil for a minute or two. Remove a few at a time, and peel inner and outer skins while still warm. Place peeled chestnuts in a heavy saucepan and add butter, stock, and Madeira. Simmer for 30 to 40 minutes, until liquid is absorbed. Meanwhile, crumble sausage meat and sauté slowly for about 10 minutes; pour off all but about 4 tablespoons of fat and sauté onions and celery in it for about 10 minutes. Combine with thyme, sage, parsley, bread cubes, and cooked chestnuts, adding salt and pepper to taste; amount of seasoning depends on seasoning of sausage.

MAKES ENOUGH FOR 10-LB. TURKEY

Chapter 16

Fish
and
Seafood

West Coast Abalone Steak

Abalone, considered a great treat in California where it can be bought fresh, is one of the foods that Chinese cooks introduced to American bills of fare.

1½ lbs. abalone steaks, about ½ inch
    thick
½ tsp. salt
    freshly ground pepper
    flour
2 eggs, beaten

½ cup sweet butter
⅛ cup California olive oil
    juice of ½ lemon
2 Tbs. minced parsley
4 lemon wedges

If abalone has not been previously tenderized, it must be well pounded with a wooden mallet until soft but not mushy. Season the steaks with salt and pepper; dredge them with flour, dip into beaten eggs, then dredge again with flour. Heat half of butter and the oil in a skillet and brown abalone quickly on each side. Overcooking will make fish tough. Put steaks on a warm serving platter, pour fat from skillet, and add remaining butter; let it get brown but not burned and add lemon juice and parsley. Pour sauce over abalone and serve with lemon wedges.

MAKES 4 SERVINGS

When Dr. Carleton Ray was one of the directors of marine life at the New York Aquarium he was also a champion of fish as food for mankind, and his earlier acquaintance with Chinese in San Francisco had made him a devotee of Oriental ways of cooking. One day in his Coney Island office he gave us this recipe for cooking striped or black sea bass, carp, red snapper, or Pacific coast rockfish with vegetables.

4 dried Chinese mushrooms	4 water chestnuts, fresh preferred
8 dried Chinese lichens	2 fish, about 2 lbs. each
2 scallions	flour
12 snow pea pods	vegetable oil
6 slices of fresh or pickled gingerroot	

SAUCE:

4 Tbs. soy sauce	2 Tbs. cornstarch
4 Tbs. sherry	2 tsp. salt
4 Tbs. white vinegar	1½ cups water
1 Tbs. sugar	

Cover mushrooms and lichens with water in separate containers and soak for 2 hours. Cut scallions into thin horizontal slices, including tenderest part of green leaves. Trim ends from snow pea pods; cut gingerroot into ⅛-inch cubes and chestnuts into ⅛-inch slices. Set aside. Meanwhile combine sauce ingredients, eliminating any lumps of cornstarch. Clean fish; chop off fins but leave head and tail on; slash sides at ¾-inch intervals from gills to tail; dust with flour. Heat enough oil to come to about middle of fish's thickness. When oil is sizzling fry fish for 1 minute on each side. Turn heat low and cook for 3 minutes more on each side. Outside should be crisp while interior is tender and moist. Remove cooked fish to warm place and pour off all but 2 tablespoons oil. Drain mushrooms and lichens, pat dry, and cook with scallions, snow pea pods, gingerroot, and chestnuts in remaining oil; stir over high heat for 1 to 2 minutes so vegetables are barely cooked. Stir in sauce mixture and cook until it thickens and becomes clear. Turn down heat and add cooked fish, spooning sauce over for 1 to 2 minutes. Serve immediately with rice.

MAKES 4 SERVINGS

Herman Deutsch's Catfish (or Flounder) Paupiettes

Catfish are not easy to buy in markets, but they make delicious eating when dusted with white cornmeal and fried in bacon fat, or baked in a garlicky Creole sauce of lemon and thyme-flavored tomatoes and green peppers. A New

Orleans friend, the late gastronome and newspaper columnist Herman Deutsch, developed a stuffing for catfish fillets which, in the absence of the real thing, is sometimes made in our kitchen with flounder and with a high respect for the cuisine of the Crescent City.

8 small fish fillets, 1½ by 5 inches	1 Tbs. minced white onion
salt	¼ cup minced mushrooms
2 Tbs. capers	½ tsp. dried basil
18 pecans, finely chopped or pulverized	18 oysters
	1 egg, beaten
2 cups dry white wine	1 tsp. cornstarch
2 Tbs. butter	freshly ground pepper

Wipe fillets and sprinkle with salt. Mash the capers and the ground pecans together and spread this paste evenly over the center of the fillets, then roll them up, securing them with a toothpick or thread. Place them in a saucepan snugly in one layer, cover with wine, bring gently to a boil, and simmer for 3 or 4 minutes. Remove and keep warm, covered with foil, while preparing the sauce. Melt butter; add onion, mushrooms, basil, and 1 cup of wine in which fish cooked, bring to a boil, and let cook down for about 10 minutes. Meanwhile drain oysters and add oyster liquor, no more than ½ cup to simmering wine. Combine beaten egg with cornstarch dissolved in a little water, gradually blend in some of the hot liquid, then turn egg mixture into the wine sauce and warm, but do not boil, stirring until smooth and thick. Add the oysters, correct seasoning, and warm just until oysters curl at the edges. Pat dry the paupiettes, then pour the oyster sauce over them and serve.

MAKES 4 SERVINGS

Flaming Bluefish Fillets with Fennel

4 bluefish fillets, about 8 inches long, approximately 3 lbs. altogether	4 Tbs. butter
flour	1 to 2 Tbs. minced fresh herbs: thyme, savory, or combination of chives and parsley
salt	
freshly ground pepper	⅓ cup brandy
2 tsp. whole fennel seeds	

Wipe fish with damp cloth. Season flour with salt, pepper, and whole fennel seeds and dust fillets. Melt butter, heating until sizzling but not brown. Put in fillets, skin side up; turn after 3 minutes and sauté other side for 3 to 5 minutes, depending on thickness. Sprinkle top with a little salt, pepper, and the fresh herbs. Heat brandy, pour over fish, and set aflame; spoon over fish until flames die out.

MAKES 4 SERVINGS

Impressive as swordfish can be when broiled, it is so good a fish that it should be used in lots of ways; we found this so delicious a stew that it deserves a less prosaic title.

1½ lbs. swordfish, cut 2 inches thick	1 medium-size onion, chopped
1 qt. fish stock or clam juice diluted with equal amount water	½ cup chopped carrot
1 cup diced celery	½ tsp. dried thyme
2 tomatoes, peeled and chopped, or canned tomatoes	½ tsp. dried basil
	1 tsp. salt
1 Tbs. tomato paste	freshly ground black pepper
½ green pepper, trimmed and chopped	4 bacon slices, cut into squares
	2 small potatoes, diced
	2 Tbs. minced parsley

Wipe fish and cut into 2-inch cubes. Heat fish stock (or diluted clam juice) in a 3-quart pot and add celery, tomatoes, tomato paste, green pepper, onion, carrot, herbs, salt, and several turns of pepper grinder; simmer for about 30 minutes. Meanwhile sauté bacon squares, drain fat, and when crisp add squares to chowder. Add diced potatoes, continue cooking for 10 minutes, then add swordfish chunks and cook for about 20 minutes, until potatoes are tender but firm. Sprinkle with parsley when serving.

MAKES 4 SERVINGS

An old story maintains that New Englanders who came to settle in the Northwest resorted to making their traditional hash with clams when they had no corned beef.

1½ cups peeled and chopped baked potatoes	¼ cup finely minced onion
	salt
2 cups chopped cooked clams	freshly ground pepper
¼ cup butter	½ cup heavy cream

Toss chopped potatoes with chopped clams. Melt about 2 tablespoons butter in a heavy skillet and lightly sauté onion for about 1 minute. Stir onion into potato-clam mixture. Season to taste. Melt remaining butter in skillet and spread hash over bottom, pressing down evenly, then let it brown. After about 10 minutes pour cream over and let it sink in. Let hash cook over very low heat for about 30 minutes; fold like an omelet.

MAKES 4 SERVINGS

Baked Herb-Stuffed Clams

32 medium-size clams
½ cup water
2 scallions
½ cup minced parsley
¼ cup minced fresh basil and/or
    fresh thyme and/or
    tarragon
1½ Tbs. butter

1½ Tbs. flour
⅓ cup milk
salt
freshly ground pepper
5 or 6 drops of Tabasco
2 Tbs. dry sherry
⅓ cup fresh bread crumbs
¼ cup melted butter

Preheat oven to 500°

Place clams in a heavy pot with ½ cup water, cover tightly, and steam over high heat until shells open, about 5 minutes. Scrape clams from shells and set shells aside. Chop clams very fine with scallions, parsley, and other herbs. Melt 1½ tablespoons butter in a saucepan, stir in flour, and cook for 1 or 2 minutes. Off heat, beat in milk; return to heat and stir until smooth and thickened. Add salt to taste, several turns of pepper grinder, and Tabasco; stir in sherry. Stir minced clams into sauce, then fill reserved clam shells, using about 20 shells. Sprinkle with bread crumbs, dribble melted butter over, and run under broiler or bake at 500° until browned and sizzling.

MAKES ABOUT 6 SERVINGS

Fried Clams

The first time we tasted a "clamburger" was in an unprepossessing café in Coos Bay, Oregon, but fried clams, in or out of a sandwich, are characteristic of New England.

24 to 30 clams, shucked
1 cup cracker crumbs, bread crumbs
    or cornmeal
2 eggs, beaten

½ tsp. salt
½ cup milk
2 cups corn oil
tartar sauce

Dip clams into crumbs or meal, then into beaten eggs seasoned with salt and mixed with milk, then again into crumbs or meal. Preheat oil to about 385° and fry coated clams, not too many at a time, until golden brown. Drain on paper, and serve piping hot with tartar sauce.

MAKES 4 SERVINGS

New England Codfish Balls

½ lb. salt cod
4 raw potatoes
1 celery rib
1 small onion
1 small carrot

3 peppercorns
1 Tbs. butter
1 egg
freshly ground pepper
½ cup vegetable or peanut oil

Soak fish under dripping tap for 24 hours, or change water several times. Drain and flake. Peel and slice potatoes to make 2½ cups, and put in a saucepan with codfish, celery, onion, carrot, and peppercorns; add enough water to cover fish and vegetables by 1 inch. Bring to a boil and simmer until potatoes are soft, about 20 minutes. Discard celery, onion, carrot, and peppercorns. Drain water off fish and potatoes, then shake saucepan over heat until all moisture has evaporated. Off heat, mash mixture until potatoes are free of lumps; stir in butter. Beat egg thoroughly, then stir into mixture with freshly ground pepper. Heat oil in a skillet. When almost smoking drop spoonfuls of mixture into fat, taking care not to crowd the pan. Turn balls when underside browns, and fry until crisp. Drain on paper towel and keep warm. Make 12 balls in this manner, or shape mixture into flat cakes and fry the same way. Serve with catsup or tomato sauce.

MAKES 4 SERVINGS

Cape Ann Codfish Pie

½ lb. frozen cod
1 Tbs. minced onion
1 garlic clove
6 Tbs. butter
3 Tbs. flour
¾ cup chicken stock
3 Tbs. heavy cream
2 Tbs. lemon juice

1 tsp. salt
¼ tsp. white pepper
½ tsp. dried thyme
¼ cup white wine
3 egg yolks
¾ cup mayonnaise
1 pie shell, 9 inches, prebaked for
8 to 10 minutes

Preheat oven to 375°

Bring fish to room temperature and grind very fine. Finely mince onion and garlic. Melt 4 tablespoons butter in a saucepan and sauté fish, onion, and garlic, stirring constantly, for about 3 minutes. Remove with slotted spoon, then melt remaining butter in same pan and blend in flour. Off heat, stir in stock; when free of lumps return to heat and cook until sauce thickens, then stir in cream. Add fish mixture to sauce, mix, and stir in lemon juice, salt, white pepper, thyme, and wine. Beat egg yolks with mayonnaise until smoothly blended, then fold into sauce with fish. Pour into prebaked pie shell, and bake for 35 to 40 minutes, until golden brown.

MAKES 6 SERVINGS

Falmouth Codfish with Shrimps

1 lb. salt cod
2 Tbs. bacon fat
1 small green pepper, chopped
5 or 6 shallots, chopped
2 garlic cloves, minced
½ cup chopped celery
1 cup sliced mushrooms

Tabasco
salt
¼ lb. raw shrimps, peeled
butter
2 small potatoes
¼ cup grated Cheddar cheese
¼ cup fresh bread crumbs

Preheat oven to 375° *

Soak fish under dripping tap for 24 hours, or change water several times. About 1½ hours before serving, melt bacon fat in a skillet and sauté green pepper, shallots, garlic, celery, and mushrooms. Flake soaked fish and drain well before stirring into vegetables. Add several dashes of Tabasco, and a little salt if necessary. Stir in shrimps. * Butter a 1½-quart casserole and put half of fish mixture in it. Peel potatoes and slice with vegetable peeler, very thin; spread potatoes over fish mixture. Sprinkle in cheese, and cover with rest of fish. Melt 1 tablespoon or more of butter and stir in crumbs, then sprinkle crumbs on top. Bake for about 1 hour.

MAKES 4 SERVINGS

Cod Steaks in Orange Sauce

½ cup flour
1 tsp. salt
½ tsp. cayenne
4 cod steaks, about ⅓ lb. each
3 garlic cloves, minced
½ cup minced parsley

3 to 4 Tbs. olive or corn oil
1 to 1½ Tbs. lemon juice
¾ cup fresh orange juice
slivered almonds or crushed
hazelnuts

Preheat oven to 475°

Mix flour, salt, and cayenne and dredge cod steaks with the mixture. Stir together garlic, parsley, oil, and lemon juice and saturate all surfaces of fish, letting steaks marinate for at least 1 hour. Put them in a baking dish with orange juice and bake for about 25 minutes, basting at least twice with juices; when done most of juices will be absorbed. Sprinkle nuts over fish before serving.

MAKES 4 SERVINGS

4 Tbs. butter
1 shallot or scallion, minced
4 large mushrooms, about ¼ lb., sliced
2 Tbs. white wine
2 Tbs. flour
1 cup milk
1 cup fresh lump crab meat, about
    ¼ lb.

salt and pepper
1 tsp. dried tarragon
2 Tbs. dry sherry
1 egg yolk
1 Tbs. heavy cream
4 tsp. mixed grated cheese and
    bread crumbs

In a small enamelware saucepan melt 2 tablespoons butter and sauté minced shallot for 1 minute. Add sliced mushrooms, then stir in the white wine and simmer for 5 minutes. Remove vegetables to dish; keep warm. In same pan melt remaining 2 tablespoons butter and blend in flour; off heat, stir in milk, eliminating all lumps before returning to heat; stir constantly till sauce thickens. Scrape mushrooms, shallot, and juices from warming dish into sauce. Stir in crab meat, salt and pepper to taste, tarragon, and sherry. While this gets hot, beat egg yolk with cream, adding to it a bit of hot sauce; whisk again, then add more hot sauce. Now pour all of yolk mixture into hot sauce, stirring constantly as it comes to boiling point. Divide the crab-mushroom mixture among 4 scallop shells or small baking dishes and sprinkle each with cheese and bread crumb mixture. Slide under broiler to brown.

MAKES 4 SERVINGS

¾ lb. fat salt pork, cut into ½-inch dice
2 lbs. thick eels, unskinned, cut into
    2-inch slices
3 large onions, sliced
    freshly ground pepper

3 medium-size potatoes, cut into
    ½-inch dice
3 Tbs. flour
    salt
2 Tbs. very dry sherry

Fry salt-pork dice in a skillet until crisp, then remove and keep warm in heated oven; pour off and reserve half the fat; leave remainder in skillet. Set aside tails and skinny end pieces of eel, and sear the other chunks in fat in skillet; remove, put in metal bowl and keep warm in oven. Sauté onion slices in fat that remains in skillet, sprinkling with pepper. Turn heat as low as possible and cover skillet. Meanwhile, put end pieces of eel in a separate pot, cover with 3 cups slightly salted water, and bring slowly to a boil; let simmer for 10 minutes. Remove eel pieces and discard, replace with diced potatoes, and boil gently for 10 minutes. Now add some reserved salt-pork fat to skillet containing onions and stir in flour. Drain cooked potatoes and stir potato water into onions and flour to make a thin sauce; when this is smooth and creamy add potatoes and

the eel pieces from the oven. Cover skillet and let eel and potatoes simmer gently in sauce for 15 to 20 minutes. Add salt to taste and blend in sherry. Serve in hot soup plates with crisp salt-pork dice scattered in each. Knives and forks are as necessary as spoons.

MAKES **6** SERVINGS

Seafood Gumbo

Happiness for a cotton factor or rice planter of the Old South has been defined as a midday meal with a long mint julep to begin, a slice of iced watermelon to end, and a thick pottage based on okra as the *pièce de résistance*. Varying as they do throughout the South, such gumbos are often mixtures that include two or more kinds of shellfish and one or more kinds of meat. Lafcadio Hearn, whose *La Cuisine Créole* was published in 1885, recommended enriching a beef or chicken gumbo with oysters, crab or shrimps, "as all improve the gombo." Goose or waterbirds (*poules d'eau*) may be used in Louisiana, and in Tennessee some cooks make the cabbage gumbo of the central hills that leaves out poultry and seafood in favor of tangy country ham, Tennessee pork sausage and milk.

½-lb. piece of ham
1½ lbs. raw shrimps
1 garlic clove, minced
4 white onions, chopped
¾ lb. okra, trimmed and sliced
2½ cups chopped peeled tomatoes
1 can (6 oz.) tomato paste
3 cups chicken stock

Tabasco
1 Tbs. Creole seasoning,* optional
1 green pepper, chopped
1 lb. crab meat
1 Tbs. filé powder
1 lemon
18 mussels

Trim fat from ham, cut lean meat into cubes, and render enough fat to make about 2 tablespoons in bottom of a heavy skillet; reserve remainder. Peel and wash shrimps; pat dry. Sauté garlic and onions in ham fat with okra, adding shrimps after 10 minutes; continue to cook for 5 minutes. Remove shrimps and okra to refrigerator. Stir tomatoes into skillet and add tomato paste, stock, several dashes of Tabasco, and Creole seasoning. Simmer for 2 hours or more. Thirty minutes before serving add okra, reserving shrimps, crab meat and filé powder. Heat some of reserved ham fat and sauté chopped green pepper and crab meat for about 10 minutes, and add. Grate lemon rind and add. Stir in filé powder and reserved shrimps, then top with mussels. Cover tightly and steam until mussels open. Serve over hot rice.

MAKES **6** TO **8** SERVINGS

* Creole seasoning may be found in specialty food stores.

California Fish Fillets in Red Wine

2½ Tbs. butter
2 white onions or shallots, minced
4 fillets of rex sole or flounder
 salt

freshly ground white pepper
¾ cup Pinot Noir or other red wine
2 Tbs. minced parsley

Preheat oven to 350°

Use a baking dish just large enough to hold fillets that can also be used on top of stove. Melt 1½ tablespoons butter in it, reserving the rest, and cook minced onions for 2 or 3 minutes. Lay fillets on onions, sprinkle with salt and freshly ground white pepper, pour in wine and dot with remaining butter. Bring to a boil, then put baking dish in oven and bake, basting frequently. When sauce reduces to about ¼ cup, remove dish from oven (about 10 minutes), sprinkle fish with parsley, and serve with buttered and parsleyed new potatoes.

MAKES 4 SERVINGS

Halibut with Avocado and Mushroom Stuffing

4 halibut fillets
 salt

freshly ground pepper
lemon juice

STUFFING:

⅛ lb. mushrooms, finely chopped
4 scallions, finely chopped
3 Tbs. butter
2 Tbs. flour
1 fresh tomato, peeled and chopped,
   or canned tomato

1 large ripe avocado, mashed
½ cup dry white wine
½ cup chicken stock
 salt
 freshly ground pepper
2 egg yolks

Preheat oven to 400°

Wipe fish with damp cloth and season with a little salt, freshly ground pepper, and a liberal sprinkling of lemon juice. Put chopped mushrooms, scallions, and butter in a skillet and sauté for 5 minutes. Stir in flour and cook for 2 or 3 minutes more. Add chopped tomato and mashed avocado; stir in wine, chicken stock, and salt and pepper to taste. Off heat, stir in egg yolks. Cook over low heat as sauce thickens. Put 2 fillets in a greased baking dish and cover with half of stuffing. Top with 2 more fillets and remaining stuffing. Bake for about 20 minutes.

MAKES 4 SERVINGS

Halibut Fillets in Aspic

1 lb. halibut fillets
2½ cups fish stock
¾ cup white wine
1½ envelopes unflavored gelatin

1 cup seedless white grapes, peeled
fresh tarragon
watercress

Wash fish fillets, fold in half, and put in enamelware pan or heatproof baking dish just large enough to hold comfortably. Pour over fish the stock and ½ cup of the wine. Bring to just below boiling point and simmer gently, covered, for about 5 minutes, or until fish is flaky. Remove fish and set aside to cool. Strain stock, through several layers of cheesecloth lining a strainer or colander, into a clean pan. Stir gelatin into remaining ¼ cup wine; when completely dissolved add to stock and bring liquid back to boiling point. When all traces of gelatin have vanished remove stock from heat. Meanwhile chill a fish-shaped (or other) mold that holds at least 1½ quarts. When aspic mixture is cool, cover bottom of mold to ½ inch in depth; chill in freezer for 15 minutes, until aspic is jellied. Spread decorative layer of peeled grapes over and return mold to freezer for 5 minutes. Spoon in more stock and let set. Flake cooked fish and make one layer in mold, sprinkling with salt and minced tarragon leaves. Repeat layers of stock, grapes, fish, finishing with stock. Let set in refrigerator for 4 to 5 hours. Turn out on chilled platter and decorate with watercress.

MAKES 4 SERVINGS

Pontchartrain Jambalaya

One of the greatest of American dishes, Jambalaya is one of the most instantly recognizable of Creole dishes. Recipes vary from one household to another; this one we find has delighted guests many times.

1 Tbs. bacon fat or rendered ham fat
2 medium-size onions, chopped
6 pork link sausages, highly seasoned
1 Tbs. flour
½ lb. country ham, diced
3 medium-size tomatoes, peeled, seeded, and chopped
1 cup uncooked rice
1 large garlic clove, minced

2 cups chicken stock
1½-inch piece of dried red pepper pod, crushed, or ¼ (or more) tsp. Creole or cayenne pepper
½ tsp. dried thyme
1 medium-size green pepper, diced
3 Tbs. minced parsley
1½ lbs. raw shrimps, peeled
1¼ pts. raw oysters

Use a heavy pot with tight-fitting cover and in it melt fat. Add onions and sausages and stir over moderate heat until sausages brown a little and onions are translucent. Stir in flour and cook slowly, stirring constantly until the "roux" has turned the color of peanut butter. Add ham and tomatoes and cover tightly, simmering over low heat for about 30 minutes. Add rice, garlic, stock, seasonings, green pepper, and parsley. Cover tightly and simmer over very low heat for 40 minutes or more, until rice is cooked but not mushy; do not stir. Stir in shrimps and cook for 2 minutes. Stir in oysters and cook for 3 minutes. Country ham should eliminate need for salting; taste and adjust seasoning as desired.

MAKES 6 SERVINGS

Charles Scotto's Lobster Américaine

This version of a fabled dish—given verbatim—is attributed to Chef Scotto of New York's Hotel Pierre who was regarded as Escoffier's favorite pupil. Imprecise though they are, these instructions may be followed by experienced cooks. The technique here avoids cutting up live lobsters, but it does not go as far as some other American variations, which call for removing the shell from the lobster pieces in the kitchen.

lobster	¼ cup burnt-off brandy
salt, pepper	1 Tbs. meat glacé
⅓ cup olive oil	3 small fresh tomatoes, chopped
10 Tbs. butter	and pressed
2 shallots, chopped	pinch of minced parsley
1 garlic clove, minced	few grains cayenne
2 Tbs. Chablis wine	2 or 3 sprigs parsley
2 Tbs. fish stock	boiled rice

Plunge lobster into rapidly boiling water for 5 minutes. Remove and drain. Sever and slightly crush the claws; cut tail into sections; split into halves lengthwise; remove the green tomally. Remove intestines and coral, and season lobster with salt and pepper. Then place lobster pieces, still in shells, in saucepan with olive oil and 2 tablespoons butter, melted and hot. Fry covered until meat has stiffened, then tilt the pan to empty grease, while holding lid. Sprinkle lobster with shallots and garlic, add the wine, fish stock, burnt-off brandy (heated and set aflame), meat glaze, tomatoes, parsley, and cayenne. Cover and cook in oven for 18 to 20 minutes. Then turn out lobster pieces onto a dish; take meat from sections of tail and claws, and put it in a timbale (with larger pieces still in shells). Keep hot. Now reduce the cooking sauce of the lobster to ⅛ pint. Add intestines and chopped coral together with 2 tablespoons of butter; cook for a moment and strain. Put this into a pan, heat it without letting it boil, and add, away from fire, remaining butter cut into small pieces. Pour sauce over pieces of lobster and garnish with fried parsley. Serve with rice.

Delmonico's Lobster Newberg

Ben Wenberg was a sea captain whose ship regularly brought in Cuban fruit. In 1876 he brought something else to his favorite eating place. Home from a cruise, he entered Delmonico's and called for a blazer in which to demonstrate his new method of preparing lobster, then offered the result to his friend Charles Delmonico. The restaurateur was so pleased that he added the dish to his menu and called it *Lobster à la Wenberg*. He was as quick to strike it from the bill of fare after a falling-out with Wenberg, and when popular demand forced him to compromise he reversed the spelling of the first syllable of Wenberg's name. The misspelling of the second syllable came later. Here is Delmonico's recipe, adapted for use at home.

2 live lobsters, 2 lbs. each
6 Tbs. butter, clarified
½ tsp. salt
1 cup heavy cream

2 Tbs. Madeira wine
3 egg yolks, well beaten
cayenne

Cook lobsters in boiling salted water for 25 minutes. Remove and cool. Cut lobster meat into slices and put slices in a saucepan with most of the butter, making sure that each piece lies flat; season with salt and sauté lightly on both sides without coloring. Moisten to their height with good raw cream, and reduce liquid quickly to half. Add Madeira and boil once more only. Remove from heat and thicken sauce with beaten egg yolks. Reheat without boiling, incorporating a little cayenne and remaining butter. Arrange lobster pieces in serving dish and pour sauce over.

MAKES 4 TO 6 SERVINGS

Mackerel Grilled with Buttermilk

2 mackerel, 1 to 1½ lbs. each,
    beheaded and split
¾ cup buttermilk
¼ cup minced fresh herbs: parsley,
    dill, or fennel leaves, or
    combination

coarse salt
freshly ground pepper

Wipe fish with damp cloth. In flameproof baking dish large enough to hold fish in one layer, pour enough buttermilk to cover bottom ⅛ inch deep. Put in fish, skin side down, cover with remaining buttermilk, then sprinkle with minced herbs, coarse salt, and freshly ground pepper. Turn on broiler and put in baking dish, about 5 to 6 inches from source of heat. Grill for 12 to 15 minutes, basting with the liquid once or twice.

MAKES ABOUT 4 SERVINGS

Oysters Baked with Blue Cheese Sauce

6 oz. blue cheese
6 Tbs. butter
6 Tbs. finely chopped celery
4 tsp. Worcestershire sauce

½ cup sour cream
1 qt. oysters
½ lemon
2 hard-cooked eggs, chopped

Preheat oven to 400°

Crumble cheese and melt with butter in top part of a double boiler over simmering water, stirring; add chopped celery; cook for about 5 minutes. Add Worcestershire and sour cream. Divide oysters among 6 individual ramekins, and sprinkle with lemon juice. Stir chopped eggs into cheese sauce and pour over oysters, dividing evenly. Bake for about 10 minutes, and serve piping hot.

MAKES 6 SERVINGS

Oyster Stew

5 Tbs. butter
2 small carrots, minced
1 young white turnip, minced
2 small white onions, minced
2 celery hearts, minced
2 Tbs. flour

1 cup scalded milk
12 shelled oysters and their juice
1 cup heavy cream
   salt and pepper
   paprika
2 Tbs. chopped parsley

Melt 2 tablespoons butter in a skillet and gently sauté finely minced vegetables, stirring constantly, for about 20 minutes, until they just begin to take color. In a saucepan melt 2 tablespoons butter, stir in the flour, and when this mixture is smooth and has cooked for about 2 minutes stir in the scalded milk, blending well to make a smooth sauce. In an enamelware saucepan, melt remaining 1 tablespoon butter and turn oysters into it, letting them plump up over heat before adding their juice. Season with salt and pepper, add cream to white sauce and stir in cooked minced vegetables before mixing with oysters. Bring stew to point just below boiling, stirring constantly. Pour into hot soup tureen, dust with paprika, and sprinkle with chopped parsley.

MAKES 2 SERVINGS

Ocean Perch with Lobster Tail, Chervil Sauce

Rosefish, redfish, sea perch, and red perch are all apt to be sold under the name "Ocean Perch," and they are easily found frozen in most supermarkets. The delicate flavor is enhanced in this recipe by contrast with the texture of lobster tails and the flavor of chervil and sour cream. The fillets run about six to a pound.

1½ to 2 lbs. frozen ocean perch
2 cups fish stock or diluted clam juice or chicken stock
4 Tbs. butter
¼ cup minced red onion
1 Tbs. parsley
½ cup diced lobster tail
2 Tbs. flour

salt
freshly ground pepper
¼ to ½ tsp. dillweed
2 Tbs. minced fresh chervil leaves, or canned puréed chervil, drained
3 to 4 Tbs. sour cream, at room temperature

Thaw fillets in refrigerator overnight or at room temperature for 3 to 4 hours. Poach in simmering stock for about 8 minutes. Remove fish and keep warm while reducing stock to 1½ cups. Meanwhile melt butter in a saucepan, stir in onion, and sauté briefly; stir in parsley and lobster tail; cook for 5 minutes. Sprinkle lobster and onion with flour, stir over heat for 2 or 3 minutes, then gradually add reduced stock, blending to make a smooth sauce. Add salt only if necessary, and a little pepper. Stir in dillweed, drained chervil, and sour cream; heat but do not boil. Pour over warm perch fillets and serve.

MAKES 4 SERVINGS

Polish-American Stuffed Pike

Old-world ways with fish have been much adapted, and the Northern Pike of the Upper Midwest have been turned into delicious dishes like this one when brought home by Polish-American anglers. If the pike comes from a market, look it in the eye and be sure it is absolutely fresh.

2 whole pike, about 1¼ lbs. each, split open
4 Tbs. butter
½ cup chopped onions
½ cup chopped celery
½ cup chopped apples

½ cup chopped mushrooms
¾ cup fresh bread crumbs
1 egg, beaten
¼ tsp. dried thyme
softened butter
salt and pepper

Preheat oven to 450°

Rinse fish and pat dry. Melt butter and sauté onions and celery over low heat for about 5 minutes. Add chopped apples and mushrooms and sauté for 2 or 3 minutes more. Off heat, stir in bread crumbs, blend in beaten egg, and add thyme, salt to taste, and several turns of pepper grinder. Stuff this fruit-vegetable-crumb mixture into cavities of fish, skewering or sewing them to hold in stuffing. Rub fish with softened butter, sprinkle with salt and pepper, and bake, under foil cover, in a buttered baking dish for 30 minutes. Remove foil, brown in oven for 5 minutes, and serve with Warsaw Sour-Cream Sauce (p. 329).

MAKES 4 SERVINGS

Sautéed Pompano in Chervil Butter

Some Americans consider pompano to be one of the most elegant fishes on which to dine, and it is easy enough to find in Florida and other markets near the Gulf of Mexico. It is good enough when broiled, and excellent with herbed butter, as sometimes done in our kitchen.

Pepper

2 pompano, 1¼ to 1½ lbs. each, split and boned	freshly ground pepper
¼ lb. butter	¾ cup dry vermouth
coarse salt	3 Tbs. chopped fresh chervil, or
	2 tsp. puréed chervil

Wipe fish with damp cloth. Melt about 6 tablespoons butter in a skillet large enough to hold fillets of pompano. When butter has foamed, skim off white froth, turn heat to moderately high, and sauté fillets, flesh side down, for 3 minutes; turn, sprinkle with a little salt and pepper, and sauté on other side for 5 minutes, spooning hot butter over fish. Remove, and keep warm on serving plate. Sizzle vermouth in hot skillet, boiling to reduce by half; then add chervil and swirl in remaining butter. Pour sauce over fish just before serving.

MAKES 4 SERVINGS

Seafood Pilau

Pilau is probably originally a Turkish word, but the kind of food described is known all over the Middle East, often as *pilav*, or *pilaf*; in India the usual spelling is *pullao*. Recipes arrived in the United States some time after rice was first planted in Carolina, perhaps brought by Charleston trading vessels, and both spelling and pronunciation were soon distorted. In places like Savannah and New Orleans it is still frequently referred to as "purloo," and spelled sometimes "perlew," sometimes "purlow." Southerners consider a variety of combinations to be their own, from okra or tomato pilaus to those made with lamb, pork, chicken, fish, or shellfish.

2 Tbs. bacon fat
¼ cup chopped shallots or scallions
¼ cup chopped green pepper
½ cup uncooked rice
1 cup fish or chicken stock
½ canned red pepper, minced
½ tsp. sage

½ tsp. dried thyme
  salt
1 cup fresh or canned oysters
1 cup minced clams
1 cup fresh or canned crab meat
1 cup cooked, sliced okra
1 cup diced country ham

Melt fat and sauté shallots and green pepper for 3 or 4 minutes, then stir in rice, coat rice with fat, and cook for 2 or 3 minutes. Add stock, bring to a boil, then simmer under tight-fitting cover for 20 to 25 minutes, until rice is fluffy and rather dry. (You may use half chicken or other white stock and half liquid from oysters and/or clams; or you may add seafood liquids if rice absorbs stock before it is done.) Season with red pepper, sage, thyme, and very little salt if using country ham. Mix in oysters, clams, crab meat, okra, and ham. Flavors meld better when this dish is made early so it can be set aside to steep under tight cover; heat carefully just before serving.

MAKES 4 SERVINGS

Antoine's Pompano en Papillotte

From the late Roy Alciatore, grandson of the founder of one of New Orleans' most famous watering places, there came the inscribed recipe on which this is based. The spelling is that used in the *Vieux Carré*.

3 medium-size pompano
1 small carrot, roughly chopped
1 stalk celery
1 small onion, roughly chopped
2 cups water
2 finely chopped shallots or scallions
1¾ cups dry white wine
  salt and freshly ground pepper
6 Tbs. butter

3 or 4 drops of Tabasco
2 cups cooked small shrimps
2 cups crab meat
1 garlic clove, finely minced
1 pinch of dried thyme
1 bay leaf
2 Tbs. flour
  vegetable oil

Preheat oven to 450° *

Clean the pompano and cut into 6 fillets. Use the head and bones to make a fish stock, simmering them with the carrot, celery, and onion in the water and 1 cup of the wine for about 30 minutes, until somewhat reduced. Strain the stock and pour over the fillets, seasoning them with salt and pepper and adding ½ cup of the wine. Let fish simmer, covered, very gently, for about 8 minutes, then let it rest in the stock. Meanwhile make the sauce: cook the shallots or scallions in half of the butter for a few minutes, then add Tabasco, shrimps, crab meat, garlic, thyme, and bay leaf. In a separate pan melt remaining butter; blend in flour, and cook slowly, stirring constantly, for a minute or two, then blend in 1 cup of the warm stock and remaining ¼ cup wine. Combine with the shrimp and crab-meat mixture and correct the seasoning. * Now cut 6 pieces of parchment paper in the shape of hearts 8 by 12 inches and oil each piece well. Remove fillets from poaching liquid with a slotted spoon, saving remaining stock for another purpose. Place one fillet in the center of each piece of parchment, top with one sixth of the seafood sauce, and fold the oiled paper over. Seal the edges by making a tight, firm rolled fold all around the open edge. Don't rub oil on the outside. Place the parchment hearts on a baking sheet and bake for 15 minutes, until the paper has browned. Serve immediately in the paper hearts, the *papillottes*.

MAKES 6 SERVINGS

Porgy Baked with Herbs and Tomatoes

4 porgies	coarse salt
3 Tbs. peanut oil	4 small ripe tomatoes
1 medium-size onion, chopped	freshly ground black pepper
2 Tbs. minced fresh basil	½ cup water
1 bay leaf	2 to 3 Tbs. minced parsley

Preheat oven to 350°

Run cold water over fish and pat dry. Put oil, onion, basil, and bay leaf in a saucepan and simmer for 3 or 4 minutes, stirring occasionally. Salt fish lightly inside and out. Prepare a shallow casserole, large enough to hold fish flat, by straining enough oil from saucepan to cover bottom. Lay fish side by side and scrape onion, seasonings, and remaining oil on top of them. Cut tomatoes into 1-inch slices and arrange around fish. Sprinkle fish and tomatoes with 8 to 10 turns of pepper grinder. Pour water into bottom of casserole, then bake in oven for 30 minutes. Fish should flake easily when done. Sprinkle tomatoes with minced parsley and serve.

MAKES 4 SERVINGS

Pan-Fried Porgy

4 porgies, about ¾ lb. each*	½ cup corn oil
1 cup cornmeal	¼ lb. butter
1 Tbs. coarse salt	¼ cup minced shallots or scallions
½ tsp. freshly ground pepper	⅔ cup dry white wine

* Small trout, sea squabs, flounders, or soles may be substituted.

Clean porgies but leave whole; rinse and pat dry. Mix together cornmeal, salt, and pepper and dredge fish with mixture. In one very large or two medium-size frying pans heat oil until almost smoking. Fry fish for 5 minutes on each side, then remove and keep warm. Wipe pan clean of any burned bits, then melt 3 to 4 tablespoons butter and sauté minced shallots until soft and slightly browned; turn up heat, pour in wine, let sizzle, and reduce to half. Swirl in remaining butter and pour over warm fish.

MAKES 4 SERVINGS

Smoked Salmon on Bed of Spinach

½ to ¾ lb. sliced smoked salmon
2 pkg. (10 oz. each) frozen spinach, or 1 lb. fresh spinach

1½ cups Lemony Mustard Sauce (p. 329)
2 to 3 Tbs. minced parsley

Bring salmon to room temperature. Prepare spinach according to package directions, or cook in usual fashion until tender, then purée or chop. Heat (prepare if not on hand) lemony mustard sauce. Heat drained spinach, placing salmon slices on top to heat also. Put spinach on hot platter, topping with salmon slices and sauce; sprinkle with parsley. Serve sauce separately.

MAKES 4 SERVINGS

Poached Salmon Steaks with Dill Sauce

4 salmon steaks, about ½ lb. each
1 bunch of dill
4 onion slices
½ cup dry white wine
1 to 2 cups fish stock, or half clam juice, half water
2 Tbs. butter

2 Tbs. flour
½ cup light cream or milk
1 egg yolk
salt
freshly ground pepper
nutmeg
1 Tbs. minced parsley

Put salmon steaks in flameproof dish or skillet and top each with 1 sprig of dill and 1 onion slice. Pour in wine and stock. Bring slowly to a boil and simmer gently, covering pan, for 10 minutes. Meanwhile melt butter in a heavy saucepan, stir in flour, and cook over low heat for 1 or 2 minutes. Off heat, stir in hot stock ladled from fish; when smoothly blended cook, stirring constantly, until thickened. Beat a little of cream or milk with egg yolk, add to it a little hot sauce and remaining cream, and stir into sauce; bring just to boiling point. Add a little salt and pepper, 1 tablespoon minced dill, a little grated nutmeg, and the parsley. Drain salmon steaks, scraping off cooking vegetables, and distribute hot sauce over them.

MAKES 4 SERVINGS

A West Coast member of the flounder family that only Californians enjoy regularly, sand dabs have an indescribable, delicate flavor when sautéed quickly in butter as we first tasted them; or they can be baked in the oven in paper hearts.

2 sand dabs or rex sole, filleted
    salt and freshly ground pepper
4 slices of boiled ham, slightly
    smaller than fish pieces
3 to 4 Tbs. butter

8 mushroom caps
4 sheets of parchment paper or bond
    writing paper, 8½ by 11 inches
1½ Tbs. minced chives and parsley

Preheat oven to 450°

Sprinkle fillets with salt and pepper and put a slice of ham on top of each. Melt 1½ tablespoons butter in a skillet and cook mushroom caps lightly, turning often. Cut each sheet of paper in the shape of a heart, folding lengthwise; butter one half thoroughly, and place on it a fillet and ham slice topped by 2 mushroom caps and a sprinkling of mixed chives and parsley. Bring edges of heart together and crimp well to hold in juices. Bake in hot oven for 10 minutes, or until paper browns and puffs up.

MAKES 4 SERVINGS

Broiled Scrod

Pollock, haddock, or other fish are often sold as scrod, but the uniquely American scrod is really a young, small codfish, weighing between 1 and 2 pounds, to be broiled as a strictly New England dish. Kenneth Roberts wrote that "State-of-Maine and Boston gourmets confronted with such fish delicacies as pompano, Great Lakes whitefish or broiled scrod, are as apt to take the scrod as the whitefish or pompano." When the young codfish is split wide open and the head, tail, and bones removed, it becomes a scrod; nothing else will do, nor can anything else duplicate the fresh flavor of this Yankee specialty.

2 whole scrod, 1 to 1½ lbs. each,
    split and boned
½ cup melted butter

salt
freshly ground pepper
1 Tbs. lemon juice

Brush scrod with melted butter and sprinkle with salt and pepper. Grease the grill and broil about 3 inches from high heat for 8 minutes. Serve with a sauce made of the remaining melted butter, adding more if desirable, to which the lemon juice has been added.

MAKES 4 SERVINGS

Scrod with Minced Mushrooms and Artichokes

2 lbs. scrod
3 cups fish stock, or 1½ cups clam
    juice and 1½ cups water
¼ cup white wine
1 cup finely chopped mushrooms
2 shallots, minced
4 Tbs. butter
1 cup finely minced cooked artichoke
    (see below)

salt
freshly ground pepper
2 Tbs. flour
½ cup heavy cream
2 Tbs. dry sherry
3 Tbs. grated cheese, aged Cheddar
    or Parmesan

Place scrod side by side in Teflon or enamelware skillet; pour in stock and wine and bring to a boil. Cover and simmer gently for 5 minutes, until fish flakes easily. (Be careful not to overcook.) Sauté minced mushrooms and shallots in 2 tablespoons of butter for 3 or 4 minutes. Scrape edible pulp from tips of artichoke leaves and combine with minced hearts, or mince frozen parboiled artichokes. Mix with shallots and mushrooms to warm, adding salt and pepper to taste. Spread mixture on bottom of shallow casserole large enough to hold fish pieces in a single layer. Lift fish with slotted spoon, pat dry, and lay on vegetable bed, sprinkling with a little salt and pepper. Melt remaining butter, stir in flour and cook slowly for 2 or 3 minutes. Off heat, stir in 1 cup of liquid in which fish cooked, beating to eliminate lumps; stir over heat until thickened, then add cream and sherry. Taste and add salt and pepper if needed. Pour sauce over fish in casserole and top with sprinkling of cheese. Put under broiler to brown. (This can be made ahead of time and brought to room temperature; then bake at 450° for 10 minutes.)

MAKES 4 SERVINGS

Shad Stuffed with Sorrel Sauce

2 pairs shad roe
2 Tbs. butter
2 Tbs. minced shallots or scallions
¾ cup white wine
    salt
    freshly ground pepper

1 shad, 4 lbs., cleaned, boned,
    and split
1 tsp. cornstarch
1¼ cups heavy cream
⅓ cup tightly packed puréed cooked
    fresh sorrel, or canned sorrel

Preheat oven to 375°

In an enamelware pan, sauté roes in butter with shallots for about 2 minutes on each side; add wine and simmer for 10 minutes. Remove roes with slotted spoon, sprinkle generously with salt and pepper, then break up and stuff into the flaps on the two sides of shad. Butter a baking dish just large enough to hold fish; put stuffed fish in it and cover loosely with foil. Bake for about 30 minutes. Meanwhile reduce by one third the pan juices from the roe, cooking over brisk heat. Dissolve cornstarch in a little of the cream, mix with remainder, and stir into boiling juices. Simmer until sauce has the consistency of cream, then add puréed sorrel and stir until the sauce is hot again. Test fish to see if it flakes easily. If so, it is done; if you like it a little drier, bake for another 5 minutes. Remove to a platter, pour some hot sorrel sauce over, and serve remaining sauce in sauceboat.

MAKES 6 SERVINGS

Shad with Mushroom and Corn-Bread Stuffing

1 shad fillet, about 1 lb., boned
3 Tbs. butter
1 Tbs. chopped shallot or scallion
1 Tbs. chopped green pepper
3 or 4 medium-size mushroom caps, chopped fine
⅓ cup crumbled corn bread
⅓ cup crumbled baking powder (or commercial water) biscuit
salt
freshly ground pepper
1 tsp. chopped dill
1 Tbs. minced parsley
lemon wedges

Preheat oven to 375°

Wipe shad with a damp cloth and put in lightly buttered shallow baking pan. Make stuffing: melt 2 tablespoons of butter in a skillet, add shallot, green pepper, and mushrooms, and cook slowly for about 5 minutes. Stir in crumbled corn bread and biscuit; sprinkle generously with salt, freshly ground pepper, and herbs. When well mixed, spread stuffing on inside of fish, fold top piece over, and tie with string in 2 or 3 places. Dot with remaining butter and sprinkle with salt and pepper. Pour 2 or 3 tablespoons water into baking pan and cover fish loosely with foil. Bake for 30 minutes. Remove strings, cut fish in two, and garnish with lemon wedges.

MAKES 2 SERVINGS

Chesapeake Bay Shad Roe

In Maryland shad roe is frequently cooked with mushrooms, sometimes being baked instead of poached or sautéed. After many waits for spring to come and the shad to run, this is one of the ways we like to prepare this delicacy.

4 pairs shad roe
3 Tbs. butter
6 to 8 shallots, minced
3 or 4 Tbs. minced parsley
½ lb. small mushrooms
1 cup dry white wine
1 cup heavy cream
1 Tbs. flour

Wipe shad roe with a damp cloth. Melt butter in a large skillet, stir in minced shallots and parsley, and cook slowly for 1 minute. Stir in mushrooms and cook for 5 minutes, shaking pan frequently. Carefully add shad roe, cover with wine, and simmer under cover for 15 minutes, letting steam escape occasionally. Put cream and flour in a jar and shake until free of lumps. Remove roe from pan and reduce liquid to half, then stir in cream and flour mixture and cook to thicken slightly. Put roe on a flameproof platter, pour sauce over, and broil for 3 or 4 minutes.

MAKES 4 SERVINGS

Creole Shrimps

2 medium-size Bermuda onions, finely chopped	1 bay leaf
	1 thyme sprig
2 medium-size green peppers, seeded and chopped	1 tsp. salt
	ground cayenne or Creole pepper
2 Tbs. butter	dash of Tabasco
3 tomatoes, peeled and chopped	1½ lbs. raw shrimps, peeled
2 cups chicken stock	cooked rice

Sauté onions and green pepper in butter for about 4 minutes. Add tomatoes, chicken stock, bay leaf, thyme, salt, and cayenne or Creole pepper to taste. Bring to a boil and simmer for 45 minutes. Add a dash of Tabasco, then stir in raw shrimps and cook for 5 minutes. Serve on hot fluffy rice.

MAKES 4 SERVINGS

Spiced Lagoon Shrimp Flambé

1 lb. large raw shrimps	salt
3 Tbs. olive oil	freshly ground pepper
½ tsp. ground cinnamon	¼ cup rum
¼ tsp. grated nutmeg	lemon juice
3 whole cloves	

Peel shrimps but leave tails on. Rinse under running water; drain. Heat oil in a skillet large enough to hold shrimps in one layer. Pat shrimps dry with paper towel, then sauté in oil until they turn pink; remove from heat. Stir in cinnamon, grate nutmeg over, and stir in whole cloves. Sprinkle with a little salt and a turn or two of pepper grinder, then let shrimps steep, covered, for 30 minutes or more. Reheat shrimps when ready to serve and warm up rum. Set rum aflame and pour over shrimps in pan, stirring while flame burns. Squeeze on lemon juice and serve hot. Creamed pearl onions make an interesting side dish.

MAKES 4 SERVINGS

Southern Shrimp Pie

Shrimp is one of the traditional favorites on Southern menus, including break-fast dishes. In Charleston shrimp pie is made with bread crumbs, which are replaced by boiled rice in Savannah. Sometimes a pastry crust is used, sometimes not.

2 lbs. raw shrimps
4 slices of white bread
1½ cups white wine
⅛ tsp. grated mace

grated nutmeg
salt
cayenne pepper

Preheat oven to 400°

Put shrimps in boiling salted water and cook for about 3 minutes. Tear up bread, spin in blender for a second or two, then soak in wine. Peel shrimps and add to wine and crumbs, seasoning liberally with mace, gratings of nutmeg, salt, and cayenne, enough cayenne so one can taste it. Turn into a buttered baking dish and bake for about 50 minutes.

MAKES 6 SERVINGS

Spiced Smelts

These scaleless silvery fish run in spring and fall in many coastal streams, in Lake Champlain and in tributaries of the Great Lakes. Smelts of the Pacific Northwest are a fatter variety and so rich in oil when found in the Columbia River that the Northwest Indians used them, after drying, as candles. Seasonal smelt runs, when the fish are so numerous they can be scooped up with bushel baskets, are traditionally celebrated in places like Michigan and New England. The silver splinters are cooked very simply, often deep-fried, baked, or broiled. In Maine, panfuls are crisscrossed with strips of salt pork and baked into a solid slab of matchless crispness with a subtle blend of flavors. The following unusual preparation is a favorite of James Beard's.

2 lbs. smelts
1 large onion, thinly sliced
1 garlic clove, minced
1 large bay leaf
6 peppercorns
½ lemon, sliced
⅓ cup olive oil
¼ cup vinegar

2 tsp. salt
½ tsp. paprika
4 whole allspice
½-inch cinnamon stick
4 whole cloves
1 cup water
½ cup dry white wine or cider

Preheat oven to 400°

Make sure you have 3 or 4 smelts per person. Combine all other ingredients in a saucepan and bring to a boil, then simmer for 15 minutes. Meanwhile wash and clean smelts, leaving heads on. Dry them and arrange in a single layer in large baking dish; cover with simmered liquid, cover with a tight lid or foil pinched around edges, and bake for 15 minutes for good-size fish, 10 to 12 minutes for small. Let them cool in the spicy liquid, then chill in refrigerator for several hours.

MAKES 4 SERVINGS

Cutchogue Fish Stew

2 lbs. fish fillets, sea bass, haddock, flounder
1 eel, skinned and cut into pieces
1 Tbs. wine vinegar
¼ cup olive oil
2 garlic cloves, minced
3 Tbs. minced sorrel leaves, or 1 Tbs. puréed sorrel
1 bay leaf
2 Tbs. minced parsley

⅓ cup chopped onion
1½ cups Muscadet or other dry white wine
2 tomatoes, peeled and chopped, or 1 cup canned tomatoes
1 tsp. salt
freshly ground pepper
2 lbs. fresh mussels
stale bread

Put fillets and eel pieces in a mixing bowl and cover with vinegar and oil seasoned with garlic, sorrel, bay leaf, parsley, and onion; add wine, tomatoes, salt, and several turns of pepper grinder. Refrigerate for 2 hours or more.

Wash mussels under running water, using brush to scrub thoroughly. When ready to cook, put fish and marinade in a heavy pot and spread cleaned mussels over; cover tightly and bring to boiling point, then simmer for 12 to 15 minutes. Stew will be done when eel is tender. Do not overcook. Put slices of bread in hot soup plates and pour stew on top.

MAKES 6 SERVINGS

Pinebark Stew

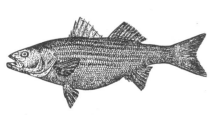

On the coast of the Carolinas fish stews have colloquial names. Along Albemarle Sound people get together outdoors to cook a kind of chowder famous in those parts as a "muddle." Some recipes start out with 50 pounds of rockfish and 10 pounds of bacon. Even bigger amounts have been needed when the annual Mullet Festival at Swansboro has drawn as many as 5,000 persons. In the South, mullet is also combined with yams and onions to make a stew "unjustly ignored by cookbook makers" according to a South Carolinian. "Pinebark Stew" is another local delight. "Since seasonings were unavailable during

Revolutionary War days," a Carolina newspaper asserted, "the small tender roots of the pine tree (found by digging about 20 feet from the trunk of the tree) were used for flavoring. With homemade ketchup as a base, the only other seasoning was red pepper." Bacon is important to make a good pinebark stew, and the Carolinian cook would use blue bream, redbreast, bass, trout, or even such saltwater fish as sheepshead.

4 bacon strips
1 cup chopped onions
1½ cups finely diced potatoes
1 qt. boiling water
2 tsp. salt
½ tsp. dried thyme
½ tsp. dried marjoram
2-inch piece of dried red pepper pod
1½ lbs. bass
1 lb. perch
4 or 5 small tomatoes, peeled, or
    equivalent canned

Cut bacon into squares and sauté for 13 to 15 minutes over very low heat. Drain off all but about 3 tablespoons fat. Stir in onions and cook for about 5 minutes. Stir in potatoes, cover with boiling water, and season with salt, herbs, and dried pepper pod. Simmer for 15 to 20 minutes. Add whole fish and continue to simmer for 10 minutes. Add tomatoes and cook for 5 to 10 minutes more, until fish flakes easily. Remove pepper pod before serving.

MAKES 4 SERVINGS

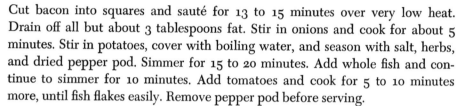

Floridian Sea Squab

12 to 16 sea squabs (3 or 4 per
    serving, depending on size)
½ cup flour, seasoned with salt and
    pepper
3 to 4 Tbs. butter
3 Tbs. olive oil
½ cup dry white wine
4 Tbs. minced shallots or scallions
1 garlic clove, minced
1 can (28 oz.) plum tomatoes
1 pkg. (9 oz.) frozen baby arti-
    chokes, blanched for 10 minutes
12 pitted black olives
2 Tbs. minced parsley

Rinse sea squabs (sometimes called blowfish), pat dry and roll in seasoned flour; shake off excess. Heat 1½ tablespoons butter and equal amount of oil in a large skillet until sizzling, then sauté fish, six to eight at a time, for 5 minutes on each side. Remove to heated platter and keep warm. Add more butter and oil while cooking remaining fish. When all fish have been removed from skillet, add wine and boil down quickly, scraping up brown bits. Stir in minced shallots or scallions and brown lightly, adding extra butter if necessary. Stir in garlic and drained tomatoes with about 1 tablespoon of tomato liquid; cook down. Add cooked artichokes and olives; when warm through put in sea squabs and spoon tomato mixture over them. Taste to correct seasoning. Serve piping hot with sprinkling of parsley.

MAKES 4 SERVINGS

Sturgeon Baked with New England Hard Cider

1 cup finely chopped onion
1½-lb. sturgeon steak, 1 piece 1½ to
    2 inches thick
4 very thin slices of salt pork
2 cups very dry cider or white wine
5 Tbs. softened butter
3 Tbs. flour

½ cup heavy cream
salt
freshly ground black pepper
¼ tsp. dried thyme
¼ tsp. dried basil
1 Tbs. applejack
1 tsp. minced parsley

Preheat oven to 350°

Cover bottom of an 8-inch baking dish with chopped onion, laying fish steak on top and covering steak with salt pork slices. Pour cider (or dry white wine if only sweet cider is available) over fish. Cut brown paper slightly larger than top of baking dish, saturating it well with about 2 tablespoons butter, then tuck paper in around edges of baking dish to enclose fish and onion. Bake for about 35 minutes, removing from oven when fish flakes easily. Meanwhile knead 3 tablespoons flour with 3 tablespoons butter. Remove fish and set aside to keep warm. Put baking dish over direct flame and slowly stir cream into onion-cider sauce; when hot but not boiling blend in butter-flour paste. Taste as sauce thickens and add seasonings. Stir in about 1 tablespoon applejack and cook for about 1 minute. Pour sauce over hot fish and sprinkle with chopped parsley.

MAKES 4 SERVINGS

Broiled Tilefish with Caviar

It is said that tilefish appeared off the New England coast in 1879 and that the name derives from its tilelike coloring. When they disappeared early in 1882 fishermen supposed them to have become extinct. They returned a decade later with no explanation, and in the twentieth century they have been netted along the Atlantic Coast and sometimes made available in metropolitan New York markets. A large, rather bland fish with firm, moist flesh, tile can be cut into good-size slices for broiling. Whitefish caviar from Wisconsin adds a lovely accent.

5 Tbs. butter
4 slices of tile, about ½ inch thick
    coarse salt
    freshly ground pepper

lemon
4 tsp. whitefish caviar
2 Tbs. minced parsley

Smear about 1 tablespoon of the butter on the bottom of a baking pan just large enough to hold the pieces of fish in one layer. Place the fish in, season with salt and pepper, and squeeze several drops of lemon juice over each piece. Broil under hot flame for 3 to 5 minutes, depending on the heat of your broiler, then turn fish over and broil for 3 or 4 minutes longer. While broiling, cream remaining butter, then blend in caviar. Now spread equal amounts of the caviar-butter on the fish steaks, spoon hot juice over, and run under the broiler for another minute to heat through. Spoon juice over again, sprinkle parsley on top, and serve with slices of lemon.

MAKES 4 SERVINGS

Lake Trout Sautéed with Fresh Sage

Anyone who has grown up in Minnesota knows what the taste of freshly caught trout can do to one, and there is some reason to think the effect is greater on visitors. Before this recipe was tried, an acquaintance told a story about being the state's hostess for the Duke and Duchess of Windsor. When she served trout for the fish course, "the duke ate his first trout in two minutes flat and asked for a second." He might have liked the following presentation even better.

4 lake trout, 1 lb. each
  butter
¼ cup chopped fresh sage

salt
freshly ground pepper

Wash trout in cold salted water, and pat dry. Melt enough butter to cover bottom of a large skillet 1 inch deep. Add chopped sage and simmer for 1 minute. Slip in fish. Cook for 10 minutes on first side, turn, sprinkle with salt and pepper, then cook for 5 minutes on second side. Zucchini cooked with chopped black walnuts (p. 206) makes a delicious accompaniment.

MAKES 4 SERVINGS

Black-Walnut-Breaded Pan-fried Trout

4 Rocky Mountain trout, about 1 lb.
  each, cleaned
  coarse salt
  freshly ground black pepper
⅔ cup ground black walnuts
½ cup fresh bread crumbs
¼ cup crumbs from Montpelier water
  biscuits or soda crackers
1 egg

3 Tbs. butter
3 to 4 Tbs. walnut oil
½ cup dry white wine or hard cider,
  or tea plus 5 to 6 drops of lemon
  juice
2 Tbs. mixed minced herbs, parsley,
  chives, basil, or tarragon
1 lemon, quartered

Rinse trout under cold water, pat dry, and sprinkle inside and out with coarse salt and freshly ground pepper. Mix walnuts, bread crumbs, and cracker crumbs, and spread out on wax paper. Break egg into large saucer, beat lightly with a fork, then dip each trout into egg, coating each side. Dip fish next into crumbs, coating thickly. Heat 2 tablespoons of the butter and 2 tablespoons of the oil in a large skillet; when almost smoking put in trout and fry over medium heat for 8 to 10 minutes, depending on size, on one side and 4 to 5 minutes on other side. Add remaining butter and oil as needed. Remove fish to warm plate. Sizzle wine (or other liquid) in hot skillet; swirl around and let it reduce for about 1 minute. Add fresh herbs and pour over fish. Serve with lemon quarters.

MAKES 4 SERVINGS

Planked Great Lakes Whitefish

Once on a cold, dreary day outside Anacortes, Washington, we had the warming reward of eating salmon that had been cooked outdoors on a plank. The method was that of the American Indians and it was a common way to cook fowl, lobster, shad, and other fish from eastern rivers, and whitefish from the Great Lakes. The latter "has gained much favor," Fannie Farmer pointed out in 1896. "Our plank had been used long and often, gaining virtue with every planking," a man who grew up in nineteenth-century Michigan remembered; "it held two medium-sized whitefish cut down the back and pressed firmly on the board." For those who needed a recipe one was provided in the 1857 edition of the *New Cookery Book* of Eliza Leslie who cited the method as "superior to all others."

3½- to 4-lb. whitefish, cleaned and   freshly ground pepper
    boned   butter
   coarse salt   3 bacon strips

Preheat oven to 375°

Season fish inside and out with salt and pepper. Butter plank liberally, and put fish in center. Cover exposed part of plank with coarse salt to keep from burning. Spread bacon strips on top of fish, then bake for 45 minutes.

MAKES 4 TO 6 SERVINGS

Chapter 17

Salads

Artichoke and Grated-Carrot Salad

1 pkg. (9 oz.) frozen baby artichokes	½ lemon
⅓ cup water	¼ cup olive oil
½ tsp. salt	2 medium-size carrots
6 to 8 peppercorns	¾ Tbs. mixed minced parsley and
6 to 8 coriander berries	fresh basil

Put artichokes in saucepan with water, salt, bruised peppercorns and coriander, juice of ½ lemon, and oil; cover, bring to a boil, and simmer for 5 minutes. Remove cover and boil until liquid is evaporated. Chill for several hours. Scrape carrots and grate. Put chilled artichokes in center of salad bowl and arrange grated carrots around. Sprinkle with a little more lemon juice and olive oil, then scatter minced herbs over all.

MAKES 4 SERVINGS

Beet and Apple Salad

½ cup heavy cream	¾ cup mayonnaise
¼ cup sour cream	½ tsp. prepared mustard
¼ cup yoghurt	2 Tbs. chopped parsley or fresh dill
4 medium-size beets, cooked	salt
2 tart apples, peeled and cored	freshly ground pepper

Mix the cream, sour cream and yoghurt thoroughly and let stand at room temperature for several hours. Dice beets and apples into equal-size pieces. Mix mayonnaise and cream mixture, blend in mustard and parsley or fresh dill. Toss with beets and apples. Taste, and add a little salt and a few turns of pepper grinder, as needed.

MAKES 4 SERVINGS

Beet, Celery and Cucumber Salad

3 garlic cloves, minced
½ tsp. salt
1 cup fresh bread crumbs
½ cup pine nuts
½ cup olive oil
2 to 3 Tbs. vinegar
  lemon

salt
freshly ground pepper
1 cup diced boiled beets, drained on
  paper
¾ cup finely chopped celery
¾ cup finely diced peeled cucumber
  lettuce leaves

Stir together minced garlic, salt, bread crumbs, and pine nuts, adding a little oil and vinegar alternately, and a squeeze or two of lemon juice; mix constantly. Mixture should be moist but still granular, not soggy. Taste, add salt only if needed and a few turns of pepper grinder. Toss this mixture with drained beets, celery, and cucumber. Arrange on lettuce leaves and serve cool but not chilled.

MAKES 6 SERVINGS

Beaver Bay Cabbage, Ham and Chicken Salad

12 red radishes
 2 cups shredded white cabbage
 2 cups shredded red cabbage
 2 cups shredded leaf lettuce
 1 cup strips of cooked chicken breast
 ¼ cup strips of country ham

2 Tbs. chopped anchovies
6 Tbs. salad oil
2 Tbs. tarragon vinegar
1 to 2 Tbs. mayonnaise
  freshly ground pepper
  Wisconsin whitefish caviar

Slice radishes very thin and put in a large salad bowl with shredded cabbage and lettuce (or other salad greens). Toss, adding chicken, ham, anchovies, oil, vinegar, mayonnaise, and pepper to taste. (Salty flavor of ham, anchovies and caviar should eliminate need for salt.) Add caviar just before serving, or divide salad on plates and garnish with caviar.

MAKES 6 TO 8 SERVINGS

Pennsylvania Pepper Cabbage

 1 green or sweet red pepper
 2 cups thinly sliced cabbage
1½ tsp. salt
 1 cup thick sour cream
 1 Tbs. grated onion

2 Tbs. vinegar
1 Tbs. lemon juice
  freshly ground black pepper or
  cayenne
2 Tbs. mayonnaise

Remove white ribs and seeds from pepper and cut into thin juliennes, about size of wooden matchsticks. Toss cabbage and pepper strips with 1 teaspoon salt. Mix ½ teaspoon salt with sour cream, grated onion, vinegar, lemon juice, and 6 or 7 turns of pepper grinder, or shake on cayenne to your own taste. Blend mayonnaise into this mixture and toss with vegetables.

MAKES 4 SERVINGS

VARIATION:

Pepper Cabbage with Hot Dressing

1 green or sweet red pepper
2 cups thinly sliced cabbage
1½ tsp. salt
2 tsp. sugar
½ tsp. dry mustard
   freshly ground black pepper

½ cup vinegar
1 Tbs. butter
1 tsp. flour
½ tsp. salt
1 egg yolk

Put sugar, mustard, a few turns of pepper grinder, and vinegar in a saucepan and bring to a boil. Melt butter in another saucepan and stir in flour, salt, and egg yolk. Blend with vinegar and simmer for 4 minutes. Pour over pepper cabbage (preceding recipe) in place of sour-cream dressing.

Chef's Salad

The origin of this salad is not, apparently, a matter of record, but it may have been made first in the kitchen of the Ritz-Carlton where a recipe used by Louis Diat called for smoked ox tongue as one of the meats and watercress as the only green leaf.

DRESSING:

½ tsp. salt
3 Tbs. vinegar

9 Tbs. olive oil
   freshly ground pepper

SALAD:

½ head iceberg lettuce, finely
   shredded
1 scallion, finely minced
1 cup strips of cooked ham or tongue,
   ¼-inch wide by 2 inches long
1 cup similar strips of cooked chicken
   or turkey

1 cup similar strips of Swiss cheese
⅛ green pepper, cut into similar strips
1 medium-size tomato, cut into
   ½-inch wedges
   fresh parsley, basil or tarragon, or
   combination, minced

Mix dressing and pour about half of it over lettuce and scallion; toss thoroughly. Arrange lettuce in bottom of salad bowl and over it arrange other ingredients in decorative patterns. Pour remaining dressing over all and sprinkle with one or more of minced herbs.

MAKES 6 SERVINGS

Judith's Chicken and Grape Salad

1 chicken, 3 to 4 lbs., steamed (p. 246)	24 green seedless grapes, peeled
2 cups Homemade Mayonnaise (p. 294)	lettuce leaves
salt	⅓ cup toasted almonds
freshly ground pepper	optional: 1 tarragon sprig, minced
1 tsp. lemon juice	1 Tbs. mixed minced chives and parsley

Cut good white and dark meat from chicken into fair-size dice (save wings and drumsticks for a picnic). Toss with mayonnaise and season to taste with salt, pepper, and lemon juice. Fold in peeled grapes. Toast almonds in 400° oven for about 5 minutes. Serve salad over fresh lettuce leaves, topped with almonds and a sprinkling of herbs.

MAKES 6 SERVINGS

Pennsylvania Dutch Coleslaw

½ cabbage or the heart of a small cabbage	1 small white onion, or 2 or 3 scallions
1 carrot	1 tender celery rib

DRESSING:

1 Tbs. sugar	¼ tsp. salt
2 Tbs. vinegar	freshly ground pepper
½ cup heavy cream	minced parsley

Cut away hard core of cabbage and shred remainder very fine. Peel and grate carrot; mince onion and celery, and mix all vegetables together. Combine ingredients for the dressing, dissolving sugar in vinegar before adding cream. Toss with vegetables, then let mature in refrigerator for 2 to 3 hours before serving.

MAKES 4 SERVINGS

Blue-Cheese and Avocado Salad

1 large, very ripe avocado
¼ cup sour cream
1 Tbs. grated onion
  Tabasco
½ cup crumbled blue cheese

¾ cup California olive oil
¼ cup wine vinegar
¼ cup California Chablis
1 tsp. lemon juice
  lettuce leaves

Peel avocado, remove seed, and mash until smooth, blending in sour cream a little at a time. Stir in grated onion, a few dashes of Tabasco, and crumbled cheese. Add oil, vinegar, wine, and lemon juice gradually, tossing to mix lightly. Chill, and serve on lettuce leaves.

MAKES 4 SERVINGS

Fisherman's Salad

1 can (2 oz.) flat anchovy fillets,
  well drained
3 Tbs. red salmon or whitefish caviar
1 cup diced mozzarella or other bland
  cheese

1 cup cooked marinated artichoke
  hearts, coarsely chopped
3 hard-cooked eggs, minced
1 Tbs. minced fresh thyme
  lettuce
  romaine

Chop anchovies very fine and combine with caviar, cheese, artichokes, and eggs. Sprinkle with thyme. Clean, wash, and dry enough lettuce and romaine for 4 persons, tear the leaves into pieces, and toss with other ingredients.

MAKES 4 SERVINGS

Garbanzo Salad

1 cup cooked garbanzos (chickpeas)
1½ Tbs. minced scallions
1½ Tbs. minced green pepper
1½ Tbs. red-wine vinegar
3 Tbs. California olive oil

½ tsp. salt
  freshly ground pepper
½ tsp. minced green chilies
½ tsp. ground cuminseed
  romaine lettuce

If cooking your own chickpeas, soak them overnight like any dried legume. Cook them for several hours in water or, better yet, in liquid left from boiling ham, tongue, or corned beef. Drain. Mix with remaining ingredients, arranging romaine leaves around.

MAKES 4 SERVINGS

Jellied Fresh Fruit Salad

2 envelopes unflavored gelatin
1 cup cold water
¾ cup sugar
1¼ cups fresh orange juice, or mixture
  of orange and grapefruit juice
¼ cup mixed fresh lime and lemon
  juice
½ cup dry sherry

pinch of salt
1 small avocado, or ½ large, peeled
  and sliced
1 medium-size pear, peeled, cored,
  and sliced
1 large navel orange, peeled and
  sectioned
2 dozen grapes, peeled and seeded

GARNISH:

cream-cheese balls rolled in fresh herbs (minced parsley, chives, basil, or
  tarragon)
watercress

Dissolve gelatin in ½ cup cold water. Meanwhile heat the sugar with another ½ cup water until sugar is thoroughly dissolved. Remove from heat and blend in gelatin. Add freshly squeezed and strained orange juice, the lemon and lime juice, sherry, and salt. Oil a ring mold that will hold 8 cups. Pour a little fruit juice aspic over the bottom and chill. Meanwhile prepare the fruits. When gelatin has set, arrange the fruits in alternating patterns around the ring attractively and fill the mold with the rest of the fruit juice. Chill for several hours. Serve with cream-cheese balls in the center and sprigs of watercress around.

MAKES 8 SERVINGS

Bailey Avenue Potato Salad

New potatoes are waxier and, we think, just right for a summer picnic salad like this one. Don't be deterred if the vegetable bin has only baking potatoes, however. The texture of the potatoes will be mealier and they will absorb more mayonnaise, but the result is, in either case, perhaps the most American of all vegetable salads.

6 medium-size potatoes, cooked
1 Tbs. white-wine vinegar
2 tsp. coarse salt
  freshly ground pepper
1 cup freshly made mayonnaise
  (p. 294)
  lemon juice or cream

2 scallions, or more to taste
2 Tbs. finely chopped green pepper
¼ cup minced parsley mixed with
  fresh basil, tarragon, or dill
  hard-cooked eggs
  tomatoes
  watercress

Scrub new potatoes and boil in their jackets in salted water for 35 to 40 minutes. Pierce to test for doneness; new potatoes will take less time. Cool a bit, peel, and dice. Toss with vinegar, salt, and pepper, then set aside while making mayonnaise. Gently fold in mayonnaise thinned with a little cream or lemon juice. Season with salt and pepper, and add minced scallions, green pepper, and herbs. Chill before serving. Garnish with sliced or quartered hard-cooked eggs, tomatoes, and watercress.

MAKES 4 TO 6 SERVINGS

Ham and Cheese Salad

1 cup diced cooked country ham	¼ to ½ cup chopped raw mushrooms
1½ cups diced mozzarella or other mild cheese	¼ cup mayonnaise
½ cup finely chopped celery	¼ tsp. dried basil
¼ cup minced scallions	¼ tsp. dried marjoram
3 to 4 Tbs. chopped ripe olives	¼ tsp. dried orégano
	lettuce leaves

Combine ham, cheese, celery, scallions, olives, and mushrooms with enough mayonnaise to bind, and sprinkle in herbs. No other seasoning is needed if well-flavored country ham is used. Arrange lettuce in a salad bowl, and mound salad mixture in center.

MAKES 4 SERVINGS

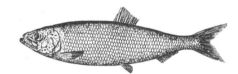

New England Herring Salad

6 to 8 kippered herring	freshly ground pepper
2 small beets, cooked, peeled and sliced	6 Tbs. olive oil
2 tart Greening apples, peeled and sliced	2 Tbs. tarragon vinegar
	1 tsp. dry mustard
2 or 3 scallions, minced	2 to 3 Tbs. minced fresh dill, or
salt	½ to 1 tsp. dried dillweed
	lettuce leaves

Tear kippers into small strips, then blot with paper towel. Toss in salad bowl with beets, apple slices, scallions, and a little salt only if needed; grind in several turns of pepper mill. Add oil, vinegar, mustard, and dill, and toss again. Chill and serve on lettuce leaves.

MAKES 6 SERVINGS

Heart of Palm Salad

2 celery ribs, diced
2 Tbs. carrot shavings
2 Tbs. slivers of green pepper
1 scallion, minced
¼ tsp. dried marjoram
¼ tsp. dried orégano

freshly ground pepper
1 tsp. salt
1 can hearts of palm, diced
  juice of ½ lemon or lime
1 Tbs. mayonnaise
  about 1 Tbs. vinegar

Mix prepared vegetables with herbs, seasonings and hearts of palm. Add citrus juice and mayonnaise, and toss. Add vinegar according to taste. Chill well before serving.

MAKES 6 SERVINGS

Sausage and Green-Bean Salad

1½ cups crisp cooked green beans
  oil and vinegar dressing with garlic
1 garlic clove, split
¾ cup matchstick strips of dry
  Lebanon smoked beef sausage
1 hard-cooked egg, chopped fine

1 Tbs. minced chives
1 tsp. dried savory
  salt
  freshly ground pepper
4 large canned sardines

Put cooked beans in a glass bowl. Make a garlicky French dressing and pour over beans, then set aside for 2 or 3 hours. Rub wooden salad bowl with cut side of garlic clove, and put in sausage, egg, chives, savory, salt to taste, and a few turns of pepper grinder; toss well. Add beans and dressing and toss again. Serve on lettuce cups and top each serving with a sardine.

MAKES 4 SERVINGS

Shrimp, Bacon, Tomato and Egg Salad

6 bacon strips
1½ cups cooked small shrimps
3 to 4 Tbs. mayonnaise
2 Tbs. lemon juice
2 or 3 sprigs of fresh dill, or
  ½ tsp. dried dillweed
1 tsp. minced fresh tarragon
  (optional)
½ tsp. salt

1 Tbs. vinegar
3 Tbs. olive oil
  freshly ground pepper
1 small head of Boston lettuce
  watercress
2 large tomatoes, cut into wedges
2 hard-cooked eggs (10 minutes
  only)

Fry bacon until well cooked, then drain on paper. Wash cooked shrimps and pat dry; mix with mayonnaise, lemon juice, and herbs. In a salad bowl, mix salt and vinegar, and add oil, stirring hard with wooden spoon. Add several turns of the pepper grinder. Crumble bacon. Put lettuce leaves in salad bowl, add a few sprigs of watercress, tomato wedges, eggs peeled and cut into quarters, and bacon bits; toss until well mixed. Pile shrimps in center and serve salad with toasted rye bread.

MAKES 6 SERVINGS

Spinach, Bacon and Mushroom Salad

¼ lb. very fresh young spinach
8 bacon strips
4 medium-size fresh mushrooms
1½ Tbs. lemon juice

4 Tbs. olive oil
salt
freshly ground pepper

Wash spinach leaves thoroughly, remove tough stems, then shake or spin dry. Fry bacon until crisp, drain on paper, and crumble. Slice mushrooms thinly after removing only tough end of stems. Tear spinach leaves into 3 or 4 pieces each, and toss with mushrooms and bacon. Sprinkle with lemon juice, oil, salt, and several turns of pepper grinder. Toss again, taste for seasoning, adding salt and pepper if necessary. Serve immediately.

MAKES 2 SERVINGS

Louisiana Sweet-Potato Salad

1 cup grated raw sweet potato
2 cups diced apples
½ cup broken pecans
¾ cup seedless raisins

½ cup finely chopped celery
Homemade Mayonnaise (p. 294)
lettuce

Put grated sweet potatoes in a salad bowl and add apples, pecans, raisins, and celery. Stir in a spoonful of mayonnaise at a time to make salad as moist as desired. Serve in lettuce cups.

MAKES 8 SERVINGS

Cheese-Stuffed Tomato Salad

4 large ripe tomatoes
6 oz. cream cheese
6 oz. dry-curd cottage cheese
1 egg
1 Tbs. flour
1 Tbs. sugar
½ cup milk

1 Tbs. wine vinegar
1 Tbs. minced fresh basil
1 Tbs. minced fresh tarragon
1 tsp. salt
freshly ground pepper
2 hard-cooked eggs, finely chopped
2 to 3 Tbs. minced chives

Hollow out tomatoes to make cases with shells about ½ inch thick; remove all seeds and chill for several hours. Bring cheese to room temperature. Mix egg, flour, and sugar, stir in milk, and cook over low heat for about 5 minutes, stirring constantly as mixture thickens. Off heat, add vinegar, then stir into cheese, mixing until smooth. Mix in herbs, salt, and several turns of pepper grinder. Spoon cheese mixture into chilled tomatoes, sprinkle liberally with finely chopped eggs, then with chives. Return to refrigerator and chill for 1 hour or more.

MAKES 4 SERVINGS

Vegetable Salad

1 medium-size cucumber
1 cup cooked peas
1 cup diced cooked carrots
¼ green pepper, chopped
2 medium-size tomatoes, diced
½ medium-size red onion, thinly sliced
¼ cup minced parsley

1 cup Homemade Mayonnaise
  (p. 294)
2 Tbs. chili sauce
salt
freshly ground pepper
1 Tbs. chopped fresh basil (optional)
salad greens

Peel cucumber, slice into quarters lengthwise, scrape out seeds, and cut into bits about size of peas and carrots. Mix all vegetables and toss with mayonnaise and chili sauce. Season to taste with salt and pepper, and sprinkle with fresh basil, if available. Serve in bowl lined with salad greens.

MAKES 4 SERVINGS

Waldorf Salad

Oscar Tschirky, who became famous as Oscar of the Waldorf and was *maître d'hôtel* from that hotel's opening until his death, created this salad for a "society supper" to which 1,500 persons from Boston, Baltimore, and Philadelphia were invited to a preview of the Waldorf when it opened in March, 1893. For Sheila Hibben of *The New Yorker* his creation was a mixed blessing. She thought his combination of apples and mayonnaise headed American housewives in the wrong direction "and bred the sorry mixture of sweet salads" that remain very much on the gastronomical scene. Someone else seems to have added nuts to Oscar's salad which, truth be told, can be a happy mixture when homemade mayonnaise is used, particularly with some walnut oil added, rather than the more common sweet salad dressing.

1 cup diced crisp tart apples
1 cup diced crisp celery
½ cup coarsely chopped walnuts

¾ cup Homemade Mayonnaise
   (p. 294), using walnut oil
   lettuce leaves

Toss apples and celery with nuts, then fold in mayonnaise. Chill and serve on lettuce leaves.

MAKES 6 SERVINGS

Minnesota Wild-Rice and Beef Salad

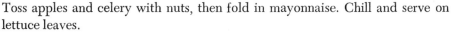

2 cups julienne strips of rare roast
   beef
1½ to 2 cups cooked wild rice or
   other rice
2 to 3 Tbs. pine nuts
1 small white onion, minced
2 to 3 Tbs. chopped green pepper

1 cup sour cream
1½ to 2 Tbs. Dijon mustard
2 to 3 Tbs. wine vinegar
   sugar
   dried chervil
   lettuce leaves

Mix beef, rice, pine nuts, and vegetables. Season sour cream to taste with mustard, vinegar, very little sugar, and ½ teaspoon or more of dried chervil. Toss meat and rice mixture with dressing and refrigerate for an hour or so. Serve on lettuce leaves.

MAKES 6 SERVINGS

Green Goddess Dressing

George Arliss, the British actor who was later a great Hollywood star, made such a hit in the early 1920s in a play called *The Green Goddess* that its run in San Francisco inspired the creation at the Palace Hotel of an anchovy-flavored, meadow-colored mayonnaise to dress salad greens and to be served as Western style dictates at the beginning of a meal.

8 to 10 anchovy fillets	3 cups Homemade Mayonnaise
1 or 2 scallions, minced	(p. 294)
3 to 4 Tbs. minced parsley	3 Tbs. tarragon vinegar
1½ Tbs. minced tarragon leaves	3 Tbs. minced chives

Chop anchovies, then stir in scallions, parsley, and tarragon. Mix well with mayonnaise, adding enough vinegar to give the consistency of heavy cream; stir in chives. For a green salad, rub a wooden bowl with garlic before putting in washed and dried mixed greens. Add dressing and toss until well mixed.

MAKES ABOUT 3½ CUPS

Poppy-Seed Dressing

Poppy seeds were among the many things that American Shakers raised, packaged and sold, as well as used in their own simple but imaginative cooking. Mennonite cooks dressed orange and grapefruit slices, or red cabbage, with oil and vinegar flavored with poppy seeds and onion juice, and Helen Corbitt, whose knowledge of United States gastronomy stretches from Pennsylvania to Texas and from sea to sea, perfected a poppy-seed dressing to be made in a blender. The recipe below is good on all combinations of fruit and on avocado slices.

½ cup sugar	1 Tbs. grated onion
1 tsp. salt	1 cup vegetable oil
½ tsp. dry mustard	1 tsp. poppy seeds
⅓ cup vinegar	

Mix sugar, salt, mustard, and vinegar. Stir in grated onion. Add oil very slowly, a little at a time, and beat constantly until thick. Stir in poppy seeds.

MAKES ABOUT 1½ CUPS

Homemade Mayonnaise

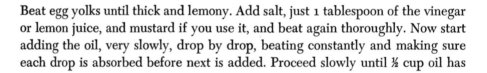

3 egg yolks, at room temperature	optional: ¼ to ½ tsp. dry mustard
½ tsp. salt	up to 2 cups good oil, or combination
2 Tbs. vinegar or lemon juice, or	of olive, vegetable, or other oil
1 Tbs. of each	

Beat egg yolks until thick and lemony. Add salt, just 1 tablespoon of the vinegar or lemon juice, and mustard if you use it, and beat again thoroughly. Now start adding the oil, very slowly, drop by drop, beating constantly and making sure each drop is absorbed before next is added. Proceed slowly until ½ cup oil has been assimilated, then start adding more quickly. When mayonnaise is very thick, add a little of remaining vinegar or lemon juice, and continue adding oil until you have desired consistency. Correct seasoning. If storing, keep refrigerated in tightly sealed jar.

Variations: For a more mustardy mayonnaise, halfway along add 1 tablespoon of whole-seed mustard, and as much more as you like when correcting seasoning at the end.

For a variation in flavor, try using half walnut oil, particularly delicious with Waldorf Salad (p. 292–293).

Chapter 18

Casseroles, Lunch and Supper Dishes

Stuffed Artichokes

4 large artichokes
1 lemon
4 Tbs. butter
3 Tbs. olive oil
3 Tbs. finely minced shallots or
   scallions
1½ cups finely diced cooked ham
1 garlic clove, finely minced

1 cup cooked wild rice
2 Tbs. chopped parsley
   pinch of dried thyme
1 tsp. tarragon
   salt
   freshly ground pepper
2 Tbs. grated Parmesan cheese

Preheat oven to 425°

Trim the tops and stems from the artichokes, snip off thorny tips of leaves, and remove small, tough outermost leaves. Rub the cut surfaces with lemon. Steam the artichokes on a trivet over boiling water in a heavy, tightly lidded pot for 45 to 50 minutes, or until a leaf pulls out easily. Melt 2 tablespoons of the butter in a skillet with 1 tablespoon of oil. Sauté the shallots or scallions for a few minutes, then add ham, garlic, wild rice, herbs, salt (if necessary), and pepper to taste. When the artichokes are done, scrape out the center down to the heart and spoon out all the choke. Fill the centers with the ham and rice mixture so that it heaps over the tops and spills down some between the leaves. Sprinkle freshly grated Parmesan and bread crumbs over the top, dribble on remaining oil, and bake for 10 minutes.

MAKES 4 SERVINGS

Asparagus with Ham Sauce

3 Tbs. butter
2½ Tbs. flour
2 cups milk
4 Tbs. puréed chervil
2 cups finely minced cooked ham

1½ lbs. fresh asparagus, or 2 pkgs.
    (10 oz. each) frozen asparagus,
    cooked
4 hard-cooked eggs

Melt butter in a saucepan, stir in flour, and cook for 3 or 4 minutes. Off heat, stir in milk; return to heat when smooth and cook until sauce thickens. Stir in puréed chervil and minced ham. Be sure asparagus is hot. Chop 3 hard-cooked eggs and stir into sauce. Slice remaining egg. Garnish each serving of asparagus with sauce and slices of hard-cooked egg.

MAKES 4 SERVINGS

Avocado with Creamed Pheasant

1 ripe avocado
  lemon juice
  salt
  freshly ground pepper
1½ cups small chunks of cooked
    pheasant

¾ cup leftover gravy from pheasant,
    or stock made from pheasant
    carcass thickened with a little
    cornstarch
¼ cup heavy cream

Preheat oven to 425°

Peel the avocado, remove the pit, and cut fruit into ¼-inch slices. Place in the bottom of a buttered shallow baking dish. Sprinkle with lemon juice, salt, and pepper. Toss pheasant chunks on top and pour over the gravy or the thickened stock mixed with heavy cream. Bake for 10 to 15 minutes.

MAKES 4 SERVINGS

Avocado Baked with Chicken and Ham

¼ lb. butter
2 Tbs. chopped onion
4 Tbs. flour
¾ tsp. salt
¾ tsp. paprika
¾ tsp. mulled dried rosemary
1½ cups chicken broth

1½ cups sour cream, at room
    temperature
2 cups diced cooked chicken
1 cup finely diced country ham
1 medium-size avocado, peeled
    and diced
½ cup fresh bread crumbs

Preheat oven to 350°

Melt 6 tablespoons of the butter and sauté chopped onion until golden in color. Stir in flour, salt, paprika, and rosemary. Cook over low heat until mixture is smooth and bubbling. Off heat, stir in chicken broth, return to very low heat, and stir constantly until sauce comes to a boil. Remove from heat and stir in sour cream, a little at a time. Fold in chicken and ham, then add avocado. Pour into a 1½-quart baking dish. Blend bread crumbs and remaining butter over medium heat, then spread over contents of baking dish. Bake for 30 minutes.

MAKES 6 SERVINGS

Baked Tuna-Stuffed Avocado

2 cans (7 oz. each) tuna	½ tsp. dried rosemary
2 Tbs. butter	1 tsp. salt
2 Tbs. flour	freshly ground pepper
1½ cups heavy cream	lime juice
milk	2 medium-size avocados
½ tsp. dried thyme	sesame seeds

Preheat oven to 350°

Drain tuna and reserve. Melt butter in a saucepan, stir in flour, and heat and stir for about 2 minutes, until smooth. Off heat, stir in cream and continue to stir until smooth; return to heat and cook for about 5 minutes, until sauce thickens. If it seems too thick, add a little milk. Stir in thyme, rosemary, salt, some freshly ground pepper, and a squeeze of lime juice. Peel avocados, cut into halves, and remove seeds; cut into ¼-inch-thick slices. Cover bottom of a small baking dish with avocado slices. Stir tuna into sauce, letting it warm up, then pour sauce over avocado slices. Sprinkle with sesame seeds and bake for 12 to 15 minutes.

MAKES 4 SERVINGS

Black-Eyed Peas with Ham, Sausage, Duck

2 cups dried black-eyed peas	leftover pieces cooked duck
1 Tbs. salt	1 cup diced country ham
1 strip bacon, cut in squares	1 lb. pork sausages, cooked
2 onions, chopped	1 tsp. sweet red pepper, minced
1 stalk celery, chopped	2 Tbs. butter
1 small green pepper, chopped	1 cup stale baking powder biscuit
½ cup rendered duck fat	(or bread) crumbs

Preheat oven to 350°

Soak peas overnight. Drain; cover amply with fresh water. Add salt and bacon, bring water to boil, and simmer 1 hour. Melt 2 tablespoons duck fat in skillet and sauté onion, green pepper and celery 5 minutes. Cook sausages, cut them in sections and add them with diced ham to vegetables; stir well, then add with duck and sweet pepper to peas. Stir in rest of duck fat, and transfer to 3-quart casserole with enough liquid in which peas cooked to barely cover. Melt 2 tablespoons butter and into it stir 1 cup crumbs made from biscuits; mix well and spread evenly over casserole. Bake for 1 hour.

MAKES 6 SERVINGS

Grandfather's Baked Beans and Duck

More Americans descend from families who moved south from Canada than many people think. In the Maritime Provinces where this recipe began its journey into the Upper Midwest, baked beans are as popular as they are in "Boston, home of the bean and the cod."

1 lb. dried pea beans	½ cup blackstrap molasses (no sulfur)
6 cups beer	2 Tbs. Worcestershire sauce
2 cups beef stock	1 Tbs. Dijon mustard
2 bay leaves	½ tsp. ground cuminseed
1 medium-size onion, chopped	1 tsp. dried savory
½ cup chopped candied gingerroot	freshly ground pepper
1 lemon, sliced and chopped	½ cup diced salt pork
¼ cup maple sugar	1 duck, 4 to 5 lbs.

Preheat oven to 350°*

Soak beans in 4 cups of beer overnight. Mix 2 cups of beer with the beef stock, combine with beans and the beer they soaked in, and pour all into 4-quart baking dish. Add bay leaves, onion, gingerroot, lemon, maple sugar, molasses, seasonings, and salt pork.* Cover and bring to a boil, then put baking dish in oven and bake for 3 hours, adding a little water every 30 minutes as necessary; there should be enough liquid to cover beans by 1 inch.

Cut duck into 4 or 6 pieces, pulling fat away from meat. Render fat in a skillet large enough to hold all of duck pieces flat. Brown the pieces for 8 to 10 minutes, turning often so that all surfaces are seared; when browned, transfer to baking dish and push down into beans and liquid. Pour off duck fat from skillet and stir in ½ cup of water, scraping up brown bits on bottom of pan and letting liquid sizzle for about 1 minute; pour over duck and beans in baking dish. Cover and continue baking for 3 to 4 hours, checking occasionally and adding water, if necessary, to keep beans covered. When done they will have absorbed most of the liquid, including any fat that may still come from duck; the meat should be falling off the bones.

MAKES 6 TO 8 SERVINGS

Mashed Lima Beans in Sausage Ring

1 lb. highly seasoned bulk sausage	2 eggs, lightly beaten
1½ cups soft bread crumbs	6 Tbs. crushed cornflakes (or stale
4 Tbs. grated onion	corn bread)
1 tsp. prepared mustard (optional)	2 cups mashed lima beans
4 Tbs. chopped parsley	

Preheat oven to 350°

Grease an 8-inch ring mold thoroughly. Mix sausage with crumbs, onion, mustard if desired, chopped parsley, and beaten eggs. When thoroughly blended, press crushed cornflakes to greased surface of mold, coating evenly. Pack meat mixture in mold, then bake; after 15 minutes draw off fat that has collected and continue baking for 15 minutes more. Meanwhile heat mashed lima beans until bubbles appear. Turn baked sausage ring upside down on plate and fill center with mashed beans.

MAKES 4 SERVINGS

Dried Beef and Sweet Potatoes

4 medium-size sweet potatoes	salt
¼ lb. dried beef	freshly ground white pepper
1 small onion, grated	pinch of grated nutmeg
2 Tbs. butter	½ cup bread crumbs
2 Tbs. flour	¼ cup grated store cheese
1¾ cups milk	

Preheat oven to 350°

Cover sweet potatoes with boiling water and cook for 10 to 15 minutes, until skin slips off easily. Cut into 1-inch dice. Shred dried beef and mix with grated onion. Melt butter over low heat and stir in flour, cooking for 2 or 3 minutes, slowly. Off heat, stir in milk, return to heat, and whisk continuously until smooth and thickened. Add salt sparingly, then white pepper and nutmeg. Mix together sauce, sweet-potato dice, and beef, and turn into a 1½-quart casserole. Sprinkle top with bread crumbs, then with grated cheese. Bake for 30 to 40 minutes, until mixture is bubbling and the top has turned golden.

MAKES 4 SERVINGS

1 recipe basic pastry (p. 349)
1 calf's brain
1 Tbs. vinegar
  salt
1 pkg. (10 oz.) frozen spinach

1 Tbs. butter
½ cup chopped ham
  freshly ground pepper
¼ tsp. ground cloves
1 Tbs. minced parsley

SAUCE:

2 Tbs. butter
2 Tbs. flour
1 cup milk

salt
freshly ground pepper
2 Tbs. prepared horseradish

GLAZE:

1 egg mixed with 1 Tbs. water

Preheat oven to 450° ❋

Roll out pastry to a rectangle 6 by 12 inches and place on a greased cookie sheet; chill while preparing filling. Soak brains in cold water for 30 minutes; then put in a saucepan, cover with water, and add vinegar and 1 teaspoon salt. Bring to a boil and simmer very gently for 15 minutes. Meanwhile, cook spinach in salted water for 5 minutes, drain thoroughly, then return to pan to toss with butter until moisture has evaporated. Chill. Now drain poached brains and rinse with cold water until cool enough to handle; remove membrane and cut into ¾-inch pieces. Toss with chopped ham and add seasonings, cloves, and parsley; amount of salt depends on saltiness of ham.

Make sauce by melting butter, blending in flour, and cooking gently for 1 minute, stirring continuously. Off heat, whisk in ¾ cup milk and return to heat long enough to thicken. Season to taste with salt and a few turns of pepper grinder. Stir ¼ cup of sauce into meat mixture. Thin remaining sauce with remaining milk, add horseradish, and set aside in a warm place.❋

Spread spinach on pastry, leaving 1-inch border. Spread brain-ham mixture on top. Draw long sides of dough toward each other and paint nearer side with egg glaze; overlap farther side by 1 inch, gently pressing into glaze to seal. Then flip roll over so seam is on bottom; tuck in two ends. Paint the roll, top and sides, with egg glaze. (Use leftover dough, if you wish, to make decorative shapes; place these on top and paint with glaze.) Bake for 10 minutes; reduce heat to 375° and continue baking for 20 to 25 minutes, until crisp and golden. To serve: cut into slices and serve horseradish-cream sauce separately.

MAKES 4 SERVINGS

Baked Broccoli with Ham and Cheese

1 large bunch of fresh broccoli
salt
3 Tbs. butter
3 Tbs. flour
3 cups milk
3 Tbs. puréed chervil, or 1 tsp. dried
chervil

freshly ground pepper
1 cup flakes of country ham
butter
½ 8-oz. package of mozzarella cheese
sweet paprika

Preheat oven to 350°

Cut buds away from broccoli stalks and put in a bowl of cold water with a little salt. Peel and cut up stalky pieces, making them about thickness of bud stems and about 1 or 1½ inches in length. After 30 minutes of soaking put stalk pieces in boiling water and cook for 5 minutes. Then add buds and continue cooking for 10 minutes. Meanwhile make sauce; melt butter in a saucepan and stir in flour to make a thick paste. Off heat, gradually stir in milk, blending until smooth. Return to heat and cook slowly, stirring occasionally as sauce thickens. Blend in chervil and several turns of pepper grinder; a salty country ham eliminates need to add salt. Stir in ham flakes about the size of postage stamps. Drain broccoli thoroughly and pat dry with paper towel. Butter a 1½-quart casserole and put in broccoli, then cover with ham and sauce. Cut enough ¼-inch slices of mozzarella to cover contents of casserole. Sprinkle with sweet paprika and bake for 25 minutes, until cheese blisters and has taken on color.

MAKES 4 SERVINGS

Pennsylvania Dutch Stuffed Cabbage

2 cups chopped cooked fresh pork
1 cup chopped cooked ham
½ cup finely chopped mushrooms
1 tsp. dried savory
½ tsp. salt
freshly ground black pepper

8 large cabbage leaves, blanched
1 qt. pork or chicken stock, boiling
2 Tbs. butter
2 Tbs. flour
1 Tbs. minced chives

Mix chopped pork, ham, mushrooms, savory, and salt, and grind in fresh pepper. Carefully peel 8 large leaves from blanched head of cabbage without tearing. Divide stuffing mixture among leaves, tuck in ends of each, and wrap like a package. Put these side by side in one layer in pan, cover with boiling stock, and simmer for 30 minutes. Remove and keep hot. Mix butter, flour, and chives into smooth paste, then add paste stock just enough to liquify, and stir into stock. Let sauce thicken over medium heat before pouring over stuffed cabbage leaves.

MAKES 4 SERVINGS

Baked Cabbage with Chopped Meat

4 cups finely chopped cabbage
1 small onion, minced
⅓ cup slivered sweet red pepper
2 eggs, separated
½ cup heavy cream or evaporated milk

1½ tsp. salt
freshly ground black pepper
½ tsp. dried rosemary
1½ to 2 cups cooked veal heart and ham, chopped together

Preheat oven to 375°

Cook prepared vegetables in boiling water 7 or 8 minutes; drain and pat dry. Beat egg yolks with cream or evaporated milk, adding salt, a few turns of pepper grinder, and rosemary. Mix drained vegetables with veal and ham (any leftover meat can be used), then stir into sauce. Beat egg whites until very stiff, and fold carefully into vegetable-meat mixture. Transfer to buttered casserole and bake for about 45 minutes.

MAKES 4 SERVINGS

California Carne con Chile

6 red *ancho* chilies
1 large onion
2 garlic cloves
4 Tbs. fat
1 Tbs. flour
2 lbs. beef chuck, diced

½ tsp. ground coriander
½ tsp. dried thyme
¼ tsp. ground cuminseed
salt and pepper
2 or 3 canned green chilies

Split open red chilies and soak in hot water for 1 hour. Drain and remove seeds and pith, then put through meat grinder with onion and 1 garlic clove. Heat 2 tablespoons fat in a skillet and stir in 1 tablespoon flour, cooking slowly until flour takes on color. Stir in ground chili mixture and cook for 5 minutes. In another pan sauté diced beef in remaining fat until well seared on all sides. Mash remaining garlic clove and add to beef with seasonings. Add ground chili mixture and cook for about 10 minutes, until meat is tender. Mince green chilies and stir in. Serve with cooked pinto or pink beans.

MAKES 6 SERVINGS

Cauliflower with Shrimps

1½ Tbs. butter
1½ Tbs. flour
2 cups milk
½ tsp. salt
½ tsp. sugar

2 Tbs. sour cream
1 lb. freshly boiled shrimps, peeled
  and cleaned
1 large cauliflower
2 Tbs. dry sherry

Melt butter in saucepan and stir in flour until smooth. Off heat, stir in milk, blending well, then return to heat and cook until sauce thickens. Stir in salt, sugar, and sour cream; taste for seasoning and add shrimps. Cook cauliflower, whole, in boiling water for 20 to 25 minutes, until tender, adding a little salt just before it is done. Drain well but keep warm. Reheat shrimps and sauce, stirring in the sherry. Pour over cauliflower.

MAKES 4 SERVINGS

Crab-Meat and Mushroom Scallop

4 medium-size mushrooms
4 Tbs. butter
1 shallot or scallion, minced
2 Tbs. dry white wine
2 Tbs. flour
1 cup milk
1 generous cup fresh lump crab meat
  salt

freshly ground black pepper
1 tsp. dried tarragon
2 Tbs. dry sherry
1 egg yolk
1 Tbs. heavy cream
4 tsp. mixed bread crumbs and
  grated Cheddar cheese

Rub mushrooms with damp cloth but do not wash; slice thin. Melt 2 tablespoons butter in a skillet and sauté minced shallot or scallion and sliced mushrooms, coating well with butter; add wine and simmer for 5 minutes. Remove from skillet and keep warm. Melt remaining butter and blend in flour. Off heat, stir in milk, whisk well, return to heat, and let thicken, stirring constantly. Add mushrooms, shallots, crab meat, a pinch of salt, 2 or 3 turns of pepper grinder, tarragon, and sherry. Beat egg yolk with a little cream, add a little hot sauce and stir, then a little more sauce; combine with crab mixture and bring to a boil, stirring gently. Fill 4 scallop shells or small shallow baking dishes, sprinkle each top with a teaspoon of cheese-crumb mixture. Put under broiler and serve when bubbling and golden.

MAKES 4 SERVINGS

2 Tbs. butter

2 whole eggs

2 egg yolks

2 cups grated sharp Vermont Cheddar
cheese

9 large Montpelier water biscuits or
unsalted crackers

salt

freshly ground pepper

3 Tbs. chopped celery leaves or
mixed parsley and chives

dusting of paprika

Preheat oven to 350°

Butter a 1-quart casserole liberally. Beat whole eggs with egg yolks and add cheese. Crumble the biscuits with a rolling pin and sprinkle one third of them over the bottom of the casserole; add salt and pepper and half of the egg-cheese mixture. Repeat, then strew chopped greens over and top with last layer of biscuits dusted with paprika and dotted with remaining butter. Bake for 35 to 40 minutes, until puffed up and set. Serve with broiled fresh tomatoes.

MAKES 4 SERVINGS

Cabot Cheddar and Onion Pie

CRUST:

1⅓ cups flour

2 Tbs. lard

5 Tbs. butter

½ tsp. salt

3 Tbs. ice water

FILLING:

10 bacon slices

2 eggs

1 cup milk

1 Tbs. granulated flour

½ tsp. salt

freshly ground pepper

pinch of cayenne

2 good-size onions, finely chopped

2 Tbs. butter

¾ lb. Vermont Cheddar cheese,
grated

Preheat oven to 450°

Mix crust and chill for a few hours, or 1 hour in the freezer will do. Roll out and fill a 9-inch pie tin, crimping the edges. Set a slightly smaller pie tin on top to hold down crust, or line with aluminum foil filled with dried beans. Bake for 8 minutes, then remove extra tin or filled foil, prick bottom all over, and bake for another 2 or 3 minutes.

Cook bacon slowly, squeezing out all fat. Beat the eggs with milk, flour, salt,

pepper, and cayenne. Drain the bacon and wipe skillet free of grease. Melt butter in same pan and sauté onions slowly until translucent. Now blend together crumbled bacon, egg mixture, sautéed onions, and grated cheese and pour into partially baked shell. Turn oven down to 375° and bake for 30 minutes. Let set for a few minutes before cutting.

MAKES 6 SERVINGS

Souffléed Cheese Sandwiches

4 slices of cheese, ¼ inch thick
8 slices of white bread, trimmed of crust
2 eggs, beaten

2 cups milk
butter or bacon fat
½ tsp. salt
freshly ground pepper

Preheat oven to 325°

Put each cheese slice between 2 slices of bread and press firmly together to make 4 sandwiches. Beat eggs and milk until blended. Use a shallow rectangular pan or heatproof dish just large enough to hold 4 sandwiches; butter it well, or use bacon fat for added flavor. Cover bottom with sandwiches and pour egg-milk mixture evenly over all. Sprinkle with salt and a turn or two of pepper grinder. Let stand for 45 minutes. Put in oven and bake for 45 minutes, until puffy and golden brown.

MAKES 4 SERVINGS

Minced Chicken Sam Ward

Lately Thomas, Sam Ward's distinguished biographer, points out that in the seventies and eighties of the nineteenth century Ward was recognized as America's premier authority on all matters pertaining to food and wine. "The evidence is ample of Sam's preeminence in the American hierarchy of the table, ranking second to none," Thomas wrote, adding that "his worthiness of association with the brightest luminaries of the French firmament" is beyond doubt. Here is Ward's own recipe:

1 large chicken
1 lb. fresh mushrooms
3 Tbs. butter, or more
2 cups white wine

1 large potato, cooked
heavy cream
4 bacon slices, crisply fried

Clean chicken and boil until done. Remove all meat from bones and chop into fine dice. Chop mushrooms and sauté in about 3 tablespoons butter for 4 or 5 minutes, stirring occasionally. Add white wine, bring to a boil, and let it reduce to one third. Meanwhile put potato through grinder. Add chopped chicken to reduced wine-mushroom mixture, and stir in potato to bind mixture. Add just enough cream to make a smooth, thickish blend. Serve piping hot, topped by crisp bacon in half slices.

MAKES 8 TO 10 SERVINGS

Old Dominion Chicken and Oysters Over Corn Bread

American cooks have been combining chicken and oysters since the earliest colonial days. In one method, called Chicken Smothered in Oysters, chicken pieces were baked in milk, then "smothered" in a mixture of cream and oysters with their liquor. Following is a seventeenth-century shortbread which proves why cornmeal was so accepted when wheat flour was in short supply; it is delicious.

2 cups diced cooked chicken	4 or 5 drops of Tabasco
1½ pints oysters	1 tsp. lemon juice
4 Tbs. butter	1 recipe Everyday Corn Bread
5 Tbs. flour	(p. 162), freshly made and
1¾ cups chicken stock	still warm
½ cup heavy cream	2 Tbs. minced parsley
½ tsp. salt	

Have chicken and oysters at room temperature. In a saucepan melt butter and stir in flour until smooth. Off heat, stir in chicken stock until mixture is free of lumps, then return to heat and simmer over lowest heat for about 5 minutes. Stir in cream, salt, Tabasco, and lemon juice. Poach oysters in oyster liquor for 5 minutes or less, until they have just become plump. Drain and fold into sauce, adding diced chicken. To serve: cut squares of warm corn bread, split, and put bottoms on platter. Cover with half of chicken-oyster sauce, top with remaining corn squares, and pour sauce over. Sprinkle with parsley.

MAKES 6 SERVINGS

Chicken Livers Madeira

1 lb. chicken livers	1 tsp. dried sage
¼ cup finely diced country ham	salt
1½ Tbs. butter	freshly ground pepper
1½ Tbs. oil	8 bread triangles
	¼ cup Madeira

Trim livers of connective tissues, and combine with ham. Heat butter and oil over brisk heat and stir in meats, searing livers quickly and turning constantly.

Add sage and salt and pepper. After no more than 5 minutes (livers should be rosy inside), remove meats with slotted spoon and keep warm. Fry bread triangles in same pan, remove, and put on hot serving plates. Heat Madeira in same pan and stir in warm meats. Let bubble up and pour over triangles.

MAKES 4 SERVINGS

Chicken Soufflés with Mushroom Sauce

1 cup finely chopped cooked chicken	freshly ground pepper
1 tsp. dried tarragon, or 1 Tbs. chopped fresh tarragon	4 Tbs. butter
	3 Tbs. grated Parmesan cheese
1 Tbs. chopped parsley	3 Tbs. flour
2 shallots or scallions, very finely chopped	1 cup strong chicken stock
	3 egg yolks
salt	4 egg whites

SAUCE:

¾ lb. mushrooms	salt
3 Tbs. butter	freshly ground pepper
2 Tbs. flour	optional: leftover chicken (up to
1 cup chicken stock	¼ cup), minced
¼ cup Madeira	

Preheat oven to 400°

Mix finely chopped chicken with herbs, shallots, and salt and pepper to taste. Set aside while making the soufflé base. Prepare 4 individual straight-sided baking dishes of at least 1 cup; or, if a single soufflé is preferred, use a 1½-quart mold; smear with 1 tablespoon of the butter, then sprinkle the bottom and sides with Parmesan, using about 1½ tablespoons altogether. Make collars of foil to extend the molds by 1 inch and butter insides of foil. Melt remaining butter over low heat, add flour, and blend and cook for 1 minute. Off the heat, add chicken stock, beat until smooth, return to heat, and stir as sauce thickens. Let simmer for a minute, then remove and add egg yolks, one by one, beating in thoroughly. Add the flavored chicken, season with remaining Parmesan and salt and pepper (the base should be highly seasoned). In a clean bowl beat the egg whites, adding a pinch of salt, until they form soft peaks. Beat one third of egg whites into soufflé base, then gently fold in remaining two thirds. Turn into prepared molds and place in top third of oven. Turn heat down to 375°. Small soufflés will be done in 20 minutes; the larger in 30.

Meanwhile prepare the sauce by wiping the mushrooms clean, chopping them roughly, then sautéing them in sizzling butter, tossing occasionally, for about 5 minutes. Sprinkle on flour, then add chicken stock and stir until thickened. Add the Madeira and let the sauce simmer to reduce a bit. If there is an extra bit of chicken, mince it very finely and add it to the sauce for body. Serve in a large sauceboat.

MAKES 4 SERVINGS

Stuffed Cucumbers with Ground Lamb

4 cucumbers, 7 inches long
4 cups ground cooked lamb
1 Tbs. minced fresh orégano
1 Tbs. puréed chervil

salt
freshly ground pepper
½ cup pine nuts

Preheat oven to 325°

Soak cucumbers in cold water for 15 minutes. Cut into halves lengthwise and scoop out seeds, leaving a shell ¼ to ⅓ inch thick. Boil them for 15 to 20 minutes. Mix ground lamb with orégano and chervil, add salt and pepper to taste, and stir in pine nuts. When cooked cucumbers are cool enough to handle, divide meat mixture evenly, spooning into cucumber hollows and mounding neatly on top. Bake on a rack in a shallow pan for about 1 hour.

MAKES 4 SERVINGS

Cambrian Baked Eggs with Cheese Sauce

butter
8 eggs, at room temperature
salt
freshly ground pepper

2 cups cheese and pimiento
    sandwich spread (p. 148)
minced chives

Preheat oven to 375°

Thoroughly butter 4 individual heatproof serving dishes. Carefully break 2 eggs into each dish. Sprinkle with a little salt and several turns of pepper grinder. Crumble about ½ cup of cheese spread over each dish of eggs, then sprinkle with minced chives. Bake for 15 minutes; check to see if eggs are set. Finish by turning oven to 500° for 5 minutes.

MAKES 4 SERVINGS

Eggplant with Beef and Cheese

1 medium-size eggplant
2 to 3 Tbs. bacon fat
½ cup chopped onion
¼ to ½ cup chopped green pepper
¾ lb. ground beef

1 cup tomato sauce
1 cup grated Cheddar cheese
1½ tsp. salt
   freshly ground pepper

Preheat oven to 350°

Peel and dice eggplant. Put in a saucepan, cover with boiling water, and cover pan. Let stand for 15 minutes, then drain. Melt bacon fat in a saucepan and sauté onion and green pepper for about 5 minutes; stir in ground beef, tomato sauce, cheese, drained diced eggplant, salt, and several turns of pepper grinder. Heat thoroughly, turn into 2-quart casserole, and cover. Bake for about 30 minutes; remove cover and continue baking for 15 minutes longer.

MAKES 4 SERVINGS

Game Bird Croquettes with Mushroom Sauce

3 Tbs. butter
⅓ cup flour
1 cup stock made from game-bird
   bones, or canned broth
2 cups minced meat from roasted
   partridge or other game birds

flour
1 egg, well beaten
¾ cup fresh bread crumbs
1 qt. or more oil for deep frying

Melt butter in a saucepan and stir in flour until it is smooth and thick. Off the heat, stir in stock, a little at a time, then return to heat and stir constantly for about 10 minutes as sauce cooks and thickens. Stir in minced partridge or other meat; chill for 1 hour or more. Shape chilled partridge mixture into 4 cylindrical croquettes; roll them first in flour, then in beaten egg, then in bread crumbs. Chill overnight.

Heat oil to 375° to 385°. Immerse croquettes. In 2 minutes turn them over and fry for 1 or 2 minutes more. Remove with slotted spoon and drain on paper; keep warm in 350° oven. Serve with mushroom sauce (p. 328).

MAKES 2 TO 4 SERVINGS

Flaming Hot Dogs

Scores of guests have consumed this dish with relish and with little clue to its ingredients. Hostesses not so surreptitious serve it from a chafing dish.

1 lb. skinless frankfurters	salt
6 Tbs. butter	freshly ground pepper
½ lb. mushrooms	1 Tbs. minced parsley
1 garlic clove, minced	¼ cup applejack, heated

Cut frankfurters into quarters lengthwise, then into ½-inch pieces. Heat butter and sauté frankfurters for 5 minutes. Wipe mushrooms with damp cloth, trim stems, and cut caps into quarters. Add mushrooms with garlic, a teaspoon or less of salt, and several turns of pepper grinder to frankfurters. Cover and cook for 5 minutes, stirring occasionally to coat mushrooms with butter. Sprinkle with minced parsley. Just before serving pour heated applejack over all and set aflame.

MAKES 4 SERVINGS

Ham Soufflé with Mushroom Sauce

1 cup finely ground country ham	4 egg yolks
6 Tbs. butter	2 Tbs. grated cheese, Wisconsin
2 Tbs. minced scallions or shallots	Asiago, Parmesan or very dry
3 Tbs. flour	sharp Cheddar
1 cup milk	5 egg whites

Preheat oven to 375°

Bring ground ham to room temperature. Melt 4 tablespoons of the butter and sauté scallions or shallots for about 5 minutes. Stir in remaining butter and flour and cook over low heat for 2 or 3 minutes. Remove from heat and stir in milk, eliminating all lumps; return to stove to thicken sauce. Off the heat, drop in egg yolks, one at a time, stirring briskly with wire whip as each is added. Stir in ham and half of cheese; sprinkle bottom and sides of buttered soufflé dish with remaining cheese. Beat egg whites until stiff, and fold 1 to 2 tablespoons into cheese-ham mixture, then turn mixture into egg-white bowl and fold gently until barely blended. Tie a buttered paper or foil collar on soufflé dish and pour mixture into it. Bake for 35 to 40 minutes. Meanwhile make mushroom sauce (p. 328). Top each serving of soufflé with some sauce.

MAKES 4 SERVINGS

Pepper

Jambalaya Soufflé

2 cups leftover jambalaya or less	4 eggs
2 cups milk	½ tsp. salt
½ cup flour	freshly ground black pepper
2 Tbs. butter, plus 1 tsp.	1 Tbs. grated cheese

Preheat oven to 350°

Bring leftover jambalaya (p. 264) to room temperature and chop so all ingredients are of uniform size. Heat milk in 2-quart saucepan. Meanwhile carefully stir just enough water into flour to make a smooth, almost runny mixture. Melt 2 tablespoons butter in hot milk (do not let it boil), then gradually add flour mixture, stirring constantly for about 5 minutes, until thickened. Stir in chopped jambalaya and set aside. Separate eggs and beat yolks, then beat into hot jambalaya mixture. Add salt and a little pepper. Let cool. Beat whites to form peaks and fold into mixture. Use 1 teaspoon of butter to grease 2-quart soufflé dish, then sprinkle in cheese, turning and shaking dish to distribute cheese evenly. Pour in soufflé mixture. Bake for 40 minutes or more, until soufflé is firm in center and the risen top is delicately brown.

MAKES 4 SERVINGS

Lamb and Eggplant Casserole

1 large eggplant
1 medium-size onion, chopped
1 lb. lean uncooked lamb, cut into
    1-inch cubes
5 to 6 Tbs. melted butter
½ cup heavy cream

salt
freshly ground pepper
2 tomatoes, peeled, seeded, and cut
    into 1-inch pieces
3 Tbs. minced parsley

Preheat oven to 450°

Bake eggplant 45 minutes. Mix onion, lamb, and 2 tablespoons of the melted butter. Put it in a 1½-quart casserole and bake alongside of eggplant for 30 minutes. Remove eggplant when soft inside, peel it, and mash the pulp; stir in remaining butter and the cream, and add salt and freshly ground pepper to taste. Blend the eggplant and tomato pieces into the casserole meat and return to oven, reducing heat to 350°. Bake casserole for 20 to 30 minutes. Sprinkle top with parsley just before serving.

MAKES 4 SERVINGS

Lasagna Baked with Ham and Spinach

This is uncompromisingly American—wide noodles so common in Italian neighborhoods, spinach in a style reminiscent of the *spanakopita* of citizens with Greek and Turkish backgrounds, and ham from a country smokehouse in the Ozarks, Piedmont Virginia, or a hillside village like East Hardwick, Vermont.

SPINACH SAUCE:

4 Tbs. corn or other vegetable oil
1 large onion, finely chopped
2 lbs. uncooked fresh spinach,
    finely chopped
4 Tbs. minced fresh dill, or 1½ Tbs.
    dried dillweed
1 tsp. dried lemon thyme

½ tsp. salt
    freshly ground black pepper
¼ cup heavy cream
½ lb. mozzarella cheese, finely diced
4 eggs, beaten
    butter

PASTA:

1 lb. lasagna

HAM SAUCE:

6 Tbs. butter
½ cup flour
1 to 2 cups milk

3 cups finely chopped country ham
    pepper
½ cup grated Swiss cheese

Preheat oven to 300°

Heat oil in a large skillet and sauté chopped onion over low heat for about 5 minutes, then add the chopped spinach, cover, and cook for 5 minutes. Remove cover, add dill and other seasonings, and cook slowly for about 10 minutes. Scrape out into bowl and let mixture cool. Add cream, cheese, and beaten eggs. Butter a 2-quart baking dish.

Cook the pasta and let it drain well.*

Melt 6 tablespoons butter in a saucepan and stir in flour until a thick, smooth paste is formed. Add milk a little at a time to make a thick sauce; it should be too thick to drop off spoon. Stir in finely chopped ham and a few turns of pepper grinder; salt will not be needed if ham has good country character.

Cover bottom of a buttered baking dish with a layer of lasagna. Spread half of spinach mixture over this, and cover with a layer of lasagna. Spread this with half of ham mixture. Repeat layering until all of spinach is used and the dish is topped by ham mixture. Sprinkle top evenly with cheese to form crust. Bake for 1 hour; then turn up oven to 500° for last 5 minutes to brown cheese slightly, or put dish under broiler.

MAKES 4 TO 6 SERVINGS

Lentils with Spanish Sausages

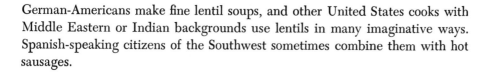

German-Americans make fine lentil soups, and other United States cooks with Middle Eastern or Indian backgrounds use lentils in many imaginative ways. Spanish-speaking citizens of the Southwest sometimes combine them with hot sausages.

¾ cup dried brown lentils

1 tsp. salt

4 cups boiling water

½ lb. chorizo sausages

1 large onion, chopped

1 green pepper, chopped

2 garlic cloves, minced

1 cup drained plum tomatoes,
   chopped

salt

freshly ground pepper

2 bacon strips

Wash and drain lentils. Add salt to boiling water and dribble in lentils. Cook over medium heat until water has been absorbed and lentils are tender but not mushy, about 35 minutes. Meanwhile, in a skillet simmer sausages in ¼ cup water, pricking them several times. When water is absorbed and pan is covered with fat from sausages, add chopped onion, green pepper, and garlic, and sauté until soft. Add drained tomatoes and mix well; add salt and pepper to taste. Cut sausages into bite-size pieces. Put a layer of lentils in a casserole, spread sausage and tomato mixture on top, then another layer of lentils. Cut bacon strips into halves and arrange on top. Put casserole under broiler until bacon becomes crisp and the lentils bubble.

MAKES 4 SERVINGS

Mushroom, Egg, Barley Casserole

¼ cup uncooked barley

3 Tbs. chopped green pepper

2 cups sliced mushrooms

5 Tbs. butter

2 Tbs. flour

2 cups milk

¼ cup grated Sardo or Parmesan
   cheese

4 eggs, hard-cooked

1 tsp. salt

freshly ground black pepper

Preheat oven to 350°

Pour barley slowly into 2 cups boiling water and cook for about 30 minutes, until tender; drain and set aside. Sauté green pepper and mushrooms in 2 tablespoons butter for 5 or 6 minutes. Meanwhile in a 1½- to 2-quart flameproof casserole melt 2 tablespoons butter, stir in the flour, and cook over gentle heat, stirring constantly, for about 2 minutes. Off the heat, blend in the milk, then return to heat and whisk until smooth and thickened. Stir cheese into the sauce, then mix in the hard-cooked eggs, drained barley, sautéed vegetables, and remaining butter. Season to taste with salt and freshly ground pepper. Bake for 30 to 40 minutes, until crusty surface forms.

MAKES 4 SERVINGS

314

Legends left behind in many United States cities after Jenny Lind's triumphal tour in 1851 refused to die, leaving among other things several dishes bearing her name. The singer wrote letters home that told of her longing for familiar foods, but she also cooked, while in this country, some of her favorites herself. Before a concert she often had a creamy soup to which she added sago or tapioca, and she is said to have prepared a tomato-oyster chafing-dish supper for some St. Louis admirers. Oysters and Ham Jenny Lind were first done this way, the story goes, by a St. Louis doctor at whose house she was entertained.

1 Tbs. butter	⅛ tsp. red pepper
1 Tbs. bacon fat	½ tsp. celery salt
2 Tbs. flour	¼ tsp. paprika
½ pint oysters, juice reserved	½ cup chopped cooked ham
½ cup heavy cream	2 Tbs. sherry, cider, or white wine
½ tsp. salt	2 patty shells

Melt butter and bacon fat in a chafing dish over hot water. Stir in flour to make a smooth paste. Off the heat, add oyster liquor and slowly stir in cream. Cook for about 4 minutes while mixture thickens. Add seasonings, oysters, and ham. Cook until oysters plump up and curl at edges. Stir in sherry, cider, or wine, and serve immediately in patty shells.

MAKES 2 SERVINGS

Oyster-Spinach Casserole

24 large fresh oysters	1 tsp. salt
2 pkgs. (10 oz. each) frozen chopped spinach, cooked and drained	Tabasco
	¼ cup sour cream
5 Tbs. butter	2 eggs, beaten
2 medium-size onions, chopped	lemon juice
½ cup small whole mushrooms	1 cup loosely packed fresh bread crumbs
1 garlic clove, minced	

Preheat oven to 350°

Drain oysters and set aside 12 whole ones; chop remainder and mix with chopped cooked spinach which has as much moisture as possible pressed out. Melt 2 tablespoons of the butter and sauté onions, mushrooms, and garlic for about 5 minutes, stirring often to cook mushrooms evenly. Stir in spinach and oysters, salt, a dash or two of Tabasco, and the sour cream. When mixture is hot, remove from heat and stir in beaten eggs and a liberal sprinkling of lemon juice. Butter a 2-quart casserole and put reserved dozen oysters on bottom, then pour in hot spinach mixture. Melt remaining 2 tablespoons butter and stir in bread crumbs; spread over spinach. Bake for 30 minutes, until mixture bubbles and crumbs turn golden.

MAKES 4 SERVINGS

Wallis Windsor's Oyster and Hominy Pie

During World War II the Duchess of Windsor put together a small book of her native Maryland recipes, and turned the proceeds over to charity. She said her husband had great appreciation for food that was typically American; few dishes are more so than this one.

1½ cups cooked whole hominy (canned)
1 qt. oysters, liquor reserved
3 Tbs. butter

½ cup milk
½ tsp. salt
freshly ground pepper
plain pastry (p. 349)

Preheat oven to 400°

Put alternate layers of hominy and oysters in a buttered casserole. Combine oyster liquor, milk, remaining butter, salt, and a few turns of pepper grinder; pour over oysters. Roll pastry dough very thin and trim to fit over top of casserole; make slashes for steam to escape. Bake for 30 to 40 minutes, until crust is well browned.

MAKES 6 SERVINGS

Pancakes with Ham-Fruit Sauce

1 recipe for thin pancakes (p. 170)
¼ cup seedless raisins
⅓ cup lemon juice
3 to 4 Tbs. applejack
3 Tbs. red currant jelly
¼ cup orange-fruit preserves

1 Tbs. butter
2 cups finely diced cooked country ham
⅓ cup maple sugar
¼ cup slivered almonds

Make a stack of thin pancakes and keep warm. Soak raisins in cold water for about 30 minutes, then drain. Put them in a saucepan, cover with cold water, and bring to a boil; continue boiling until raisins have absorbed all the water. Add lemon juice, applejack, currant jelly, and preserves (a combination of apricot and orange is good, or plain marmalade). Bring this mixture to a boil and remove from heat. Melt butter and brown diced ham in it. Sprinkle with maple sugar and stir for 1 minute or more, then stir in fruit mixture and slivered almonds. Serve hot pancakes with plenty of butter and a sauceboat of this tangy sauce.

MAKES 4 SERVINGS

Buttermilk Cakes Stuffed with Chicken, Ham, and Walnuts

This is one of those dishes of the harvest century that used the bounty of the farm, but it can be a treat today when made with cultured buttermilk and, if necessary, chopped dried beef instead of country ham.

2 cups diced cooked chicken
1 cup chopped or diced cooked
    country ham
¼ cup finely chopped black walnuts
½ tsp. dried rosemary
3 Tbs. butter
3 Tbs. flour

1 cup chicken stock
½ cup buttermilk
¼ cup heavy cream
3 to 4 Tbs. bourbon
1 recipe for Buttermilk Pancakes
    (p. 170)
3 Tbs. grated Cheddar

Preheat oven to 400°

Mix diced chicken and ham, and add black walnuts and rosemary. Melt butter and stir in flour over low heat for about 4 minutes. Off the heat, stir in stock, blending until smooth; then stir in buttermilk, cream, and bourbon. Return to heat and cook until sauce thickens, stirring constantly. Reserve half of sauce and stir meat mixture into remainder; keep warm. Make 12 Buttermilk Pancakes. Have a casserole large enough to hold 4 cakes flat on the bottom. Spread each cake with chicken-ham mixture, making 4 stacks 3 cakes high; divide mixture evenly. Pour reserved sauce over all and sprinkle with cheese. Bake in oven for about 5 minutes, until all is bubbling.

MAKES 4 SERVINGS

Cornmeal Pancakes Stuffed with Game

A delicious dish made with leftover game—Canada goose, mallard duck, teal, or any wild bird dinner of which enough might be left so that by assiduous picking the cook may have 2 cups of finely minced meat. Carcass and separate bones must be stewed for several hours to make a broth first.

BROTH:

2 to 3 game-bird carcasses, or other
    poultry parts
2 carrots
2 unpeeled onions

2 stalks celery
salt
freshly ground pepper

Break and flatten carcass, put in a pot with vegetables, and cover with at least 6 cups of water. Add seasoning after simmering for 3 hours or more during which stock is considerably reduced; it must be rich in flavor. You should have about 3 cups.

PANCAKES:

½ cup yellow cornmeal   ½ cup milk
1 tsp. salt   ¼ cup water
½ cup boiling water   ¼ cup corn oil
½ cup flour   1 egg, well beaten
1 Tbs. baking powder

Mix cornmeal, salt, and boiling water; beat well, then add flour, baking powder, milk, water, corn oil, and beaten egg, blending thoroughly.

FILLING:

2 Tbs. butter   2 Tbs. Madeira
¼ cup finely chopped shallots or   2 cups finely chopped game-bird
    scallions   meat
1 cup coarsely chopped mushrooms   salt
2 Tbs. flour   freshly ground pepper
1 cup game broth (as above)

Melt butter in a skillet and sauté shallots for 4 or 5 minutes. Add mushrooms and cook for about 7 minutes. Stir in flour and let it brown slightly. Off the heat, stir in broth, returning to heat when flour is absorbed; stir until it comes to boil, then add wine and simmer for 5 minutes. Add meat and seasoning to taste, and let it heat.

While this meat filling is simmering, start baking the pancakes: *Preheat oven to 400°.* Brush an 8-inch skillet with a little butter, heat until almost smoking, and pour in enough batter to thinly cover bottom of pan after pan is tipped to spread batter evenly to edges. Cook over medium heat, turning when bubbles appear on surface; cook other side until lightly browned. Repeat, making 8 pancakes in all.

Divide filling into 8 portions; spread 1 portion in a line in middle of each cake, turn up edge nearest, and roll. Put in buttered ovenproof dish just large enough to hold 8 stuffed rolls. Bake for 15 minutes. Reserve skillet in which filling cooked.

SAUCE:

2 Tbs. butter   freshly ground pepper
2 Tbs. flour   1 Tbs. Madeira (optional)
2 cups game-bird broth   3 Tbs. chopped parsley
    salt

Melt butter in skillet in which filling cooked, scraping brown bits and letting butter turn almost brown without burning. Blend in flour. Add hot game broth when bubbles appear. Cook, stirring constantly as sauce thickens, and add salt and pepper to taste and optional Madeira. When stuffed pancakes are piping hot, spoon sauce over them and sprinkle with parsley.

MAKES 4 SERVINGS

Rice Croquettes

¾ cup uncooked rice
¾ cup boiling water
1½ cups milk, scalded
1½ Tbs. butter

3 egg yolks, plus 1 egg yolk beaten
　with 1 Tbs. water
1 cup fine bread crumbs
　lard for deep frying
　raspberry and currant jelly

Wash rice in several changes of water. Put it with the boiling water in a deep saucepan; cover tightly. Cook till rice has absorbed all the water. Add scalded milk. Fork rice over lightly. Cook over hot water until soft; take from heat. Stir in butter; cool for 5 minutes. Stir in 3 egg yolks. Spread mixture on a platter to cool. Make balls the size of a golf ball. With your thumb, press a good hollow in the top of each ball. Chill.

Heat fat to 375° to 385°. Roll croquettes in egg yolk beaten with water, then in crumbs, then in egg again. Fry croquettes until golden brown and drain on brown paper. Keep warm. At serving time put some jelly in the hollow of each croquette.

MAKES 4 SERVINGS

Dixie Baked Rice and Sausage Meat

2 cups cooked rice
½ cup minced parsley
1 lb. Southern-style smoked pork
　sausage
½ cup finely chopped green pepper

2 cups chopped peeled fresh
　tomatoes, or canned
3 Tbs. melted butter
½ cup fresh bread crumbs
¼ cup grated mild cheese

Preheat oven to 350°

Mix rice and parsley in a large bowl. Spread sausage on bottom of a cold skillet and cook very slowly until meat browns lightly. Pour off all but 2 table-spoons fat and push cooked meat to one side; sauté green pepper in sausage fat for about 10 minutes, but do not burn. Stir meat and vegetable together and add chopped tomatoes; mix well. Stir sausage mixture into rice, blending

thoroughly. Brush baking dish lightly with melted butter and pour in rice-sausage mixture. Mix remaining melted butter with bread crumbs and spread over top. Sprinkle with cheese and bake for 30 to 40 minutes.

MAKES 4 SERVINGS

Rice with Duck and Ham

2 Tbs. bacon fat or butter
1 medium-size onion, chopped
1 celery rib, chopped
1 cup uncooked rice
2½ cups rich duck stock or chicken stock
1 cup canned tomatoes with juice

¼ tsp. dried orégano
¼ tsp. dried basil
¼ tsp. dried marjoram
1½ to 2 cups diced cooked duck meat
½ to 1 cup diced country ham
salt
freshly ground pepper

Preheat oven to 300°*

Melt fat and sauté onion and celery for about 8 minutes, stirring frequently so vegetables turn color slightly, but do not brown. Stir in rice and sauté for 2 minutes, mixing with vegetables and coating each grain with fat. Pour in hot stock (made from yesterday's carcass). Add tomatoes, chopping them a bit with a knife. Sprinkle in herbs, then stir in duck and ham. Add very little salt if ham is country cured; grind in a few turns from pepper mill. Cover pan tightly and simmer over very low heat for about 45 minutes.* Remove cover from rice (there should be some liquid) and put in oven for 5 minutes; turn off heat and leave rice in oven for 5 minutes more before serving.

MAKES 6 SERVINGS

Rice with Tomatoes, Chilies and Cheese

3 small canned green chilies, seeded and chopped
1 garlic clove, minced
½ cup canned tomatoes, drained, juice reserved
2 Tbs. drippings or other fat

1 white onion, chopped
½ cup uncooked rice
butter
½ cup stuffed olives, halved
¾ cup shredded Monterey Jack cheese

Preheat oven to 350°

Put chopped chilies, garlic, and tomatoes in a blender. Add enough water to reserved tomato juice to make about 1½ cups; add this gradually while spinning vegetables to make a thin purée. Melt fat in a skillet, add onion and rice,

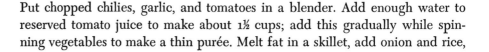

and sauté until rice is golden; stir almost constantly. Stir in puréed tomato mixture, bring to a boil, cover, and simmer for about 40 minutes, until rice absorbs all liquid and each grain remains separate. Butter a 1½-quart casserole and spoon in half of rice, then sprinkle in olives and grated cheese; top with remaining rice, and cover casserole. Bake for 30 to 45 minutes.

MAKES 4 SERVINGS

Little Vienna Souffléed Sandwich

3 eggs, separated
½ tsp. dry mustard
¼ tsp. salt
½ tsp. paprika

¼ tsp. cayenne
1 lb. skinless frankfurters
8 slices of toast

Preheat oven to 350°

Beat egg yolks until lemon colored. Stir in mustard, salt, paprika, and cayenne. Beat egg whites stiff enough to form peaks; gently fold into beaten yolks. Split frankfurters and arrange on toast in a shallow pan large enough to hold all pieces side by side. Pour soufflé mixture over and bake for 25 to 30 minutes, until slightly browned.

MAKES 4 SERVINGS

Spaghetti with Blue Crab and Tomato Sauce

Delicious! a labor of love that is worth the effort.

4 Tbs. olive oil
2 medium-size onions, chopped
2 or 3 garlic cloves, minced
¼ cup minced celery
½ cup minced parsley
¼ cup fish stock, or 2 Tbs. clam juice and 2 Tbs. water
4 medium-size tomatoes, peeled and chopped

8 blue crabs (live hard-shell), about 5 inches in diameter
1½ Tbs. salt
   freshly ground black pepper
½ tsp. sugar
3 Tbs. chopped fresh basil
¾ lb. spaghetti

In a large heavy pot sauté chopped onions in 3 tablespoons of the oil, adding garlic, celery, and parsley; cook over very low heat for about 10 minutes. Add liquid and chopped tomatoes with their juice and bring to a boil with salt, pepper, and sugar. Pick up 4 of the crabs with tongs and very quickly drop them into the tomato mixture and cover. Reduce heat to medium and cook for 10 minutes, then remove crabs and set aside. Repeat with remaining four crabs.

Heat a large pot of water to boiling. Keep tomato sauce simmering over low heat. Meanwhile crack shells of crabs and remove all of the meat and juices. This can be done over the pot so you don't lose any of the juice; scrape all meat away from shells, breaking claws and using skewer to loosen bits of crab. When water is boiling, toss in spaghetti in big handfuls, pushing top ends down into water, and add 1 tablespoon salt and 1 tablespoon oil. Cover and boil for about 12 minutes. Drain well and serve on piping hot plates with hot crab sauce and chopped basil divided equally.

MAKES 4 SERVINGS

Spinach with Braised Chestnuts and Livers

⅓ lb. chestnuts
4 Tbs. butter
½ cup chicken stock
1 Tbs. Madeira

1 lb. fresh spinach, washed and
   trimmed of stems
salt
¾ lb. chicken livers

SAUCE:

2 Tbs. butter
3 Tbs. flour
1½ cups milk
   salt

freshly ground pepper
freshly grated nutmeg
2 Tbs. dry white wine or vermouth
¼ cup grated Parmesan cheese

Use a sharp knife to cut a cross in each chestnut, then drop into pan of cold water; bring to a boil and boil chestnuts for just 1 minute. Use a slotted spoon to remove a couple at a time, and peel away both shell and inner skin. Then braise chestnuts slowly in a tightly covered small pan with 2 tablespoons butter, the chicken stock, and Madeira for about 25 minutes; shake pan occasionally and check to make sure liquid does not evaporate; if necessary add a little water or more stock. Meanwhile blanch spinach in 1 cup boiling water with a little salt for 3 to 4 minutes, until spinach is barely tender. Drain; chop coarsely. Clean and trim chicken livers, cutting each into 2 or 3 pieces. Sauté them in remaining 2 tablespoons butter over fairly high heat for 1 or 2 minutes on each side.

Make the sauce: Melt butter, stir in flour, and cook for 1 or 2 minutes. Add milk off the heat, mixing until smooth. Return to heat and whisk as mixture cooks and thickens, adding salt to taste, some pepper and nutmeg, and the wine.

In a shallow baking dish spread out half of spinach. Slice chestnuts and return them to pan in which they cooked; then use a rubber spatula to scrape chestnut juice and sliced nuts into baking dish, spreading evenly over spinach. Scrape out chicken livers and juices and spread over chestnuts. Top with remaining spinach, then pour sauce over all. Sprinkle with cheese. Put under broiler until everything bubbles and cheese turns golden.

MAKES 4 SERVINGS

322 | *Casseroles, Lunch and Supper Dishes*

Butternut Squash Stuffed with Pork, Apples, and Chestnuts

2 medium-size butternut squash
6 Tbs. softened butter
  salt
  freshly ground pepper
2 cups small dice of cooked pork

1 large tart apple, peeled and diced
  about 8 roasted and peeled
    chestnuts, diced
3 scallions, chopped
1 tsp. crumbled dried sage

Preheat oven to 350°

Split the squashes lengthwise and scoop out seeds. Rub with a little of the butter and fill centers with a small knob of butter. Salt and pepper them and bake for 40 minutes. Remove from the oven, pour the hot butter from the centers into a bowl, and mix it with the other ingredients. Now scoop out the partially cooked flesh from the shells, trying not to break the skin. Chop squash pulp coarsely and fold into the filling; correct seasoning. Pile filling mixture evenly into the shells, dot remaining butter on top, and cover loosely with aluminum foil. Bake for 30 to 35 minutes.

MAKES 4 SERVINGS

Tacos de Carne

1 lb. lean beef chuck
5 Tbs. vegetable oil
1 small onion, chopped
1 garlic clove, minced
¼ tsp. whole cuminseeds
½ tsp. ground coriander

1 Tbs. chili powder
8 tortillas
  shredded lettuce
½ avocado, sliced
  sour cream

Do not grind meat, but chop it with a sharp knife to ¼-inch pieces. Heat 4 tablespoons oil; sauté onion and garlic for 1 or 2 minutes, then stir in chopped meat and let it brown. Mull cuminseeds and add with coriander and chili powder; stir in ½ cup water and let mixture absorb it. In a skillet heat remaining oil and heat tortillas until soft; while they are hot fill them with shredded lettuce, 2 or 3 avocado slices, some sour cream, and some of seasoned meat mixture. The contrasts of hot and cold temperatures, spicy and bland flavors, are exquisite.

MAKES 4 SERVINGS

After it opened in August, 1905, The White Turkey Inn near Danbury, Connecticut, gained many enthusiasts for its American bill of fare. It often served turkey slices with broccoli under a cheese sauce, and so, a half century later, did Albert Stockli at his airport restaurant called The Newarker. When chicken was substituted, a similar dish became known as Chicken Divan.

1 lb. broccoli, cooked	1 Tbs. arrowroot starch
2 Tbs. butter	½ cup heavy cream
8 slices of cooked turkey breast	1 cup hollandaise sauce
½ cup milk	½ cup grated Vermont cheese
½ cup chicken stock	¼ cup bread crumbs

Preheat oven to 375°

Break up broccoli in individual buds. Butter a shallow baking dish, cover the bottom with turkey slices, and top them with broccoli. Heat milk, stock, and 1 tablespoon of butter. Mix arrowroot with cream and stir this paste into hot milk mixture; cook slowly until sauce thickens, stirring constantly. Off the heat, stir hollandaise into the cream sauce, blend well, and pour over broccoli and turkey. Sprinkle with bread crumbs and cheese. Bake for about 15 minutes.

MAKES 4 SERVINGS

Chapter 19

Sauces

Richmond Barbecue Sauce for Pork or Spareribs

This sauce complements all meats and is an especially poignant accent for pork. Spit-roast—indoors or out—a pork shoulder with its skin still on for 5 to 6 hours, basting often so that meat almost falls off the bone when finished.

1 Tbs. dry mustard
2 to 3 Tbs. grated maple sugar, or other sugar
1 tsp. celery seeds

1 tsp. salt
½ to ¾ tsp. red pepper flakes
1 tsp. freshly ground black pepper
1 cup tarragon vinegar

Combine mustard, sugar, celery seeds, salt, red pepper, and black pepper. Stir into vinegar and boil for about 5 minutes.

MAKES ABOUT 1 CUP

Peppery Barbecue Sauce for Beef

1 cup melted butter
2½ cups water
¼ cup red wine
1¼ tsp. dry mustard
1 Tbs. sugar
2 tsp. salt
2 tsp. chili powder
⅛ tsp. cayenne
1½ tsp. Worcestershire sauce

1 tsp. Tabasco
¼ tsp. freshly ground black pepper
1 Tbs. paprika
½ cup finely minced onion
1 garlic clove, finely minced
1 tsp. dried marjoram
1 tsp. dried thyme
1 Tbs. lemon juice

Put all ingredients in an enamelware saucepan; stir to blend flavors. Boil over moderate heat for 20 minutes, stirring occasionally. Brush on meat while broiling, or use as marinade.

MAKES ABOUT 4 CUPS

Mary Kelleher's Never-Fail Béarnaise Sauce

Sarah Tyson Rorer, whose *Philadelphia Cook Book* was published in 1886, urged Americans to serve Béarnaise sauce with broiled steak, smelts, or "lobster chops," but she offered no help in ways to avoid failure in the kitchen. For her part, Mary Kelleher enhances her promises by suggesting the use of dry vermouth instead of wine for "a somewhat richer taste." We have found it to be delicious and foolproof, but a more subtle Americanization of the classic sauce than the garlic- (and sometimes nutmeg-) flavored New Orleans Béarnaise Sauce.

1 generous tsp. dried tarragon
1 generous tsp. chopped shallots
  salt
  freshly ground pepper
4 Tbs. wine vinegar

⅓ cup dry vermouth
2 egg yolks, mixed with 1 tsp. water
¼ lb. sweet butter (1 stick divided into 8 Tbs.)

Place tarragon, shallots, salt and pepper to taste, vinegar, and vermouth in a small saucepan and bring to boil, reducing to two thirds of original volume. Bring water to a boil in bottom part of a double boiler. Strain tarragon mixture into the cool top part of double boiler and place pot over (but not touching) water, which should be kept at a slow, steady boil. Gradually stir in egg yolks with a wire whisk. Stirring steadily, add the butter, tablespoon by tablespoon, allowing each to melt before adding the next. When all butter is used and sauce has become thick enough, put top half of double boiler into a pan of cold water for a few minutes to stop the cooking.

MAKES ABOUT 1 CUP

White Clam Sauce

4 Tbs. butter
⅓ cup olive oil
½ to ¾ cup chopped onion
1 tsp. dried basil
1 tsp. dried orégano
1 tsp. dried rosemary
¾ cup minced parsley

2 cans (7 oz. each) minced clams
¼ cup white wine
½ cup grated Parmesan cheese
¼ cup grated Sardo cheese
  salt
  freshly ground pepper

Heat butter and oil in skillet and sauté onion over very low heat for 25 minutes, stirring frequently. Mull dried herbs between fingers and sprinkle over onion; cook for 5 minutes. Stir in minced parsley, cover, and cook for 10 minutes. Add clams, their juice, and wine and cook for 5 minutes, then stir in grated Parmesan and Sardo; add very little salt and freshly ground pepper to taste. Toss with buttered pasta—rigatoni, shells, linguini, etc. Be sure serving plates are hot, and have plenty of extra cheese.

MAKES ABOUT 4 CUPS

Chop coarsely enough of each of the following to make:

1 cup watercress	2 Tbs. fresh basil
1 cup fresh spinach	2 Tbs. fresh tarragon
2 Tbs. green leaves of scallions	2 Tbs. fresh dill
2 Tbs. Italian parsley	2 Tbs. fresh chervil

Put greens in blender and add:

1 hard-cooked egg	1 Tbs. tarragon vinegar
2 Tbs. cottage cheese	4 canned sardines
1 cup yoghurt	1 dill pickle

Blend until smooth, adding salt and pepper to taste. Excellent with cold fish and seafood or poultry; also delicious as a dip for crisp raw vegetables.

MAKES ABOUT 4 CUPS

1 pint oysters	1 tsp. good brandy
3 Tbs. butter	salt
3 Tbs. flour	freshly ground white pepper
½ cup heavy cream	pinch of cayenne
½ cup white wine	1 Tbs. minced parsley
1 Tbs. lemon juice	

Poach the oysters in their own liquor until the edges curl. In a separate pan melt the butter, add flour, and stir over low heat for a minute or two. Off heat, add drained oyster liquor, cream, and white wine plus another ¼ cup of oyster liquor reserved from stuffed chicken breasts (p. 241). (If making the sauce independently and there is no additional oyster liquor at hand, use an equivalent amount of pungent fish stock or chicken broth diluted with a little water.) Return to the heat and stir until well blended and fairly thick. Let cook slowly for a minute or so, then add lemon juice, brandy, and seasonings to taste; taste carefully and correct. If too thick add a little more liquid. Finally, add drained oysters; if they are large cut each into 2 or 3 pieces. Serve in a sauceboat sprinkled with minced parsley.

MAKES 2 CUPS

Ferry Farm Maple-Honey Sauce

This syrup, an absolutely brilliant complement to buckwheat cakes for breakfast or lunch, is also uniquely American and a fine example of native cookery. Dating from colonial days, it is still served in Kentucky and Virginia and was a favorite sauce for waffles and pancakes that Washington's mother, some say, frequently made at her Ferry Farm.

½ cup strained pure honey
¾ cup pure maple syrup

2 tsp. ground cinnamon
⅛ tsp. caraway seeds

Combine honey and maple syrup and heat slowly. Add cinnamon and caraway and bring to a hard boil. Serve hot.

KENNEBEC FRENCH-CANADIAN MAPLE BUTTER

½ cup grated maple sugar
¼ cup sweet butter, softened

Blend maple sugar into softened butter. Serve on waffles, pancakes, or hot toast.

OZARK MAPLE-BUTTER WHIP

¼ cup maple syrup
½ cup butter, softened

Combine syrup and soft butter and whip until fluffy. Serve on waffles, pancakes, or hot corn bread.

Simple Mushroom and Madeira Sauce

For hamburgers, leftover beef, game, croquettes, and many other uses.

¼ lb. mushrooms
2 Tbs. butter
2 Tbs. flour
¾ to 1 cup beef stock or canned
    consommé

salt
freshly ground pepper
1 tsp. minced fresh tarragon, or
    ½ tsp. dried
1 to 2 Tbs. Madeira

Wipe mushrooms clean. Remove stems and chop fine; slice caps. Melt butter and sauté stems and caps for 3 or 4 minutes. Sprinkle in flour; cook and stir gently for 1 more minute. Pour in beef stock and add seasonings to taste along with Madeira; stir until thickened and smooth.

MAKES ABOUT 1½ CUPS

4 egg yolks	½ tsp. salt
1½ cups sour cream	1 to 2 Tbs. rose paprika
1½ to 2 Tbs. lemon juice	3 Tbs. minced fresh parsley

Beat egg yolks in top part of a double boiler; stir in sour cream and lemon juice over simmering water; beat continuously until sauce thickens. Add salt, enough paprika to turn the sauce to a subdued pink, and stir in parsley just before serving. Excellent with Polish-American Stuffed Pike (p. 248), other fish, or cooked vegetables.

MAKES ABOUT 2 CUPS

¼ cup butter	juice of 1 lemon
2 Tbs. flour	½ tsp. aromatic French mustard
1½ cups boiling water	salt
3 large egg yolks, beaten until light	cayenne

Melt butter in a saucepan and stir in flour to make a smooth paste. Add boiling water slowly, stirring constantly to eliminate all lumps. Off heat, stir in egg yolks, mixing thoroughly with sauce. Blend in lemon juice, mustard, a scant teaspoon salt, and a liberal sprinkling of cayenne. A tangy accent for fish, or cauliflower, celery, asparagus, and for Jerusalem Artichoke and Celery-Root Salad (p. 157).

MAKES ABOUT 2 CUPS

Chapter 20

Desserts

Apple Crunch or Delight—or Heaven

Just about every American household had its favorite simple, crunchy apple dish in days when a meal wasn't complete without a homemade dessert. This was a favorite in our family, handed down by parents and cherished by our children. It can be made with peaches, when in season, or with rhubarb (with additional sugar), but apples always ranked first and the dish went by any of the above names.

6 to 8 medium-size tart apples   ½ cup sugar
½ tsp. ground cinnamon   nutmeg

TOPPING:

⅔ cup flour   4 Tbs. butter
⅔ cup sugar

Preheat oven to 375°

Peel and core apples and cut into slices. Toss in a baking dish with cinnamon and sugar; more or less may be added according to how sour, or flavorful, the apples are; add a sprinkling of grated nutmeg. For the topping, mix flour and sugar together. Cut butter into small pieces and blend lightly with fingertips into dry mixture. Sprinkle this crumblike mixture over apples. Bake for about 45 minutes, or until apples are bubbling over onto browned, crusty top.

    MAKES 6 SERVINGS

Bananas Baked with Guava Jelly

Some Key West cooks, and those in tropical Florida, have homegrown, small, tart Cattley guavas from which they make excellent jelly. But the commercial jelly, available throughout America, makes an interesting dessert when served with cream cheese, and an even better one in this combination that is accented by coconut cream.

1 cup heavy cream
½ cup shredded nonsweetened
    coconut
4 firm bananas

⅓ cup guava jelly
2 Tbs. butter
2 Tbs. warm rum (optional)

Preheat oven to 350°

Several hours ahead mix cream and coconut and set aside. Peel and slice bananas, and place them in a buttered dish. Distribute the guava jelly over them and dot with butter. Bake for 20 minutes, turning once and spooning melted jelly over bananas. Serve warm with coconut cream, pouring flaming rum over the dish if desired.

MAKES 4 SERVINGS

Black Walnut Cake

A veteran retailer of nuts of all varieties once said he could be sure anyone who asked for black walnuts was either a Southerner or a Midwesterner. This recipe migrated to eastern Pennsylvania.

½ cup butter
1 cup plus 2 Tbs. sugar
2 whole eggs
1 tsp. vanilla extract
1 tsp. orange juice
2 cups cake flour

2½ tsp. baking powder
¾ tsp. salt
¾ cup milk
¾ cup black walnut bits
    powdered sugar

Preheat oven to 350°

Cream butter and sugar; add eggs, vanilla, and orange juice, mixing thoroughly. Sift together flour, baking powder, and salt, then stir into first mixture with milk and nuts. Spoon batter into a greased and floured loaf pan (9 x 5 x 3 inches). Bake for 1 hour and 10 minutes. Remove from oven and cover top with powdered sugar.

Michigan Applesauce Torte

2⅛ cups fresh bread crumbs, made
    from white homemade bread
5 Tbs. butter
3 eggs, separated
2 cups applesauce
2 Tbs. vanilla sugar*

salt
2 Tbs. sugar
⅓ cup mixed chopped walnuts and
    filberts
1 cup chilled boiled custard, or
    1 cup whipped cream

Preheat oven to 350°

Reserve 2 tablespoons of bread crumbs; sauté remainder in 4 tablespoons butter, tossing continuously over very low heat until they turn golden brown. Beat egg yolks thoroughly, then add applesauce, sautéed bread crumbs, and vanilla sugar. Beat egg whites with a pinch of salt until almost stiff, then add plain sugar and beat until peaks form. Mix one fourth of stiff egg whites into applesauce batter, then carefully fold in remainder. Fold in chopped nuts. With remaining butter generously grease a shallow cake tin (8 to 9 inches) and sprinkle with reserved bread crumbs. Pour in applesauce mixture and smooth out. Bake for 1 to 1¼ hours. Chill overnight and serve with cold boiled custard or whipped cream.

MAKES 8 SERVINGS

* Before vanilla extract was readily available American cooks would keep a bruised vanilla bean embedded in about 1 pound of sugar in a well-sealed jar. This vanilla sugar gives a fresh and delicate flavor. You can, of course, use plain sugar with a little vanilla extract instead.

Carole Lowenstein's Blintzes

BATTER:

1 tsp. sugar
2 eggs
2 Tbs. salad oil
1 tsp. vanilla extract

1 cup milk
¾ cup sifted flour
½ tsp. salt

Beat sugar, eggs, oil, vanilla, milk, flour, and salt until smooth, or spin in a blender for 1 minute or a little more. Refrigerate for at least 1 hour.

FILLING:

½ lb. cottage cheese
¼ lb. cream cheese
1 egg
2 Tbs. sugar
½ tsp. salt

1 tsp. vanilla extract
½ tsp. ground cinnamon
½ tsp. grated lemon rind
matzoh meal to thicken

Combine ingredients for filling, adding just enough matzoh meal to make mixture quite thick.

TO MAKE BLINTZES:

8 Tbs. butter
1 cup sour cream (optional)
   cinnamon

Melt butter, and brush bottom of 6- to 7-inch skillet with enough to cover lightly. Pour about 2 tablespoons of batter into pan, tilting to spread batter evenly around bottom. Cook over medium heat for about 1 minute, until lightly browned on one side only. Turn out, brown side up. Brush butter lightly into pan again and repeat, buttering and making blintzes until batter is used up. Pancakes may be stacked with layers of filling or, as each blintz is baked and turned out, place a spoonful of filling in center and carefully roll. Before serving, brown rolls in butter. Add a dollop of sour cream to each hot blintz and dust with cinnamon; or, if you prefer, omit sour cream and dust with sugar and cinnamon.

MAKES 6 TO 8 SERVINGS

Chocolate Custard Cake

3 oz. unsweetened chocolate
½ cup condensed milk
1 cup granulated brown sugar
1 egg yolk
2 cups cake flour
1 tsp. baking soda

½ tsp. salt
¼ lb. (1 stick) butter
1 cup white sugar
2 eggs
¾ cup milk
1 tsp. vanilla extract

FROSTING:

1 cup condensed milk
1¼ cups sugar
5 oz. unsweetened chocolate

¼ lb. (1 stick) butter
1 tsp. vanilla extract

GARNISH & DECORATION:

2 Tbs. mint jelly
12 pecan halves

Preheat oven to 350°

Melt the chocolate with condensed milk, brown sugar, and egg yolk over hot water, stirring until smooth and thickened. Remove from heat. Sift together flour, baking soda, and salt. Cream the butter and add white sugar gradually, beating constantly until fluffy. Separate the eggs and add yolks to the butter mixture one at a time, beating after each addition. Now add the flour alternately with the milk. When thoroughly blended stir in the chocolate custard and the vanilla. Beat the egg whites until they form soft peaks and fold them into the cake batter. Butter well and flour lightly, knocking out excess flour, two 9-inch cake tins, and distribute batter evenly into them. Bake for 30 minutes, then cool in the cake tins for about 10 minutes; turn out on racks.

Make the frosting: Combine condensed milk and sugar in a heavy saucepan. Bring to a boil, stir once, then turn down heat and let simmer, without stirring, for 6 minutes. Remove from heat. Blend in the chocolate, then the butter, then vanilla; let cool, stirring occasionally. When sufficiently cool and thick, spread about one third over one layer, place the next layer on top and coat the surface of that with the mint jelly. Spread the rest of the frosting over the top surface and sides of the cake. Place the pecans around the edge for decoration.

Date and Nut Cakes

3 eggs	1 cup chopped walnuts
1 cup chopped dates	1 Tbs. bread crumbs
3 Tbs. sugar	softened butter

GARNISH:

1 cup heavy cream	½ tsp. vanilla extract
1 tsp. sugar	

Preheat oven to 375°

Separate the eggs; beat the yolks until lemon-colored. Toss the chopped dates with the sugar so they don't stick together, then mix with walnuts and bread crumbs and add to yolks. Beat whites until they form stiff peaks, then fold into date mixture. Butter 12 muffin tins, and fill three-quarters full. Bake for 12 minutes. Remove and cool a little on cake racks. Beat the cream, add the sugar, and continue to beat until stiff; then blend in vanilla. Serve a dollop over each slightly warm cake.

MAKES 12

Devils' Food Cake

1 tsp. baking soda	3 egg yolks
½ cup sour milk	1 tsp. vanilla extract
2 oz. chocolate	½ cup hot coffee
½ cup shortening	2 cups sifted flour
2 cups brown sugar	

Preheat oven to 350°

Stir baking soda into sour milk. Shred chocolate; put in a ½-cup measure and fill with boiling water to make ½ cup of liquid chocolate. Cream together shortening and 1 cup brown sugar; beat remaining sugar into egg yolks, then blend with shortening and sugar, beating thoroughly. Stir in liquid chocolate, vanilla, and hot coffee, and continue thorough beating. Stir in sifted flour alternately with sour milk, beating the mixture for 3 more minutes. Spoon into a loaf pan (9 x 5 x 3 inches) and bake for about 35 minutes.

Filbert Cake

Pioneer cooks found American hazelnuts abundant in the South and in Midwestern states like Kansas, but nowhere were these nuts turned into tempting desserts more often than in Oregon. This excellent version is not unlike a very popular Salem dessert.

7 eggs	½ lb. filberts
1 cup vanilla sugar (see footnote p. 332)	¼ tsp. cream of tartar
	butter
2 Tbs. flour	flour
⅛ tsp. salt	confectioners' sugar
⅛ tsp. ground cinnamon	1 cup heavy cream, whipped
freshly grated nutmeg	(optional)
1 tsp. rum	

Preheat oven to 325°

Separate eggs, putting whites into a very clean stainless steel or copper bowl. In another bowl, beat yolks until lemon-colored, then add vanilla sugar gradually, beating continuously until sugar is all absorbed. Sift in flour and salt, then add cinnamon and a few gratings of nutmeg along with rum. Pulverize filberts in a blender, half at a time. When very finely ground stir small amounts into batter by lightly crumbling the nuts through your fingers to loosen their density; beat well into mixture. Beat egg whites, adding a pinch of cream of tartar, until they form peaks. Mix one fourth of beaten whites into batter to lighten, then turn batter into the bowl of remaining whites, carefully folding to keep lightness. Butter a 10-inch tube pan generously; sprinkle with flour and shake out excess; pour in batter and bake for 1 hour. Let the cake cool in the pan. Turn out on rack. To serve, slip onto a cake plate and sprinkle well with confectioners' sugar, or heap with whipped cream and sprinkle with extra nuts.

MAKES 10 SERVINGS FOR DESSERT CAKE WITH CREAM

There are plenty of stories to go with this splendid cake, almost as many as there are recipe variations. It seems to be true that novelist Owen Wister, tarrying in Charleston, was so taken by the city and a cake he first ate there that he borrowed the name of the cake for the title of his 1906 romance, *Lady Baltimore*. It also may be true that the "original" recipe became the property of the Misses Florence and Nina Ottolengui who managed Charleston's Lady Baltimore Tea Room for a quarter of a century and annually baked and shipped to Owen Wister one of the very American cakes his novel had helped to make famous. The following method is simpler than some but results in a cake that tempts one to eat it with a spoon.

½ lb. sweet butter	1 cup milk
2 cups sugar	¼ tsp. almond extract
3½ cups cake flour	8 egg whites
4 tsp. baking powder	pinch of cream of tartar
½ tsp. salt	butter and flour for cake tins

FILLING:

1 cup chopped mixed nuts	8 dried figs
½ cup raisins, yellow and brown mixed	Optional: ¼ cup sherry or rum

ICING:

3 egg whites	½ tsp. cream of tartar
1⅛ cups sugar	pinch of salt
4 Tbs. cold water, or substitute 1 Tbs. with rum or brandy	1½ tsp. vanilla extract (less if liquor is used)

GARNISH:

pecan halves

Preheat oven to 375°

In a large bowl cream the butter, add the sugar slowly, and beat until fluffy. Sift the flour before measuring; then sift again with the baking powder and salt. Add flour alternately with the milk and finally the almond extract and beat batter until smooth and light. Beat egg whites with a pinch of cream of tartar (unless using a copper bowl) until stiff but not dry. Mix well one fourth of the whites into the batter, then fold in the rest. Butter well three 9-inch cake tins, dust with flour, and shake out excess. Turn equal amounts of the batter into the tins and bake for 25 minutes. Cool on racks.

Prepare the filling: Chop nuts, raisins, and figs together; if you like, steep them in sherry or rum for a while, then drain. Spread equal amounts of filling on the top of two layers, then place one over the other. Add third layer.

Prepare the icing: Mix egg whites, sugar, water (with rum or brandy if desired), cream of tartar, and salt in the top part of a double boiler and place over boiling water. Beat continuously for 7 minutes, maybe a little more, until the mixture will stand in peaks when beater is lifted and turned up. Remove from the heat. When cool, add vanilla. Spread generously over the top and sides of cake. Decorate the rim with halved pecans and a little wheel of pecans in the middle.

Maple Layer Cake

2 cups all-purpose flour	5 egg whites
2½ tsp. baking powder	salt
¼ lb. butter, softened	⅛ tsp. cream of tartar
1¼ cups powdered sugar	½ cup milk
1 tsp. vanilla extract	

Preheat oven to 375°

Sift flour and baking powder three times. Cream softened butter with sugar until light and lemon-colored. Add vanilla. Beat egg whites with a pinch of salt and cream of tartar until they form peaks. Add milk and flour alternately to butter-sugar mixture, blending well. Finally mix in about one fourth of whites to lighten, then gently fold in remaining whites. Turn into two buttered and floured 9-inch cake tins, and bake for 25 minutes. Cool on cake racks. Spread with Aunt Lucy's Vermont Maple Frosting, coating sides and decorating with walnuts.

AUNT LUCY'S VERMONT MAPLE FROSTING:

1½ cups pure Vermont maple syrup
 2 egg whites, beaten with a little salt

Boil syrup till it spins a thread. Egg whites should be stiff but not too dry. Add syrup gradually and keep beating till cool and of spreadable consistency.

Marble Cake

¼ lb. butter	½ tsp. baking soda
2 cups sugar	½ tsp. salt
2 eggs, beaten	1 cup milk
3 cups cake flour	1 tsp. vanilla extract
1 tsp. cream of tartar	3 Tbs. unsweetened powdered cocoa

Preheat oven to 375°

Cream butter and add sugar slowly, beating constantly until sugar is absorbed and mixture is fluffy. Add the eggs. Sift dry ingredients together, then start adding alternately with the milk, beating with each addition. Then add vanilla. Moisten the cocoa with just enough boiling water to make a smooth paste. Remove about one third of the cake batter to another bowl and beat in cocoa until smooth. Grease a 10-inch tube pan or a decorative round cake mold. Using two spoons, start adding the two batters, first the white, then a dollop of the chocolate here and there, swirling it slightly to form a marbled pattern. Knock tube pan on the counter to even the batter; don't smooth and mix up two batters. Bake in the top third of the oven for 1 hour. Remove and cool in the pan for about 10 minutes before turning out. Marble cake can be served simply sprinkled with powdered sugar, or it can be frosted with chocolate icing (p. 333).

Leslie Jones' Oatmeal Cake

1¼ cups boiling water	2 eggs, beaten
1 cup rolled oats	1½ cups flour
¼ lb. butter, softened	1 tsp. baking soda
1 cup white sugar	½ tsp. salt
1 cup brown sugar	¾ tsp. ground cinnamon
1 tsp. vanilla extract	¼ tsp. grated nutmeg

Preheat oven to 350°

Pour boiling water over oats, cover, and let stand for 20 minutes. Beat butter until creamy; gradually add both sugars and beat until fluffy. Blend in vanilla and eggs, then stir in oats. Sift together flour, baking soda, salt, cinnamon, and nutmeg; add to creamed mixture and mix thoroughly. Pour this batter into a well-greased and floured 9-inch square pan. Bake for 50 to 55 minutes. Leave in pan and spread on topping.

TOPPING:

¼ cup melted butter	⅓ cup chopped nuts
½ cup brown sugar	¾ cup shredded coconut
3 Tbs. half and half or evaporated milk	

Combine all ingredients, blending until smooth. Spread over top of cake, then put it under the broiler just long enough to glaze. Good either hot or cold.

MAKES 9 SERVINGS

Charlotte Russe may have been created by the great French confectioner, Carême; it may have received its appellation because it resembled a French hat style called "charlotte" which, as Parisians said, was "garnished with shuttlecocks." But Charlotte Russe became the American hostess's most festive dessert in the latter part of the nineteenth century. Six Southern ladies, contributing to *Housekeeping in Old Virginia*, published in 1879, each gave her own version, each as different as plantation hostesses could be.

12 to 18 ladyfingers
½ cup Madeira
2 envelopes unflavored gelatin
4 cups heavy cream
¾ cup powdered sugar

1 tsp. vanilla extract
optional: ¼ cup slivered toasted
    almonds or ¼ cup
    crumbled macaroons

Line a 2-quart glass bowl with ladyfingers. Sprinkle with about half of the Madeira to help make them adhere. Soften the gelatin in 2 to 3 tablespoons cold water and the rest of the Madeira. Whip the cream in a metal bowl over ice; when thickened, whip in sugar and finally the softened gelatin. Add vanilla. Pile the cream mixture into the lined bowl. Chill for at least 8 hours. If desired sprinkle toasted almonds or crumbled macaroons over the top before serving.

MAKES 6 TO 8 SERVINGS

2 cups oatmeal flour (made from
    whole oats—see preparation
    below)
¼ lb. butter, softened, plus extra for
    pan

⅓ cup condensed milk
½ tsp. salt
4 Tbs. maple syrup

Preheat oven to 325°

Make the oatmeal flour by spinning a handful of whole oats in a blender until it has the consistency of stone-ground flour. When you have 2 cups, add softened butter with a pastry blender or mix with fingers. Mix in the condensed milk, salt, and maple syrup. When well mixed, spread onto a generously buttered pan about 6 x 10 inches. Bake for 15 to 20 minutes, until oatcake shrinks from the sides and is slightly brown on top. Remove and immediately cut into 18 cakes, but let cool in the pan before trying to remove the pieces; they will be crumbly. Eat still slightly warm; if kept, reheat, spread with a little butter, in a medium oven for 4 or 5 minutes. They can also be kept frozen. Delicious for tea.

MAKES 18 THIN CAKES

Ninth-Floor Brownies

Brownies have been made on the ninth floor of a certain apartment building in New York for probably as many years as the vintage building has stood. Nobody seems to know who made these chocolate confections for the first time, but they vary from one region to another, sometimes having almost fudge-like consistency. The rich taste is very American in character and chocolate has been available to American cooks since early colonial days.

¼ lb. butter	1 tsp. vanilla extract
2 oz. unsweetened chocolate	½ cup flour
1 cup sugar	pinch of salt
2 eggs, slightly beaten	½ cup chopped walnuts

Preheat oven to 325°

Melt butter with chocolate in top part of a double boiler, over hot water, and mix well. Sift sugar and stir in slightly beaten eggs, then fold in the chocolate mixture and the vanilla. Stir in flour a little at a time, then salt. Finally stir in walnuts. Pour this batter into a greased 8-inch-square pan. Bake for about 30 minutes; don't bake too long, for brownies should be slightly moist and chewy and never dry. When cool, cut into squares.

MAKES 16 TO 24 SQUARES

Louise Sheldon's Fudge Bars

Just before the turn of the century the word fudge, which until then was used almost entirely to connote deceit of one kind or another, was given a new definition as the term for a candy mixture that in New England was often made with maple syrup. As the availability of chocolate increased throughout the country that flavor became the most popular, resulting in many variations, like fudge bars, or the Wellesley Fudge Cake that long was a campus favorite in Massachusetts.

1 cup flour	1 cup sugar
1 tsp. baking powder	1 egg, well beaten
⅛ tsp. salt	½ cup chopped nut meats
3 Tbs. shortening	1 tsp. vanilla extract
2 oz. unsweetened chocolate	

Preheat oven to 375°

Sift together flour, baking powder, and salt. Melt shortening with chocolate over very low heat. Beat sugar into beaten egg; stir in melted chocolate and butter, then sifted flour. Stir in nuts and vanilla, and mix well. Spread batter very thin on a greased 17 x 14 baking sheet, and bake for 20 minutes or less. When cool, cut into squares.

MAKES ABOUT 2 DOZEN

Banana Cookies

In *The Notions of a Travelling Bachelor* James Fenimore Cooper listed bananas among tropical fruits "as common as need be" in New York markets in the nineteenth century. But the great popularity of the fruit in the United States had to wait until the improvement of refrigeration and transportation facilities, a generation or so after Captain Lorenzo Baker of Wellfleet in 1870 brought the first ship loaded exclusively with bananas into Boston harbor. Breads, pies, cakes made with bananas—and cookies, too—were soon thereafter being turned out by innovative American cooks. A delicious variation of traditional banana cookies results when a little finely minced candied gingerroot is scattered over the tops just before baking. The sharp ginger gives a pungent accent to the banana flavor.

2 large ripe bananas
⅔ cup butter
1 cup sugar
1 tsp. vanilla extract
2 eggs

2¼ cups flour
2 tsp. baking powder
¼ tsp. baking soda
¾ tsp. salt

TOPPING:

cinnamon and sugar, mixed, in
    shaker or, finely chopped
    candied gingerroot

Preheat oven to 400°

Mash bananas, making about 1 cup or a little more. Cream butter and sugar, beating until fluffy, then blend in vanilla. Stir in mashed bananas, then eggs, one at a time, beating well after each addition. Sift dry ingredients together, then stir into batter. Scoop up batter with a teaspoon and drop onto ungreased cookie sheets. Sprinkle liberally with cinnamon and sugar, or with about 3 tablespoons finely chopped candied gingerroot. Bake for 12 minutes, then remove to racks to cool.

MAKES ABOUT 4 DOZEN

Peanut-Butter Cookies

The flavor improves when freshly roasted peanuts are shelled, peeled, and chopped, then combined with freshly ground peanut butter, as the original recipes dictate. But as long as the ingredients are the best available, this recipe results in cookies that are perhaps more exclusively American than any others.

1 cup peanut butter	2 eggs
¼ lb. butter	2½ cups flour
2 tsp. vanilla extract	1 tsp. baking soda
½ cup light brown sugar	1 cup peanuts, finely chopped
1 cup honey	

Preheat oven to 375°

Cream together peanut butter and butter; add vanilla. Beat in sugar and honey, then stir in eggs, one at a time; beat until batter is smooth and light. Sift flour and baking soda and stir into batter, then finally fold in chopped nuts. Scoop up batter with a dessert spoon and drop onto lightly greased cookie sheets. Press down with the flat of a fork to smooth the top of each mound, making cookies about ⅛ inch in height. Bake for 12 minutes.

MAKES ABOUT 6 DOZEN

Winter Squash Cookies

All the varieties of winter squashes, as well as pumpkin, and carrots of course, turn up often in old recipes for cookies and sweets and always seem to add a good color and special texture.

6 oz. butter	grated rind of 1 orange
¾ cup sugar	2 cups flour
1 cup grated raw winter squash or pumpkin or carrot	2 tsp. baking powder
	½ tsp. salt
1 large egg	

Preheat oven to 375°

Cream the butter, then add the sugar gradually, creaming until smooth. Beat in the grated vegetable and the egg and continue beating until light. Sift the dry ingredients into this batter a little at a time and mix well. Drop the batter from a teaspoon onto well-greased cookie sheets, pressing the mounds down lightly with your fingers. Bake for 12 to 15 minutes, until golden brown at the edges. Remove while warm to racks to cool.

MAKES ALMOST 40 SMALL COOKIES

¼ lb. butter
2 cups brown sugar
2 eggs, well beaten
1 cup nut meats, finely chopped
1 cup dates, chopped

3½ cups flour
1 tsp. baking soda
1 tsp. salt
1 tsp. vanilla extract

Preheat oven to 375°

Cream butter and sugar, gradually adding a little of each and beating until smooth. Add beaten eggs, nuts, and dates. Sift flour, baking soda, and salt together, then add to dry ingredients. Add vanilla, and stir well. Turn dough out on floured surface, divide in two, and shape 2 long sausagelike rolls. Wrap each in floured wax paper and refrigerate for several hours. Remove from refrigerator and cut into slices about ⅛ inch thick. Place slices on greased cookie sheet and bake for 10 minutes.

MAKES ABOUT 50

PASTRY:

1¾ cups all-purpose flour
¼ lb. (1 stick) butter
4 Tbs. lard

1 tsp. salt
6 Tbs. ice water

4 rather small tart, firm apples
4 tsp. brown sugar, mixed with 4 tsp. butter

or

3 or 4 tsp. raisins, steeped in 2 Tbs. rum, plus 4 tsp. butter

SYRUP:

1 cup dark brown sugar
1½ cups water

2 Tbs. butter

Preheat oven to 450° ❋

Prepare the pastry by cutting butter and lard into flour; add salt and enough ice water to hold together. Chill for at least 30 minutes. Peel and core the apples and spoon one of the two fillings into the centers, topping with butter to fill holes completely. Roll out the pastry fairly thin. Divide pastry into four parts. Place a stuffed apple in one section; trim dough roughly in a circle around apple so there will be enough dough to cover as you draw it up around the apple. Pinch top together with a little water. If the folds seem too thick, trim them and seal seams with water. Repeat with the remaining apples and put them all in the refrigerator for about 20 minutes. * Mix syrup ingredients in a small saucepan and boil slowly for 5 or 6 minutes. Paint the apples with the syrup and quickly put in preheated oven for 10 minutes; then turn down heat to 350° and bake for 35 minutes longer. Continue to paint the dough with syrup every 10 minutes while baking. Serve with thick or slightly whipped cream.

MAKES 4 SERVINGS

Charleston Benne-Seed Wafers

1 cup flour
½ tsp. baking powder
¼ tsp. salt
¾ cup butter
2 cups brown sugar

2 eggs, beaten
1 tsp. vanilla extract
¾ cup sesame seeds (called benne-seeds in Charleston)
vegetable or peanut oil

Preheat oven to 325°

Sift flour, baking powder, and salt. Cream butter and gradually add brown sugar, beating constantly until it is all absorbed and mixture is fluffy. Beat in eggs, then vanilla. In a large skillet heat sesame seeds, shaking and stirring constantly to distribute heat evenly, and toast seeds until they turn taffy color. Add them to batter. Oil a large cookie sheet. Drop batter by the teaspoon, leaving at least 1½ inches between the drops on the cookie sheet for batter to spread; bake in upper third of oven for 10 minutes, *only one sheet at a time*. Let wafers cool for about 1 minute, then scrape them up briskly but gently with a spatula and cool on cake racks. Repeat until batter is all used.

MAKES ABOUT 6 DOZEN

Maple Crème Brûlée

Crème brûlée had its origins in the grilled cream that was a seventeenth-century favorite at King's College, Cambridge. It appeared in at least one early American cookbook as "Burnt Cream," and is said to have been prepared often by Thomas Jefferson's cook, Julien. In St. Louis and on the West Coast toasted California almonds are added, and sometimes the local brandy or sherry. A Montpelier, Vermont, cook devised this truly American recipe.

6 egg yolks
¼ cup vanilla sugar
1 cup milk, scalded

¾ cup heavy cream, scalded
¼ to ⅓ cup maple sugar

Beat egg yolks and add vanilla sugar, continuing to beat for 2 or 3 minutes. Gradually add scalded milk and cream in a steady stream, then put mixture in a heavy saucepan over very low heat, or in the top part of a double boiler over simmering water, and stir continuously as mixture slowly thickens; it must not boil and should not exceed temperature of 165°. Remove from heat when custard coats the spoon. Let cool, beating several times, then turn into a buttered shallow heatproof 1-quart casserole and chill thoroughly, for at least 4 hours or overnight. Just before serving, sprinkle maple sugar over top to make layer ⅛ inch thick. Run under hot broiler until sugar bubbles. Chill again briefly and serve from baking dish.

MAKES 4 TO 6 SERVINGS

Phyllis' Orange Jelly

2 envelopes unflavored gelatin
½ cup cold water
1¾ cups boiling water
¾ cup sugar

1½ cups freshly squeezed orange
    juice
    juice of 1 lemon
1 bunch of green seedless grapes,
    1 lb. or less, peeled

GARNISH:

1 cup lightly whipped cream
    (optional)
    Cointreau

Dissolve the gelatin in the cold water, then pour on the boiling water and mix well. Add sugar and fresh orange and lemon juice, and blend thoroughly. Spread the peeled grapes around a 1-quart mold, then pour the liquid jelly on top. Set in the refrigerator to chill thoroughly. Serve turned out if you wish, garnished with lightly whipped cream, which can be flavored with a little Cointreau.

MAKES 6 SERVINGS

Baked Fresh Peaches

4 medium-size fresh ripe peaches
½ lime
2 Tbs. chopped hazelnuts
2 Tbs. butter

2 Tbs. brown sugar
⅓ cup sauterne or Scuppernong wine
½ to ¾ cup sour cream

Preheat oven to 400°

Peel peaches, cut into halves, and remove pits. Rub with cut half of lime. Mix chopped hazelnuts with butter and sugar, then spread in even amounts over peaches. Place in baking dish just large enough to hold fruit and pour wine around them; bake for 20 minutes, basting once. Serve warm with dollops of sour cream.

MAKES 4 SERVINGS

Fresh Peach Cobbler with Peach or Apricot Jam

12 peaches
    juice of ½ lemon
2 Tbs. flour

¼ cup sugar
2 Tbs. peach or apricot jam
2 Tbs. butter

TOPPING:

1½ cups sifted all-purpose flour
½ tsp. baking powder
1 Tbs. sugar

5 Tbs. butter
1 egg
½ cup soured cream or milk

GARNISH:

½ cup heavy cream
1 tsp. vanilla sugar

Preheat oven to 425°

Butter a 9- or 10-inch cake tin or round shallow casserole. Slice peaches, sprinkle with lemon juice, and arrange loosely in baking dish; mix flour and sugar and sprinkle over fruit. Spread fruit with jam and dot with 2 tablespoons butter. Sift flour, baking powder, and sugar, cut in 5 tablespoons butter, and mix lightly. Beat egg with soured milk or cream, then stir into flour until mixture is smooth, but don't overmix. Divide dough into 8 portions and drop in small mounds on fruit. Bake for 30 minutes. Serve with cream whipped with vanilla sugar.

MAKES 8 SERVINGS

Helen Knopf's Medford, Oregon, Prize Pear Torte

Fruit growing is profuse in each of the Pacific States, but no orchard was more prolific than the Medford acres once presided over by the distinguished New Yorker who, in more youthful days, won a ribbon for this original recipe.

2 eggs
1 cup sugar
½ cup flour
2½ tsp. baking powder
¼ tsp. salt

1½ cups stewed (or canned) Bartlett
    pears, drained and well mashed
1 cup English walnuts, broken
    cooking oil
    extra flour

Preheat oven to 350°

Beat eggs until light; add sugar and continue beating. Sift flour, add baking powder and salt, and sift again. Fold the flour mixture into the egg and sugar alternately with the mashed pears. Fold in walnut meats. Oil a shallow rectangular pan about 14 x 12 inches, then dust it lightly with flour; pour in batter. Bake for 30 to 40 minutes. Torte is done when tooth pick or straw comes out clean. Serve warm.

MAKES 6 TO 8 SERVINGS

Plum Duff with Cherry Liqueur

1 lb. fresh plums, about 5 medium-
    size, split and pitted
½ cup sugar
⅓ cup kirsch
2 tsp. tapioca
1 large egg

3 Tbs. vanilla sugar
    salt
⅛ tsp. cream of tartar
3 Tbs. sifted flour
⅛ tsp. almond extract
    heavy cream

Preheat oven to 325°

Use a flameproof dish that will hold pitted plum halves snugly; distribute plums in a single layer. Mix sugar, kirsch, and tapioca, and pour over fruit, then stew for about 10 minutes on top of the stove. Meanwhile separate egg and beat yolk in a small bowl. Slowly add vanilla sugar, or plain sugar with ¼ teaspoon vanilla extract, until smooth and lemon-colored. In a separate bowl, beat egg white with a small pinch of salt and cream of tartar; when stiff fold in beaten yolk, then stir in flour and almond extract. Spread this batter over plums, and bake for 30 minutes. Keep warm and serve from baking dish with heavy cream.

MAKES ABOUT 4 SERVINGS

This recipe for frozen lime pie is adapted from one by a cook who brought the style of Virginia to New York when she opened a tiny restaurant. Called Mr. & Mrs. Foster's Place, it is a reservations-only oasis where cosmopolitans sample American food untainted by institutionalized kitchens. Lime pie made in this fashion is common in parts of the South. It uses neither evaporated milk nor the gelatin common to most Florida lime pies; it is as fresh as any fruit ice cream. Two kinds of limes are grown in Florida; the Persian, sometimes called Tahiti, is about the size of a small lemon; the so-called Key lime is juicy, yellowish, small and seedy; it grows from Miami to Fort Myers. Key limes are preferred by many Floridians who grow their own. A third type of lime, planted by Spanish explorers, grows along Georgia's Ogeechee River, but it is rarely found in the twentieth century except by blacks who know the Georgia back country.

CRUST:

1¼ cups graham-cracker crumbs   ¼ cup butter at room temperature
¼ cup superfine sugar

Preheat oven to 350°

Mix all ingredients thoroughly, then press evenly into a 9-inch pie pan. Bake for 10 minutes; cool to room temperature.

FILLING:

5 eggs, saparated   2 tsp. grated lime rind
¼ cup superfine sugar   salt
⅔ cup freshly squeezed lime juice

Beat egg yolks in top part of double boiler over hot but not boiling water until very thick. Gradually beat in ½ cup of sugar until mixture turns pale yellow and is thick enough to form a thread when dribbled off beater. Stir in lime juice and grated rind and heat again over simmering water until mixture will coat a spoon. Mixture should not boil. Turn out into a large bowl and cool to room temperature. Beat egg whites with pinch of salt until soft peaks form. Gradually beat in remaining sugar until mixture is stiff and shiny. Stir one third of this into cooled yolk mixture, then fold in remainder and turn into cooled pie shell. Bake for 15 minutes and set aside to cool; then chill in refrigerator before freezing. Cover with plastic wrap when frozen.

TOPPING:

1½ cups heavy cream, whipped   sugar
1 lime, thinly sliced, or fresh
    strawberries

Take pie from freezer about 10 minutes before serving. Cover with whipped cream and arrange thin slices of lime or fresh strawberries dipped into sugar on top.

MAKES 6 SERVINGS

Basic Pie Crust

In older American cookbooks pie dough was made with pork lard, a method still used by some people who prefer the traditional flavor and texture. Tastes, however, do change. We use mostly butter with a little lard, preferring animal fat to vegetable shortening. The latter of course can be substituted for lard by those who watch cholesterol counts, or for any other reason. This recipe will make a 2-crust 8-inch pie or 1 10-inch bottom crust; if a smaller crust is called for leftover dough can be wrapped and frozen for future use.

2 cups unbleached flour	3 Tbs. chilled lard
½ tsp. salt	about 5 Tbs. ice water
¼ lb. chilled butter	

Mix flour and salt together. Cut in chilled butter and lard; use pastry blender or fingers to mix until dough is the consistency of cornmeal. Dribble enough ice water into mixture so it holds together. Scoop up this dough and put on a floured board. Smear the dough out in about two or three strokes with the heel of the hand, then scrape together into a ball. Flour the ball lightly and refrigerate 2 hours or more.

To make 2 double-layer pie crusts: divide the dough into 2 slightly uneven portions. Roll out the larger portion; if it cracks just pinch it together, then line an 8-inch pie tin, pressing the dough firmly into angles of sides. Refrigerate the lined pie tin and the remaining dough while making the pie filling. After putting the filling into the pie shell, roll out the smaller portion of chilled dough and drape it over the filling; then press together the dough along the rim, crimping with a fork and trimming away excess.

To bake empty pie shells, line a 10-, 9-, or 8-inch pie tin according to need; press in firmly, then cut around the edge, leaving a ½-inch overhang. Fold this margin under and press all around with the tines of a fork, or crimp with fingers. Butter the outside of another pie tin just one size smaller and press it on top of dough lining original pie tin. Bake for 8 minutes at 425°, then remove top tin and prick the bottom of the pastry with a fork in several places. Reduce oven heat to 375° and return pastry shell for 2 minutes more (for partially baked), 10 to 15 minutes more or until lightly golden for fully baked. For a sweet pie or tart, take the shell from oven after first 8 minutes, brush the bottom with 1 tablespoon of apricot jam or currant jelly, as indicated in specific recipes, then return to 375° oven.

To make small pastry shells, follow the method above, lining small tart molds or small muffin tins with pastry. To bake blind, cut aluminum foil to fit individual mold and fill with dried beans or rice for first 8 minutes of cooking, then remove and bake at lowered heat another 3 to 4 minutes.

St. Anthony Falls Salt Pork and Apple Pie

A New Englander who came to Minnesota as a girl in 1856 wrote down this recipe 60 years later: "You cut the pork so thin you can almost see through it. Cover the bottom of a pie tin with it, then cut the apples up on top of this. Put two thin crusts one on top the other over this, then when cooked, turn upside down in a dish and serve with hard sauce. This recipe," she added, "is over a hundred years old but nothing can beat it." Calvin Coolidge was equally partial to pie of this kind, as are hundreds of contemporary Americans.

8 to 10 tart cooking apples
¾ cup maple sugar, or brown or
    white sugar
½ tsp. ground cinnamon
½ tsp. grated nutmeg

1 Tbs. flour
salt
8 to 10 slices of salt pork, size and
    thickness of postage stamps
pastry dough (p. 349)

Preheat oven to 450°

Peel and core apples and slice very thin; spread slices in bottom of a deep pie dish. Sprinkle with sugar, cinnamon, nutmeg, flour, and very little salt. Arrange salt pork slices on top; if they are sufficiently thin, they will disappear leaving nothing but an ineffable old-fashioned flavor. Cover with pastry dough and pinch down edges; make slits in dough to allow steam to escape. Bake for 10 minutes, then reduce heat to 350° and continue baking for 30 to 40 minutes longer.

MAKES 8 SERVINGS

Apricot Chiffon Pie

In France the word "chiffon" has been used to describe fabric that is smooth and silky and sometimes in the vernacular as a synonym for gossip, conversation of airy nothingness. Nowhere but in America is it a description for smooth and silky confections from the kitchen that are among desserts characteristic of the twentieth century.

Prebaked 8-inch pie shell (p. 349)
    or graham-cracker crust (p. 348)
½ box (11-oz. box) dried apricots
¾ cup apricot or orange juice

¾ to 1 cup sugar
1 envelope unflavored gelatin
¼ cup cold water
2 egg whites

Place apricots in top part of double boiler, cover with water, and cook over boiling water, uncovered, for 20 minutes. Remove from heat; spin in blender with apricot or orange juice to purée. Return to double boiler with as much sugar as needed, depending on sweetness of juice. Meanwhile soften gelatin in ¼ cup cold water, then stir in sweetened purée and mix well; set aside to cool. Beat egg whites until stiff, then fold carefully into cooled purée. Turn into the baked pie crust or the crumb crust and chill for several hours before serving.

MAKES 6 SERVINGS

Boston Cream Pie

Harvey D. Parker, who opened his Boston hotel in 1856, was host to distinguished people from all walks of life, including such members of the Saturday Club as Ralph Waldo Emerson, Henry Wadsworth Longfellow, Oliver Wendell Holmes, Nathaniel Hawthorne, and John Greenleaf Whittier, who came to the Parker House regularly to stimulate each other intellectually and praise the hostelry's American bill of fare. Boston Cream Pie had been on that menu since the day Parker House opened, yet the fact that it is really a cake disguised by this misnomer remains unexplained. When the layers of vanilla cream filling are transformed into stratifications of raspberry jam this dessert is equally famous, again for reasons unknown, as Washington Pie.

CAKE:

6 Tbs. butter	½ tsp. salt
1 cup sugar	2 tsp. baking powder
2 eggs	½ cup milk
1¾ cups all-purpose flour	½ tsp. vanilla extract

FILLING:

⅔ cup sugar	2 cups milk, scalded
⅓ cup all-purpose flour	2 egg yolks
pinch of salt	½ tsp. lemon extract

TOPPING:

powdered sugar in a shaker

Preheat oven to 375°

Cream the butter with all but 2 tablespoons of the sugar. Beat eggs until lemon-colored, add remaining sugar, and beat. Blend eggs into creamed butter and beat until fluffy. Sift together dry ingredients, then add, alternately with the milk, to the batter and continue beating until all is absorbed. Add vanilla. Turn into 2 well-buttered 8-inch cake tins and bake for 25 minutes. When done, turn out onto cake racks to cool.

Prepare the filling: Mix sugar, flour, and salt together in top part of double boiler. Blend in the hot milk slowly and let cook gently over barely boiling water, stirring occasionally, until thickened, about 15 minutes. Beat egg yolks, blend a little of the hot mixture into the eggs to warm them, then add to the rest of the mixture and continue cooking for another 3 or 4 minutes. Remove from the heat and season with lemon extract. When custard is cool, spread between the cake layers. Sprinkle the top liberally with powdered sugar. To serve, cut into pie-shaped wedges.

Bourbon Pecan Pie

Westering Southerners found pecans growing wild as they moved into Louisiana and Oklahoma, but it was a black gardener named Antoine who grafted 16 trees on a plantation in Louisiana sugar country to produce the best pecans the South had known. Pecan pie is one of the reasons gastronomes come to the Lowell Inn in Stillwater, Minnesota, where it is made with white sugar. In Louisville, a traditional recipe calls for maple syrup and maple meringue. Here the mystery flavor is a sip of Kentucky's own bourbon.

⅛ cup butter
½ cup dark brown sugar
3 eggs
¼ tsp. salt
1 cup dark corn syrup

1 Tbs. Kentucky bourbon
1 cup chopped pecans
1 Tbs. flour
1 recipe for pie dough (p. 349)

GARNISH:

8 to 10 whole pecans, in halves

OPTIONAL:

¼ cup heavy cream
2 Tbs. sugar
2 to 3 Tbs. Kentucky bourbon

Preheat oven to 450°

Cream butter and add brown sugar slowly, beating constantly until all is absorbed and mixture is fluffy. Add eggs, one by one, beating continuously, then add salt, corn syrup, and bourbon. Toss pecans in flour, then fold them into filling. Line a 9-inch pie tin with dough and hold down pastry by placing another tin on top, or line with foil filled with beans; bake for 10 minutes. Remove from oven, remove extra tin or foil, and prick bottom of crust with fork. Pour in filling. Lower heat to 350° and bake for 35 minutes, or until pie is firm. Decorate top by making border of pecan halves and bake for 5 minutes more. Serve tepid; pie may be garnished with whipped cream flavored with sugar and bourbon.

MAKES 8 SERVINGS

The birth of the Brandy Alexander Cocktail may be obscured in alcoholic mists, but the first brandy Alexander pie seems to have been made some time after the end of Prohibition. Not that brandy hadn't been almost essential to good mincemeat pies for generations; it's simply that some temperate cooks seem to think that evolving a pie filling from a cocktail recipe is a little like gilding the lily. In the freewheeling 1970s the gilding of pies of all flavors took the form of paintings; top crusts of some pies baked commercially by New York artists looking for added income were decorated with portraits, landscapes, patchwork, even pornography.

1 envelope unflavored gelatin	¼ cup Cognac or applejack
¼ to ½ cup water	¼ cup crème de cacao
⅔ cup sugar	1½ to 2 cups heavy cream, whipped
⅛ tsp. salt	1 recipe graham-cracker crust
3 eggs, separated	(p. 348)

GARNISH:

grated chocolate or chocolate curls

Sprinkle gelatin into a saucepan containing water; add half of sugar, salt, and egg yolks; stir thoroughly. Over low heat continue stirring until gelatin is entirely dissolved and mixture thickens. Do not boil. Off heat, stir in Cognac and liqueur. Let cool, then chill in refrigerator until mixture starts to thicken at edges. Beat egg whites until peaks form, gradually beat in remaining half of sugar, and fold all carefully into thickened gelatin mixture. Fold in about 1 cup of whipped cream. Pour pie mixture into a 9-inch pie tin lined with graham-cracker crust. Chill for several hours or overnight. Garnish with remaining whipped cream and chocolate gratings or curls.

MAKES 6 TO 8 SERVINGS

Honey Cheesecake Pie

pastry for 8-inch pie (p. 349)	3 eggs
8 oz. cream cheese, at room	¼ tsp. salt
temperature	1½ cups milk
½ cup honey, warmed	cinnamon

Preheat oven to 450°

Cream cheese until soft. Mix honey, eggs, salt, milk, and about ¼ teaspoon cinnamon. Stir into cheese and blend thoroughly. Pour into pastry-lined 8-inch pan and sprinkle with cinnamon. Bake for 10 minutes; reduce heat to 325° and bake for 25 to 30 minutes longer. Cool before putting in refrigerator.

MAKES 6 SERVINGS

Green Tomato Pie

This has long been a favorite among New Englanders who are apt to have lots of green tomatoes on hand when the frost comes early and the still unripened tomatoes have to be gathered in a hurry. Crusts, of course, were almost always made with lard but we've found that our standard more buttery, crumbly crust (p. 349) holds its own well with the long cooking required before the tomatoes soften and yield their lovely surprising flavor.

1 recipe for pie dough (p. 349)	½ tsp. freshly ground allspice
6 medium-size green tomatoes	½ tsp. ground cinnamon
2 Tbs. butter	¼ cup cider vinegar
1 cup sugar	1 tsp. flour

Preheat oven to 425°

Slice the tomatoes paper-thin. Dot a little of the butter on the pastry in the tin, then spread on layers of tomatoes, topping each layer with some sugar and spices, some vinegar and butter, and a sprinkling of flour to make a full pie. Roll out remaining dough and cover pie, crimping edges and trimming. With remaining scraps of dough roll out a small piece, curl it around a finger, then insert it in a small cross in the center of the top crust, forming a chimney to allow steam to escape; turn out edges for a more decorative rosette. Bake for 20 minutes, then turn down heat to 375° and continue baking for 35 to 40 minutes. Serve slightly warm with a wedge of Vermont cheese.

MAKES 6 SERVINGS

Lemon Meringue Pie

A pie can always be turned out for dessert as long as there are lemons in the house, and American cooks have devised many recipes. President Calvin Coolidge is said to have favored a simple lemon custard pie. The even more common lemon meringue, ever present in public eating places, is one more dish served at Boston's Parker House that has become a classic in the American repertoire. And a special version gained fame swiftly when it went on the menu of the Lion House Social Center in Salt Lake City. The version below is based on a method worked out in the 1960s by the late Michael Field in collaboration with Dr. Paul Buck, a food scientist at Cornell University. The determined Mr. Field devoted days to making one lemon meringue pie after another until he eliminated the "weeping" common to meringues that sit around on counters; his trick was to use a little calcium phosphate powder, a food-grade phosphate product available in drugstores and suggested by Dr. Buck, and the gingersnaps sprinkled on the crust help to keep it from getting soggy.

¾ cup sugar
¼ cup cornstarch
    pinch of salt
1¾ cups cold water
6 eggs
2 Tbs. grated lemon rind
2 Tbs. butter
½ cup strained fresh lemon juice

2 Tbs. pulverized gingersnaps
1 prebaked 9-inch pie shell (p. 349)
½ cup vanilla sugar, or ½ cup granu-
    lated sugar mixed with 1 or 2
    drops of vanilla extract
½ tsp. cream of tartar
½ tsp. calcium phosphate (optional)

Preheat oven to 325°

Prepare the filling by blending sugar, cornstarch, salt, and water and cooking slowly, stirring constantly, for 2 minutes. Remove from heat. Separate eggs and drop yolks, one at a time, into the hot mixture, beating thoroughly after each addition. Set aside 5 egg whites in a large mixing bowl. Return cornstarch-egg mixture to heat, add lemon rind, and simmer for 6 or 7 minutes, until smooth and very thick, beating constantly as it thickens. Off heat beat in the butter, a little at a time, then the lemon juice. Let custard cool to room temperature. Sprinkle pulverized gingersnaps on the bottom of the precooked pie shell, then pour filling in evenly. Now beat the 5 egg whites until foamy, then add mixture of vanilla sugar, cream of tartar, and calcium phosphate (optional), a little at a time, until whites form stiff peaks. Spread the meringue over the lemon filling, making decorative swirls and peaks, if you wish. Bake for 25 minutes, until meringue is golden. The pie must cool at room temperature for at least 3 hours before serving, but don't refrigerate to hurry it.

MAKES 6 SERVINGS

Key West Papaya and Pineapple Tart

1 papaya
2 slices (½ inch thick) fresh pineapple
½ cup sugar
½ cup water

2 limes
⅓ cup apricot jam
1 pie shell, 10 inches, baked with
    coating of apricot jam (p. 349)

Peel papaya, split into halves, scoop out seeds, and slice flesh into ¼-inch strips. Cut pineapple slices into small wedges. Put sugar and water in a saucepan, bring slowly to a boil, and cook for 1 minute, then remove from heat. Add juice of 1½ limes, and steep papaya strips in this syrup. Cut remaining ½ lime into very thin slices and cut slices into halves. Add pineapple wedges to syrup and let stand for 15 to 20 minutes. Remove pineapple and papaya pieces from syrup and add lime slices to it; boil syrup for 3 or 4 minutes and remove lime slices with slotted spoon. Combine apricot jam with half of remaining syrup and boil for about 5 minutes, until reduced to a glaze and quite thick. Arrange papaya

strips as spokes in bottom of precooked pie shell. Fill spaces in between with pineapple wedges and slivers of lime. Spoon the apricot glaze over all. Serve cool, but do not refrigerate.

MAKES 8 TO 10 SERVINGS

Rhubarb and Strawberry Tart

1 10-inch prebaked pie shell (p. 349)	1 cup sugar
⅓ cup currant jelly	1 tsp. cornstarch
2 lbs. rhubarb	1½ pints fresh strawberries

GARNISH:

1 cup whipped cream flavored with 1 tsp. sugar and 1 to 2 Tbs. strawberry or other liqueur

Preheat oven to 375°

Melt currant jelly and brush bottom of cooked pie crust with some melted jelly, reserving rest.

Cut rhubarb into large chunks and place in a casserole; sprinkle sugar mixed with cornstarch over and cover the casserole. Bake for 20 to 25 minutes, until fruit is soft but not mushy. Remove rhubarb with slotted spoon and place in cooled pie shell. Add rhubarb juice to remaining currant jelly and cook over medium-high heat until it forms a thick syrup. Remove stems and halve the strawberries, then arrange them, rounded side up, over the rhubarb. Brush the strawberries generously with the syrup, letting it penetrate to rhubarb underneath. Let the tart cool, but do not refrigerate. Serve with flavored whipped cream spooned over in stripes, or piped through a pastry tube over the fruit.

MAKES 8 TO 10 SERVINGS

Connecticut Maple-Topped Squash Pie

1 recipe pie dough (p. 349)	½ tsp. freshly grated nutmeg
3 eggs, well beaten	½ tsp. ground ginger
¾ cup brown sugar	2 cups hot milk
1 tsp. salt	2 cups cooked squash, strained
½ tsp. ground cinnamon	

GARNISH:

1 cup heavy cream
¼ cup maple syrup

Preheat oven to 450°

Line a 9-inch pie pan with rolled-out pie dough and flute edges with fingers. Mix beaten eggs, brown sugar, salt, cinnamon, grated nutmeg, and ginger, then gradually stir in hot milk and strained squash. Pour into uncooked pie shell and bake for 10 minutes; reduce heat to 325° and bake for 30 minutes longer. Remove from oven and cool. Whip heavy cream until peaks form, then carefully pour syrup in a fine stream over whipped cream, turning cream to fold in syrup. Spread lightly over pie in swirls.

MAKES 6 SERVINGS

Sweet-Potato Pie

1½ to 2 cups mashed cooked sweet
    potatoes
4 eggs
⅛ cup sugar
⅔ cup milk
⅓ cup orange juice

2 Tbs. honey
salt
2 Tbs. applejack or brandy
1 recipe pie crust (p. 349)
13 pecan halves

Preheat oven to 450°

Make sure sweet potatoes are free of lumps. Beat eggs until very light, then add sugar and sweet potatoes, stirring until well mixed. Stir in milk, orange juice, honey, and a pinch of salt, then stir in applejack or brandy. Line a 9-inch pie tin with pastry, pour mixture into it, and bake for 10 minutes. Reduce heat to 350° and bake for 30 minutes longer. While pie is hot, put 1 pecan in center and arrange other nuts around edge.

GARNISH:

1 cup heavy cream
1 to 2 tsp. sugar

1 Tbs. grated orange rind
1 Tbs. applejack

Beat cream over ice until it peaks, then beat in sugar, grated orange rind, and applejack. Use as garnish for each wedge of pie cut.

MAKES 6 SERVINGS

Tyler Pudding Pie

A recipe popular for many decades in Virginia and other parts of the South, Tyler Pudding Pie was named for President John Tyler and has been made by so many generations of Tyler women that each of several variations is said to be authentic. Whether made by Miss Mary Lee Tyler of Haymarket, Virginia, by a granddaughter in Richmond, a great-granddaughter in Louisville, or a relative in Washington, D.C., the Tyler dessert has been extolled as "a culinary masterpiece." If it isn't truly that, it is characteristic of southern plantation food and a fitting end to a good meal. "Rich?" asked Harriet Ross Colquitt in presenting her Savannah version. "Of course, but was it not presidential fare?"

pastry for 9-inch pie tin (p. 349)	½ cup heavy cream
¾ cup white sugar	3 eggs
¾ cup granulated brown sugar	1 tsp. vanilla extract
¼ lb. butter	2 Tbs. grated coconut

Preheat oven to 450°

Line a 9-inch pie tin with pastry, making a scalloped edge, and partially bake (see p. 349). Let cool while preparing filling. Lower oven heat to 350°. In the top part of a double boiler mix both sugars; add butter in pieces, and the cream, and heat until butter has melted. Beat the eggs well and then pour the warm mixture slowly into them, continuing to beat. Add vanilla and turn into the partially baked shell. Bake for 35 minutes, then sprinkle coconut over the top and bake for another 5 minutes, until coconut is lightly toasted.

MAKES 6 SERVINGS

Pineapple Lime Bavarian Cream

3 eggs	⅔ cup pineapple chunks, or 3 slices
1 lime	canned pineapple cut into chunks
⅔ cup syrup from canned pineapple	½ cup heavy cream
1 to 2 Tbs. wine jelly (optional)	pinch of salt
1 envelope unflavored gelatin	

GARNISH (optional):

½ cup whipped cream
1 or 2 additional pineapple slices

Separate eggs and beat the yolks. Grate the lime and squeeze the juice from it, then add rind and juice to egg yolks. Boil pineapple syrup, adding some wine jelly if you have some (wine jelly with ginger is particularly delicious). When syrup is reduced to ½ cup, remove from heat and pour in a slow steady stream into the yolk mixture, stirring constantly. Place in the top part of a double boiler over simmering water and heat, continuing to stir, until thickened. Remove from heat. Soften gelatin in ⅛ cup cold water, and stir into the hot custard, then add the pineapple chunks. Chill, while beating first the cream until stiff and then the egg whites with a pinch of salt until they form soft peaks. Fold both into the pineapple custard. Pour into a 1-quart ring mold or 6 sherbet glasses and refrigerate, for 6 to 8 hours if Bavarian cream is to be unmolded, for only 3 or 4 hours if served in individual glasses. The center of the mold can be filled with whipped cream and additional pineapple slices cut into whatever shape one wants.

MAKES 6 SERVINGS

Georgia Sweet Potato Pudding

4 Tbs. sugar
½ cup Georgia cane syrup
½ cup milk
2 cups grated raw sweet potatoes
¼ tsp. ground cloves

½ tsp. ground allspice
¾ tsp. ground cinnamon
4 Tbs. butter
2 small eggs, beaten

Preheat oven to 375°

Mix all ingredients except eggs and butter. Put butter in flameproof casserole over low heat to melt, and beat eggs into sweet potato mixture. When butter is melted pour mixture into casserole, stirring until it is hot. Put in 375° oven for 20 minutes, then stir crust developing on sides and bottom into pudding. Repeat twice before removing casserole after pudding has baked total of 40 to 45 minutes. Serve with lemon sauce.

Brown Sugar Pudding

3 slices of homemade white bread
2 Tbs. butter
1½ cups brown sugar
2¼ cups milk
2 eggs

1 tsp. vanilla extract
pinch of salt
½ tsp. grated nutmeg
½ tsp. ground cinnamon

Preheat oven to 350°

Trim crusts from bread and butter well on both sides. Sprinkle brown sugar over the bottom of buttered 1-quart casserole. Warm the milk, beat in the eggs, and add vanilla and salt. Tear the bread into small pieces and distribute over the sugar, then add warmed milk-egg mixture. Sprinkle spices on top and bake for 45 minutes. Serve warm or chilled with heavy cream.

MAKES 4 SERVINGS

Nutmeg

Miss Leslie's Indian Pound Cake

6 Tbs. butter
1 cup sugar
4 eggs
1¼ cups sifted pastry flour
¾ tsp. baking powder

¼ cup sifted white cornmeal
⅛ tsp. freshly grated nutmeg
¼ tsp. ground cinnamon
½ tsp. vanilla extract
2 tsp. applejack

Preheat oven to 325°

Cream butter, gradually working in sugar until mixture is fluffy. Beat in eggs, one at a time. Sift together flour and baking powder, then stir in cornmeal and spices. Blend dry ingredients with egg-butter mixture, adding vanilla and applejack a little at a time. Pour this batter into greased shallow 10-inch cake pan and bake for 1½ hours. Let the cake cool in the pan for 10 minutes after baking, then turn upside down on cake rack.

MAKES ABOUT 8 SERVINGS

Bailey Family Blueberry Bread Pudding*

1 pint blueberries
2 Tbs. water
⅛ cup sugar (more or less, depending upon tartness of berries)

about ¼ loaf homemade white bread, 1 or 2 days old
1 to 2 Tbs. butter

Place picked-over berries in a heavy saucepan with water and sugar, and bring slowly to the boiling point. Simmer for 5 to 10 minutes, depending upon ripeness of berries, until they are soft but still holding their shape. Meanwhile slice bread very thin; if it is presliced, split slices into halves; remove crusts and butter one side lightly. Line a small bowl (less than 3 cups) with bread slices, buttered side down, cutting and shaping more slices to press in and fit snugly so bottom and sides are lined and leave no gaps. Spoon berries into bread-lined bowl, reserving some of juice, and fold bread slices over, adding a slice to cover top completely. If juice does not saturate all of bread, spoon some of reserve over top. Set a saucer on top and press down. Refrigerate bowl for at least 6 hours. Serve with heavy cream.

* May be made with raspberries, huckleberries, or blackberries.

MAKES 4 SERVINGS

Hominy Pudding with Apricots

¾ cup dried apricots, chopped
2 Tbs. butter
2 cups hot milk
1 cup hominy grits, cooked
¼ cup sugar

¼ tsp. salt
¼ cup slivered almonds
2 eggs, well beaten
⅛ tsp. ground cinnamon

Preheat oven to 350°

Soak dried apricots in water for 30 minutes or more, until soft. Melt 1 tablespoon butter in hot milk; stir in cooked grits. Combine sugar, salt, almonds, and apricots with beaten eggs. Add cinnamon, then stir slowly into milk mixture. Butter a 1-quart casserole, fill with mixture, then set casserole in a pan of hot water. Bake for 45 to 50 minutes.

MAKES 4 SERVINGS

Maple-Flavored Indian Pudding

In early Ohio, when some of the eastern counties were known as the Western Reserve, a common frontier dish, adapted by pioneer cooks from the Indians, was a mixture of cornmeal and maple syrup cooked with wild fruits or berries. With eggs and milk added, maple-flavored Indian pudding can be delicious, with or without fruits but with a dollop of rich cream on top. One of the best ways to achieve at least a semblance of old-fashioned, heavy, unpasteurized cream is to mix "heavy cream" from store or milkman with cultured sour cream, as indicated below. It must, however, be made ahead of time, and left to mature in the refrigerator at least 1 hour or overnight.

5 Tbs. yellow cornmeal
4 cups scalded milk
2 Tbs. melted butter
1 cup maple syrup
2 eggs, beaten

1 tsp. ground cinnamon
¾ tsp. ground ginger
1 tsp. salt
1 cup cold milk

GARNISH:

1 cup heavy cream
⅓ cup sour cream

Preheat oven to 300°

Add cornmeal to scalded milk, stirring constantly to make sure no lumps form; continue cooking and stirring over low heat until thickened. Off heat, stir in butter, maple syrup, beaten eggs, cinnamon, ginger, and salt. Pour into a

buttered 2-quart baking dish, and bake for about 45 minutes. Stir pudding and whisk in cold milk, then continue baking for about 1 hour longer. Garnish should be made ahead of time: Shake sour cream and heavy cream in a bottle and set aside in a warm place for 2 hours, then put in refrigerator for 1 hour or more. Serve pudding warm and top each serving with heavy or slightly whipped cream.

MAKES 8 TO 10 SERVINGS

Lemon Pudding

2 Tbs. butter	3 Tbs. flour
1 cup sugar	1 cup milk
1 lemon	2 large eggs
salt	¾ cup heavy cream (optional)

Preheat oven to 350°

Cream butter and work in sugar until all is absorbed. Grate lemon, then squeeze it, and add both grated rind and juice, and a pinch of salt. Stir in the flour alternately with the milk, blending until smooth. Separate eggs; add yolks to mixture and blend thoroughly. Beat egg whites until they form soft peaks, then fold in. Turn pudding into a 1-quart baking dish, set dish in pan of hot water, and bake for 40 minutes. Serve tepid, or chilled with thick cream.

MAKES 4 TO 6 SERVINGS

Bess Truman's Ozark Pudding

The food preferred by President Truman and his wife was as American as it could be. When Winston Churchill came to Fulton, in the Truman's home state, to make his "Iron Curtain" speech, he was the guest of honor at a dinner for which the menu included the famous Missouri country ham and this plain but wonderful dessert.

1 egg, beaten	½ cup chopped walnuts, or
¾ cup sugar	mixed nuts
⅛ cup all-purpose flour	1 tsp. vanilla extract
1¼ tsp. baking powder	1 cup heavy cream, whipped
salt	3 to 4 Tbs. rum
1 medium-size apple, peeled, cored, seeded, and chopped	

Preheat oven to 325°

Put beaten egg and sugar in mixing bowl and beat until very light. In another bowl sift together flour, baking powder, and a pinch of salt. Blend this well with egg mixture and fold in apple, walnuts, and vanilla. Pour into a greased shallow 1½-quart baking dish, and bake for 30 minutes. Add rum to whipped cream. Serve pudding when cooled, and garnish with whipped cream.

MAKES 8 SERVINGS

Ohio River Persimmon-Buttermilk Pudding

1 large, not-too-ripe persimmon
1½ cups buttermilk
1 cup sugar
2 Tbs. melted butter
2 eggs, well beaten until foamy
1 cup all-purpose flour

1 tsp. baking soda
1 tsp. baking powder
¼ tsp. salt
½ tsp. ground cinnamon
½ tsp. freshly grated nutmeg
   whipped cream or custard sauce

Preheat oven to 450°

Peel persimmon, cut into small pieces, and spin in blender with buttermilk until fruit is puréed and smooth. Add sugar and melted butter and stir well; stir in foamy eggs. Sift dry ingredients into a large bowl and beat in fruit mixture, a little at a time, until well blended. Pour into a high-sided 1½-quart baking dish. Bake for 15 minutes, then reduce heat to 375° and bake for 30 minutes longer. Pudding will be nicely puffed up and browned. Serve warm with whipped cream. Also good cold with custard sauce mixed with a little sherry.

MAKES 6 TO 8 SERVINGS

Southern Rice-Fruit Pudding

2 cups cooked rice
1 egg, beaten
½ cup sugar
2 cups half and half, or rich milk
½ cup chopped dried apricots
½ cup chopped dates

½ cup chopped pecans
2 or 3 pieces of candied gingerroot,
   chopped
nutmeg
½ tsp. vanilla extract
2 Tbs. melted butter

Preheat oven to 350°

Put rice in a large mixing bowl. Combine egg and sugar and stir into rice. Add half and half, apricots, dates, pecans, and candied gingerroot, then grate in about ¼ teaspoon nutmeg. Add vanilla and melted butter and stir well. Pour into a greased 1½-quart baking dish and bake for about 1 hour, until pudding is firm in center. Serve with Lemon and Wine Sauce (p. 364).

MAKES 6 SERVINGS

Welsh-American Snowdon Pudding

Welsh-Americans include the father of Thomas Jefferson, and numbers of them live in every part of the country. This recipe is a part of the heritage of family cooks in Minnesota and Wisconsin, and the accent of lemon marmalade that distinguishes it from other boiled puddings makes it worth the effort. If necessary, an orange marmalade can be substituted.

½ cup seedless raisins
   butter
1 cup bread crumbs
1 cup chopped suet
3 Tbs. flour

¼ cup lemon marmalade
¾ cup light brown sugar
6 eggs, well beaten
   grated rind of 2 lemons

Cut raisins into halves with a very sharp knife. Butter a 2-quart mold, and press raisins, cut side down, into butter, making a decorative pattern. Stir together bread crumbs, suet, flour; then stir in marmalade, sugar, beaten eggs, and grated rind of lemons. Beat well, pour into mold, and cover it with wax paper and a lightly floured cloth; secure with a length of string. Place filled mold on a rack in a kettle and pour in boiling water to reach three fourths of height of mold. Cover and steam for 2 hours. Serve with Lemon and Wine Sauce.

MAKES 8 TO 10 SERVINGS

Lemon and Wine Sauce

½ cup sugar
2 Tbs. cornstarch
1½ cups water

1 lemon
4 Tbs. butter
½ cup sherry

Put sugar, cornstarch, and water in top part of double boiler and cook over boiling water, stirring constantly, for 10 minutes. Grate half of lemon rind, then squeeze all of juice. Remove thickened sugar mixture from heat and stir in lemon rind and juice along with butter and wine.

Rhubarb Stockli

Swiss-born Chef Albert Stockli, who was responsible for the creative dishes featured at New York's Four Seasons in the 1960s, was a great enthusiast for the natural bounty of the United States. A genuine lover of rhubarb, as are we, he originated this splendid dessert in response to a request for a dish that would celebrate the tart, colorful fruit that is seldom used except in pies or stews served as desserts.

1 lb. rhubarb, peeled and diced
¾ cup water
½ cup sugar
⅔ cup Madeira

1 lemon
½ cup dry vermouth
7 egg yolks
8 slices of zwieback, diced

Combine rhubarb, water, sugar, and about ⅓ cup of Madeira in a saucepan, and simmer for 5 minutes. Squeeze lemon and add juice with vermouth; continue to simmer for about 5 minutes longer, until rhubarb is tender. Drain rhubarb and reserve liquid. In a glass or stainless-steel bowl, beat egg yolks lightly and blend in rhubarb liquid; place bowl over boiling water and beat vigorously with wire whip until mixture is light and frothy. Off heat, stir in remaining Madeira, and fold in cooked rhubarb. Divide zwieback cubes among dessert bowls and pour rhubarb on top.

MAKES 6 SERVINGS

Cold Rhubarb Soufflé

4 cups chopped unpeeled rhubarb
1¾ cups sugar
1 envelope unflavored gelatin
2 tsp. crème de cassis
1 cup heavy cream

4 egg whites
pinch of cream of tartar
½ cup vanilla sugar, or ½ cup plain
    sugar and 1 tsp. vanilla extract

GARNISH:

12 large fresh strawberries
   whipped cream

Preheat oven to 350°

Toss rhubarb and sugar in a casserole and put in oven to stew for about 20 minutes, until rhubarb is soft. Drain, reserving juice; purée rhubarb in a blender or put through food mill. Dissolve gelatin in crème de cassis. Boil reserved juice until reduced to ½ cup; cool, then stir into dissolved gelatin. Use a balloon whisk to whip cream in a metal bowl over ice cubes, letting in as much air as possible so volume is almost doubled. Beat egg whites with a pinch of cream of tartar until almost stiff, then add vanilla sugar and continue beating until stiff peaks form. Fold whipped cream into rhubarb purée, then fold in egg whites. Make a collar of wax paper or aluminum foil about 2 inches high and fit it to a 2-quart soufflé dish, tying it a little below rim; pour in rhubarb mixture. Chill overnight, or for at least 6 hours. To serve, remove collar. Garnish with strawberries cut into halves and whipped cream squeezed in swirls from pastry tube, if desired.

MAKES 6 TO 8 SERVINGS

Plum-Guava Latticework Tart

FOR VERY FLAKY CRUST:

1 cup all-purpose flour
  salt
  sugar

6 Tbs. butter
2 Tbs. vegetable shortening or lard
3 Tbs. ice water

FILLING:

  about ⅓ cup guava jelly
12 small fresh plums, halved and
    pitted

1 tsp. sugar
1 tsp. flour
  heavy cream (optional)

Preheat oven to 425°

Mix dough lightly and refrigerate for at least 2 hours before rolling out to a very thin sheet. Line an 8-inch pie tin with thin layer of dough. Spread about half of guava jelly evenly on bottom. Arrange halved pitted plums, skin side down, over the bottom, fitting them in snugly. Put a little jelly in center of each half plum, then sprinkle with mixture of sugar and flour. Roll out remnants of dough left from lining pie tin, and cut into strips. Make loose latticework across top of tart, and pinch down ends to join with bottom pastry. Bake for 15 minutes, then reduce heat to 350° and bake for 20 minutes more. Serve warm with heavy cream if desired.

MAKES 6 SERVINGS

Ken's Upside-Down Cake

Most Americans grow up on upside-down cakes of one kind or another, usually made of pineapple rings with a cherry in the middle and a gooey brown bottom; sometimes apples are used, or bananas, or another fruit in season, and the fluffy white cake with one egg is usually puffy and rather bland. Ken Wollitz, a gifted musician from California with a fine palate, is addicted to upside-down confections. His contention is that the cake should have far more substance and texture to balance against the candied fruits it supports, and after much study he devised this recipe calling for a pumpkin bread-cake with nuts and an unusual combination of fruits. It may sound far out but it is delicious.

20 dried apricots, approximately
 ½ recipe Pumpkin Bread (p. 164)
 ½ cup chopped walnuts
 4 Tbs. butter

¾ cup dark brown sugar
¾ cup whole cranberries, cooked
   (canned whole cranberry sauce
   is fine)

GARNISH:

2 cups whipped cream

Preheat oven to 350°

Soak apricots in boiling water to cover while preparing cake. Follow directions on page 166 for mixing pumpkin bread batter, using half the amount and adding chopped walnuts at the last. Melt butter in a skillet and add brown sugar, heating until melted and blended. Pour into a well-buttered pan 7 x 11 inches or equivalent and arrange apricots on the bottom in a decorative pattern; surround apricots with cranberries, filling in all the interstices. Pour batter over fruits and bake for 45 minutes to 1 hour, or until a straw inserted comes out clean. Turn out onto a platter and serve warm with whipped cream.

MAKES 12 SERVINGS

Avocado Ice Cream

1 cup milk
1 cup light cream
½ cup sugar

3 egg yolks, well beaten
1 cup avocado pulp
½ cup chopped pistachio nuts

Combine milk, cream, and sugar, and heat to boiling point, stirring constantly. Pour over beaten egg yolks and blend well. Add avocado pulp and pistachios, stirring till smooth. Cool and turn into refrigerator trays; freeze. When firm, put in a chilled bowl and beat until smooth. Return to trays and freeze. Repeat beating in chilled bowl. Freeze for 2 hours and serve.

MAKES ABOUT 1½ QUARTS

Mocha Frosting

3 Tbs. strong fresh coffee
3 Tbs. butter
¼ cup heavy cream

⅛ tsp. salt
1 tsp. vanilla extract
2 cups confectioners' sugar

Pour hot coffee into a saucepan and stir in butter. Heat cream; add to coffee when warm. Stir in salt, then remove from heat. When mixture is cool, add vanilla and beat in sugar, a little at a time. When smooth and spreadable, frost any suitable cake.

MAKES ENOUGH FOR ONE 2-LAYER CAKE

Old Dominion Greengage Ice Cream

Some time after small, green, delicious plums were first cultivated in England, they acquired the surname of Sir William Gage and colonial plum orchards were started in Virginia before the Revolution. Mrs. Raffold's cookbook provided Old Dominion ladies with a recipe for ice cream that required no mechanical freezer, and her cookbook also told them how to make greengage preserves. The two combined became a favorite dessert at the King's Arms in Williamsburg.

1 jar (11½ oz.) greengage preserves
2 small lemons, juiced
1 cup sugar
¼ tsp. salt
3 cups heavy cream
3 cups milk

Mix all ingredients and pour into a flat freezer container. Freeze for 2 hours. Remove from freezer and beat; return to freezer. Continue freezing; remove and beat again. Freeze until firm.

MAKES 2 QUARTS

Plum Pudding Ice Cream

Frances Parkinson Keyes, a transplanted Virginian who lived in New England and later spent much time in Louisiana, was a novelist with a probing interest in American food; she wrote once of finding in an old newspaper a recipe for a Christmas dinner ice cream invented by Yankee cooks. This is the way Plum Pudding Ice Cream was made for a recent twentieth-century holiday.

1 cup seedless raisins
½ cup chopped candied orange peel
   or dried currants
   applejack or other brandy
1 cup sugar
4 oz. unsweetened chocolate
1 qt. buttermilk
¾ tsp. ground cloves
¾ tsp. ground cinnamon
1 tsp. vanilla extract
4 egg whites

Day before making, put fruits in a bowl and barely cover with applejack; set aside to macerate at least overnight; most of liquid should be absorbed. Put sugar, chocolate, and about 3 tablespoons of the buttermilk in a saucepan or top part of a double boiler over hot water and heat just enough to melt chocolate and meld it with sugar; stir in cloves, cinnamon, and vanilla. Beat egg whites until peaks form. Combine sugar-chocolate mixture with remaining buttermilk, then fold in egg whites. Pour into freezer containers and freeze for about 3 hours, then stir well. Repeat at 3-hour intervals twice.

MAKES 12 OR MORE SERVINGS

1½ cups heavy cream
3 egg yolks
¾ cup brown sugar
1 scant Tbs. cornstarch
   salt
1¼ cups mashed cooked pumpkin
¾ tsp. ground ginger
¾ tsp. ground cinnamon

¾ tsp. grated nutmeg
¾ tsp. grated lemon rind
2 Tbs. dark rum
1½ cups heavy cream, whipped
¾ cup finely chopped walnuts
⅓ cup finely minced preserved
   gingerroot
1 prebaked 10-inch pie shell (p. 349)

MERINGUE:

2 egg whites
   cream of tartar
¼ cup vanilla sugar (scant)

Scald cream. Beat yolks until lemon-colored; stir in brown sugar and cornstarch, then add hot cream. Cook over boiling water until custard begins to thicken (180°), adding a pinch of salt. Remove from heat; mix pumpkin with ginger, cinnamon, nutmeg, and lemon rind, then stir into custard. Beat mixture over ice while adding rum. When cool, fold in whipped cream, chopped walnuts, and minced gingerroot. Freeze in ice-cream freezer, or in a metal bowl in refrigerator freezing compartment. Beat twice during first 2 half-hour periods of freezing. Soften ice cream made in refrigerator by removing to lower shelf; when it reaches a stiff but spreadable consistency fill pie shell and return to freezing compartment.

Just before serving beat 2 egg whites with a pinch of cream of tartar until peaks form; add sugar gradually until mixture has firm meringue consistency. (If vanilla sugar is unavailable add a little vanilla extract to plain sugar.) Spread meringue over ice cream, making sure edges are neatly sealed; put under broiler until lightly browned. Serve immediately.

MAKES 6 TO 8 SERVINGS

Vermont Maple Parfait

2 large egg yolks
¾ cup pure maple syrup
2 cups whipped cream

GARNISH:

½ cup heavy cream, whipped
½ tsp. sugar

1 tsp. rum, optional
⅓ cup chopped walnuts

Beat egg yolks in a heavy pot or top part of double boiler until lemon-colored. Heat syrup to boiling point, then slowly add to the eggs, beating continuously. Cook over boiling water until eggs coat spoon, or reach 170° on a candy thermometer. Cool mixture over ice, beating well; set aside. Over same ice beat 2 cups of heavy cream, preferably with a whisk, until stiff and doubled in volume. Fold in maple-egg mixture until well blended, then turn into parfait glasses, filling not quite full. Cover with plastic wrap, and chill in freezer for at least 6 hours. Before serving, whip remaining ½ cup of cream, and add sugar and optional rum. Spoon a little cream over each parfait glass, and top with walnuts.

MAKES 8 SERVINGS

Indexes

Index
of American Food

The Gastronomic Story

In addition to the section of recipes from personal files, the text of this book includes descriptions of numerous American dishes as well as documentary receipts reproduced as they were originally used. They provide guidance for the good natural cook and are indexed below.